# The Kilimanjaro Club Adventure Series: Book 1

# A GRAVE INVITATION

## RON LAMBERSON

**A Grave Invitation: The Kilimanjaro Club Adventure Series Book 1**
Published by Hydra Heads Press
Denver, CO

Publisher's Cataloging-in-Publication data

Names: Lamberson, Ron, author.
Title: A grave invitation : the Kilimanjaro Club adventure series book 1 / Ron Lamberson.
Description: Denver, CO: Hydra Heads Press, 2022.
Series: The Kilimanjaro Club Adventure Series
Identifiers: ISBN: 979-8-9852013-1-4
Subjects: LCSH Family--Fiction. | Adventure and adventurers--Fiction. | Rome--Fiction. | Morocco--Fiction. | Ethiopia--Fiction. | Thriller fiction. | Adventure fiction | BISAC FICTION / Action & Adventure
Classification: LCC PS3612.A54628 G73 2022 | DDC 813.6--dc23

Cover and Interior Design by Victoria Wolf, wolfdesignandmarketing.com.
Copyright owned by Ron Lamberson

**HYDRA HEADS PRESS**

*To Gretchen, my muse*

# CHAPTER

# ONE

Stuart Mancini had never missed a single day of work in his life. He was riding a streak that had just hit 4,490 days since starting at D'Artagnan Group. From the time he took his first job at fourteen, washing dishes at Zen Wok in Englewood, through a half dozen jobs that carried him through high school and college, and throughout his current job, he never missed a day. Early on he took the rare vacation—three or four days strung together, including a weekend or a holiday—but never an entire week. The last time he'd taken such an extended leave, he conveniently contracted appendicitis late on a Friday night and was back at work the following Tuesday after Memorial Day, still not racking up a single unplanned absence.

As it would turn out, day 4,490 would be the last day of Stuart Mancini's streak.

Stuart had been on the phone with his senior trader in London, off and on, the entire morning. Markets overseas were ping-ponging due to a 6.7 earthquake in Japan and what was being deemed a "highly credible terrorist threat" to the Metro system in Paris. By 7:30 a.m. New York time, Stuart and his man in London had completed over $70 million in transactions. Despite the turmoil, Stuart calculated they'd managed to stay roughly three hundred thousand dollars ahead.

While Jerold, the London trader, was rattling off quotes from a German columnist at the *Financial Times*, Stuart's boss, Heath, popped into his doorway and said, "Jesus, Stuart. What the hell is happening? The Dow was down over a hundred and fifty when I stepped onto the subway and was up nearly seventy by the time I got off."

Stuart shielded his phone against his chest and said, "The buyers and sellers are at odds today, Heath."

"Really. Don't give me that crap. Who's the culprit?"

"Just a second," Stuart said into the phone and re-shielded it. "Everyone's panicked. There's a big earthquake in Japan, tsunami warnings going off all over, and some no-name terrorist group threatened to destroy the entire Paris underground. It's crazy."

Heath paused a second, leaning against the doorframe, and said, "Don't they know it's Friday? We don't need this on a Friday." Stuart forced a smile and shrugged. Heath shook his head and disappeared into the hall.

As CFO of D'Artagnan, Stuart was not only responsible for managing and reporting the firm's financial performance, but he was also responsible for ensuring that its capital—the liquid assets on hand to fund customer deals—was readily available, safe, and when not in use, flourishing. That meant he and his team had to funnel cash into a hodgepodge of investment options that promised a jaw-dropping level of growth and security. And, as anyone who has ever invested in any stock market knows, guaranteeing growth and security is impossible.

"Look, Jerold. I trust you. If you think the Hammond Fund is our best option this morning, then go for it. I don't see anything to the contrary." Stuart felt a slight hitch in his chest as his last comment floated through the phone lines. He hadn't had time to review the Treasury group's most recent fund analysis, or, for that matter, anything else they had produced in recent weeks. For the past three months, he'd focused every waking moment on the pending merger with Rhinegold, Fletcher and Hobbes, another successful boutique—and frequently adversarial—firm.

"The beta was really low, right? Then it's a safe landing place. We ride out the day and reevaluate Monday," Stuart said. He turned his focus back to the draft memo he'd brought up on his screen while Jerold spouted off about British mistrust and something about an upcoming bank holiday.

"We're up three hundred grand right now, or something close. Make the trade and call me … call me in like ninety minutes, okay?" Stuart paused a moment. The line was silent and then Jerold said, "Consider it done." Stuart planted the receiver into the phone's base and exhaled loudly.

"Don't pick that phone up again," he heard Olivia, his assistant, say. Stuart looked up and saw her approaching his desk, a ceramic coffee mug the size of a softball clutched in her hand. Stuart raised an eyebrow. "You've got a busy day, mister. You're with Heath and Jessup from ten to at least eleven, then you've got a call with Goldman at 11:30 and lunch with Helmut."

Stuart slumped and let his chin hit his chest.

"Come on. You like the Plaza, remember?"

"Yes, but it's Helmut. I never taste my lunch when I'm with Helmut," Stuart said.

Stuart Mancini was the Chief Financial Officer of a mid-sized investment firm that catered to a neo-conservative, purposefully obscure segment of Manhattan's point-one percent. The D'Artagnan Group had swept Stuart from a smaller, avantgarde firm based in Boston a few years after he completed his MBA at Harvard. Stuart turned out to be the brilliant automaton the organization needed. He logged ridiculous hours, rarely uttered a complaint, and did not, and chose not to, maintain any semblance of a social life. It wasn't just his diligence that created value for the firm. Stuart wielded an innate knack for rapid, complex financial analysis. His ability to maneuver the serpentine regulatory landscape was eclipsed only by his ability to concisely and effectively deliver the right message in the right way to customers and board members alike. But when the ink dried on the biggest deals and the first cork was launched from a bottle of Krystal by D'Artagnan's leadership team, Stuart's characteristic absence was disregarded the moment the first toast was proposed.

After a dozen of highly lucrative years with D'Artagnan, Stuart found himself at a crossroads. The firm's principal owners—three roguish school-boy friends whose startling fusion of bravado, legitimate brilliance, and remarkable luck had brought them fortunes in the tens of millions—were calling it quits. They were in the final stages of closing a deal that would transfer all of D'Artagnan's assets and clients to Rhinegold, Fletcher and Hobbes. The sale would net the three owners nearly half a billion dollars. Stuart, who'd earned a minority stake in the business, stood to make a significant sum and, if all went as planned, the new entity would provide him a similar role in the reconstituted firm's structure.

Stuart's conundrum resulted from the smoldering hated he'd harbored for Rhinegold, Fletcher and Hobbes. Throughout his entire career at D'Artagnan, Stuart had drawn a significant amount of his drive and commitment from the adversarial relationship that had evolved between the two firms. When T. Heath Robinson, D'Artagnan's original numbers guru, shared the firm's plans with Stuart earlier that year, Stuart nearly vomited. It was as if the Yankees were merging with the Mets. It was unfathomable.

After the morning's mayhem, Stuart sunk into his office chair and passively listened to a parade of analysts on Bloomberg debating the merits of renewable energy sources while rereading one of a dozen pro-formas that accompanied the final draft agreement between the two firms. He glanced at the screen of his laptop and saw that it was 10:47 a.m. In three minutes, Olivia would reappear and remind him that his lunch meeting with Helmut Rhinegold was in forty minutes. He sighed loudly, tossed the documents on his desk, and closed his eyes. Almost immediately, Olivia popped into his office and delivered her reminder.

Helmut Rhinegold was the original founder of Rhinegold, Fletcher and Hobbes and the financial mastermind behind the firm's success and mystique. Although Stuart's loathing for the rival organization propelled his desire to lead D'Artagnan to record heights, he maintained a conflicting soft spot for Rhinegold. The two regularly found themselves at the same conferences and industry events, in New York or Chicago, as well as overseas. In many ways, Rhinegold was the inverse of Stuart. Helmut was a rumbling mammoth of a man, physically in complete contrast to Stuart's elongated wispiness. Perched on Helmut's boulder-like shoulders was a highly animated caricature of a human head, airbrushed a vivid pink and topped with a wily shock of white-blond locks, fueled by Russian vodka and lava-hot tacos. Helmut, without fail, would storm toward Stuart at these meetings, hurl some outlandish insult about D'Artagnan, erupt in laughter, and smother Stuart in a sloppy hug. Then he'd grab Stuart by the shoulders, instantly transforming into the epitome of a dangerous uncle, and tell Stuart how sincerely amazed he was by one of D'Artagnan's recent successes.

Heath had informed Stuart of the buyout after a late-night dinner at Acappella, a common occurrence as Heath shared Stuart's manic work ethic. Heath's news effectively ended the dinner, with Stuart mumbling an abrupt apology and nearly running from the restaurant. He walked fifteen blocks before relenting to the subway and returning to his apartment. By the time he reached his building, he had two messages on his answering machine. The first was from Heath, apologizing profusely for upsetting him. The second was from Helmut. His message said he knew Heath was planning to share the news that evening, and he wanted to immediately follow up with Stuart because he knew he wouldn't be enthusiastic about the move. "I hope, for my sake, that this may mean we have an opportunity to work *together* rather than against each other. I know there's quite a bit I could still learn from you, and I hope vice versa. Call me tomorrow if you're interested in sharing your thoughts."

Ultimately, it was Helmut's continuous interventions throughout the complicated negotiation process that made the effort tolerable for Stuart. There was nothing Helmut could do that would alter Stuart's predisposition for despising his future employer, but he played a critical role in defusing the insufferable posturing and egotistical backstabbing that ravaged most business deals. Now, six months later, Helmut had scheduled an unnecessary celebratory lunch with Stuart as both leadership teams prepared to take the deal across the goal line. For Stuart, this culmination was anything but appetizing.

"Mr. Mancini, you're due at the Oak Room in fifteen minutes. The car is waiting," Olivia chimed again. Stuart flapped a hand at her and grunted. He closed his laptop, grabbed his cell phone and the newspaper, and left the office.

When the D'Artagnan driver pulled up to The Plaza, the surrounding area was utter chaos. What appeared to be a disintegrating parade of Mardi Gras stilt walkers had melded with a flood of poodles and their harried owners.

The driver caught Stuart in the rearview mirror as he attempted to maneuver the black Lincoln Town Car around the hotel's signature fountain. "Mr. Mancini, I'm not sure how close I can get to the front. Do you … do you want me to keep trying?"

Stuart glared out the tinted window, shook his head sharply, and sprang from the car.

The madness outside the hotel was disorienting. A cacophony of barking dogs, distorted Cajun music, and blaring car horns electrified the air. Stuart squeezed between two stilt walkers clad in lion costumes, nearly crushed a miniature poodle, and leaped to the sidewalk. A narrow gap opened in the crowd just outside the hotel doors, and he darted through to escape the pandemonium.

Once inside, the delicately balanced elegance of The Plaza, simultaneously contrived and authentic, masked the bedlam that had been extruded from Central Park. Where the throngs congregated outside threatened to siphon the soul out of any unsuspecting onlooker, the hotel's interior—sparsely populated with a peculiar combination of prim business men and women and antsy Midwestern tourist families—soothed the festering anxiety Stuart felt in the car. He made his way around the rear of the lobby and approached the Oak Room podium.

"May I help you, sir?" an ageless, tuxedoed maître d' purred as Stuart rested a hand on the podium.

"Mancini. We have a twelve o'clock reservation. It's probably under Rhinegold."

"Oh, yes," the man said, his eyes closing in slow motion. "Mr. Rhinegold has yet to arrive. Would you care to be seated, Mr. Mancini?"

"Please," Stuart said and scanned the already crowded dining room. As Stuart was escorted to the table, the maître d' glanced back and asked, "Are you visiting us from out of town, Mr. Mancini? London perhaps?"

"No. I live in Manhattan," Stuart said flatly.

"My apologies. I thought I heard a hint of a brogue."

Stuart smirked, then sat as the host motioned toward a banquette table set for two.

"I'll show Mr. Rhinegold in once he arrives. Leo will be taking care of you this afternoon."

Stuart settled into the banquette seat and opened the *Wall Street Journal* he'd brought with him. He glanced at his watch. It was exactly noon. Rhinegold was only ever on time by accident. Stuart knew he had at least fifteen minutes before he sauntered in.

"Good morning, sir."

Stuart looked up and saw a server standing before him. "I'm Leo and I'll be taking care of you today. Can I get you something to drink while you wait for Mr. Rhinegold?"

"An iced tea would be fine, thank you," Stuart said, returning to the paper.

A moment later, Stuart heard a chirp from his cell phone, signifying either a missed call or a voicemail. He pulled the phone from his pocket, frowning. He hadn't heard nor felt the phone ring. The cell coverage in the city was often unpredictable, though. The pervasive forest of steel and concrete continued to wreak havoc with signals and connectivity. He flipped open the phone and saw that he had a voicemail.

It started with static. Again, a common occurrence in the city. "Stuart, it's Helmut. I …" The message broke up. More static. Helmut didn't sound quite right. There was an edge of anxiety to his tone. Something Stuart had rarely, if ever, heard before. "… not sure … may need your help …" and then the message ended. Stuart replayed the message but couldn't pull anything of significance from it other than it sounded as if Helmut was trapped in a wind tunnel. The gist seemed, though, that he was canceling. Stuart dialed Olivia to see if Helmut or anyone from his office had called to cancel. As the phone rang, he realized that Olivia would have, of course, called him if any such message came in.

"Hi, Stuart," Olivia said.

"Olivia, have you heard anything from Helmut? He left me a very garbled message a minute ago. It sounds like he's canceling."

"I haven't heard a thing. I'll call over to his office and see what I can find out."

Stuart sat back and considered whether to stay for lunch. Leo arrived with his tea and said, "Would you care for an appetizer, or would you prefer to wait?"

"It looks like I'm going to be dining alone," Stuart said. He flipped open the menu and said, "I'll have the Cobb salad."

Leo nodded and left just as Stuart's phone rang. It was Olivia.

"Hi, Stuart. I just talked to Helmut's assistant, and she said Helmut hasn't been in today. She hasn't heard from him and he has nothing on his schedule. Her guess is that he has something going on outside the office and just forgot to tell her. Sounds like you're on your own."

"Well, that's really not good. We actually had a few critical things to cover before Monday. Can you work with her to see if you can locate him? I can meet him later this afternoon or have dinner, drinks, or whatever tonight, if necessary." Olivia promised to do her best.

Stuart returned to the paper but could not focus on any one story. He was frustrated that Helmut had blown him off and, at the same time, worried that something had gone awry. While the critical details necessary to close the deal the following week were complete, he'd been depending upon Helmut's insight and, frankly, his encouragement, to make Stuart feel comfortable about finalizing the sale. It was to be a rare acquisition. Both firms were highly successful, relatively lean from a staff standpoint, and weren't seeking any daunting financial synergies. Most of the employees were enthusiastic about the deal, and a celebratory atmosphere had been building within D'Artagnan for weeks. Stuart had tried his best to feign a similar level of anticipation, not that he ever demonstrated anything that others would deem as "emotion," so that Heath and the others leaders wouldn't develop some unnecessary concern for the transaction.

Stuart gave up on the paper and focused on his tea. He scanned the teeming restaurant and checked to see if there was anyone present whom he recognized. No one looked familiar. He noticed two men dressed in oddly out-of-date clothing—bulky tweed sports coats, vests, and the smaller of the two had a pocket watch—who had just left the podium and were walking unaccompanied through the dining room. They were of contrasting height, one a hair or two over six feet and the other five foot eight or nine, and entirely different builds. The gentleman who appeared to be in the lead was barrel-chested and sported an immense mustache, which, from a distance, could have been mistaken for a miniature ferret. The second appeared to weigh a third of what his companion weighed, and sported a jet-black comb-over that streaked his shining pate in perfect parallel streams. Stuart watched with growing interest to see where the men were headed. The gaze of the larger, leading man locked onto Stuart's. His eyes actually twinkled in the lighting and, within a moment, both men were flanking Helmut's vacant chair.

"Please do pardon us, but … are you Stuart Mancini?" The man spoke with a thick English accent, a curious mixture of cockney and more proper Queen's English.

Stuart shot a nervous gaze around the room. This had to be a setup.

"I'm sorry, have we met?" Stuart responded.

"Most certainly not," the large man chirped, shoving a meaty paw toward Stuart and nearly clobbering his iced tea. "How rude of me. I'm Bailey Honeybourne and this …" he said, nearly bowing and raising a hand toward his companion.

"… is Parnell Sumner," added the wiry man, as if the act had been orchestrated. The second man was obviously English, too. His accent and diction were flawless.

Stuart attempted to stand with some form of grace, having been wedged into his seat. He grappled for both men's hands and managed something of a handshake with both.

"Yes, I'm Stuart Mancini. I'm afraid you caught me at a bit of a loss."

Both men chuckled and Bailey added, "Which I hope is infrequent."

Stuart glowered and sat back down. "How … do you know who I am? I don't believe I'm familiar with either of your names."

The men exchanged knowing glances. "It is curious," Bailey said. "You see, Parnell and I were very good friends with your maternal grandfather, Malcolm Buckley."

Stuart bristled at the mention of his grandfather's name. He couldn't remember how long it had been since he'd heard the name or had even a thought of the man.

"I can see we've caught you a bit by surprise. Mind you, it wasn't our intention, but sometimes these things can't be helped."

Stuart shook his head slightly and said, "I'm not sure I understand. Is there something you need from me? If you know anything about me, and my grandfather, then you're certainly aware that we are … estranged, at best. I really know nothing about him."

Bailey looked down at the empty chair, paused, and then said, "May we join you, just for a few minutes? We won't delay your meal."

Stuart sat back and spread his hands out somewhat dramatically. "Be my guest. Please, pull up a chair," he said to Parnell.

"Splendid!" Bailey barked and plopped into the open seat. Parnell grabbed a neighboring chair and slid it up to the small table.

"I suppose I should start by asking you if you're aware of your grandfather's condition," Bailey said in a hushed voice.

Stuart frowned and said, "His condition? Of course not. I haven't had contact with him for … I don't know, thirty-five years? He's my mother's father. She severed their relationship when I was little. I met him once or twice. I remember him sending letters at one point, but not much else. I don't … *we* don't consider him family."

"Yes, we're aware of your tempestuous relationship."

Stuart laughed. "I'm not sure how something that doesn't exist can be tempestuous? You make it sound like part of this is my fault."

"Oh, no, no, no, Mr. Mancini. Please don't misunderstand me. It's just that …"

"Your grandfather died recently," Parnell blurted out. Bailey glared back at him. "Bailey, you were prattling on. You promised not to interrupt the man's lunch, and yet here we are, and you can't seem to get a rational thought out of your mouth."

"I'm so sorry, Mr. Mancini. We …" Bailey glared again at Parnell "I had planned to employ some degree of tact when delivering this, surely, troublesome and unfortunate news."

"Mister … I'm sorry," Stuart said, fluttering his hands at both men. "I've forgotten your names. At any rate, your news doesn't mean anything to me. I don't wish for anyone to die, but I assumed he'd been dead for years. Now, if you don't mind, my salad should be here any minute, and I'd prefer a quiet lunch."

Bailey sighed loudly and bowed his head toward his clasped hands. Parnell merely stared back at Stuart. "Mr. Mancini, please trust that Parnell and I wouldn't have so rudely interrupted your day, unannounced, of course, if we didn't feel we had something important to share."

"Well, I wouldn't go as far as to say that you were rude, but …" Stuart said, opening his hands to the table. "Here you sit, continuing to talk about a now dead relative who had been dead to *me* for ages. I really don't …"

"Malcolm bequeathed something to you in his will," Parnell spat out as if he'd been holding his breath.

"Parnell, for God's sake, man," Bailey said, suddenly breaking from his poised demeanor.

"I have to tell you … Bailey, is it? I prefer your partner's direct approach to yours."

Parnell nodded slightly and grinned.

"I can't imagine anything of value that the man would want to leave to me. As I said, we had virtually no contact. By choice."

Bailey stuck his chin out and dug two sausage-sized fingers into his collar and tugged. Parnell leaned forward and said in a low voice, "Mr.

Mancini, I certainly understand. This, we feel, is important. I assure you; this is something of distinct value." Parnell reached into his breast pocket and revealed a cream-colored envelope that appeared to be sealed with a red wax stamp. Black calligraphy adorned the front. Parnell turned the envelope face up and slowly slid it across the table toward Stuart.

To Be Delivered to Stuart Kane Mancini
Immediately upon my Death
Malcolm Seymour Buckley, Jr.

Stuart read the envelope and looked up at Bailey. "You've got to be kidding. What the hell is this?" Stuart said, scooting away from the envelope as if it radiated poison.

"It is ..." Bailey said, leaning forward and staring deep into Stuart's eyes, "an invitation."

"What, to a ball? Is the Queen acknowledging his ... his damage to British Society? And if it's to the funeral, you can ... you can just leave. I'd die of dehydration from spitting on his grave."

Bailey and Parnell both squirmed in their chairs. Bailey cleared his throat and leaned forward again. "As I mentioned, I'm acutely aware of the lack of affection you had for your grandfather. I'm not here to convince you otherwise. I'm simply here as a messenger. For better or worse, Malcolm was a dear friend to Parnell and I, and we swore to uphold his last wishes. This ... delivery of sorts being most important to him."

Stuart looked away from both men for a moment and allowed his eyes to wander as he processed the day's events. This bizarre interruption was only amplifying the frustration, concern, and stress he was feeling over the upcoming sale of D'Artagnan. His chief desire was to return to the office and track down Helmut.

"Mr. Mancini, it's obvious our timing has been unfortunate at best," Parnell said. He placed two business cards on top of the envelope. "While our preference would be to walk you through the contents of this envelope in person, I'm convinced you wouldn't welcome the discussion at this time. Please," he said, tapping the business cards, "call either me or Bailey this evening if you have questions or would like to continue our conversation. I think … I think the contents will be somewhat self-explanatory. You will, I'm sure, want to talk again if you have any interest in responding to your grandfather's invitation."

Both men stood together. Bailey shoved his paw out again and half coughed. Stuart put his napkin down and stood, shaking Bailey's hand and then Parnell's.

"You're right. Your timing wasn't good. I realize that I'm the one who's being rude. It wasn't my intent. It's just …"

"No, no, Stuart. No apologies necessary," Bailey said raising a hand and beginning to back away.

"Please call, though. We'll be in town …" Parnell said, shooting a look at Bailey, "as long as necessary," he finished, grinning again. Parnell slid a simple business card next to the invitation. Stuart noticed it included only his name and a phone number.

"No promises, gentlemen. Have a good afternoon," Stuart said, and returned to his seat. Leo arrived with Stuart's Cobb salad just as the two men disappeared into the swarm of restaurant patrons.

# CHAPTER

# TWO

The sterile abode belonging to Stuart Mancini was perched on the thirty-sixth floor on Manhattan's Upper East Side, hovering above Lexington Avenue. At this time in the early afternoon, the residence was silent. Thick, triple-paned glass, dense concrete and fiber walls, and the building's surrounding neighbors deflected and absorbed the distinctive sounds of the bustling hive of humanity coursing through the city. Even when inhabited, the sparsely furnished apartment, uncomfortably immaculate and chic, rarely registered a noise that could be heard between rooms. When Stuart purchased the property eight years earlier, he wondered, briefly, what he would do about decorating his new home, about making it habitable. Recalling the fourteenth-floor model that had convinced him to forward an offer, he asked the agent for the name of the designer who constructed the model's interior. His instruction to her was simple. Recreate the model, whatever the cost.

The layout was symmetric and predictable—safe. Each floor of the building housed either two or four apartments. Stuart, living alone, opted for a unit that consumed a quarter of a floor. Four elevators serviced the building, each opening into the foyer of the corresponding apartment.

Outside the etched stainless-steel elevator doors, a narrow, well-appointed entry led into a striking main room that overlooked the east side of the island. To the right was a short hall that led to the master suite. To the left, the kitchen and dining area opened off the main room. A half bath, laundry room, and storage area, plus a study, were tucked behind either side of the entry hallway.

A series of six Renaissance prints framed in rusty patina-coated wood lined the off-white walls of the entry hallway. Earth-tinted travertine tile flowed toward the floor-to-ceiling windows that accentuated the main room. Cold, minimalist furniture sprang from the landscape. A Breuer chair, an Eames lounge and ottoman, and a low glass and chrome coffee table were separated by a black leather sofa. An inconspicuous Bang & Olufsen system flanked the opposite wall. The only incongruity was a bulky Life Fitness treadmill that faced the windows in one corner.

This immaculate atmosphere greeted Stuart each evening when he returned from the office, often around 8:00 p.m. This particular evening, he stepped from the elevator just after 5:30. The sun was setting, reflected into the span of windows facing east off the two towers positioned across the street. Stuart halted abruptly as the door shut behind him. It had been years, he realized, since he'd seen anything like it. Even on the weekends, he was either at the office or holed up in his study, isolated from this million-dollar view. He ambled into the main room, gently set his briefcase on the abstract Persian rug, and soaked up the skyline. Stuart grinned and headed into the kitchen. He laid the envelope Bailey and Parnell had left him with on the dining table, opened the refrigerator, and pulled out a stoppered bottle of Viognier. He filled a bistro tumbler with wine and sat at the table.

The earlier aversion he'd felt upon hearing his grandfather's name had subsided during the afternoon. Stuart had spent the remainder of the workday trying to determine how concerned he should be about Helmut's message and absence, the bizarre materialization of Bailey and Parnell, and the cryptic invitation they had given him. Most people would have ripped the envelope open before the lunch check arrived at the table, regardless of how they felt about the source. Stuart had a sixth sense that this wasn't just some odd, post-death party invitation. Too many years had passed since any form of contact had taken place between Malcolm Buckley, Malcolm's only child, and *her* only child, for the letter to be a mere courtesy.

Stuart took a long drink of wine, smacked his lips, and stood the envelope up in front of him, rereading the carefully scripted text that adorned the parchment. He flipped it over and stared at the red wax seal. The design was remarkably intricate and appeared to be a mixture of medieval, African, and Asian design elements. *TKC* was centered on the mark. He peeled the seal off the paper, opened the envelope, and pulled out its contents—a single page, folded neatly in half, framed with rough-cut edges. He laid down the envelope, took another swig of wine, and unfolded the letter.

Dearest Stuart,

I am pleased, and I would have to admit if were I present, somewhat shocked, to find you reading this letter. As you would have been informed, I have passed from this weary world. I hope I have done so with some degree of dignity. In reluctant anticipation of the circumstances that will prompt delivery of this letter, I have placed considerable thought into what actions will be taken once I am gone. One only has a single chance to initiate this sort of deed. I have arranged for most of the typical items that are involved in wills to be handled. Those details need not be anything that concern you. Among other assets, I have something unique that I believe has great value, and I am compelled to share it with you.

This letter shall serve as my sanctioned and rightful decision to pass membership to The Kilimanjaro Club, a rare and exclusive organization that I joined before World War II, to you. I have asked Mr. Bailey Honeybourne and Mr. Parnell Sumner, assuming they themselves remain "of sound mind and body," to hand deliver this invitation to you upon my death. You should know, regardless of the actions you take, or do not take, from this point on, that these two men are remarkable, trustworthy confidants and friends. I have no doubt they will treat you with impeccable respect and humility.

I am quite confident you have no knowledge of this organization. New members are rarely initiated. Membership may also be bequeathed by existing members who pass away. I will allow Bailey and Parnell to provide you with the more critical and interesting elements of membership. I think you will find we are truly a unique clan.

One final, very important, element of this invitation is that it is time sensitive. Once you have received the envelope containing my letter, you have 24 hours to accept the invitation, no exceptions.

On a more personal note, I hope this letter finds you well, happy, and productive in your life. While you may have absolutely no interest in my feelings, I do wish to share with you that I have thought of you often, if not daily, since the very day you were born. Regardless of what your mother, my beloved daughter, has told you, I care for and love you both deeply.

Kindest Regards,

Malcolm Seymour Buckley, Jr.

May 29, 1987

Stuart flattened the letter on the table and scowled. A swarm of conflicting thoughts and emotions buzzed behind his tired eyes. Twenty-four hours? Why hadn't those bumbling fools told him about the expiration? Nineteen eighty-seven? He'd been twenty-seven, nearly twenty-eight, when Malcolm had written the letter. Over a decade had passed. What the hell was this Kilimanjaro Club? Some bizarre fraternity of old Englishmen who betrayed their loved ones and sent cryptic messengers on scouting trips after they died? He buried his face in his hands and rubbed deeply at his eyes. Way too much was going on right now.

As he exhaled, he was jolted by the buzz of the intercom. It was the signature double beep of Larry, the doorman. Stuart grabbed his wine glass and walked over to the intercom panel on the kitchen wall. He pressed the talk button and said, "Yes, Larry?"

"I'm sorry for disturbing you, Mr. Mancini, but there's a man here for you … 'if you want,' he says."

Stuart frowned and responded, "Do you have a name for me, Larry? I'm not expecting anyone." Larry was surely just as surprised as Stuart. It had been at least two years since anyone had visited.

"Uh, yeah, that would help, huh?" Larry said. Stuart could hear voices away from the speaker. "He says his name is Carlton and that he was asked to come here at the behest of Mr. Honeybourne. Does that mean anything to you?"

Stuart began to respond when his cell phone rang. He'd left it in the main room on the console table. "Larry, hold on for a second." He darted into the other room and grabbed the phone before the call went to voicemail.

"Mancini," he blurted. He hadn't looked to see what the caller ID had reported, if anything.

"Good evening, Stuart," a newly familiar voice called. "Bailey Honeybourne here. I hope I'm calling at a convenient time."

"Yes, hello, Bailey," Stuart said. "I … please hold on for a moment. The man you sent over is with my doorman." Stuart jogged back into the kitchen and hit the talk button again.

"Larry, can you please ask … Carlton, was it, to hold on? I have his boss on my cell phone."

"Sure thing, Mr. Mancini. I'll be right here." Stuart retrieved his wine glass and sat back down at the table.

"Bailey, this is kind of crazy. What's going on? And why didn't you tell me what this letter was about? What if I hadn't opened it until Monday? And it's awfully presumptuous sending someone over to fetch me—"

"Stuart! Stuart! Stuart!" Bailey barked into the phone. Stuart stopped, then took a breath to continue.

"… to fetch—"

"Stuart, please stop for a moment. Hear me out."

Stuart stopped, sensing his heart rate climbing.

"Okay, okay … I'm … I'm sorry. This has been an overwhelming day."

Bailey paused a moment, then continued. "Again, Stuart, I truly apologize for barging in on you now twice in the same day. As Parnell and I mentioned earlier, though, this is important."

"Okay, I guess I understand that … at least to some degree. Now, why is there a man downstairs?"

"I believe for you to truly appreciate the … magnitude of you grandfather's gift—"

"Gift?" Stuart said.

"Please, if possible, Stuart, let's leave the history aside for a moment. This invitation from your grandfather is indeed a rare and valuable gift. But you need more information to get a better sense of what's being offered to you."

Stuart felt his breathing steadying. His pulse followed suit, dropping down to where he couldn't feel it any longer.

"So, I assume I should go with this man, correct?"

"Yes," Bailey said, seeming chipper again. "Carlton will drive you to the local chapter of our club. Parnell and I are here now. We'd like to dine with you and give you an opportunity to see the club—learn more about it."

"Come on, Bailey. This sounds like a timeshare pitch. What are you really trying to sell me? A country club membership? You really *don't* know me, do you?"

"The Kilimanjaro Club is *not* a country club, Stuart Mancini. We do not play golf nor bat tennis balls around a court."

"Then what in the hell *do* you do? You can at least tell me that."

"Stuart, that's why we want to have you visit tonight. You need to see it." Bailey paused a beat. "Please. Pick out a sport coat and meet Carlton downstairs. You won't need a tie. It's Friday."

Stuart took a pair of deep breaths and said, "Ten minutes. Give me ten minutes to … to get down there."

"Splendid! You'll not regret it. Oh, and please don't forget your grandfather's letter. You'll need to present it when you arrive." Stuart rolled his eyes at Bailey's last comment.

"Okay, sure. I'll see you in a bit," Stuart replied and ended the call.

CHAPTER

# THREE

Carlton drove a standard, non-descript, black Lincoln Town Car limousine. While the matching black leather interior was flawless, it boasted none of the stereotypical limo amenities Stuart had experienced while being wined and dined by clients or business partners. There were no crystal decanters of liquor, no video screens, and no console cell phones. Light strains of jazz—it sounded like Coltrane—seeped from surrounding speakers. The glass partition between the front and back seats was lowered about three-quarters. Carlton slid into the driver's seat and shut the door with a cushioned thump. He punched a button on the dash and Coltrane disappeared. The partition closed.

"I sincerely apologize for any misunderstanding, Mr. Mancini. Mr. Honeybourne assured me you'd be expecting my arrival," Carlton's voice emanated from the surround sound speakers.

"It's okay, really," Stuart said. He looked around, unsure of where to direct his reply. Carlton had already apologized twice before letting Stuart into the car. It was beginning to be a bit much.

"So, where is this club, Carlton? Lower east side? Soho perhaps?" Carlton didn't reply. "Is there any chance you could lower the glass? It's a little awkward. I feel like I'm talking to myself."

There was a pause, then the partition lowered. In the rearview mirror, Stuart watched a smile spread across the driver's taut face. Carlton looked ageless. His rich mocha-toned skin was smooth, marked only by minute crow's-feet that branched from the outside corners of his eyes. Carlton wore a traditional driver's cap. Faint tufts of grey peeked from just beneath the brim.

"Now, Mr. Mancini, the precise location of The Kilimanjaro Club is something I'm not at liberty to share this evening. In fact, I need to let you know I'll be closing the window again between us in a moment. It's tinted, as you saw. Your windows are locked and tinted on the inside. There's nothing to be afraid of, Mr. Mancini. It's just that tonight you're a guest of the club, not a member. So … you know, we need to keep this whole thing under wraps. For the time being." He smiled again. Carlton's reassuring smile provided a sense of calm rather than amping up the creepiness of the evening's events.

"We'll be driving for a while. Would you care for some music? I like a little jazz myself, but I have just about everything at my fingertips."

"What you had on is fine. I'll just try to sit back and … wait, I guess."

Carlton chuckled. "That sounds good. You know what, Mr. Mancini? The worst thing that can happen tonight is that you get a fantastic free meal. The chef's special is amazing. Kobe beef and truffles. Never had anything like it in my life."

Stuart forced a smiled and nodded. Carlton saluted him and the divider rose. As it closed, Stuart realized just how deeply it was tinted. He couldn't see Carlton, or even his profile, through the glass. He glanced to his left, realized that the side windows were similarly opaque, and turned around. The rear window was essentially black. As he turned to face forward, a lone trumpet filled the air, and the car eased from the curb. Stuart checked his watch. It was five after six.

At exactly 6:45, Stuart felt the car slow and turn into what felt like an alley. After the turn, the car dipped down. Underground parking, Stuart realized, feeling better that he at least knew what altitude he might be at. He'd attempted to track Carlton's route—at least during the first few minutes—but after several consecutive right turns Stuart gave up, recognizing that Carlton was purposely trying to disorient him.

The car's tires rumbled and squealed through the parking garage. Finally, Carlton eased the car to a halt and retracted the partition.

"We have arrived," he said, turning to look at Stuart. "Everything go okay back there? I know it can be a bit … unnerving."

"No, I'm fine, Carlton. Thank you."

"Good," he said, with a short laugh. "Believe it or not, I've had more than one passenger lose their lunch during the ride. Said it felt like a damn pitch-black roller coaster, if you'll pardon my French." Before Stuart could respond, Carlton whirled to his left and slid from the car. A moment later Stuart's door was open. As he stepped out, he realized they weren't in a typical parking garage. In fact, there didn't appear to be parking anywhere in the vicinity. They had stopped in an underground alley. Soaring red brick walls, at least twenty feet high, lined the pale concrete lane. The roadway emerged from a corner fifty feet behind the limo and disappeared around a similar curve a short distance beyond. Adjacent to the car, carved into the brick façade, was an ornately etched concrete wall that framed two brass elevator doors. After shutting the car door, Carlton approached the elevator. A discrete black speaker cover lined with dark wood separated the doors.

"Carlton," the driver said into the speaker. A round red light came on above the elevator door on the right. Carlton stepped back and faced Stuart.

"Well, Mr. Mancini. It was a pleasure meeting you this evening. I hope you enjoy your time with Mr. Honeybourne and Mr. Sumner. They're amazing gentlemen." He smiled and bowed quickly. "Oh, and, my condolences as well."

For a moment, Stuart wasn't sure what he meant.

"I only met your grandfather on a few occasions, but he was in a whole 'nother ballpark. We'll all miss him." Just then the elevator doors slid open. The car was empty, not that he was expecting anyone.

"Please," Carlton said, stepping aside and gesturing toward the open elevator. "Just press the black button when you get in. It'll take you up to the club."

Stuart thanked the driver and stepped into the elevator. He found the black button—it was the only button in the entire elevator—and punched it as instructed. As the door closed, Carlton nodded and saluted again. Stuart forced a smile and gave a quick wave.

The elevator opened into a spacious square anteroom, featuring an arrangement of plush upholstered chairs, assorted tables, and lamps in its center. An array of high-backed chairs were spaced around the perimeter of the room. A lush Persian rug covered most of the parquet floor, and deep mahogany paneling draped the walls. A series of paintings—portraits and scenes from British fox hunts—paraded along the windowless walls. Broad double doors, sporting massive brass handles, flanked the opposite side of the room. Stuart stepped from the elevator and, as the doors slid closed behind him, the double doors opened, and Bailey strode through.

"Ah, Stuart!" he bellowed. "So, *so* good to see you. I do hope you'll forgive our shenanigans this evening, but I think you'll enjoy yourself, nonetheless."

Stuart made his way around the seating arrangement and grasped Bailey's outstretched hand. Bailey gave his hand one quick shake, and then slid around beside him and slipped an arm behind Stuart's back.

"Welcome … to The Kilimanjaro Club!" he said dramatically as they crossed the threshold. As if on cue, a distant piano began to play, knifing through the din of conversation that filled the air. They stepped into a wide hallway that stretched in both directions. Directly across the way, the hall opened into an expansive, low-lit dining room. To the right was an enormous bar that extended toward them, into the dining room, and then bent ninety degrees to the right and continued on beyond Stuart's line of sight. Every table in the dining room appeared to be occupied. Service staff clad in white tuxedo jackets hovered throughout the room. As Bailey guided him through the entryway, he caught sight of the pianist, situated on a small stage at the opposite end of the room.

The stage appeared to be a set within a small-scale replica of a historic theater. Rich burgundy velour curtains hung in pleats at the rear of the stage. An elaborately carved wooden frame rose to form a proscenium arch that crossed the ceiling. Low wattage stage lights beamed from under cover at the foot of the stage. A gleaming grand piano dominated the modest stage. The musician, a fragile gray-haired man, was hunched over the keys, swaying with the strains of the music.

"We have a table over there," Bailey said, motioning toward the back of the dining room. Stuart saw a series of prominent semi-circular booths that stretched from the bar to the foot of the stage. He saw Parnell rise from the dark leather upholstery of the booth nearest the bar and raise a hand.

"Friday nights are almost always a full house," Bailey shouted as they made their way through the tables. Stuart scanned the establishment's inhabitants and realized the room looked as if the United Nations had emptied into the club. Dozens of men and women—each dressed in a variety of outfits; some draped in robes or saris, several in military uniforms and field jackets—mingled throughout the room. Others, mixed among the more elaborate costumes, wore evening gowns and suits. Stuart noticed one patron with an actual pith helmet carefully positioned on his table. Stuart wasn't quite sure what he had expected from a Kilimanjaro Club, but this was closer to a Halloween party.

As his eyes adjusted to the dim lighting, he noticed the paneled walls were covered with hundreds of small, framed photographs, most of which appeared to be black and white. By the time they reached the booth, Parnell was standing in front of the table. He greeted Stuart with an enthusiastic handshake, smacking him on the shoulder with his left hand. Parnell's smile was so broad it looked like it hurt.

"Welcome, Stuart! Welcome. I'm overjoyed that you've joined us this evening," he said, ushering Stuart into the booth.

"Well, it wasn't for a lack of coercion on your part."

"Oh, we do tend to get ahead of ourselves at times," Parnell said, eyeing Bailey. The two men slid in after Stuart, who felt his anxiety begin to wane.

"I was telling Parnell earlier, Stuart, just how much I enjoy visiting the New York club."

"We have many, many fond memories from this place," Parnell added.

Stuart spied a server heading toward the table. Bailey seemed to follow Stuart's gaze and said, "Would you like something to wet your whistle before we dine?"

Stuart looked at the table in front of both men and asked, "What are the two of you having?"

"Good evening, Mr. Honeybourne, Mr. Sumner," the server said as he arrived at the booth. He was a stocky, spectacled man in his late thirties or early forties. He had a pleasant, disarming smile.

"Rodney!" Parnell yipped, recognizing the server.

"May I serve you gentlemen something from the bar?" Rodney asked, folding and unfolding a side-towel absently.

"The usual," Bailey said. Parnell nodded as Rodney looked his way.

"Mr. Mancini, my name is Rodney, and I'll be taking care of you this evening," Rodney said, his smile disappearing under a serious gaze. Stuart half stood and shook Rodney's outstretched hand.

"Good to meet you," Stuart said. "I suppose I'll have a glass of wine. Do you … have a recommendation for a Syrah or Zinfandel?"

"Oh, I do," Rodney said, rising up a bit on his toes. "My personal favorite is Rust en Vrede, a lovely Syrah out of South Africa. Stellenbosch."

"Sounds good," Stuart said and sat back into the plush, worn leather booth.

"Excellent, Mr. Mancini," Rodney said, and shot away to the bar.

The three men sat in relative silence for several seconds. Stuart stared straight ahead. He could feel the tension in his jaw return and creep into his gut. How had this happened? What was he doing here? He was days away from wrapping up the biggest transaction of his career. A key partner in the negotiations was MIA and the Queen's version of Laurel and Hardy had dropped from the sky to tell him a despised relative was bequeathing a mysterious gift to him. A sudden heat seemed to percolate within him. Finally, Bailey leaned over toward Stuart.

"Stuart, I …"

Stuart raised his hand and glared at Bailey. "Let's put aside all the …" he said, waving his hands, "pageantry here? What in the hell is going on? I feel like I'm aiding my own kidnapping. I don't like games, Mr. Honeybourne, and I most certainly don't play games with men who seem to have a … a feeble grasp of reality."

Bailey slid back looking astonished.

"You did your job. You delivered your little note," Stuart said and then looked at Parnell. "This isn't for me. Call your driver and have him take me home."

"Now, Stuart—"

"Are you listening to me? You two … *lunatics* and your … your," Stuart said, gesturing to the room, "International Boys' Club are just about the last thing I need. Now get the car here, Parnell. Do it!" Stuart snapped, his voice attracting the attention of a few nearby patrons.

Parnell sat still for a moment, looked at Bailey, then rose from the booth. Stuart fumbled his way out behind him. Stuart grabbed Parnell's arm and marched him back through the dining room toward the entryway. They roughly bumped several patrons as they made their way through the room, triggering a slight hush throughout the dining room.

"Stuart, this really isn't necessary," Parnell said, pulling away from Stuart's grip. They had reached the main hall that separated the lobby from the dining room. Parnell yanked on the bottom of his suit jacket to straighten it out. Stuart was breathing heavily, his jaw clenched. He stared at Parnell then turned and walked toward the double doors. Stuart shoved both doors open simultaneously and stormed into the anteroom. Parnell paused a second then followed him into the lobby.

"There's a phone on that table. Call Carlton," Stuart said, pointing to an old rotary phone on one of the room's side tables.

"Stuart, if I can ask you to just calm down for one moment, I think I can provide you with the explanation you deserve."

"I'm not interested in calming down. I don't have time for this. I have a significant responsibility for an acquisition that's now at risk. What I *deserve* is to be left alone," Stuart growled.

"Helmut Rhinegold is missing," Parnell said.

"What …" Stuart said, taking a step toward Parnell. "How do you know Helmut?"

Parnell pivoted to his right and pointed to a framed eight-by-ten photograph hanging above a leather club chair. The dim yellow lamp light cast a shadow over the image. Stuart walked over to the chair and peered at the photo. Helmut Rhinegold was flanked by two Tibetan monks. Behind them, over Helmut's left shoulder, was The Potala Palace in Lhasa. Stuart turned back to Parnell, confused.

"Helmut … Helmut's a member? Here?"

"Indeed, and a dear friend of Bailey's. Me as well, but he and Bailey have a bit more history together. He scheduled your lunch today so that the three of us could extend your grandfather's gift. But we know he's a busy man. We obviously thought he had something come up. A change in plans."

"Change in plans? I haven't been able to find him. No one has. I'm extremely worried."

Stuart took a few steps toward Parnell.

"As are we. Bailey has been trying to reach him all day. No one seems to know where he is. Not his assistant, not his family. It's disturbing. And as far as this deal you've been constructing, Stuart, it's on indefinite hold. Without Helmut—"

"I know. It *can't* be consummated. At least not without some serious, unlikely concessions from the other owners," Stuart said, his gaze glued to the photo. He struggled to make sense of the onslaught of emotions, data, and images that flashed through his mind. He was tired, confused, and still angry.

Parnell held his right palm out toward Stuart. "Come. Let's begin again. I think Bailey and I can answer some of your questions and help you with your decision."

Stuart looked down at the floor, exhaled, and began walking back toward the double doors. Parnell grinned and led him across the hall and into the dining room.

Bailey swirled the beet red wine around the humongous bowl. He watched the spin die down and took a lengthy drink.

"I still remember meeting Malcolm for the first time," he said. "Nairobi, fittingly enough. Nineteen twenty-eight, late April. He was quite a figure in his RAF uniform."

"That's a little lofty for a deserter," Stuart said.

Bailey guffawed and looked at Stuart from the corner of his eye. "'Deserter,'" he scoffed again. "We have quite a lot to tell you about your grandfather, Stuart. Although it's a long and complicated story, I can assure you that Malcolm was the furthest thing from a deserter. He was a loyalist through and through."

"The Queen's charge," Parnell chimed in.

The trio was on their second round by this time, the first having passed for the most part in silence. Bailey and Parnell appeared to be giving Stuart whatever time and space he needed to recover from his initial reaction.

Rodney delivered generous pours, and as Stuart worked on the last half of his glass, he did feel less agitated and, to some degree, a bit embarrassed about his earlier reaction. Bailey and Parnell seemed relatively harmless.

"Okay, we've dodged this long enough, Bailey," Stuart said, planting his goblet firmly on the table. "I have until noon tomorrow to accept or refuse this invitation you delivered today. I need to know what it's all about."

His hosts smiled at one another and took turns swigging from their glasses. Stuart was somewhat surprised to hear Parnell begin.

"Tonight, you're a guest, albeit an honored guest, of the New York chapter of The Kilimanjaro Club. As I believe the letter from Malcolm stated, this is a private and highly exclusive club. There are, officially, twenty-four chapters located across the globe. The founding and original location is in Nairobi, Kenya. A group of British explorers and military men initiated the club in the private room of the Long Bar in Nairobi proper. As membership grew—and it did so in a highly controlled, selective manner—the individual members, many of whom were quite renowned, elected to open charter clubs in or near their home cities. London, rather predictably, was the first. Paris followed soon after. By the end of World War II nearly a dozen chapters were operating full time."

"So, what was the purpose? Why create a private club?" Stuart asked.

"At first these were men who were drawn together because of their passion for adventure and exploration," Parnell continued. "Remember, at the turn of the century, there were still vast areas of the globe that had been undiscovered by civilized man. Africa and her myriad lands were an obvious draw for much of Europe. This *fraternity*, as it truly was, thrived on the testosterone-driven egos of men who couldn't stand to be one-upped by a fellow gentleman."

"Initially," Bailey said, "the clubs were meant as a sort of escape from the traditional pubs and men's clubs that sprang up in many cities. While you could certainly find a fine drink and a decent meal at most of these establishments, they lacked, in many cases, a … a mutual objective.

"The Kilimanjaro Club filled a portion of that gap. Back when the Nairobi Club, as it was originally dubbed, came into existence, its members instituted the tradition of dramatically recounting the details of their journeys into the jungles and swamps of what were then East Africa, the Congo, and the Sudan. Mind you, we're talking about a time when members numbered in the dozens. Early on, the club's small membership regularly supplemented its ranks with a significant number of guests, often women, and the atmosphere, typically, was rather raucous."

"Ah, the good old days," Parnell said, toasting Bailey. The two men laughed and drank.

"I'm still struggling a bit with this," Stuart said to Bailey. "I understand my grandfather wished to will his membership to me, but his decision obviously doesn't carry the same weight with me as it does the two of you, or for someone who might be interested in joining some social or … or adventurers' club. Like I said, you don't know me very well. You don't know me at all. My life is my career. I live to work and I'm proud of that. It's what I do. It's what I love. I spend a great deal of time—by choice—either in front of a computer or in meetings talking to people about what I do in front of the computer. There's just no … no appeal to me. Do you understand?"

Bailey stuck his bottom lip out a bit, nodded, and stroked his mustache.

Stuart continued, "In my experience, any club like this has all kinds of requirements and expectations. I imagine there's some sort of minimum that members are required to spend here, too. And while I certainly eat a fair number of meals out, I can't imagine that I'd be compelled to visit this club—wherever the hell we are—frequently enough to meet that requirement. It just wouldn't be worth it."

Rodney interrupted what could have turned into another uncomfortable silence by delivering their entrees. He carefully positioned plates carrying softball-sized filets balanced upon a steaming mound of risotto. Stuart had ordered a red snapper dish with steamed vegetables.

"Another bottle of Syrah?" Rodney asked.

Stuart began to shake his head to decline when Parnell shouted, "Most definitely!"

"Stuart, we know how dedicated you are to your work. Malcolm talked about it frequently. He was quite proud. But it's Friday evening. Even you can appreciate a night of frivolity," Bailey said.

"I'm not sure I would categorize this as *frivolity*, but I suppose you're right. I do need to leave once we finish dinner."

They spent several minutes dining in silence, allowing the piano and surrounding conversation to fill the air.

"As you've probably noticed," Bailey said, having devoured half his entrée, "Parnell and I can take a while to get to the point. Frankly, we're social beasts. We tend to thrive as much on the gab as we do on the thrust, if you know what I mean."

Stuart nodded, chewing.

"The bottom line, as you business folk like to say," Parnell added, "is that Malcolm's gift to you includes the membership, obviously, but also the initiation fee, and, I must say, a substantial sum of money."

"Money?" Stuart said mid-chew. Parnell nodded.

"The initiation fee itself is one million dollars," Bailey said.

Stuart set his knife and fork down slowly and gaped at Bailey. "What?"

Bailey smiled. "Malcolm predicted you would react … negatively. That's part of the reason he included the fee in your inheritance."

"That sum is in a trust of sorts. It can only be accessed if you accept the membership invitation," Parnell said.

"And the additional funds can only be released after you've completed initiation."

Stuart stifled a laugh and sat back. "Well, I guess you've hit the bottom line alright. Either I join this place or I say goodbye to some sort of windfall."

"That," Bailey said and took a sip of wine, "is correct."

Stuart glanced at his watch. "I have, what? Fourteen hours now to deal with this?"

Bailey nodded and Parnell said, "I can't believe it's much of a decision. You were correct earlier. There are annual minimums. They're sizable, too, but I would imagine the additional money Malcolm set aside for you would cover those costs for quite some time."

"Humor me. What are the fees?"

"Twelve thousand dollars a year. A thousand a month," Parnell said.

It was actually less than what Stuart had imagined. There were a number of his colleagues at D'Artagnan who paid significantly more to maintain memberships at private golf, tennis, and polo clubs.

"What's the other catch?"

"I'm sorry?" Bailey said.

"Well, as you said, Parnell, there doesn't seem to be much of a decision. From what you've shared, I should be able to simply accept and, if I feel like it, just forget that I'm a member. I'm assuming there's something else significant. It's too good to be true."

"Of course it's too good to be true. It's The Kilimanjaro Club," Bailey said. "But the *catch*, as you say, is actually what compels our members to seek out and maintain their memberships. As our club title implies, this is an adventurers' club. We pride ourselves on living vigorously—on seeking out opportunities to explore, experience, and share our lives."

"Bailey, my dear friend, I believe Stuart is looking for the bottom line again."

Bailey chuckled. "Right, the bottom line. We require members to complete an annual adventure—more if they like—that is sanctioned by the club, and share the results, the experiences, from that adventure with club members, during Friday Stories."

"Friday Stories?" Stuart said. "Like Toastmasters or AA?"

"Certainly not AA," Parnell said, lifting his glass. "We'd be bloody failures."

"But you're not too far off," Bailey said. "It harkens back to the club's beginnings I mentioned, when the founders competed rather aggressively to accumulate the most amazing and fearsome adventures."

Stuart thought it sounded like a mandatory vacation. He had never taken what would be categorized as a vacation since he'd started with D'Artagnan. He'd actually coerced the firm's administrative manager to turn off his accumulation of vacation time. He'd accrued over four hundred hours that remained untouched.

"Which takes me back to my earlier point," Stuart said. "There's no real draw for me. I don't take vacations. And I don't go on adventures."

# FOUR

He was suffocating. It was as if someone had jammed an athletic sock into his mouth. Every drop of moisture seemed to have been drained from his mouth and throat. Panic set in. His heart pounded. And just as quickly as he felt the last trace of oxygen pass through the tiny bronchi of his lungs, life returned. Air rushed back down his windpipe, followed by a dry burn. Shafts of bright light seared his eyes as he pried them open. A second later the intensity of the light faded and he was able to focus. He recognized the teak table a few inches in front of his face. It was one of his nightstands. Stuart was in bed, and in agony.

He rolled onto his back and took another deep, shuddering breath. As he did so, the entire room hesitated and tracked behind the path of his head, like a bad soundtrack lagging the actors' lip movements. When he closed his mouth, his lips stuck together, and the inside of his mouth clung to his teeth. He dropped a hand on his chest and realized he was still wearing his dress shirt. He slid his hand down further and found he was wearing his pants as well. A quick glance confirmed what he feared. Shoes on, too. What the hell happened? What day is it?

Stuart propped himself up on his elbows and took another deep breath, hoping the following exhale would relieve some of the throbbing and fatigue that was pulsing through his veins. It did little good. *Water*, he thought. *I've got to start with water.*

He lurched off the bed, kicked off his shoes, and shuffled into the main room toward the kitchen. A blinking red light off to his right caught his eye. *Answering machine. It can wait.*

Midway through the third glass of water, his stomach began to protest, but his mouth and throat were hoarding every drop. Almost immediately he began to feel ... human.

Saturday. It was Saturday, he realized. *Thank god.*

The intercom system was integrated with the apartment's alarm and thermostat. Stuart walked over to the wall and confirmed the day and time. Saturday, 9:27 a.m. He couldn't remember the last time he'd slept past seven, let alone nine. He filled his glass again and walked back into the main room.

"Okay," he said out loud. "If today is Saturday, and yesterday was Friday, what the hell did I do last night?" The void that followed this thought was frightening. The panic returned. *Work. What did I do at work yesterday?* Nothing came to him. He had a vague memory—or perhaps a manufactured memory since the routine of his days was relatively consistent—of greeting Olivia when she arrived. Was that right? Had she been wearing that pink short-sleeved blouse? Had it been warm or cold yesterday?

Whatever had happened the day before, it had definitely involved alcohol. The symptoms were beginning to clarify themselves and the diagnosis was hangover. A whopper, too. Hangover mixed with something else. A cold, perhaps. He felt nasty.

He punched a button on the answering machine and a voice announced that he had one message.

"Good morning, Mr. Mancini. It's Larry. I hate to bother you, but I have a package for you downstairs. Just an envelope, really. I thought I'd see you this morning on your way to the office, but I may have missed you. Or maybe you haven't gone in yet. Anyway, it'll be here. Have a good one." The machine beeped, then announced, "Saturday, 8:09 a.m."

Stuart trudged back into the kitchen and started a pot of coffee. He threw in an extra scoop of beans. Something had to take this pain away. He opened the refrigerator and scanned the contents. There was an impressive array of condiments, an open bottle of chardonnay—no hair of the dog, thank you—a half empty bottle of pasta sauce, and several zip-lock bags filled with cheese. What he didn't find was a giant package of breakfast sausage or a pack of bratwurst. His stomach growled in protest. Mustard on Irish cheddar wasn't going to cut it. He thought for a moment. Did Domino's deliver this early? He needed grease. He closed the door, and the phone rang.

He found the handset just before the call went to voicemail. "Hello?"

"Stuart! Where are you?" It was Heath.

"I'm at home. Where you called," Stuart answered.

"Right, right. Sorry, man. Hey, you sound like crap."

"Thanks. Feeling as such … or worse."

"Well, I'd love to spend some time learning about your uncharacteristic bender, but we've got business to take care of. Did you hear about Helmut?"

"What happened?" Stuart said, his pulse jumping.

"He's missing. No one has heard from him. That lunch he missed with you was about the last detail anyone has."

Stuart paused. A quick blast of the previous day's events registered. "Yes, you're right," he said. "We were supposed to meet for lunch. He stood me up, but … but not before leaving a bizarre message on my cell phone. I … I missed his call. The message was all garbled. I had Olivia try to track him down but she came up with nothing." The memory was still faded, but at least it was a part of the puzzle.

"I know. I know. Jesus. I got a call late last night from Hugh Fletcher. He was in a panic. Something about he and his wife throwing some dinner party for Helmut and … well, he didn't show there either. They're completely freaked out right now. No one has said it, but we're all worried that the deal's in jeopardy."

Stuart sucked in a breath and sat down on the couch. "Heath. When was the last time anyone saw him? Yesterday sometime, in the morning maybe? Have they called the police? Checked the hospitals?"

"Yeah, yeah, yeah. The cops don't like to treat these things as missing persons until they've been gone twenty-four hours, but they claim to be helping. Helmut knew people all over the city, you know. Someone in the police department escalated it. Hugh said they were checking the hospitals, too, but nothing came up. You know, your message from him may turn out to be important. I don't know if anyone saw or heard from him after about 8:00 a.m. yesterday."

Pieces of the prior day were starting to fall into place. Helmut going AWOL. The status of the deal. Way too much alcohol.

His recollection of the voicemail message materialized. Everything about it had been uncharacteristic. He glanced around the room searching for his cell phone. He needed to listen to Helmut's message again.

"Stuart? Stuart? Are you still there?"

"Yes, I am, Heath. Sorry. I haven't had any coffee yet."

"Don't worry about it. Hey, are you free this afternoon? Maybe right after lunch? I'm at the office. Carl's here. So's Kennedy. We should probably huddle. We don't have much of a contingency plan at this point."

Stuart thought for a moment. He could sleep another couple of hours and still get to the office by one.

"Yes, of course I can be there. How about one or so?"

"Sure, that's fine. Come earlier if you can. We'll see you then." Heath sounded a bit distant. "Oh, hey, Stuart."

"Yes?"

"Carl said something earlier about Helmut taking these weird, spur-of-the-moment vacations. Have you ever heard anything like that?"

Stuart felt another memory jog, but nothing clicked. "He … I know he liked to travel. I can't say I ever knew if they were spur-of-the-moment trips."

Heath was silent on the other end. Finally, he said, "Okay. We're grasping here. Just trying to help them out. I don't want this thing falling apart at the last minute." Heath hung up without saying goodbye. Stuart hardly noticed.

He peeled off the previous day's clothes and threw on a t-shirt, sweatpants, and running shoes. He rode the elevator down to the lobby and headed for the front door. The doormen maintained a small office with a large pass-through window. To the right of the window was an open door leading into the office. Larry was perched on a bar stool behind the window reading the *New York Daily News*.

"Good morning, Larry."

Larry collapsed the paper and stared at Stuart. "You … don't look so good, Mr. Mancini, if you don't mind me saying so." Larry was a hulk of a man. He'd played defensive tackle for Rutgers and had been drafted—seventh round, but still drafted—by the Raiders. A three-hundred-pound nose tackle had spiraled into Larry's knee just before halftime during his first pre-season game. It was the last time Larry ever set foot on the gridiron.

Stuart ran a hand through his short dark hair and looked at the ground. "Thanks, I feel just as spiffy."

"You know, I was gone when you came in last night but Seth told me you were in rare form."

"Seth saw me last night?"

"Course. It wasn't real late. Eleven-thirty, I think he said. Your uncle brought you back. Same one who dropped off your package."

Stuart furrowed his brow and cocked his head. "Uncle? I …"

"Yeah, Uncle Bailey. Real nice man. Brought me a box of donuts. Pies-n-Thighs, my favorite." He set the paper on the counter of the window and swiveled around on the barstool. He swung back and stuck out a small square envelope. "Here you go."

Stuart took the envelope and examined it, turning is slowly. On one side, Stuart's name was scrawled in black Sharpie. "Did … my uncle say anything?"

"Nah, just asked if I'd seen or heard from you yet."

Stuart returned his gaze to the envelope and bounced it between his fingers. "Thanks, Larry," he said and walked back to the elevator.

"Sweat it out, Mr. Mancini," Larry called after him.

"I beg your pardon," he said, turning around.

"Whatever's ailing you. Sweat it out. Always works for me," Larry said, a huge smile spreading across his face.

He waited until he was inside the apartment to open the envelope. He hesitated before sliding his forefinger under the flap. For the past twenty years, his life had been controlled, organized, simple. The volume of oddities he was attempting to process from this morning alone already surpassed the number of unexpected events he faced in a given year. Rarely, if ever, was he caught off guard or surprised by anything. He spent too much time analyzing, critiquing, and predicting the next probable steps to stumble into a surprise. Now, reality seemed to have slipped from its axis. He finished opening the envelope as he walked into the main room.

Inside, he found a Sony recordable DVD. A plain white label was affixed to the non-recordable side. The prior day's date and three letters, *SKM*—his initials he presumed—were printed across the label.

He grabbed a remote control from the credenza behind the couch and punched a button to open the tray. A moment later the monitor sprang to life. He popped in the DVD and hit the play button.

Static filled the screen for the first few seconds, then the picture shifted. It appeared to be shot from a camera mounted in the upper corner of a room. A conference table situated in a well-appointed space filled most of the screen. Voices came from off-screen. A moment later, three people entered the conference room, prompting a jump in the sound quality. Stuart recognized himself immediately. They were discussing pubs in London.

A stout man with a rather large mustache stepped over to an armoire at the far end of the room and pulled out a leather-bound portfolio. Stuart watched himself sit down at the table and pull a pen from his jacket pocket.

"At the risk of sounding like a horribly broken record, Stuart, I want to tell you again how pleased I am at your decision to accept Malcolm's offer."

Stuart punched the pause button and stared at the screen. His mouth fell open. None of what he was seeing registered. Yes, the man who had just spoken looked strangely familiar, but everything else was foreign. He squinted at the screen and realized the suit and tie he was wearing in the video were the same as what he'd worn the previous night. The same clothes he'd woken up in. He hesitated, then pressed play again.

"It's okay," he heard himself say. "I understand my grandfather placed a lot of confidence in your ability to convince me to accept. I … I'm still a little leery about what I'm committing to, but I have this … this strange feeling …" The Stuart on the screen laughed, jabbed his left hand through his hair, and finished his sentence. "… that it's the right decision." He laughed again as he uncapped his pen. "Of course, it could have something to do with that shot of ouzo you forced on me."

The two men with him laughed loudly. Stuart watched himself open the portfolio and scan through the pages within the folder. A few minutes later, he scrawled his signature and closed the folder.

"Outstanding," the second man said. Stuart shook hands with both men and the group exited the room. A few seconds later the video switched back to static. Stuart shut off the DVD player and sat still. Nothing made sense.

The phone rang.

After the third ring, he pried himself from the couch and grabbed the phone.

"Mancini," he said absently.

"Top of the day, Stuart," he heard on the other end. "Bailey Honeybourne here. Doubtful you recall much of our meeting yesterday, but your man Larry at the door just informed me that you picked up my little package. I trust it's in your machine, right?"

Stuart stared at the handset.

"Stuart? Stuart, are you there?"

It took a second, but Stuart recognized the voice from the video.

"Just who in the f—" he shouted into the phone. "Who … who in the hell are you? What are you doing to me?"

His questions were met with silence, then the man said, "Stuart, I'm in the lobby. If you don't mind, I'll ask Larry to buzz me up. It's important we get reacquainted."

Stuart's heart began pounding in his chest. He'd never felt so disoriented.

"Okay, okay, whatever," he muttered and ended the call. A moment later, he heard the elevator doors open.

Stuart walked to the entryway and saw the man from the video. He looked like a younger Kris Kringle, dressed for the off-season.

"Good morning, Stuart," he said. "May I come in?" Stuart nodded as the elevator doors closed. Bailey continued down the hallway into the main room. Stuart followed, taking slow steps and watching Bailey's casual saunter.

"I'll be straight with you," Stuart said. "You've got thirty seconds before I call the police. If you try to leave, the building security cameras have you on tape. I have a DVD with you on it, apparently coercing me into signing something, and I have no memory of it or you. You'd better start."

"Stuart," Bailey said, walking toward him, his hands outstretched. "I will need more than thirty seconds, but I think you'll understand. Please, sit."

"I think I'll stand."

"I understand your frustration. It's quite common. But some of last night will return to you. In fact, I imagine you're starting to reform a few memories just from us speaking again."

Stuart simply stared at the man. He did see flashes, though. The voice. The voice and the accent. Bailey sounded like a reformed cockney bloke who spoke through a mouthful of pea gravel.

"Go on."

"It's quite simple, really. Yesterday, around midday, my colleague, Parnell Sumner, and I met you at the Oak Room. You were scheduled to lunch with Helmut Rhinegold. He didn't arrive. Parnell and I came to you as ambassadors of sorts from your maternal grandfather, Malcolm Buckley. We shared his invitation to you to join a private club, The Kilimanjaro Club. Last night you dined with Parnell and I at the club and accepted the offer. That was what you saw on the video."

Stuart began to pace around the room. He walked toward the window and then turned back to face Bailey.

"I just received a call from one of the owners of my firm. Helmut Rhinegold is missing. Wasn't it convenient that you show up at a time when my lunch date—a key member of the merger I'm about to close—isn't available? Just what part did *you* play in his disappearance?"

Bailey laughed, then stopped himself. "I'm sorry, Stuart. We went through this last night. Helmut is a member of The Kilimanjaro Club. He was planning to meet us at the Oak Room for lunch yesterday. He, as you know, didn't show." Bailey paused. "Stuart, Helmut is an old friend. Parnell and I have had nothing to do with his disappearance. You must believe me."

Stuart began pacing again. His memory felt like a faulty slide projector. Quick, random snapshots, some blurry, some crystal clear, flashed in rapid succession through his brain. He had no frame of reference to determine what was factual and what he might have imagined.

"Mr. Honeybourne, I'm always careful how much I drink in public," Stuart said, walking around the perimeter of the room. "I can't believe I drank so much last night that I blacked out. It's not possible."

Bailey smiled, "Of course it's not possible. You *were* quite careful. You had two, perhaps three, glasses of red wine and a small shot of ouzo. Perhaps enough to make you a bit tipsy, but certainly not … snockered."

"I can't begin to tell you how uncomfortable I am with all of this. It's completely inappropriate. I will not tolerate being manipulated or patronized. Either help me understand what's going on or I call the police. Now."

Bailey raised a hand and half laughed. "Stuart, please. Allow me to continue." He paused and then sat on the leather couch.

"Our club is something we hold very dear. It's more than simply private, more than selective. It is, in many ways, sacred to its members. Not in a religious fashion, by any means, but certainly from a devotional standpoint. We take what we feel are certain, necessary precautions when considering new members. These are rare moments for us."

Stuart took a deep breath, but continued to listen. The familiarity of Bailey's voice began to settle in. While he couldn't put together two rational or related recollections, he somehow knew that Bailey was speaking the truth.

"The ouzo is the culprit. We have several doctors who are members. One of them helped us years ago with a little potion to assist with our membership interviews."

"Potion?"

"A powder, really. Have you ever heard of Scopolamine?"

"No. I have not."

"Fascinating drug, really. Frightening, too, if misused. For us, its only function is to create a short-term memory loss. Alcohol can exacerbate its effects. If a potential member chooses not to accept an invitation—a rare occurrence by the way—they have no idea that the invite occurred. They have a whopper of a headache the next day, but have no clear idea why. For those who do accept, as you did, we have a bit of damage control to do. That's my job today, and perhaps for a few days going forward."

"So, I lost most of an entire day due to you and your little potion, and your … club?"

"Stuart, surely you understand. It's a security issue. I'm confident you have similar, though probably not drug-induced, safety and security measures at D'Artagnan. Right?"

Stuart shook his head and walked toward the windows.

"Scopolamine was actually one of the first truth serums. It was rather effective, too. It's been around for ages. Nearly a century. You've heard of nightshade, perhaps? That's the source. In heavy doses it's poisonous. In smaller controlled doses, it's a highly effective amnestic. It will also cause the recipient to run a bit at the mouth, thus its value as a truth serum. We started using it at the club in the 1960s. About that time, we were losing members to, frankly, old age. They were either dying or becoming incapacitated. We wanted to maintain both the vitality as well as the secrecy of the organization. As new potential members were identified, we became worried about those who might turn us down. We didn't want them wandering out in public, talking about our exclusive society. Not that we have anything to hide, at least nothing shameful. The club is, however, much more valuable and, effective, I guess one could say, as a more covert association. It's part of the draw. At any rate, the good doctor, as I mentioned, introduced the board to the magical properties of the drug, and we quickly adopted it as our key security measure. Without post-recovery visits such as mine, and our video, it's highly unlikely that those who are considered but rejected from membership ever recollect anything about the club."

"What do you mean, 'without the post-recovery visits?'"

"Well, it's different with each individual, but I would venture to guess that right about now, perhaps a bit earlier, you began to feel some sense of déjà vu. Am I correct?"

Stuart felt a lurch in his chest. At that precise moment, he had indeed felt a powerful, yet indescribably different, feeling of déjà vu. The combination of Bailey's voice, the cadence, the subtle tones, all triggered the brain malfunction.

"Think about it, Stuart. Combine me talking with you now with what you saw on the video. Isn't there something that seems … familiar?"

Confusion. That was the only tangible feeling he was experiencing. Could he trust this stranger he'd allowed into his apartment? This potential deviant who had apparently kidnapped him, or something dangerously close, and initiated him into some secret fraternity? The erratic memory gaps were maddening. He struggled to pull his focus away from the shadowed reflections within the window.

"We'd very much like to take the next appropriate step with you, Stuart. No drugs, my promise. Tonight. Parnell and I would like to host you again at the club to celebrate your membership. Our pitch is over. You've chosen to join. Now let us share the true benefits. I think you'll be both relieved and intrigued."

Stuart paced along the windows, taking deep, purposeful breaths. He was pissed at himself for allowing such a wash of conflicting emotions to cloud his mind. He felt the primal anger and disgust his mother had instilled in him toward his grandfather. There was the panic and frustration he felt, completely unrelated to anything Bailey was connected with, regarding the jeopardy the company sale was in. And then there was the unexpected, urgent desire to escape, to see this bizarre chain of events as an opportunity to take an impulsive turn in his life, to *make* it a life. He stopped, and at least momentarily, calmed himself.

"Bailey," he said, barely audible. "I need to ask you for some time. I need … I don't know … I just need some time to organize my thoughts. A lot has happened. Surely you can see that."

Bailey rose from the couch but didn't make a move toward him. "I do understand, Stuart. I do."

"About this evening. How can I reach you? I'm not sure I can make it work. But …"

Bailey raised his hand. "I shall call you. Perhaps," he said, frowning, "perhaps this afternoon." He paused a moment. "Please know that we will understand if you can't make it. We'll both be disappointed, but there will be other opportunities. It may, however, be just the right thing for you."

Stuart nodded absently. Bailey reached down toward the couch and picked up a leather portfolio. Stuart realized that he hadn't even noticed that the man had been carrying it. Bailey held it out to Stuart.

"As a member, this is yours to retain. It's an important set of documents. Not just your commitment to the club. If you have a chance, look it over before this evening. I believe it may help."

Stuart approached Bailey and took the portfolio from his hand. As he suspected, it was the same as the one he'd seen in the video. Embossed on the front was his full name.

# CHAPTER

# FIVE

As promised, Carlton pulled up outside Stuart's building at exactly 7:00 p.m. It was the same austere limousine spotted gliding up to the entrances of elegant hotels and corporate offices throughout the city. At the same time, it appeared completely unlike any other he had ever seen—as if it were from a parallel universe. Carlton slid from the driver's side and greeted Stuart with a broad, sincere smile.

"So *very* good to see you again, Mr. Mancini."

Stuart nodded and smiled. Bailey had been right. The amnestic effects of the Scopolamine faded as he re-experienced sounds, people, and sights from the previous night. While he wouldn't have recognized Carlton outside of this particular scene, the familiarity of the situation essentially recreated a memory—a comfortable one—and he reacted in kind.

"Thank you ..."

Carlton's smile somehow broadened. "Carlton, Mr. Mancini." Carlton opened the door and stepped out of Stuart's way. "I know this day can seem, well, uncomfortable. But it's likely to be the last. You're in amazing company, Mr. Mancini. Utterly amazing."

Stuart entered the car and sat. "Carlton," he said, before the door shut. "Have you … have you been affiliated with the club long?"

This time Carlton grinned, rather than smiling. "Over thirty years now," he said, and closed the door with a light thump.

The gentle float of the limo's ride, accompanied by a pleasing low rumble, triggered another recollection from the prior night. He remembered being in this car but couldn't recall where it had taken him. Stuart began to ask Carlton, and then the memory flashed again in his mind. The windows had been tinted on the inside. He hadn't been able to see outside or where Carlton had driven them. This car, however, didn't appear to have the same windows. They were tinted, but normally, on the outside.

The electric click of the limo's intercom interrupted the silence, followed by Carlton's voice. "The windows are made of what they call privacy glass. I've got a switch up here that I can manipulate. Turn the tint off and on. Inside or out."

"Wow," Stuart muttered.

Carlton made his way down Lexington to Fifty-Seventh Street, then cut across to Fifth, up to Fifty-Ninth, and then across the south end of Central Park to Columbus Circle, finally connecting with Broadway. Several blocks later, he made a left and followed a ramp to the underground entrance. A moment later, he was in front of the elevator doors and Carlton was pulling away.

As Stuart exited the elevator that carried him to the club, Bailey stood before him, beaming.

"Good evening, Stuart Mancini," Bailey trumpeted, nearly leaping to greet him with a vigorous handshake. "I am very excited about this evening's festivities, and so grateful you could join us. I do hope you're feeling better than you were earlier, eh?"

Stuart managed a smile and nodded. "Yes. It wasn't one of my better mornings, but I am feeling better—more comfortable. Still a bit apprehensive, I have to warn you, but anxious … in a good way, I suppose."

"Splendid," Bailey said, escorting him through the double doors and into the main hallway. The dissonance of voices, randy jazz, and activity erupted as they entered the hall.

"Wow," Stuart said again.

"Yes, well, weekend evenings—Friday and Saturday nights—are quite popular. We do our best to attract the most popular musicians, and it's become something of a tradition for out-of-town members to visit. Tonight is no exception."

Bailey escorted Stuart into the crowded space and to a table near the rear of the dining room. A sea of people drifted between the tables. A jazz quartet bounced vigorously on the stage, their music and energy penetrating the room. The heady mixture of cigar, pipe, clove, and cigarette smoke swirled through the air. Stuart struggled to acclimate. It had been years since he had visited a bar or restaurant that allowed smoking. The crowd seemed to absently part for Stuart and Bailey as they approached a four-top guarded by a long, lean gentleman. The man's gaze drifted toward them as they approached. He rose from his seat and stepped over to greet Stuart.

"Hello, again, Stuart. So good to see you," he said shaking Stuart's hand and grasping his forearm with this left hand.

"Uh, yes, I'm sorry, have we …"

The man leaned back and shoved a hand to the air. "My God, my apologies. I've completely forgotten … as have you, I'm sure. I'm Parnell Sumner. As Bailey may have mentioned, we met yesterday. You would have seen me on the video. I never seem to get accustomed to some of our practices."

Bailey leaned in to join the men. "Parnell, our new friend here is still a bit hesitant, and rightly so, given what he's been through."

"Please, Stuart, have a seat. Let's find a waiter and arrange for a toast," Parnell said, pulling a chair out for Stuart.

The three men sat, engulfed by the ensuing crowd. Stuart felt deafened by the conglomeration of music and voices. He leaned toward Bailey and yelled, "What's going on here?"

Bailey laughed and said, "I wish it were something out of the ordinary, but it's truly not. Some nights are just better than others."

A moment later, a tuxedo-clad server snaked between guests and reached their table. "What may I get you, Mr. Mancini?"

"Uh, well, a red … do you have a recommendation for a red wine? A Syrah, perhaps?" The server smiled.

"Certainly. Do you have any argument with an Australian offering?" Stuart shook his head.

"Excellent, then tonight I'll bring over a bottle of d'Arenberg shiraz. Are you familiar with it?"

"As a matter of fact, I am," Stuart said, pleased. "That'll be perfect."

As soon as the server left their table, the quartet ended a song and eased into a quieter tune. As if choreographed, the audience lowered their volume to match that of the band. Stuart saw Bailey check his watch and nod to himself.

"Expecting something?" Stuart asked.

"No," Bailey said, "just checking to see when the next break may come. While I am one who thrives on the energy our entertainment brings to the club, I have a great appreciation for quality background music. Parnell and I are conversationalists, I suppose you could say. We clamor for the opportunity to chat."

Stuart forced a grin, realizing these men were completely contrary to himself. There were probably fewer than a dozen people alive in the world that Stuart felt comfortable gabbing with. He hoped the server would return soon so he'd at least have something to do with his hands.

"Stuart, I know Bailey apologized for our use of narcotics last night, but I'd like to offer mine as well. We're very protective, is all," Parnell said.

Stuart nodded, gazing around the room. "Is everyone here a member? Do you allow guests?"

The men exchanged a glance, then Bailey said, "Very rarely. And we require a strong non-disclosure agreement, along with a hefty security deposit of sorts."

A flurry of activity disrupted their exchange. Excited voices rang around him. Through the crowd he spotted two servers carrying large trays of what appeared to be champagne flutes. He felt a tap on his shoulder. He turned and saw Bailey standing next to him, motioning for him to stand, too.

"Come with me," he said, leaning in near Stuart's ear. Stuart stood slowly, immediately self-conscious. Bailey placed a hand on the center of his back and gently guided him into the crowd. Even though the room seemed to be pushing the fire code limit, the pair slipped unhindered through the masses. Stuart noticed that the music had stopped just as they broke through an opening. They were at the foot of the stage. The saxophonist, an emaciated twig of a man, skin like the leather of a forgotten catcher's mitt, extended a hand to Stuart and flashed a flawless smile.

"C'mon up and join us!" A moment later Bailey was tugging Stuart toward one of the microphones. Without a word from Bailey, the room fell silent. A subtle spotlight fell on the two men as the remainder of the stage lighting dimmed.

"My fellow adventurers, good evening," Bailey bellowed into the mike.

A rousing "Good evening, Bailey" swept the room in unison.

"Thank you all for allowing me to interrupt the program this evening. I hope everyone has found a glass of champagne. If not, look around. The service staff is swarming with them."

Stuart marveled as he watched the service staff deliver drinks to empty hands through the glare of the spotlights.

"As you all know, nights like these don't come along too often anymore. I am, therefore, honored and excited to continue our fine club's tradition.

For tonight, I introduce to you our newest member. A man who, by the look on his face right now," Bailey said, turning to Stuart, "is probably thinking, fight or flight." Stuart felt a deep blush consume his face as a polite wave of laughter rippled through the room. "I believe most of you are aware of who we're honoring this evening; but, in case you missed the memo, beside me is Stuart Kane Mancini, the sole heir of one of our most illustrious and beloved members, Malcolm Seymour Buckley. I'm sure some of our newer members might recall—frankly because old buzzards like me can't remember where our hats are once we've donned our heads—the warm haze of panic and potential insanity that accompanies initiation night. Stuart here, I'm sure, is experiencing that same gut-wrenching feeling." Bailey slapped Stuart on the back and pulled him closer to the mike.

"I'm prattling on, I know. Let's get to it. Ladies and gentlemen of the New York Kilimanjaro Club, please join me in officially accepting and welcoming our newest member, Stuart Kane Mancini, into our exclusive little family."

The room erupted into a chant of sorts—Bailey joining them—that couldn't have been English. It went on for about three brief phrases and then ended with what sounded like, "Tukio!" The crowd raised their glasses in a toast and cheered. Bailey grasped Stuart in a bear hug and nearly lifted him off the ground. He released him and grabbed him by the shoulders.

"Stuart, old man, I know, I truly know that you think someone is either playing a gargantuan trick upon you or that you've completely lost your marbles, but trust me when I tell you this is—and for all the right reasons—a life-changing night for you. Now, let's go celebrate, shall we?"

From behind them, the band sprang into "Tuxedo Junction," essentially blowing him and Bailey off of the stage.

Over the next hour, Stewart entertained an unending parade of well-wishers representing every corner of the globe. Many regaled Stuart with peculiar anecdotes about his grandfather. A few had been familiar with Stuart for years, recalling how Malcolm had bragged about his grandson's success on Wall Street. It was all too bizarre to sort out.

During a rare lull, Stuart wondered what his mother would think of the day's events. He assumed he was barred from talking to her about the club, but that wouldn't likely stop him. Her reaction, he knew, would hinge solely upon her mental state, which was unpredictable.

Stuart's mother had moved into the Pendergrass Assisted Living Estate nearly two years earlier. Within months, she'd faded from the vibrant, physically active member of the Boston theater community to a docile, lost soul. Her doctors attributed her setback to Lewy Body Dementia, a rare neural disease. While she frequently recognized Stuart and some of her close friends, she rarely connected with the real world outside of this narrow group of loved ones. Since Stuart hadn't heard his mother talk of her father for decades, it was impossible to know if she would even remember who her father was, or why she'd chosen to exclude him from her life.

Since the onset of her illness, Stuart regularly made the trek north to visit her every month. The "Estate," as the administrators referred to it, offered a handful of apartments to family who wanted a convenient extended stay. Prior to each visit, he struggled to determine if this arrangement was healthy—for him, not her. The undercurrent of depression that permeated the environment was suffocating. He was confident that the care she received was of the highest quality available. The ratio at times was two to one—two medical professionals, a nurse and a medical doctor to each patient. The grounds and facilities had been designed by the same teams who had created the newest Four Seasons resorts, and the similarities were striking. Still, there was something about spending the night in a home where none of the full-time residents maintained a rational connection with reality that siphoned the hope from him.

He was due to see her again within the next couple of weeks. Her periods of delusion frequently caused her to believe she was either living in the past or channeling the experiences of a conjured persona. Stuart wondered if the mention of her father would trigger a similar incident. During these episodes, her flailing grasp on her surroundings would slip away, and she would act as if she were surrounded by a group of friends—often referred to as co-workers or former schoolmates—who, from what Stuart knew, never existed. Lately, she claimed she was living in Houston—a city she'd never visited—with three other women in their mid-twenties. On rarer occasions, she claimed to be on an archeological dig outside of Cairo, just after the turn of the twentieth century. Oddly enough, she remained Sylvia Mancini, to Stuart and any other "real" human in her midst; she just happened to be functioning in a distant, parallel universe. What other fantasies did she bury within her fragile psyche that might illuminate these unexpected revelations about his grandfather?

Stuart went to drink from his wine glass and found it empty. A bolt of fear shot through him. Had he succumbed to the same malady as his mother? Did that explain the extreme apparent shift in his existence? Was any of this real? He stopped breathing, watching the cartoonish gaggle of humanity circulate around him. A hand grasped his upper arm.

"Are you okay, Stuart?" He turned and saw Parnell at his side. A sincere look of concern washed over Parnell's face.

"I am. I am. Just … daydreaming a bit, I guess."

Parnell laughed, looking relieved, and said, "Yes, well if you can pull that off in the middle of this crowd, you've got tremendous focus."

Stuart was about to ask if there was a less frenetic place to talk when Parnell said, "Why don't we retire to the lounge?" He motioned toward the bar with his glass. "It's located on the other side of the main bar. Much quieter there. Civilized."

Stuart nodded and followed Parnell through the crowded room. A hallway lined with the requisite mahogany paneling, relic photographs, and tribal paraphernalia that blanketed most of the club opened just past the primary service station flanking the short side of the bar. Halfway down the hall, the dissonance of music and voices they left behind fell to a faint buzz. Parnell followed the hallway as it turned right. A large, ornately carved wooden door truncated the hall just past the turn. A delicate brass plate adorned the door with the words The Lounge carved in Old English calligraphy. Parnell pulled the door open and motioned Stuart past him.

The interior was the epitome of every gentlemen's club he'd either seen in a film or read about in a novel. Like the remainder of the club, the unexpectedly soothing mahogany blanketed the mammoth walls. The lamplight, infused with a mellow gold tone via the sheer lampshades shielding the bulbs, mimicked the firelight emanating from the colossal fieldstone fireplace. Numerous groupings of leather club chairs and couches, speckled with a small number of wooden legged lounge chairs, reflected the cozy aura. There were fewer than twenty people in the room, mostly groups of two or three, chatting quietly, drinking, and smoking.

A maître d' materialized next to them once they entered the lounge.

"Mr. Sumner, so good to see you this evening. Mr. Mancini, I presume?" the man said, smiling at Stuart and bowing slightly.

"Yes, thank you," Stuart responded.

"Excellent. Please allow me to share my congratulations on your recent membership. Now, may I offer you gentlemen a comfortable place to sit, and perhaps some brandy?"

"Arthur, I believe we'll sit over near the stacks," Parnell motioned toward a far corner of the lounge that was encased in floor-to-ceiling shelves full of books. "I think this evening, if it's agreeable to you, Stuart, I should prefer some Port."

Stuart felt himself blush a bit. "I'm willing to join in, but honestly I've never tried Port."

"Really? Well, this is quite an occasion. Please bring us the entire bottle, Arthur. I expect Bailey any moment now. We have things to celebrate," he said, leading them to the seating area near the bookshelves. "Never had Port?" Stuart heard Sumner say quietly. "How splendid."

Stuart settled into one of the large club chairs. It felt like sliding into a massive, firm beanbag chair. The leather exhaled a warm, invisible cloud of pipe smoke, cologne, and dust. Parnell took an identical chair adjacent to him. A heavy coffee table separated them, flanked by a leather love seat. As Stuart looked around, he realized that the furniture and greenery scattered throughout the room created subtle partitions between each of the seating areas. It was nearly impossible to clearly see or hear anyone else within the lounge. As Arthur appeared from outside their seating area, Stuart heard a piano from across the room. The music became the final piece that secluded their new world.

Arthur presented a squarish bottle to Parnell, who nodded quickly with a smile. Arthur laid out two small crystal glasses on the round table, stripped the bottle of its casing, pulled the stopper, and filled both glasses with an opaque, burgundy liquid. Silently, Parnell led them in a saluting toast. Stuart sipped lightly at the wine, unsure of what to expect, and was pleased by the warm, somewhat fuzzy texture of the wine. He sank back into the chair and, somehow, found the ability to exhale heavily.

The two men sat in silence, allowing the drifting notes from the piano to permeate the atmosphere. Parnell leaned forward and placed his empty glass on the table.

"Penny for your thoughts?"

Stuart cleared his throat and straightened in the chair. "My mother always says that," he said, smiling. "Quite honestly, my thoughts are … conflicted. A part of me is wanting to run from here as fast as I can, yet I … I somehow can't. I know that I shouldn't. This … this is all so contrary to … to who I am."

Parnell smiled and reached for the bottle to refresh his glass.

Stuart realized he was being prodded to continue. "Have you ever had one of those fascinating dreams that, after you wake up, you desperately want to fall back asleep and continue? It's like that. Except that I've actually managed to fall back asleep and continue the fantasy."

"You may find this hard to believe, especially given the methods Bailey and I—at least from your perspective—choose to employ, but we've attempted to be extremely careful with your indoctrination." He retrieved his glass and sat back, crossing his legs. "Your grandfather, Malcolm, was a very, *very* dear friend. He would have given, I believe, anything to celebrate this evening with you."

"But how can that be, Parnell? You're talking about a man whose last contact with me was when I was maybe four or five years old. I mean, I suppose there might be some sentimental connection he felt, being able to pass along this ... experience of his, but really, how am I different than some other stranger, or better yet, some other true friend of his who could have benefited from this club of yours?"

"Club of *ours*, Stuart. You're now a part of us."

"Yes, yes, but you see my point. Have you ever encountered someone from your distant past? Someone who chose to bestow some sort of ... of unearned valuable upon you?"

Parnell seemed to ponder the question for a moment, sipped from his glass and shook his head as he swallowed. "No. I suppose not, but we're speaking of your maternal grandfather, Stuart. Not some long-lost schoolmate."

"You're a bright man, Parnell. I can see that. I consider myself of above average intelligence, too. Please don't be coy. I told you; I don't play games."

"Really?" Parnell said, beaming. "No games, then; nothing like, say, Dungeons and Dragons?"

Stuart froze. He suddenly felt violated. This was wrong.

"Maybe I've been mistaken. I should leave," Stuart said. He set his glass down and stood. No one outside of the small group of D&D aficionados he played with each month knew of his connection with the game. These maniacs must have been eavesdropping on his conversations, having him followed—something disturbingly unethical.

Parnell's shoulders slumped. "Really, Stuart. Please stop the drama. My jab may have been unfair, but the truth is that we don't enter into a membership lightly. We need to have a completely solid understanding of what makes someone tick. Certainly, you were the heir of a monumental member, and a great friend as I've said, but we still do our due diligence. So you enjoy spending time pretending to be a knight, or wizard, or whatever with a group of friends. It's nothing to be ashamed of."

Stuart straightened himself and surveyed the room. He wasn't so much embarrassed as he was angry, and he felt manipulated. How could he trust these men? They had drugged him, coerced him into signing a contract, and now they openly admitted to spying. Even though Stuart could see that civility surrounded him, he was fuming. It was a blatant affront. He sighed in disgust and collapsed back into his chair.

"So, what other surprises do you have to share tonight? Have you got my medical records? My performance appraisals? Tax returns? You've got to see how ludicrous this is. The drugging? The snooping?"

Parnell laughed. "As I said, Stuart, you wouldn't be here if we had a significant concern. I was only teasing about the games. It's hardly a secret that one of your only vices is online gaming, as I believe it's called. We find it endearing, actually. Harkens back to our founders' ancestors, right? Dragon slaying and all that."

"Yes, well ..."

"Really, it's nothing to be ashamed of or apologize for. In fact, I believe it'll only aid in your appreciation for the club. Besides, I'm sure D'Artagnan conducts background checks, right? On potential employees?"

Stuart drained his glass and leaned forward. "Okay, I'll be blunt. What's in it for me? I mean, really? I haven't sought this out, so why is my membership in this … this place so important?"

Parnell cleared his throat and looked off to the side.

"Believe it or not, I think that's a very fair question. If I were in your shoes, I'm not sure I wouldn't have bolted long ago. But, as Bailey and I suspected, and your grandfather, too, you have not done so. Why not? I don't know. But I'm thankful for your decision, thus far, to stick it out. Honestly, I've been looking forward to becoming acquainted with you for some time. You know, Stuart, your grandfather spent a tremendous amount of time here in the States checking up on you and your mother.

"It's true. We traveled as a matter of course quite extensively and often found ourselves in New York, but Malcolm frequently took a few extra days to check up on you. He was always quite proud. Always telling us of your accomplishments, what you were up to. And your mother, he so desperately missed her. But, somehow, he managed to respect her wishes. He never attempted contact, and, as you know, neither did she."

Stuart chose not to reply. Instead, he tried to imagine how his grandfather may have spied upon them during his visits. He tried to remember if he ever noticed anyone whom he might have mistaken for his grandfather; but frankly, since he'd only seen the man in the flesh on a couple of occasions, and couldn't remember ever seeing a photograph of him, he had no frame of reference. When he boiled it down, his grandfather had been something of a myth in his youth. He recalled being in elementary school, before his father died, listening to his mother's random rants about her father's indiscretions. At that time, and honestly now, he had no idea exactly what she was referring to. Her tantrums, from what he could recall, were triggered by arbitrary events. News reports, characters in a soap opera, headlines in the newspaper. By the time he was a teenager, any notion of his mother's family had completely disappeared.

Parnell seemed to sense Stuart's discomfort. "Perhaps we should change the subject. Do you recall the travel requirement of the club?"

Stuart shook his head, returning to the present. Travel requirement?

Parnell laughed. "One of our newer members once told me he felt it was something akin to a timeshare, and I suppose that's accurate. At least once a year we require all members to partake in an adventure of sorts. Actually, not 'of sorts,' but truly an adventure. Aside from the camaraderie one experiences while visiting the various clubs around the globe, it's the annual adventure that anchors our organization's mystique."

Just then, Bailey appeared from behind Parnell. His face was grim.

"We've received word on Helmut."

# CHAPTER

# SIX

Stuart Mancini spent his entire childhood in northern New Jersey, first in Ridgefield Park, just south of I-80 and west of the George Washington Bridge, and then later outside of Englewood, nestled in an idyllic neighborhood that defied the stereotypical perceptions of New Jersey. Stuart's father was the quintessential 1960's salesman. When Stuart was born, Phillip Mancini hawked industrial cleaners and solvents. He hopscotched between factories throughout the northeast, typically five days a week. On the road Monday morning and back either late each Thursday night or in time for dinner on Friday. Phil Mancini's work ethic and desire to succeed, coupled with requisite iron-clad self-esteem, gradually paid off. A decade into his tenure with All-San Agents, he became one of the top company salesmen, eclipsing six figures. The ninety-year-old, shingle-clad two-story dwelling Phil, Sylvia, and Stuart inhabited—riddled with a seemingly infinite number of evasive cracks, holes, and crevices that peppered the home with frigid arctic air in the winters and siphoned off the meager stream of cool air produced by their in-window air conditioner—could be jettisoned.

As the Mancini's considered a new home, Phil bumped into an old college friend who worked for an investment bank in Manhattan. This friend had caught wind of Phil's sales prowess at All-San. Would he, Phil, be interested in making a move into the banking world? It had been a torturous decision. Phil had built deep, trusted relationships with the earnest, salt-of-the earth, blue collar folks who owned and operated the mid-sized manufacturing companies that comprised Phil's portfolio. The thought of working in pretentious Manhattan, rather than the isolated, grungy industrial parks—lunching with New York's elite, schmoozing wannabe millionaires, established millionaires, all dripping in European silk—was daunting and, frankly, unappealing.

Sylvia, on the other hand, was in full support of the change. From her perspective, this new opportunity meant more money, less travel, and, for her, a level of status she'd secretly coveted. The autonomy she'd enjoyed being married to a traveling spouse had its appeal, but Stuart was only twelve years old at the time. While a precocious child, he hardly provided the level of social sophistication she craved. She envied her neighbors whose spouses made it home nearly every night for a real family dinner, who were there to watch *The Carol Burnett Show* or *The Tonight Show*, who could keep an eye on the children a night or two a week in case the wife wanted to join a bridge club or do a little shopping alone for a change.

Stuart, though not officially consulted, was ambivalent. His father's routine was the only thing he knew. For him, having a father had always meant that this man showed up for the weekends and disappeared on Mondays, spent perhaps an hour each weekend day with him, either tossing a football or going for a bike ride, and, in Phil's case, silently attending dinner. Sylvia tried to explain to Stuart that a new job for his father would mean that he'd be home more often. Stuart's first response had been, "Why?" He tried to picture this man coming home every single day. Would that mean that there would be less food for him at dinner? Would he lose the attention of his mother? Did it increase the likelihood that he'd get in trouble? Something that coincidently only occurred on weekends.

For Stuart, having parents meant having an attentive mother—a reliable, built-in ally who helped you with long division, made the world's best fried baloney sandwiches, sprayed Bactine on skateboard injuries—and, as an unsolicited option, included the presence of this intrusive, sometimes gloomy, mostly stoic, male human who visited a couple days each week. Stuart wasn't sold on the fact that having this guy around six or seven days a week would be an improvement over the current situation.

Then there was the issue of moving. While no decision had been finalized, regarding either the new job opportunity or a new home, a move would mean a new school, a new set of friends, and an abundance of uncertainty for Stuart.

Unfortunately, his vote not only didn't count, but in the end, his opinion was never even solicited. Phil accepted the position in Manhattan in late May and the Mancini's planned to move over the summer. For a time, Sylvia pushed Phil to consider moving into the city. Phil's consideration for this option was short-lived. One tour of the type of apartment they could afford in Manhattan, even factoring in a significant jump in his income, stifled any enthusiasm Phil may have harbored about living in the city. In his mind, eight hundred square feet wasn't a home; it was a cell. For Stuart's father, the decision was made.

A few weeks later they found a five-year-old home in Englewood with a finished basement, an acre and a half of land, and a community composed of families just like theirs, as opposed to the questionable lot of bachelors, retirees, and transients that inhabited Gotham.

Stuart fell in love with the new house immediately. His bedroom was twice the size of the old one in Ridgefield Park, the basement was his Camelot, and the yard gave him space to safely hit baseballs, fly gas-powered airplanes, and stage elaborate fantasy battles.

When Stuart left behind the tight-knit group of friends he'd developed since preschool, Sylvia had assured him a similar set of relationships would follow in their new neighborhood. Although he was skeptical, he had no reason to doubt his mother. She'd always been straightforward and honest with him.

As it turned out, though, this time she was wrong.

The new neighborhood was laden with families whose children were within a year or two of Stuart's age, but that first summer was dreadful. Many of the Mancini's neighbors traveled during the summer, either to rental homes on the Jersey shore or, for the most fortunate, the Hamptons or other parts of Long Island. The Mancinis stayed put. Stuart was ill prepared for the shift in social status.

Stuart made several unsuccessful attempts to integrate with the remaining neighborhood kids. During the first few weeks in their new home, he cycled the tree-lined streets, dodging cars and popping over sidewalks on his Schwinn ten-speed, hoping to catch a group of kids doing anything. One afternoon, he ventured past a baseball field adjacent to the Englewood Cliffs school. A dozen or so boys were playing softball as the last remnants of a mid-June cloudburst hung in the breeze. He eased his bike near the first baseline, hoping one of the players would see him and invite him to play. He hadn't brought a mitt—no reason to at the time. He counted the boys in sight and came up with fifteen. An uneven number. Certainly they'd want to even out the sides. He watched one side finish their at-bat and scooted closer. He was no more than ten yards from first base. As the fielders changed places, Stuart watched the first baseman jog in his general direction. The boy, a bit taller than Stuart, probably a grade or two ahead of him, made eye contact for a moment, then looked away, turning toward the plate. Stuart watched the better part of three innings. During that entire time, no one acknowledged his presence other than that initial eye contact. Devastated, he rode his bike home, barely reaching a speed that kept him upright.

Community Junior High School had a relatively low enrollment, around one hundred fifty students. Stuart, as it turned out, was the only new student in the eighth grade that fall. There hadn't been a single day in his thirteen years he'd dreaded more than the first day at Community Junior High. Every night leading up to that first day, he'd fought through nightmares brought on by incessant worry, featuring the full gamut of bullying and torture. Wedgies, swirlies, tittie-twisters, pummelings in gym class, girls giggling behind his back—each of these visions materialized as he turned out the bedside lamp and clinched his eyes closed.

Stuart entered junior high without ever earning anything below an A. His success didn't end at Community. By the time he reached high school, studying became his solace. His inability to even engage with the skeptical band of outcasts at the school provoked him into fully dedicating himself to ruining any possibility of a grading curve. By the end of his sophomore year, he was not only singularly ostracized, but his intellectual prowess intimidated many of his classmates. Upon learning they were in the same class as Stuart, many classmates groaned aloud or lobbied to drop the class in favor of something Stuart hadn't enrolled in. His teachers, aside from Mr. Wooten, the Economics teacher, treated him with a similar degree of trepidation, as if he, Stuart, were a mole for the administration, sent to detect some flaw in their methods or behavior. Mr. Wooten, conversely, saw Stuart as a protégé, one of the very few students ever to pass through the high school halls who had demonstrated a deep fascination with interest rates, supply and demand, and predicting the gross national product.

The typical escapades that defined adolescence and the initial transformation into adulthood were all but absent from Stuart's last years of high school. There were no girls, or boys, no alcohol, no drugs, no run-ins with the law—only numbers and words. Intellectually and emotionally,

Stuart transformed from a clumsy, inquisitive thirteen year old to a visionary executive before his seventeenth birthday. He devoured the *Wall Street Journal, The Financial Times*, and *Business Week*. With proceeds he'd earned from investing in Pfizer, he bought three used VCRs to record CNN, Wall Street Week, and any other business-related broadcasts. Somehow he'd found a way to supplant the hormone driven angst his body was programmed to promote into an analytical fanaticism.

Stuart's maturation occurred independent of his relationship with his mother and father. Phil Mancini's career on Wall Street blossomed and left him as emotionally unavailable as he'd been physically absent in his prior job. Sylvia grew accustomed, and eventually satisfied, just to have her two men sitting at the dinner table more often than not, initiating dead-end small talk to fill the gaps between plate scrapes. Stuart eventually regained an audience with Sylvia. As his passion for all things financial swelled, he found he had to share his discoveries with someone, and that person was almost exclusively his mother. Initially, she expressed concern about his lack of friends or interest in anything social, but she soon embraced the things that brought him joy. Why was baseball any better than stock betas? He certainly wasn't going to get some promiscuous girl in trouble if his idea of gratification came from building mock mutual funds that out-performed some of the market's most successful managers. The bottom line, fitting for Stuart, was that this made him happy and it didn't harm him.

For Sylvia, Stuart's progression toward college passed by at warp speed. She seemed on the verge of beginning to appreciate what a unique individual she'd brought into the world when Stuart announced he was headed to Harvard. Stuart's acceptance was one of the few times Phil paused to focus on his son's interests and accomplishments. Phil, who had squeaked out a bachelor's degree from SUNY Plattsburg, was genuinely awed by Stuart's achievement.

Ten days before Stuart was scheduled to begin classes in Cambridge, just as he was experiencing a newfound role in the family, his father collapsed and died from a massive coronary in the hotel shower of The Drake in Chicago.

# CHAPTER

# SEVEN

Stuart's eyes eased open. He judged from the pallid light bleeding through his bedroom blinds that the sun was just about to rise. He rolled onto his back, realizing as he did so that he was wearing boxers, his typical bedtime attire. Aside from a distant, dull pain centered just inside his forehead, he felt a thousand times better than he had the morning before. And, he realized, he had a complete recollection of the previous evening's events.

As he slapped barefoot through the kitchen, piecing together breakfast and brewing coffee, Stuart continued to struggle with all that had transpired during the previous forty-eight hours. He settled into a kitchen chair and was about to dig into a bowl of Cheerios when he noticed his cell phone resting on an adjacent placemat. He punched a button with his forefinger and the screen lit up. A message scrolled across the top signaling that he'd missed three calls. His stomach tightened as he popped into the phone's menu. Two calls had come from D'Artagnan's PBX system, the third from Heath's cell phone. All had come in while he'd been at The Kilimanjaro Club. Odd. He distinctly remembered checking his phone on the way home from the club. The phone now registered three voicemail messages as well.

"Stuart, it's Heath. Hey, I know it's Saturday night and all, but I thought for sure I'd be able to reach you. I left a message at your place, too. It's … about seven, I guess. Give me a call when you get this. It's about Helmut. See you."

The second message was a hang up. The third was from Heath's cell phone. "Stuart, holy crap, it's nearly 9:00 p.m. Where are you? I'm hoping you'll get these messages tonight. I'm beginning to worry, and not just about Helmut now." There was a long pause. "Jesus, I can't think of a time when I had to leave you messages before hearing from you. Anyway, call when you can."

The kitchen clock read 6:50. It was early for a Sunday, but Stuart knew Heath was up. Perhaps not completely coherent yet, but vertical. He pulled up Heath's home number in his cell and hit the dial button. Heath picked up on the second ring.

"Stuart! It's about damn time …" He seemed to be breathing hard.

"I'm sorry, Heath. I … I was tied up last night. Somehow I missed your calls until just now. I'm truly sorry."

"Never mind, never mind. I'm just glad you called. Give me a second so I can get out of earshot of the girls." Heath and his wife had three daughters under the age of ten. Heath liked to joke that he loved coming to work each day so he could relax. "Okay, I'm good now. So, anyway, like I said in my messages, this Helmut thing is really getting out of control."

"Now what? Have they found him?" The crossover between Helmut's membership in The Kilimanjaro Club and the firm's sale was creating problems. Bailey wouldn't share what he had learned about Helmut last night—something about club regulations—but Stuart knew it was distressing.

"That's just it, Stuart. I don't really know, and no one from his firm is sharing anything significant. I talked to Carter Hobbes at least three times yesterday. His scripted answer was, 'I'm sure everything's fine. Probably just a little miscommunication on our part.' But I don't buy it. By last night he seemed rattled. Same answer, but not nearly as confident, you know?"

Stuart paused, then shifted into analytical mode. What was the worst-case scenario? Helmut was dead? Killed himself? Technically, his ownership would pass to his wife. Would that hold up the buyout? What if he'd simply disappeared, whether willfully or at the will of others? That would surely be more complicated. The deal would go into limbo until either Helmut resurfaced or some judge was ready to declare him dead. Six months minimum, but not an eternity.

"Heath, I certainly understand your concern, but we haven't even hit the forty-eight-hour mark. Have the authorities done anything?"

"Who knows? Hobbes claims he's been in regular communication with the police. They're obviously concerned and, supposedly, assisting with the search. I'm at a loss."

"I'm ... I'm not sure that I have much expertise in this area, Heath. Is there something you need me to do?"

Stuart could hear Heath's breathing again through the phone. "No, no. I was just hoping that either you'd heard from him, or had some revelation about where he might be. I guess ... I guess you could rack your brain a bit to see if you can remember him saying anything about a trip, or some outside commitment he had, anything that might explain his whereabouts."

"I ..." Stuart began, then caught himself. He'd nearly mentioned the club. Withholding information was completely foreign to him. His mind seized.

"What it is?" Heath asked.

"I'm sorry. Just thinking out loud. What's his family said, anything?"

"Oh, hell, I don't know. I've been wrestling with calling his wife, but that seems like crossing the line, you know? I've got to show some faith in what Hobbes is telling me. I just know he's not being completely up front." Heath paused. "Jesus, I guess I can't blame him. Hobbes, I mean. I wouldn't expect you or Christie to share theories about me if I fell off the face of the earth one day."

Bill Christie was one of the other founders of D'Artagnan and current CEO. While Stuart saw Christie as a trusted business associate and had always respected his vision and leadership capabilities, they had never developed the same trusting relationship that he had with Heath.

"Does Bill have any ideas?"

"No. Frankly, I've tried to stay positive. He knows about the meeting Helmut missed with you on Friday but tried to chalk it up to a schedule snafu. I know it didn't sit right with him. You know Bill—he can see through anyone's bullshit."

"Heath," Stuart said, trying to sound upbeat. "maybe I'll have an epiphany after some coffee."

Heath sighed heavily. "Yeah, yeah, that's fine. There's really nothing we can do. We all, you know, we've all put a helluva lot into this deal and quite honestly, Stuart, I'm really ready to put this thing to bed." He sounded exhausted.

"I know, Heath. I know," Stuart said, raking a hand through his hair. "I'll be in the office around lunchtime for a while. Call me if you want to talk, okay?"

"Yeah, I may see you there. Just depends ..." Stuart could hear female voices leaking in through the line. Heath had been found.

"I'll talk to you later, okay? Just to check in," Stuart said and hung up.

Stuart set the phone down on the table and realized, for one of the very few moments in his adult life, he had no idea what to do next. Or what to expect.

# CHAPTER
# EIGHT

D'Artagnan's offices were in the Financial District in the Park Row Building, a sculptured, century-old relic that had been swallowed by the modern monoliths of lower Manhattan in recent decades. The firm inhabited the entire tenth floor. Stuart's office faced north, the Woolworth Building and New York City Hall framing his view. The setting sun reflected off the windows along the skyline. Stuart glanced at his watch and decided to wrap up—it was late for a Sunday—and find something to eat. He'd accomplished very little in the previous four hours.

As he waited for his laptop to shut down, his phone rang. The red light flashed next to his direct line. Probably Heath again. It had only been a half hour since Heath had left.

"D'Artagnan, Stuart Mancini speaking," he said. It was his stock answer, no matter what day or time the phone rang, even if he could see from the caller ID that it was someone he knew.

"My good man, you are there," a now familiar voice boomed through the receiver. He instinctively pulled the phone away from his ear and winced.

"Yes, I am," he said slowly.

"Fantastic! Say, Bailey here. We were wondering if we could coax you up to the club this evening. You see—"

"Bailey, look, I'm honestly not accustomed to an active social life. Surely Malcolm mentioned that when he talked about me. I appreciate your enthusiasm for my membership, but my life isn't going to suddenly shift and revolve around this club. I—"

"Say no more, Stuart. I quite understand." Bailey's demeanor had shifted suddenly, and Stuart wondered if he'd insulted the man.

"To be perfectly frank, Parnell and I were hoping to speak with you about our mutual friend. Would that be possible? This evening?"

Stuart turned and stared out the window again. He supposed he'd been foolish to think that he would manage a quiet evening at home, given the circumstances. His mind continued to grapple with the seemingly contrary, yet intimately intertwined, conflicts that had arisen. There was the chance, too, that Bailey and Parnell could provide him with information that would be valuable in moving the firm sale ahead.

"Yes, yes, sure, Bailey. Is there any possibility of meeting downtown, near my office?"

His question was met with silence.

"Stuart, we consider this club business, and, whenever possible, club business is conducted at the club. This is one of those instances that falls into the whenever-possible bin."

Stuart sighed, probably too loudly, and agreed.

"Excellent! Carlton will meet you downstairs in … say thirty minutes. Will that do?"

Stuart muttered, "Sure."

By seven o'clock Stuart was back at the club. He was met by a young woman he hadn't seen before as he exited the elevator. She wore a vibrant red long-sleeved dress with a white V-neck collar. Her light brown hair fell to the top of her shoulders.

"Mr. Mancini, good evening," she said, extending a hand.

"Hello," Stuart said. He glanced beyond the woman, wondering if something had changed.

"I'm Angela Whitcomb, Director of Concierge Services. Mr. Honeybourne has reserved a private dining room for you and Mr. Sumner this evening. I'll show you the way."

Angela looked to be in her early thirties. He found her rather attractive, not in the runway-model sort of way, but in a confident, intelligent, and athletic way. He was somewhat surprised at his reaction. While he certainly noticed many of the women he worked with and encountered on a daily basis, nothing ever passed beyond a fleeting curiosity. He felt compelled to attempt small talk with Angela, something absolutely foreign to him.

"So, have you worked at the club long?" She turned to him and smiled as they entered the main hall and turned right, rather than heading into the main dining room.

"It'll be ten years later this month. Hard to believe. How are you liking the club so far?" she said.

"To be quite honest, I haven't had much time to absorb it all. For me, it's all a bit overwhelming."

Angela laughed and extended a hand toward one of the large wooden doors that lined the hall. An engraved Reserved sign hung from the center of the door. She grabbed the knob and paused before turning it.

"If I may say, Mr. Mancini, your grandfather was one of my favorite members. I met him during my first week with the club. I started here as a server during college. I've been anxious to meet you. I hope you do enjoy your affiliation with us. It's a special place." She smiled again and opened the door.

The private dining room Bailey had reserved was perfectly square and looked as if it had been plucked from an English estate. A large, round pedestal table centered the room. Bailey and Parnell occupied two of the barrel chairs surrounding the table. They stopped talking as Stuart and Angela entered, both looking a bit startled. Bailey recovered quickly, smiled, and stood. Parnell followed suit.

"Here he is!" Bailey trumpeted, rounding the table and greeting Stuart with an unexpected bear hug. Stuart froze. No one hugged him. Ever. Not even his own mother. Stuart stiffened, arms dangling at his side, then lifted one hand and patted Bailey awkwardly on the back.

When Bailey released him, Parnell slid in and shook his hand.

"Please join us," Parnell said, directing him to an open chair. "Angela tells us the kitchen has two specials this evening, scallops and shrimp, right? And a rib-eye. Bailey and I both opted for the rib-eye. What's your pleasure?"

Stuart turned and realized Angela was still standing in the doorway, in a servant's attention stance, arms clasped behind her back, feet together. "Um, I think I'll have the scallops."

"Wine with that, Stuart?" Bailey asked.

"No, no, ice water is fine."

Angela nodded and disappeared behind the closing door.

The three men sat. Bailey cleared his throat and took on a look that erased the joviality he'd demonstrated a moment earlier.

"Stuart, I realize we're imposing greatly on your time. Please don't take this as a slight against your priorities. I have tremendous respect for you, your profession, and your life. You must know that I wouldn't take these steps if I didn't feel it was absolutely imperative."

Stuart looked from Bailey to Parnell, who nodded as their eyes met.

Bailey continued. "It's all somewhat coincidental, actually. As we mentioned, we were aware of your relationship with Helmut. Malcolm had mentioned it in the past, and certainly Helmut himself, but I didn't expect that Malcolm's passing, your inheritance of his membership, and

Helmut's … disappearance, would all coincide."

"I will tell you, Stuart. I cautioned Bailey not to involve you," Parnell added. "I could see that this weekend's events had struck you unexpectedly. When I thought of the business impact this latest news would have on your recent work—"

"This merger, Parnell, is a still a private matter. Yes, it's what I've been focusing on as of late, but I …" Stuart sputtered. Even though it was a merger between two private organizations, both leadership teams and boards were bound by confidentiality agreements and had been diligent about protecting the details of their plans.

Parnell raised a hand. "Not to worry. We're all quite accustomed to maintaining secrecy. It's the keystone of this organization. At any rate, this convergence of events and relationships presents a complicated and, I'm sure for you, frustrating scenario. We do, truly, appreciate your position."

Stuart pulled the napkin from the table and placed it, somewhat demonstrably, in his lap.

"He's right, you know," Bailey said. "What I told Parnell, though, was that I believed these connections were present for a reason. As inopportune as they may seem, I believe you were … destined to be involved."

Stuart leaned forward and rested his elbows on the table, staring at Bailey. He felt his face warm—anger, typically a dormant emotion, bubbled in his gut again. "I'll tell you what, Mr. Honeybourne," he said, clenching his jaw. "You're exactly right. This is incredibly inconvenient and presumptuous. You … two—two perfect strangers, claiming to be the confidants of a grandfather that I've never known—waltz into my life with your adventures, your secrecy, your …" he said motioning to the walls, "private dining services, and insert yourselves into my life, my professional and personal matters, uninvited, disrupting everything I value, and expect me to accept your … lame apology. Deflecting it by inferring some emergency or … or …" He stopped, frustrated, shaking and nearly out of control.

Bailey and Parnell looked at each other. Both seemed afraid to move or speak. Stuart let out a breath and stared into his lap. His heart pounded. This sudden lack of sensibility was spiraling, and he couldn't let it continue. After a few measured breaths, he continued.

"If there's something I can actually do, somewhere I can add value, regarding Helmut, I need to know. Otherwise, I have other priorities. I told you before, I'm not a social person. I thrive on my work. I always have. I don't have any need for companionship, outside of what I get through my business. I'm perfectly content." He looked up. "I realize my frustration may seem out of place, and I apologize. You have to see, though, that this is all a mistake."

The two Brits looked at each other again. Parnell's head made the slightest downward movement.

"Stuart," Bailey said quietly. "The message we received from Helmut was delivered through … through a third party. It was encoded. It …"

Parnell interrupted. "It said, 'Get Mancini.'"

A knock came at the door, followed by Angela and a server bringing their drinks. Her presence interrupted the bewilderment that engulfed Stuart after Parnell's last statement.

"Gentleman, your entrees will be coming shortly. Is there anything else we can get you at this point?"

"No, thank you, Angela, darling," Bailey said, winking at her. She nodded, giving a slight eye-roll, and left the room with the server.

"This makes no sense. You received an … an encoded message from Helmut? What does that mean?"

Bailey cleared his throat. "None of this is easy. And we're obviously failing at handling the delivery of all this news. It's complicated, as I'm sure you can tell. You see—"

"Helmut's been kidnapped," Parnell blurted out. "At least everything we know is pointing to that fact. The message we received was part ransom note, part affirmation that Helmut was still alive. It was Helmut's message—what he said—that was encoded. There is an old club secret, of sorts," Parnell continued, wincing a bit at as he said the word *secret*. "Rarely used, of course, but our members often spent considerable time assembling contingency plans for the adventures we embarked upon. One was a method of communicating, if possible—messages to outside parties if we were ever in trouble or held captive. I can't remember the last time someone was in a position to use it," he added, looking at Bailey, "but Helmut did, and the words embedded in his statement were 'Get Mancini.'"

"But why would he ask for me? Did you receive a letter, a phone call? How was the ransom note delivered?"

"They sent a video, a DVD, actually," Bailey said.

"Really? A DVD? Is it here?"

"Certainly," Parnell said. He stood and walked to a credenza that lined the side wall. Stuart watched him punch a keypad that appeared to be set flush in the surface of the cabinet. A panel slid back on top of the credenza and a screen slowly emerged. Parnell opened a drawer, inserted the DVD, and punched another button. Bailey jumped up and locked the door.

A moment later, a picture appeared on the screen through a brief splatter of static. The screen showed a classic hostage setup. In the center, lit from above, was a person who appeared to be the same size and build as Helmut. He wore a white dress shirt, untucked and splayed open at the neck, dark pants, and a burlap bag over his head. His hands appeared to be restrained behind his back. A piece of rope closed the bag at the neck. Two other people, apparently men, dressed completely in black, ghastly Halloween masks covering their heads, stood beside Helmut. They both held intimidating rifles. Stuart knew nothing about firearms, only that the ones these men held looked menacing.

The man on the right, wearing a mask depicting a human head that had been ravaged by a machete, lifted a microphone up toward his mouth.

"Ladies and gentlemen, the man beside me is Helmut Rhinegold. He is safe and unharmed, for the time being." The voice emanating from the speaker had been digitally altered. It was flat, electronic, like a robot. "We hope to keep him in such a state until you meet our request. To preserve the value of what we seek, let me say that we're looking for a location, an exact location. I believe at least two of your members, Bailey Honeybourne and Parnell Sumner, know what we are seeking. We also have reason to believe that Mr. Rhinegold is in possession of this information, yet he has not cooperated with us. He seems …" the captor looked down at Helmut's hooded head, "unconcerned with the consequences of his lack of disclosure. However, we're confident that Mr. Honeybourne and Mr. Sumner can satisfy our request.

"We're requiring that this information be delivered in person. You have seventy-two hours to meet this requirement. Mr. Honeybourne and Mr. Sumner must be at the Hotel Hassler in Rome at precisely 6:00 p.m. this Tuesday. A representative of ours will meet them in the Hassler Bar. No one else will be in the room. Do not bring anyone else with you. Your moves will be monitored from the moment you receive this message until this meeting is completed.

"Mr. Rhinegold has asked that he be given the opportunity to let his colleagues know that he's well." The man fiddled with the microphone, apparently disengaging the voice-altering mechanism. He held the microphone in front of Helmut's hood, nudging him with his knee.

"Gentlemen, be watchful. Honestly, my handlers don't fancy deceit. Continue accordingly." The man yanked the microphone back.

"We will hold Mr. Rhinegold until the validity of this information is confirmed by our associates. If the meeting is missed, or if the information provided is false, Mr. Rhinegold will be executed." The screen briefly shifted to static again and then went blue.

"What've you got me involved in? Do you know what they're talking about?" Stuart said, standing.

"We do," Bailey said, barely above a whisper.

"What is it?" Stuart yelled, pointing at the screen. "And how did you get, 'Get Mancini' out of Helmut's message?"

"Let's answer your second question," Parnell interjected. "The code requires that we pull letters from each word he utters. The first letter of the first word, the second letter of the second word, and so forth. It's nothing too cryptic. You'll notice he says 'Honestly' in the middle. That's a marker to start the code over, so we take the first letter of the first word again after 'honestly.'"

"'Gentleman, be watchful. My handlers don't fancy deceit. Continue accordingly.' G, from gentlemen, e from be, t from watchful ..." Bailey said.

"And what about my first question?"

"Stuart, we haven't decided if the time is right to burden you with their request," Parnell said. "Right now, I think it's best if you don't know. This is something that fewer than, I presume, a half-dozen men have knowledge of. It's not something that's shared freely."

"Oh, come on. This continues to get more and more ridiculous."

"Stuart!" Parnell yelled, slamming his fist on the table. Their drinks jumped but managed to stay upright. Stuart glared at him.

"We are *not* mucking around here. I realize that we've introduced you to the club under very disturbing, bizarre circumstances. You were game enough to spend three nights with us, including this evening. But we've encountered an emergency that now, regrettably, has involved you. We certainly find our way into some difficult situations from time to time, but this is grave. And not just because of the threat on Helmut's life. Neither Bailey nor I have any idea why he's asked for you, but he did. Your choice appears to be rather elementary. Either you work with us to determine how we can help our friend, or you can return to your previous life and, perhaps, wait to hear of his death. It's your decision, Stuart."

Stuart gripped the arms of his chair. He thought through his options. He could call Heath and request time off. Heath might panic initially, but would eventually warm to the idea. Given Helmut's abduction, there was little for him to do at work. At least nothing that someone else on his team couldn't handle. Another option would be to simply walk away from this absurd adult fantasy and forget that the past three days had ever occurred. The latter option probably wasn't so simple. He'd signed something on Friday. He could involve his attorney and, rightfully, claim that he was drugged and signed whatever it was under duress. His third option was to delay.

"We'll have to decide quickly," Bailey said, his voice just above a whisper. "Parnell and I will make our travel plans immediately. We expect there'll be others within the club we'll work with to build our strategy. You, however, should travel parallel to us—different flight, similar itinerary. That is, of course, if you decide to join us."

Stuart looked at his watch. "I'll need to … I'll need to review my options. There are people I need to consider. Commitments … obligations I have."

"I think that's fine, as long as you decide this evening. I know it's short notice, but as you see, we have little time."

Stuart pushed himself away from the table and stood.

"Who should I call? I'll know before … well, before midnight, I suppose. Likely earlier."

"We'll call you at eleven sharp," Bailey said, standing. Parnell joined him.

"As unbelievable as it may seem, Stuart, this isn't at all how we envisioned your entry into the club. I truly appreciate your patience," Parnell added, stepping forward and offering Stuart his hand. Stuart hesitated and then reciprocated. Parnell grasped Stuart's forearm with this left hand and shook his arm.

In the car on the way back to his building, Stuart decided to try to reach Heath before it got too late. He had decided that a vacation request was probably the logical bet. Heath wouldn't be happy about the timing, but once news of Helmut's kidnapping got out, the deal would be on hold. If anything, Stuart thought, Heath might be congratulatory.

Heath answered the phone on the first ring.

"Hello, Heath. It's Stuart. I'm sorry to bother you on a Sunday evening."

"Hey, no problem. What's up? Have you heard anything? Anything from Helmut?"

Stuart paused, feeling a sudden pang of guilt. "No, actually I haven't. I … I've been thinking about these recent events and, well, my assumption is that we are going to be in a bit of a holding pattern for a while."

Heath sighed. "Well, that's probably right. Hobbes made a call to Helmut's wife, Cherise. She's a wreck, I guess. Hasn't heard from him since Friday morning when he left for the office. I heard they had tickets to the Met last night, *Rigoletto*, apparently Helmut's favorite. Hobbes confirmed that she's gotten the police involved. They don't have a clue."

"Oh, god …" Stuart muttered.

"So, yeah, it's not looking good. What … what were you going to say?"

"Well, Heath, this whole deal, I didn't really realize how much it had taken out of me. I … I guess it kind of hit me when I started to worry about Helmut and wondering if it might fall apart, you know, if he … if he, if something really bad happened."

The line was silent. Then Heath said, "Is everything okay?"

"Yeah, sure. I just thought, if there was ever a time when I might be able to, you know, get away for a bit, this might be it."

"Wait," Heath said, his voice changing a bit, "are you talking about a vacation?"

Stuart felt his heart take a hard thump in his chest. "Look, maybe the timing seems all wrong …"

"Wrong? Hell, no, Stuart! I'm just bowled over. Go for it. Just make sure I can reach you. What did you have in mind?"

"It's a little odd, the timing I mean. I ran into an old acquaintance who's headed to Europe for a week or so. He asked me if I wanted to join him on the trip. My first reaction was, 'No way,' given what we're dealing with, but the more I thought about it, the more I felt, for some reason, that maybe it was the right thing to do."

"When, uh, when are you planning to leave?"

"That's just it. Probably tomorrow."

"Wow," Heath said. The line was silent for a few uncomfortable seconds. "Okay, let me think this through for a second. Okay, I doubt it'll be necessary, but I can't see a problem as long as we keep in touch. Can you make sure Olivia has an itinerary?"

"Certainly, of course. I'll have my cell, too. I still have international service. It's the least I can do."

"Okay," Heath said. Some life came back into his voice. "Yeah, that's great. I think that'll be fine. I'll let Hobbes and Christie know. They'll probably grumble a bit … maybe a lot … but they'll get over it. Christ, you've never taken a vacation, have you?"

Stuart laughed. "No. I haven't. I really appreciate this, Heath. Now that I hear myself talking about it, I feel like I'm running out on you."

"Oh, hell no. We'll spend most of the time worrying about Helmut and the final steps of this deal. We certainly won't accomplish anything very productive. Besides, you can take some time now, and the rest of us will take off after the deal closes, just like we planned. You can hold down the fort later."

Stuart thanked Heath and ended the call. Within a few minutes, Carlton pulled up in front of his building. Larry was standing outside at the curb and intercepted the limo's door handle just as it came to a stop. As the door opened, Stuart noticed that Larry didn't have his trademark giant grin.

"Everything okay, Larry?" Stuart said as he stepped onto the curb with his briefcase.

"There's a detective inside. Waiting for you," Larry whispered.

"Oh," Stuart said. He walked with Larry to the revolving door and followed him through. Stuart realized he'd never been questioned by a police officer or detective, had never even been pulled over for speeding. Nothing.

"Mr. Mancini?" the detective said as he entered the foyer. She was tall, Stuart's height, and imposing. She wore a dark business suit and had her long dark hair pulled into a bun.

Stuart nodded and said, "Yes. How can I help you?"

"I'm Detective Morales from the 20th Precinct. I realize it's a little late on a Sunday, but I was hoping you might have a few minutes for me. Can we talk in your apartment?"

"Of course," Stuart said, shooting a glance back at Larry. "The elevators are right here."

After the doors closed, Detective Morales said, "I believe you know a business associate of yours, Helmut Rhinegold, has been reported missing. I'm talking with everyone I can who might have had recent contact with him." They arrived at Stuart's floor just as she finished her sentence.

"Certainly. Helmut has been my counterpart in our firms' upcoming merger," Stuart said, leading Morales along the hall into the main room. "We were scheduled for lunch at The Oak Room the day he … well, the last day we heard from him." He motioned for Morales to sit on the couch.

Morales hesitated, looking at the view of the twinkling cityscape. "This must not be too hard to come home to every night."

"I try not to take it for granted," Stuart replied as they both sat. Stuart set his briefcase on the floor next to him.

"I'll get to it, Mr. Mancini. When did you last speak to or see Mr. Rhinegold?" Morales opened a paperback-sized notepad and flipped through it to find a blank page.

"We were all on a conference call Wednesday morning. Helmut and the other partners. From what I remember, he was in their offices that day."

Morales nodded. "Mr. Hobbes mentioned the call. What about later?"

Stuart shook his head. "No. His assistant had contacted mine and arranged for the lunch on Friday, but as you know, he didn't show."

"What about prior to Wednesday's call? When did you last see him in person?"

Stuart paused, thinking. It had been at least a month since he'd been in the same room with Helmut. They spoke regularly, three, sometimes four times a week. There hadn't been a reason to get together, and that was part of why Stuart had looked forward to their luncheon.

"Four weeks, at least," he said. "The time kind of melds together. I think we had an in-person meeting at their offices."

Morales finished a note, then looked up at Stuart. She stared for a moment, then said, "What do you think happened?"

"I … I don't know. I guess I've been hoping that there's been some massive miscommunication. That he's safe someplace—on a boat or hiking somewhere. That he'll turn up soon and spend a lot of time apologizing," Stuart said.

Morales nodded. "That's what just about everyone says." She tapped her pen against the tablet then said, "Okay. I think that's all I need right now." Morales stood and Stuart followed her lead. "I appreciate you making time on no notice, on a Sunday night. You always work Sundays?"

"Yes, it's about all I do," Stuart said, forcing a smile.

"You planning to stick around the next few days? I may need to follow up with you."

Stuart cleared his throat. "Uh, yeah. No plans to go anywhere. I'll get you my card," he said, popping open his briefcase and fishing out a business card. "Cell phone's the bottom number," he said, handing her the card. Morales nodded and gestured toward the door.

When they reached the elevator, Morales pulled up short and said, "Did Mr. Rhinegold ever mention a club he belonged to? Some type of secret, uh, travelers' club or something?"

Stuart froze. His mind fluttered before he said, "I know he belonged to one of the athletic clubs. Some place up around Columbus Circle." He leaned past her and pressed the call button.

Morales shook her head. "No, that's not it. Some other thing. I can't seem to find anyone else who knows about it. His wife mentioned it but said he refused to tell her anything about it."

Stuart forced a laugh and said, "I'm not surprised. Helmut only shares what he wants to share."

The elevator arrived and Morales stepped in. "Have a good evening, Mr. Mancini."

"You do the same," he said. As the doors closed, Stuart realized that he'd lied at least twice, to a police officer.

# CHAPTER

# NINE

Stuart landed at Leonardo da Vinci International Airport just before 10:00 a.m. local time. The Alitalia flight had been smooth and uneventful, yet he'd only slept thirty minutes before the plane began its descent. By the time his taxi arrived at the Marriott Grand Hotel Flora in Villa Borghese, he was nearly delirious from sleep deprivation. Bailey and Parnell were scheduled to meet with Helmut's captors in fewer than eight hours, and he still had no idea what role he played on the trip.

The Englishmen's itineraries had them arriving in Rome two hours ahead of Stuart. Their initial plan was to meet at Harry's Bar, just down the street from Stuart's hotel, at one. Apparently, one of the bar's owners had reserved a private room for them. Stuart relished the idea of collapsing into his hotel bed for two hours prior to leaving for the meeting. As he checked in, he requested a wake-up call at 12:30 p.m. Once in his room, he kicked off his shoes and fell face first onto the bed. Sleep came immediately.

Within a matter of seconds, it seemed, the phone rang. Stuart felt paralyzed. He just needed to sleep. Why was the phone ringing already? He looked up and saw the clock on the nightstand. It was already 12:30.

He felt worse than when he'd stumbled into the room. He crawled across the bed and snatched the phone. A perky Italian woman on the other end chirped, "Buon giorno, Signore Mancini," then in tentative English, "It is your wake-up call time." Stuart grunted and hung up the phone.

Somehow, he managed to make it out of the hotel and shuffle toward Harry's with a minute or two to spare. He'd opted for a brief freezing shower that brought him the desired result. His mind was far from sharp, but at least he was vertical again and relatively coherent.

At the end of the street, just beyond the awning above his destination, stood the ancient walls that encircled the Villa Borghese. Stuart slowed as he took in the juxtaposed beauty of the ruins and the modern façades lining the street. For the first time since he'd set foot in the country he thought, I'm in Italy.

There hadn't been much time for Bailey and Parnell to prep Stuart. Truth was, they were as mystified about Helmut's request for Stuart as he was. Above all, they were concerned it might be a trap. The group holding Helmut had called all the shots, putting The Kilimanjaro Club contingency at a huge disadvantage. Although Parnell had assisted Stuart with booking his travel, Bailey and Parnell debated on where each of them should stay. Parnell's gut feeling was that they shouldn't stay anywhere near the Spanish Steps, near the Hotel Hassler. Bailey, acting on his own hunch, felt they should actually stay at the Hassler to limit their footprint and the amount of real estate they had to keep watch on. Ultimately, Bailey won out, and they arranged for accommodations at the Hassler under assumed names. Stuart's hotel was a five-minute walk from the Hassler, and Harry's was in between the two.

Stuart crossed the street and entered the bar. Given the hour, Harry's was nearly empty. A young couple sat at a small cocktail table near the front window and another single patron was perched at the bar. The bartender, a man in his fifties with thinning black hair and a grey goatee, busied himself by wiping down the brass rail along the bar. He looked up when Stuart entered and nodded. Stuart scanned the remainder of the bar hoping to spot Bailey and Parnell. Bailey had told Stuart to tell the maître d' that he was with the Smith party, and he would be shown to the private room. There did not seem to be a maître d' on staff, so Stuart approached the bar.

"Hello," he said to the man.

"Buon giorno," the bartender said, smiling.

"So, I'm with the Smith party?" Stuart said slowly, hoping the bartender understood at least a little English.

The bartender squinted, and then said, "Oh, Smith. Si. Mi accompagni, per favore." He motioned for Stuart to follow as he walked down the length of the bar toward an ornate wooden door near the back of the dining room. The bartender reached the door, knocked, and then opened it inward. Stuart hesitated before entering.

It was a smaller version of the main bar area. The same dark wood, mirrors, and brass surrounded a long dining table that sat at least a dozen. Bailey and Parnell were seated at the far end, hands clasped in front of them on the table. Stuart entered and the bartender closed the door behind him.

Once they were alone, Bailey and Parnell both stood.

"Benvenuto," Bailey said. His welcome was warm, but stern—an attitude the typically buoyant man had adopted following the news of Helmut's kidnapping.

"How was your flight? It can be rather lonely traveling alone for that amount of time," Parnell said.

"Honestly," Stuart said, pulling out a chair. "I'm exhausted. A combination of the flight, lack of sleep, and the lack of clarity about why I'm here."

"Certainly," Bailey said, returning to his seat. "We've been as … forthcoming as we feel is appropriate at this point. If I had a better idea of why Helmut asked for you, I'd share it. But we're still at a loss."

"I have to assume it has something to do with Malcolm. Helmut and your grandfather were relatively well acquainted, though I can't say I know just how well," Parnell said.

A knock came from the service door at the far end of the room, followed by a server—a young man, with ruffled short hair and a thin mustache. He stopped at the corner of the table and spat out something in Italian. Parnell greeted the server, then turned to Stuart and Bailey.

"Would either of you like something to drink or eat? Stuart, do you need a coffee?"

"Coffee would be awesome. Maybe a croissant or something like that?" Stuart said.

Parnell nodded. "Bailey?"

"Coffee and a basket of breads would be delightful."

Parnell rattled off the order to the server, who nodded, grinned, and disappeared through the service door.

"Parnell is the linguist. What, ten languages?"

"Eleven, counting American Sign Language."

"Impressive," Stuart said. He'd studied Spanish as an undergraduate, but rarely found an opportunity to put it to use.

"We should get on," Bailey said. "Our strategy hasn't changed, Stuart. We've decided to stand firm on our decision not to share what the captors are asking for, but we truly believe a direct denial of their request will put Helmut's life in certain jeopardy."

"We need to stall," Parnell added.

"Since they've elected to communicate with us up to this point only through their video, we obviously haven't had a chance to conduct a proper dialogue with them, and I believe that's our leverage point, for the time being."

"We'll have to negotiate a couple of things. First, buy some time to get approval before we share the information they're seeking," Parnell said.

"Not that we actually plan on doing so," Bailey added.

"Right, then I believe we should seek some confirmation that Helmut is actually safe. It's unlikely that they have him nearby."

"Or even in the country," Bailey said.

"Right. We hope that may pose a bit of a challenge for them."

"At what point do we drop all of this secret agent business and go to the authorities?" Stuart said. He was increasingly doubtful that he and two elderly armchair James Bonds could successfully negotiate a hostage release.

Parnell and Bailey exchanged a look, each raising an eyebrow.

"We're not completely alone, Stuart," Parnell said. "The club's membership, as I think you're beginning to see, reaches across borders and professions."

"Parnell reached out to another local member, aside from our Harry's connection, and she's conducting research as we speak through her network. She already has an aid situated at the Hassler to keep an eye on things. We're hoping she can help us identify whoever it is we end up meeting with."

"Then what?" Stuart interjected.

"That will depend," Bailey said. "Again, our main objective is to successfully stall, verify that Helmut is safe, and not divulge anything we don't want or need to."

"Contingencies?" Stuart asked. It had always been one of his main pet peeves in business. Heath and others were frequently guilty of committing to a single, linear strategy and naïvely assuming everything would go as planned. They rarely took the time, or demonstrated the patience, to establish a proper contingency plan. Stuart, always on risk patrol, would end up spending hours in the evenings and weekends putting together practical safety nets. On more than one occasion, his diligence saved the firm hundreds of thousands of dollars.

"There are none," Parnell said.

"We frankly haven't had the time to think about that," Bailey added. "Not ideal, I know."

The server knocked again and entered the room. Coffee and Danishes were served. Stuart immediately poured himself coffee and drank it as quickly as he could stand. It was unbelievably strong.

"Okay, I guess we'll get to that later. What do you need me to do?"

"I wish we had more clarity for you, Stuart," Bailey said. "Perhaps the individuals we're meeting with will give us a clue. We may receive another message from Helmut. We're hoping that our request for confirmation of Helmut's safety will spur either a brief conversation or another message from him."

"Where do you want me in the meantime?"

"Stay close to your hotel," Parnell chimed in. "You don't have to quarantine yourself, but we need to make sure we can reach you in case Prima comes across anything that points to your involvement."

"Prima? She's your local contact? She knows I'm here?"

Parnell and Bailey exchanged a glance, and then Parnell replied, "She does. We felt we needed to be completely forthright with her. We can trust her, Stuart. But we've told no one else."

"There's no reason why we should put you in any more danger than necessary, Stuart. If this group believes you have access to the same information they're seeking, they could try to apprehend you as well. Right now, the fewer people who are aware of you, the better," Bailey said.

The trio sat in silence, focusing on their coffee and pastries. Stuart had to admit that as frustrated as he had felt over the past few days, there was something unexpectedly exhilarating about the sudden shift in his world. Perhaps, he thought, it was just the jet lag taking advantage of his judgment. But that seemed unlikely. For years now, his sole focus and allegiance had been to the success and growth of D'Artagnan. It was a bit like emerging into bright light after being shuttered in the dark for an extended period. At first, the eyes screamed, protesting at the unwelcome glare, but then the mind took over as the pain and shock subsided, relishing what had been revealed from this new perspective.

"Let's discuss our next steps. Prepare for our moves for after the meeting," Parnell said, interrupting the silence.

"What if they tell you they'll kill Helmut—I can't believe I'm saying that—when you don't meet their demands?" Stuart asked.

"It's highly unlikely Helmut has what they want," Parnell said, "but they don't know that. There are others, however, who do possess that information. They don't know that either. They're fishing, Stuart. They're hoping we value Helmut's life more than the sanctity of the secret."

"And do you?" Stuart asked.

"Of course," Bailey said. "But this is a hostage negotiation. We don't walk in and hand them what they're demanding."

"We'll know more after we meet," Parnell added.

"Are you certain that there's nothing I can do?" Stuart asked. "What if something goes awry? What if it's some kind of trap? You don't have any backup plan, no safety net."

Bailey scowled at Stuart, a look he had never seen from the man. "This may come as a shock to you, Stuart, but we're hardly amateurs. Parnell and I have found ourselves in a number of equally precarious positions over the years."

"Really? Like this? When someone's life is at stake? Someone we all know and care for?"

Parnell exhaled loudly and stared at the table. "You're quite right, Stuart. This is, frankly, a frightening situation. The truth is, though, we haven't had a chance to make our move. These kidnappers, whoever they are, have made a demand and we don't have much of a choice at this point. The only way we know how to communicate with them is to attend this meeting."

"It's doubtful that they expect us to show up and give them what they want. I imagine they're waiting to see how we play this as well. I see this meeting as a sort of pre-negotiation. We know they have something we want—Helmut ... safe. We have something they want. Our showing up for this meeting grants us some credibility. That's about all that has been established," Bailey said. He turned to Parnell and asked, "Should we meet back here afterward? Say 7:30 or 8:00 p.m.?" Bailey asked.

Parnell shook his head, frowning. "No, there'll be too many people at that time. This bar is extremely popular with the tourists. I'll contact Prima for a recommendation. Our hotels obviously won't do. We'll look for another small bar or restaurant."

"Fine," Stuart said. "How will I know when and where to meet you?"

"I'll get a message to you at your hotel this afternoon," Parnell said. He then reached into his suit jacket and pulled out a piece of paper. He slid it over to Stuart. It was a business card, albeit a unique one. A solitary phone number, printed in a small font, situated the middle of the card. Stuart picked up the card. The opposite side was blank. He looked at Parnell and wrinkled his brow.

"If we don't make it to the rendezvous location by 8:30 p.m., call that number. It's the service for the Rome club. Give them your name and my name. They'll send a car for you. You only need to tell them where to find you. When you get to the club, ask for Prima."

Stuart glanced at the card again and then put it in his shirt pocket. "Will she know what to do?"

"I can only hope so," Bailey said, the smile still missing from his bulbous face.

# CHAPTER

# TEN

By four o'clock that afternoon, Stuart had exhausted the multitude of amenities offered by the Marriott Grand Flora and had grown claustrophobic in the confines of his room. He picked up a city walking guide from the concierge and decided to strike out on his own. Given that the evening's meeting was to take place near the Spanish Steps, he decided to seek out some of the other sights. The sky remained cloudless, and a slight breeze chased through the ancient streets. Every corner Stuart turned seemed to reveal more of the teeming late afternoon crowds of locals and tourists alike. He decided to head toward the Coliseum first, then perhaps Trevi Fountain.

A few blocks into his walk, he found that the city's vibrancy and stunning architecture dampened the anxiety and suspicion that had been haunting his emotions. He passed a pair of tour buses that had recently emptied dozens of foreign visitors into the streets. Their unbridled excitement, punctuated by eager expressions and animated gesturing, mimicked Stuart's sentiments. He couldn't help but hope that the evening's meeting would be successful, not just for the sake of Helmut's safety and well-being, but because it would allow him a few unencumbered days to enjoy the city before his return flight.

He slowed his gait as he caught his first glimpse of the infamous decaying relic. The afternoon sun cast lengthening shadows throughout the city, accentuating the deeply carved stone that defined the Coliseum. Although he'd seen innumerable photos of the ruin throughout his life, he found himself disappointed that he'd forgotten to bring a camera. There was something privately fulfilling about capturing this moment for himself.

A few moments later he found one of the main entrance areas and followed a group of French high school students into the Coliseum. They, too, seemed invigorated by their surroundings. As he wandered throughout the monument, he tried to envision the throngs of Romans filling the stadium's now absent seating.

Across the expanse, other groups of visitors emerged in the sunlight, perhaps trying, as he was, to conjure the lions, the bloodthirsty crowds, and the chariot races. Wasn't this where the finale of *Ben-Hur* took place? He couldn't recall. Despite how often the film ran on various cable channels, he'd never seen more than clips of the famous scene.

The threats of his world—competition, terrorism, the environment—were, to some degree, a contrast to what had been commonplace for the citizens of ancient Rome. Today, he faced his own threat, yet it certainly didn't rival the looming dread of being thrown to the lions or sold into slavery. Still, he'd somehow escaped, or more accurately, been plucked from, his sanitary microcosm of financial surety and thrust into a parallel universe of kidnapping and espionage. This sudden, otherworldly shift continued to captivate him. Being cut off from Bailey and Parnell, who at first had been annoyances, was now almost tortuous. He wanted to be in the thick of the negotiation, contribute to the excitement.

His map showed that the Trevi Fountain wasn't exactly next door to the Coliseum, but it was well within walking distance. Aside from the

Coliseum, the fountain was one of the few city sights he remembered from *Roman Holiday*, with Audrey Hepburn and Gregory Peck, where Peck's character tries to steal a camera. Again, he found himself frustrated that he hadn't brought a camera. Maybe he'd pick one up tomorrow if the outcome of the meeting provided him with more time to explore.

The fountain was tucked in a narrow piazza, hidden from the surrounding main thoroughfares. Like the Coliseum, the fountain was crowded with tourists, who were tossing coins into the water and snapping photos of each other in front of the immense sculptural background. A lone, teenage violinist pierced the din with a forlorn melody while the sweet aroma of baking waffle cones wafted from the adjacent gelaterias. A small faction of Americans vacated an area at the edge of the fountain, and he moved in and sat down. Many locals—at least he assumed they were locals—seemed dawn here to escape and lose themselves within the adoration. Couples walked hand in hand, bands of students teased one another, laughing, as if it were an adult playground. He was lost in his voyeurism when he noticed someone beside him.

"You seem quite intense."

Stuart turned and saw a woman, Italian he guessed by her accent, standing next to him, smiling. Stuart felt himself flush.

"It's my first time. I have to admit, I am a bit overwhelmed. The beauty."

The woman nodded and pursed her lips, surveying the square.

"I see what you mean. We are spoiled, I suppose. Some say we take all of this for granted."

Stuart nodded, unsure how to respond. He was struck by both her boldness and beauty. At least to him she seemed bold. Perhaps it was just how Italian women operated. He glanced at her clothes. She seemed to be dressed for a professional job—wearing a conservative, yet neatly tailored dark skirt and a simple white blouse. A pair of black heels capped her bare legs.

"Do you come here often?" he asked, then grimaced at how horrible his question sounded.

"Oh," she said, laughing. "Not really. I used to come here every week when I was growing up. I loved the fountain. Throwing coins into the water. It was wonderful for an imaginative little girl. May I?" she said, gesturing to the space beside him.

"Certainly, please," he said, nearly losing his balance as he attempted to scoot over.

"Grazie," she said, smiling. She appeared to effortlessly blend into the surrounding sculpture.

"My name is Stuart. Stuart Mancini. I'm visiting from New York." He held out his hand.

She met his hand and grasped it softly. "I know," she said, her eyes widening.

"What ..." Stuart said.

She laughed again and tapped his shirt sleeve. "I'm Prima Valdocci."

"Prima ..." Stuart said.

"Yes, I'm with the Rome Kilimanjaro Club. I believe your friends, Mr. Honeybourne and Mr. Sumner, mentioned me."

"Well, of course they did. But how did you ..."

"How did I know who you were? I have my ways of using my connections, too. I spoke with my counterpart in New York when I found out Bailey and Parnell were coming. I learned you had recently joined the club and that they'd been spending a great deal of time with you lately. Bailey mentioned that a new club member was joining them, and I had a suspicion it might be you. I had the New York club email me your photo. It didn't take long to track you down."

Stuart stared at her for a few seconds. She leaned back, propping herself up on her hands and laughed again.

"Please don't be angry, Mr. Mancini. I'm just curious. Plus, I'm trying to help out. When someone like Bailey Honeybourne asks for assistance, I do everything possible to exceed his expectations. And it was interesting watching you take in the city. I felt like a spy," she said, wrinkling her nose.

Stuart half laughed, half snorted. "I … I don't quite know how to react. To my knowledge, I've never been *tailed* before."

"It's perfectly fine to be flattered, but that wasn't my intent. Aside from my curiosity, I wanted to make sure no one else was watching you as closely as I was."

Stuart paused. "And?"

Prima looked around the fountain area again and frowned. "I think you're fine."

"I guess that's comforting. Shouldn't you be at the hotel, with Bailey and Parnell?"

"Absolutely not! I don't want to be anywhere near the Hassler while this meeting occurs. I see how upset Bailey and Parnell are—something I've rarely seen in my years of knowing them. In many ways, I'm more helpful the less I *do* know. But also, I truly want to help them, and I want to help them by keeping *you* as safe as possible."

"I … I appreciate that, Prima. To be honest, I'm a bit lost here. Just waiting on orders from Bailey."

"Oh, he'll never run out of orders. I have an idea, Stuart. Why don't we go someplace a little less public, just in case I'm not the only one *tailing* you?"

Prima walked them a block and a half away from the fountain to a narrow café tucked between a butcher shop and wine store. The bistro was half full, with patrons seated at the bar and along the banquette lining the opposite side of the room. A server pointed to an open table midway down the banquette. Prima slid into the seat against the wall and Stuart pulled up the chair.

"Do you enjoy wine, Mr. Mancini?"

Stuart nodded, "Yes, yes, I do. I can't say I'm a connoisseur, but I like most of what I try."

Prima laughed. "That's an excellent outlook." She motioned to the waiter, who was minding the tables. "Una bottiglia di Montepulciano, per favore." The waiter nodded and swung back through the kitchen door.

"Your English is amazing," Stuart said, suddenly overly conscious of his own diction.

"Yes, well, I went to school in the States."

"School? College?"

"Yes, and then law school. I had no choice other than to master the language. It's been a great benefit, though. It's enabled me to do much more with my family's business as well as the club."

"What's your family's business?" Stuart asked. Prima's casual manner and natural beauty were mesmerizing. Here was this stunning, obviously brilliant woman, talking to him, seemingly interested in the conversation, in an amazing foreign country. It felt like a dream.

"My father founded an import/export business. Furniture and food mostly. Some apparel and home decorations. Knick-knacks, you know? I have many jobs, legal advisor being one of them. I like it, though."

"Where did you attend law school?"

Prima laughed. "Indiana University. It's a good school for law. So different than California. I graduated from UCLA before going to Indiana. I loved the contrast, really. The people in Bloomington were so ... so down to earth, yes? Los Angeles was exciting. An amazing place to dive into the American culture, but Bloomington was very good for learning."

The waiter arrived with the wine, displayed the bottle to Prima who nodded and smiled, and then he served them.

Prima raised her glass. "To a new friendship," she said, clinking his glass.

"Yes, and to an amazing city."

Prima sipped her wine and said, "This is your first time in Rome?"

"Yes, Italy, for that matter—which is pretty embarrassing since my dad's family immigrated from Florence. It's … amazing. I've traveled to London numerous times on business, and made a few trips to Paris, but never here."

Prima took another drink. "I imagine that Bailey and Parnell have been filling your head with many stories of the club."

Stuart shook his head, swallowing. "No, actually the whole experience has been rather secretive, fragmented. It's … been thrust upon me, to be honest."

Prima tilted her head and looked into his eyes. "You're very fortunate, you know. All of us, I mean. Each of us who are members. It may be difficult for you to see now, but I believe you'll come around. It's inevitable."

Stuart coughed out a laugh. "I suppose you're right. I'm still struggling. This is night and day from what I'm accustomed to."

"Don't tell me," she said, pointing at him. "You're a corporate man, right? Let me guess." She scanned him from his chest up, squinting, and bringing a finger to her lips. "Certainly not sales, or marketing, hmmm. Something intellectual, right? Something complex. Engineering, perhaps? No, no. Accounting! Numbers. Am I right?" she asked, excited, as if she already knew the answer.

Stuart felt himself blush again. "Yes, actually, that's almost exactly right. I'm the CFO of a small investment firm. Accounting is one of my responsibilities."

"Aha!" she chirped, raising her glass. "I had an inkling. And I'm sure you're quite good at what you do."

Stuart forced a smile and took another drink of his wine. "This is very good," he said, hoping to change the subject.

"Oh, it's nothing fancy, but it's a favorite of mine. It reminds me of summers when I was younger. My mother's family lived in the country.

We used to visit for weeks at a time, my brothers, my mother, and I. My grandfather drank this wine all day long. It makes me comfortable."

They sat quietly a while, listening to the trumpet-laden jazz that accompanied the patrons' conversation.

"So, Bailey hasn't talked himself hoarse telling you about the club?" Prima said.

"No, he's been a wonderful host, but not particularly detailed."

Prima smiled. "I suppose I shouldn't be surprised. He can be a crazy man, all over the place. This recent issue doesn't help, I'm sure. I'd be happy to tell you what I know of the club, if that's of any value to you."

Finally, Stuart thought, a chance to get beyond this fragile, elusive veneer of the club. He took another sip of Montepulciano and urged her on.

# CHAPTER

# ELEVEN

Prima topped off her glass and sat back, slowly swirling the wine. She took a deep drink, set her glass down, stared into Stuart's eyes, and began her tale.

In the early years of the twentieth century, scores of Europeans, mainly British, migrated south to the African colonies that had been established by the empire throughout the 1800s. While instability on the continent posed a threat to long-term occupation, there continued to be an unmistakable draw to Africa's vast mysteries. The exploits of David Livingstone, Dixon Denham, and hordes of other early adventurers continued to fuel the curiosity of Europe's, and again, mainly Britain's, elite and courageous. Organized quests through East and West Africa alike were conducted by European expatriates for the well-heeled and the scientifically curious. Eventually, the men who found themselves returning to Africa began to congregate informally and, as happens when an abundance of testosterone emerges, compete with one another.

In 1920, while much of the world was still recovering from The Great War, a small group of these explorers established a club, The Kilimanjaro Club, on the outskirts of Nairobi. The wealthiest of the group, Walter Hightower, held various real estate investments throughout Kenya. One of these tracts of land boasted a meandering crevice that cut deep into the scrubland. During one of his trips to the property, Hightower happened upon a broad natural cave that burrowed several hundred feet into the west side of the gorge. Once the group formalized their organization, Hightower immediately proposed building a concealed structure where the future club members could relax, enjoy a fine glass of brandy, and tout their latest conquests. He proposed, and successfully lobbied, to construct the club within the confines of the vast cavern.

Later that year, and with the invaluable assistance of dozens of Nairobian men, Hightower's club became a reality. During the months of construction, Hightower and Elliott Fitzgerald—a retired banker from Glasgow—led a recruitment campaign to build the club's membership. Hightower was an unabashed snob who only desired to mingle with the wealthiest men. Fitzgerald, a self-made millionaire, had grown up dirt poor and wasn't nearly as comfortable with the absurdly affluent. Between the two, they managed to attract over fifty remarkably distinct— yet common in their passion for adventure—men representing six continents to join their new club. On December 31, 1920, Hightower and Fitzgerald, partnering with Henry Black and Sir Lawrence Enright, fellow Brits who'd invested heavily in the club's construction, threw a legendary New Year's Eve party to celebrate the official opening of the club's inaugural Nairobi location.

The New Year's bash solidified the new lodge as the premier watering hole for the safari and adventuring crowd. While a flood of curious visitors continued to explore the Kenyan wilderness during the first couple years of the club's existence—most who were essentially "one trip wonders"—an additional group of sixty-plus men joined and used the club as their home base between expeditions. It was the existence of this crew that led Hightower and Fitzgerald, along with Black and Enright, to craft a genuine foundation for their organization and establish a more formal membership.

Hightower had funded the majority of the original construction and did so without expecting any form of financial return. His generosity was fueled by his desire for control and his one-sided, unwavering commitment to establish the club in an obscure location. Food and drink remained relatively affordable, even after factoring in the import fees for wine, spirits, and essential European staples; and the fledging club managed to keep appropriate inventories flowing into Nairobi. As patronage grew and reached a steady level, the club began to break even during most months and even garnered a small profit during the busiest seasons.

It was Fitzgerald who pushed the idea of elevating the loose fraternity into a professional Nairobi-based establishment, replete with initiation fees, dues, formal bylaws, and such. Hightower was ambivalent; the club's current state fulfilled his desire to create an exclusive, stimulating social retreat in his home-away-from-home. Black and Enright quickly bought into Fitzgerald's concept, mostly because both men perceived a genuine risk with their investments. While financially comfortable, their fortunes were eclipsed by Hightower's. The additional structure and committed income stream mitigated most of their concerns. The club, which continued to enjoy its informal, raucous state, was wildly popular with those who went on holiday in the area and quickly gained a reputation beyond Britain and into western Europe.

The four founders initially settled on an initiation fee of ten-thousand pounds, with monthly dues of two-hundred pounds. In exchange, Hightower committed to not only upgrading the existing facility, which was far superior to anything comparable in Kenya, but remained substandard when weighed against similar clubs throughout Europe. These fees, outlandish in comparison with traditional hunting clubs, drew a membership that thrived upon occupying the highest socio-economic strata and possessed the financial resources to seal their commitment. Henry Black, a music fanatic, also pledged to bring in top-name entertainment on the weekends and for special occasions. Jelly Roll Morton, George Gershwin, and Duke Ellington were a few of the significant musicians Black imported for extended gigs. He interspersed these celebrated acts with lesser-known French and British musicians. Today, the Nairobi Club is still regarded as a prestigious, clandestine venue for top blues and jazz artists. The walls of the club remain plastered with sepia-toned photos of club members chumming it up with the stars, competing for space with the classic safari portraits. The Nairobi club evolved into a living museum to the club's origins.

Although the majority of club members were either British or American, within a few years the demand for affiliate clubs in other cities intensified. The London and New York chapters opened in the early 1930s, followed by Paris, Rome, Shanghai, and Tokyo. By 1960, a dozen chapters boasting six thousand members were thriving. The founders were all still alive at this time, but Hightower's health was faltering, and Black sustained a simmering feud with Fitzgerald and Enright. The latter were concerned about controlling the appropriate proper exclusivity for the club. Black, meanwhile, had the franchise bug long before such chains were popular. He envisioned two to three times as many clubs, along with higher initiation fees and dues. Of the four, Black stumbled financially. He was increasingly drawn to wild investment schemes and was easily goaded into financing high profile projects solely based on the press coverage they drew. After several years of infighting, the four agreed to expand to eighteen locations, substantially increasing the initiation fee, and transforming that payment into a refundable investment of one million dollars. They had no idea if the plan would work, if it would support the existing clubs and allow for expansion, but the compromise seemed to placate Black.

Each of the clubs originally elected a Chairman governed both operations and membership. The chairmen, known collectively as the Board, met several times throughout the year to discuss both the mundane and the unique issues related to their organizations. The club's mystique was consistently the main concern for the Board. While the selection committee of the Board was militant about inviting only the most credible and trustworthy members, the size of the membership had made it impossible to avoid breaches of confidentiality. Rumor of the existence of the clubs hit an all-time high in the 1960s, despite the release of any credible physical proof. Locations were tightly secured, physically cloaked, and documentation regarding the club and its operations never left the buildings. The myths continued into the 1970s when expansion ceased and the membership was finally capped. From 1972 on, no additional members were admitted. Membership could only be relinquished to others or bequeathed to heirs. These transformations snuffed the infuriating rumors and reinstated the sanctity of the fraternity.

Just as Stuart had inherited his new membership, Prima Valdocci's had been passed to her by her father, Nero Valdocci. Nero had joined the Rome chapter within a few years of starting his business. He was an experienced mountain climber, having grown up in Piedmont and scampered along the Alps bordering France and Switzerland to the north, including the Eiger and Jungfrau summits in Switzerland. The elder Valdocci introduced climbing to his only daughter when she was six, and she was hooked from the beginning. At twenty-two, she became one of the youngest Italian women to scale Mount Everest. In recent years, she'd suspended her pursuit of the tallest peaks, branching out into broader explorations in the jungles of India and the rainforests of South America.

Stuart stared into his empty glass and blinked his eyes. The bottle of wine Prima had ordered had vanished. He looked at his watch. It was 7:30 p.m. The meeting with Helmut's captors had been going on now for thirty minutes.

"I have to say, you've provided a helluva lot more information about this whole club ordeal than either of my travel mates have attempted."

"It's not that surprising, I suppose. Given all that's been happening. I mean, first Malcolm and then Helmut. I'm not privy to everything involved, but to see them this frantic is uncharacteristic, and a little unnerving."

Prima waved at their server. "We've got a bit more time to kill. Can I get you another glass of wine?"

"I don't know. I'm still battling jet lag. I …"

Prima laughed and ordered them each another glass of wine.

"I realize they were both close to my grandfather, at least that's what they've claimed. You probably don't know, but we were estranged. Actually, *estranged* makes it sound as if we had a relationship. I only met him on a couple of occasions."

"One could see that as a blessing, I suppose."

Stuart looked at her, tilting his head and furrowing his brow.

"I can't imagine it was comforting news, regardless of your relation-ship. I mean …"

"People die," Stuart said. The recent events still didn't make him feel particularly close to his grandfather. Nothing new. Prima, on the other hand, seemed shocked, almost disgusted.

"But … but Stuart, really. A murder. That's hardly the same as—"

"A what? Murder?" he said, laughing nervously. "You must be mistaken."

She sat quietly, fiddled with her cocktail napkin, and then looked up at him. "You … don't know. They didn't tell you …"

The fog that had shrouded his conscious over the past hour rapidly dissipated. The clarity was bracing. Fury suddenly displaced his fatigue.

"What … are you saying my grandfather was murdered?"

"I … Stuart …" Prima started.

"And those bastards didn't *tell* me? My god, that's … that's …" He groaned, leaning forward and shoving his fingers through his hair. He glared at the table for a moment, then shook his head. "I'm sorry, Prima. This isn't your fault, but I have *had* it with their … their constant failure to disclose all the facts," Stuart growled. He shoved his glass aside and stood.

"Stuart, Stuart, please, sit, sit, sit," Prima pleaded. She reached out and motioned for him to return to his chair. Others in the bar were staring.

"I can't, Prima. I'm going after those idiots," he said and disappeared into the bar crowd.

# TWELVE

Stuart fished two five-Euro bills from his wallet as the taxi climbed the street toward the hotel. He was regretting his decision to hold the cab for Prima. At least she wasn't pleading with him to be rational anymore, but her silence was damning. As the car halted, he flipped the bills at the driver and jumped from the taxi. Prima fumbled an apology and struck out after him. The driver examined the bills in the dome light, shaking his head.

"Stuart! Stuart, you've got to stop. This isn't safe," she called after him. His long strides made it difficult for her to catch up. She trotted carefully across the cobblestones on the toes of her heels.

The entrance to the Hotel Hassler was active. A mass of people, men in tuxedos and women in bright party dresses, clambered just outside the doors. A doorman attempted to intercept Stuart once he noticed Stuart was headed into the hotel.

"Buonasera, signore …" the doorman began. Stuart slipped past him.

"Mi scusi," Prima said, tripping and catching herself as she hurried after Stuart. "Stuart, stop!"

He took two more steps and held up just inside the doors. A slew of additional guests, dressed formally like those outside, packed the lobby.

Prima caught up to him and grabbed his sleeve. "Please," she whispered.

He turned sharply and leaned in toward her. "You know, I keep hearing that word. 'Please, Stuart, you don't understand.' 'Please, Stuart, the club is a special place.' 'Please, Stuart, forgive us for screwing up your life.'" he said. Only a nearby elderly couple seemed to pay him any attention. "I've had it with the lying and the deceit." His head snapped around again, and he scanned the lobby, seeking out the front desk. He spotted it across the room and darted toward the middle-aged gentleman behind the counter.

He looked up as Stuart emerged from the lobby crowd. "Buonasera, signore."

"Hello," Stuart grumbled. "I'm looking for the bar. The Hassler Bar."

"Yes, sir," the concierge said, quickly shifting to English. "The Hassler Bar is located just across the lobby, but I'm afraid it's closed to the public for a private function." Stuart didn't listen to the man finish his sentence. Instead, he maneuvered his way back across the lobby. As he broke into the open again, he saw Prima standing in front of the closed doors that he assumed led to the bar.

"Plea—" she began. "Ugh, Stuart. Stop. Think this through. You don't want to do anything to jeopardize your friends' safety."

"Oh, I've thought this through, all right, and I'm going to put a stop to this," he said. He grabbed the doorknob and swung the door open. For a moment, he thought he was in the wrong bar. The only person visible was a lone bartender standing guard before a wall of liquor bottles. Then, off to his left, he saw Bailey and Parnell sitting with a third man. All three were staring at him. The third man barked something in Italian at the bartender who had also frozen. The man yelled again and the bartender made a shooing motion at Stuart.

"I … uh, I am afraid this is a private meeting," Parnell said, his voice not nearly as powerful as he probably hoped it would sound.

Stuart marched over to where the men were sitting. As he approached, he could see they had a laptop open in front of them.

"Sir, please," Parnell said, standing and taking a step toward Stuart. A pathetic, pleading look slid over his face.

Stuart's heart pounded through his shoulders. Perspiration condensed along the center of his back. His eyes darted from Parnell to Bailey and finally to the slight man sitting in front of the laptop. He sucked in a sharp breath.

"What … just what the hell do you think you're doing?" Stuart barked in an exaggerated southern drawl. "My wife and I've here've been waiting twenty years to come back and have a drink at this here bar and you all have it shut down for … for a meeting?"

"I'm—" Parnell began.

"Sir, sir," Stuart heard from behind him. "I'm sorry, sir. You must leave. This is indeed a private meeting." He felt a hand grip his upper right arm. "Please, sir, come with me."

Stuart took two faltering steps backward, staring at Bailey.

"Excuse us," the third man said, nodding.

"I … well, goddamn it. Are y'all going to be open later?" Stuart said, turning toward the bartender who'd grabbed him.

"Yes, sir," he looked at his watch. "Ten o'clock, okay? We'll be open then."

"Alright, okay," Stuart said, struggling to keep up the weak charade. As they approached the doors, Stuart could see Prima just beyond the doorway. Her mouth had fallen open.

"Ten o'clock, right," Stuart mumbled as the bartender guided him out the door and closed it behind him. Prima reached out to him.

"What was that?" she said, finally.

Stuart stared out into the lobby. The opulent guests seemed to flood the room, their voices burying occasional notes of some classical refrain piped through hidden speakers. Stuart took a deep breath and returned Prima's stare.

"Stage fright? I don't know. Seeing that man with them. I had this horrible fear that I had stepped over an … an impassable boundary." He paused and looked back into the lobby. "The look on Parnell's face. I thought he was going to collapse. The fear was … you could almost physically … see it coming from him." He reached for her hand and pulled her away from the doors. "Isn't there another restaurant or bar we can get to?"

"The roof," Prima said.

"Perfect."

Prima nodded and steered them toward the elevators. When the doors opened, more couples spilled out, laughing and swinging glasses of champagne. Prima pulled him into the elevator and punched the roof button.

The seventh-floor terrace was less crowded than the lobby but still far from private. Prima continued to pull Stuart through the dining room, finally locating a small, empty balcony overlooking the city. She checked their surroundings, then jabbed him in the ribs with her index finger.

"That was idiotic! You could have gotten your friend killed, not to mention Bailey and Parnell. What were you hoping to accomplish?"

Stuart ran a hand through his hair and stepped back from her. He shook his head and said, "I know it. I know. I was just so angry, Prima. Everything is so out of control. And then to hear about Malcolm … from you, not them. It's ridiculous, Prima. It's a goddamn wild goose chase."

"Stuart, I understand that all of this is very new to you and that you don't really know me or Bailey or Parnell or anyone affiliated with the clubs enough to understand the gravity of this situation, but you have to trust us."

"*Trust* you? Why on earth should I trust anyone at this point? It's all a charade. A … an ongoing parade of little … little surprises. Prima, they drugged me. That was my introduction to the club. They slipped me something to impair my memory. Does that sound like something you do to build trust? Then they tell me one of my friends, a business associate who happens to be an integral part of my professional future, has been kidnapped, and that they know him, and that my grandfather, a man I've been cut off from for ages, has died—oh, wait, no—was murdered, but they don't bother to tell me that part. And then, and *then*, I'm dragged halfway around the world to basically sit in a hotel room. Tell me why, Prima. Why would I trust any of this?"

Prima walked away from him and stood at one of the railings overlooking the Spanish Steps and Via dei Condotti. Further off toward the horizon, the Vatican loomed over the yellowing city lights. She seemed to exhale and deflate. Stuart watched her for a moment and took a few deep breaths of his own. He was still angry but knew that Prima had little to do with his anger. She was helping her friends, fellow club members. He walked over to the railing and stood beside her.

"Prima, give me something here. Give me something to trust."

She turned slowly to face him. "These men, on both sides, are professionals. Do you know anything about Bailey or Parnell's history? Do you know where they've come from?"

Stuart shook his head. Both men looked like they had been extracted from Oxford circa 1945.

"I realize they're not young anymore, but they are, truly, trained professionals. Bailey spent at least thirty years with Scotland Yard. Before that he was in MI6. Who knows how long? He met Parnell at MI6. Parnell—well, Parnell's background is a bit spottier. Rumor has it that he was a double agent for part of his career. Others claim he isn't British at all, that he's either U.S. or Russian born. Either way, his allegiance to the British throne has been unwavering."

"Well, I can tell you from the conversations I've had with them over the past few days they seem to have no idea how to deal with Helmut's kidnapping. They can't tell me why I'm here, and they don't have any plan as to what to do with this person they're meeting with."

Prima nodded and smiled. "I can tell you that they're trying to protect you, as strange as it may seem. I believe Parnell, especially, is being extremely careful not to expose you to any danger or information that you don't need or want."

"So what *do* you know?"

She shook her head and looked down at the ground. "Not much, at least not yet. I have doubts that the captors are locals, Italians. That man in the bar, I didn't get a good look at him, but to me, he didn't look particularly Italian. I would guess German, Eastern European, perhaps Russian. But I could be wrong. My job is to help Bailey and Parnell, and you. I just don't have much more information than you do at this point."

Stuart felt his frustration rise again. "What do we do now?"

She paused then said, "I think we go to our rendezvous point, The Cowboy. Keep to the plan. If Bailey and Parnell fail to show, then we'll head to the club. If they aren't at the club, then they might leave a message for us there. We need to go quickly, though. I don't want to cross paths with that man again. It'll raise suspicion."

They rode the elevator alone as it took them down to the hotel lobby.

"By the way," Prima said, "where did you dream up that awful accent?"

Stuart shrugged, blushing again.

She laughed. "They seemed to buy it somehow. Maybe you can practice it at the Cowboy. It would seem fitting, you know," she added, jabbing him in the ribs with an elbow.

## CHAPTER

# THIRTEEN

The Cowboy was a ten-minute walk from the Hassler. Stuart and Prima managed to escape the hotel without encountering their colleagues or the captors' representative. Stuart noticed as they exited that the bartender had been repositioned outside the closed doors of the hotel bar. The swirl of partygoers remained throughout the lobby, camouflaging their departure.

It was still early when they arrived at the Cowboy, so they took a seat in a back corner table. The interior of the bar was a distorted European interpretation of a western U.S. saloon. Prima explained to Stuart on their walk to the bar that a local man who was obsessed with John Wayne had established the Cowboy in the early 1950s. A handful of patrons were congregated in the bar, and the song "Bowie Knife" played through worn speakers suspended in the corners. A plethora of western artifacts, sans the typical blanket of dust and requisite cobwebs that characterized authentic saloons, blanketed the tavern's paneled walls. Ten-gallon hats, whips, stirrups, photographs of John Wayne, unnamed cowboys, early American settlers, and other Hollywood western stars rounded out the decor.

While the walk had tamed a portion of Stuart's resurging anger, he continued to respond to Prima with one-word answers. She stopped a passing server, gave a short order in Italian, and grinned at Stuart. A moment later two cordial glasses arrived at their table filled with a clear liquid.

"I'm not sure I'm in the mood for this, Prima," Stuart said, breaking the silence and pushing the glass away.

"I know that, but it'll be good for you. It's grappa. Do you know it?"

Stuart shook his head and gazed off into the distance.

"It's a famous Italian liquor. My great-great-grandfather, my mother's grandfather, worked the vineyards throughout Tuscany nearly all of his life. Grappa comes from the remnants of the wine-making process. You know, stems, seeds, skins, pulp. It's all lumped together," she said, pantomiming the process, "and allowed to ferment further. It can be harsh, but there's something satisfying about it. Like eating the whole pig, you know? Nothing goes to waste. Come on, salute," she said, raising her glass.

Stuart let out a small snort and fingered his glass. Prima kept hers held up in front of him. She tilted her head and glared. He drew the glass toward himself with two fingers scissored around the stem, and ultimately raised the glass from the table and gave a light tap to Prima's glass. She smiled, and her expression erased any remnants of anger. "Salute," she said again and sipped from her glass.

Stuart followed suit and nearly gagged when the grappa hit his palate. He choked, struggled to swallow, and glared at her. "It's gasoline! Not a drink."

Prima laughed and patted his forearm.

"I told you it could be harsh. It is, as they say, an acquired taste. At least for some … well, *most* Americans," she said, grabbing and playfully shaking his wrist. She took another sip and sat back against the booth.

"Do you think they'll make it here?" Stuart said.

"I hope so. A delay would be bad news. But they seemed safe, even though I'm sure our unexpected entrance rattled them. Like I said, these are smart men. Brilliant. They're accustomed to handling these types of situations."

Stuart forced another sip of grappa as the music shifted to Charlie Parker. The combination provided a surprising, yet welcome, sense of calm. He watched as a steady flow of patrons continued to enter the bar, searching for the Englishmen.

"It must be eight," Prima said, nodding to the growing crowd. "They're like clockwork." He felt her scrutinizing him as he fiddled with his empty glass and a cocktail napkin.

"Well, I suppose it's my turn to launch an inquisition," she said, tapping his hand.

He looked up at her and furrowed his brow.

"I know that Malcolm was British. Were you born there or in the States?"

"I was born in Boston," Stuart said. "My mother, obviously, was English. She moved to the U.S. when she was in high school, with her mother. It was right after World War II."

"Ah, yes," Prima said. She had pushed her glass forward, a swallow of the grappa remaining, and leaned forward. "Malcolm had mentioned that."

"Just how well did you know my grandfather?" he asked. It was a bit irritating how everyone knew about his relatives and his own history.

"Oh, I can't say we were that close, really. He visited Rome regularly, so I had the opportunity to have a drink or two with him from time to time, but he had so many friends in the club. He attracted a lot of attention, and he always mentioned you."

Stuart forced a laugh and shook his head. "Parnell said the same thing. I just … it just seems odd, you know? Given I'm not even sure that I have an authentic memory of the man."

"Do you know what caused the split, with he and your mother?"

Stuart fell silent and thought of taking another sip of grappa. He lifted his glass and set it back down.

"I really don't. For as long as I can remember my mother essentially banished all talk of her father, unless of course she initiated it. And most of those discussions were peppered with a lot of colorful language."

"Really?" Prima said, smiling.

"Oh, yes. I learned 'bastard,' 'old tosser,' and 'bloody bugger' from my mother, all before kindergarten, even though I had no idea what any of them meant."

"I can see why this must be awkward for you then."

"Bizarre is more like it. My entire life has been interrupted, and to top it off, it's because of a relative that I was brought up to despise. I was programmed to cringe every time I heard his name. You just didn't talk about him in our house. By the time I was probably eight or ten, any mention of the man disappeared. I guess my mom got all of her hatred out of her system and was able to erase him by then."

"What about you grandmother, Malcolm's wife? Is she still alive?"

Stuart shook his head. "No, no. She died a few years after coming to Boston. Double pneumonia. My mom said she was a relatively frail woman, and the disease just wiped her out."

"It's funny," Prima said. "You have an accent, you know, and not American, and certainly not of Boston. No 'cahs' or 'bahs,' you know?"

"My mom. I spent a lot of time with her growing up. My dad was in sales. Worked all of the time. Mom and I became, I suppose, a support system for one another. I was pretty much a loner growing up," he said, laughing. "Still a loner, I would say."

"Are your parents still … alive?" Prima asked, wincing a bit.

"My father died when I was a senior in high school. Heart attack. He was in Chicago. I hadn't seen him for something like two weeks when …

when the news came. It was so odd," he said, returning to his glass and napkin. "I was sad because my mom was sad. It devastated her, which, now, seems strange, too. I mean, he was rarely home, at least 'present.' He was around most nights for dinner, unless he had a trip or something, but it was a non-event. I remember many evenings when he would disappear—go back to work—right after dinner. I don't think he was ever very happy, even though he was successful. And mom loved him, doted on him when she could, you know? She talked about him all the time. And I imagine he loved her, too. He just struggled, like a lot of fathers from that time. He definitely saw himself as a provider, and he was obsessed with how to maintain his role."

Prima nodded. "My father was the same way. A very passionate man. Always extremely excited about something, whether it was a customer, the government, football, anything. There was no knob on him, right?" she said, pantomiming turning a volume knob. "Everything was … was full blast, right? On high."

"If my dad was passionate about anything other than work, it never showed." He paused, conjuring the few vivid memories of his father he'd retained. A fifth birthday party, receiving a bright red two-wheeled bicycle. Another flash of a Christmas, sometime later, when the two of them put together a slot car track. It was one of the few times he specifically remembered seeing his father's smile. His father had loved those slot cars.

"What about your mother?" Prima asked.

Stuart sighed. "She's alive, to a degree, I suppose. She's in a home. Dementia. It hit her all of a sudden a few years ago."

"Oh my god," Prima said, cupping her hand over his. "I'm so sorry."

"It's a weird, horrible disease. Every once in a while, when I visit, she's almost normal. She recognizes me, seems to have a grasp on reality and what's going on in the world, but it's short-lived. It never lasts the entire visit. Other times, it's like … like babysitting a corpse. She's completely vacant. Doesn't respond to anyone or anything. I've been thinking about her a lot lately, especially during this trip. If there's anyone that I need to talk to, it's her, and she can't be here. I'm curious what she would do—what she could tell me. I truly wonder how she'd react if she knew I was chasing across the world because of something her father had been involved in."

Prima nodded and turned toward the bar. She straightened suddenly, a smile unfolding across her face. Stuart followed her gaze as she waved frantically. Then he saw Bailey, followed by the stoic Parnell, squeezing past the people crowded against the bar.

"Thank God," Prima said.

Bailey approached their table and seemed to be forcing a smile. Parnell stepped up beside Bailey without making the same cordial attempt.

"Stuart," Bailey said, his demeanor now stern, "that was one of the most foolhardy displays I've ever witnessed. What in Lucifer's name were you thinking, man?"

Parnell placed a hand on Bailey's shoulder as if to steady him. He'd gone beet red.

"Please, both of you, sit down," Prima said, motioning to the open seats. "I believe I owe you both an explanation … an apology."

"That's not necessary," Stuart said to her. "Can you give us an update, though? Is Helmut still alive?"

The men exchanged a look and sat down at the table, Parnell in the booth alongside Prima and Bailey in the open chair.

"You should know," Prima started, "I was the cause of this evening's interruption. I incorrectly assumed that Stuart here … had more information than he did."

"Whatever do you mean, dear?" Bailey asked.

"It started earlier in the day. I was a bit concerned about Stuart when you told me that he was joining you here. I followed him while he walked through part of the city and then accosted him at the Trevi Fountain. We spent part of the afternoon in a nearby café. And during our conversation we discussed Malcolm."

Parnell slumped and shook his head. "Good grief," Bailey muttered. "No wonder." He peered up at the ceiling for a quick moment then added, "We should have told you, at least before bringing you here."

"The blame's on me. Bailey pushed hard to tell you," Parnell said. "I was the stubborn, selfish one. I was grappling with Helmut's obscure message, his plea to find you, and I was afraid you'd quickly decline the offer to join us if you knew of Malcolm's murder."

Stuart failed to summon a suitable response. A scramble of thoughts and emotions seemed to seize his brain. As much as he wanted to lash out, he couldn't. It was like trying to hold a grudge against a ruthless, yet benevolent, professor. Stuart could see tears welling in the man's eyes.

"The men who are holding Helmut are responsible for Malcolm's murder. I'm sure you've figured that much out," Parnell said.

"That was my fear," Stuart responded.

"They're an odd lot," Bailey said. "They're not Italian, certainly not British. Parnell thought they were German or perhaps Austrian. Then he caught upon something I had missed. The man we met with, who cleverly gave his name as simply A, slipped and mentioned the name Thaddeus."

Prima started to speak, paused, and then said, "Ahhh."

"Exactly," Bailey said. "It was a grave error. I didn't even catch it."

"He answered a call on his cell phone when the waiter was bringing our drinks. He'd stepped away was trying to whisper. I didn't catch much of the conversation. It was brief, but I did hear him mention Thaddeus," Parnell added.

"And who is Thaddeus, since I'm obviously the only one in the dark … again?" Stuart said.

"Thaddeus Kleinreichert. One of the very few *former* club members," Parnell said.

"He was, actually still is, a brilliant explorer. A fanatical collector. He's unstoppable when he sets his sights on items he covets," Bailey said. "That's what eventually ended his affiliation with the club. He had walked a fine line for years, either beating others to the punch when it came to making significant discoveries, or somehow owning the rarest of pieces. His methods eventually caught up with him. Three different members caught his associates in the midst of theft. His membership was immediately rescinded. He did a minor stint in Maidstone, a British prison, but was released within the last five years."

"And you know this man killed my grandfather? What are you doing in a bar in Italy? Why haven't you notified the police, Interpol, whoever it is we need to inform?" Stuart said.

Parnell looked at Prima and squinted. "What else did you happen to share with our young friend?" She shrugged and smirked. Prima's playful look stunned Stuart. Her allure was beginning to distract him.

"Stuart," Bailey said, "I maintain close relations with a number of associates from MI6. I admit we use somewhat unorthodox means in these types of situations, but they're truly rare. I'm fearful that a misstep—"

"Like today," Parnell interrupted, glaring at Stuart.

"Um, yes, as I was saying, any misstep could result in another senseless murder."

"Okay, I understand. You're trained … spies or whatever. You know better. What's happened to Helmut?"

Bailey sighed. "We believe he's still alive. They shared another video."

"And he left another message," Parnell said, looking at Bailey. "It helps explain why you're here."

Prima's hand slid over Stuart's again.

"His message started the same as the previous one. 'Get Mancini.' Then he added, 'Malcolm's mirror.' Do you know what that means?"

Stuart shook his head, trying to remember. There was so little that he'd ever connected with his grandfather. Why would such a message make sense to him now?

"I'm drawing a blank," Stuart said.

"Take a moment. Think," Parnell said, leaning forward. "There must be a reason he called you out."

"Mirror …" Stuart mumbled, burying his head in his hands. What was Malcolm's mirror? Then, in a flash, it hit him. In the powder room of his apartment, a mirror hung above the basin. It was an antique his mother had given to him. He remembered the moment she discovered it. They'd been in her attic, bringing down Christmas decorations one December. The mirror—ornate and shield-shaped, about eighteen inches across— had been buried in a box marked London. His mother had pulled it out, regarded it for a moment, turning it over and running her hands around the frame.

"You should take this," she had said quietly.

"Why?" Stuart had responded. He'd just started with D'Artagnan. He lived in a barren walk-up in Chelsea.

"It belonged to my mother. Her … my father, shipped this box to me a few years ago. He gave this to her after I was born, or so she claimed. I can't keep it here. I can't keep any of this. I shouldn't," she had said. "Keep it, for me."

"I know where it is," Stuart said, his head erupting from the table.

"Good god, where?" Bailey said.

"In New York. In my apartment. In the powder room."

Parnell glared at him. "You have to go home. Now."

# CHAPTER

# FOURTEEN

Within twelve hours of leaving the Cowboy, the driver pulled the limo up in front of Stuart's building. Stuart sat in back with Bailey, trying to imagine, as he had during the entire flight, how and why his grandfather had chosen an antique mirror to harbor a valuable secret. Bailey was jumpy, and had been quick to snap at anyone, including Stuart, who tested his patience. His pudgy fingers continued to drum on the door's armrest as the car stopped.

"You're positive the building security team hasn't seen anything out of the ordinary?" Bailey asked again.

"Bailey," Stuart said. He was beginning to lose his patience as well. "I've spoken to them three times now since we arrived at the airport in Rome. We'll see Larry in about thirty seconds. He'll let us know if anything strange has happened since we last spoke," he added, flashing his watch at Bailey. "Seventeen minutes ago."

As if on cue, the car door opened. The driver, a petite brunette, stood aside the door and smiled at both men as they scooted from the car. Stuart thanked her and jogged toward the building's front doors. Bailey lingered, waiting for the driver to pop the trunk and unpack their luggage.

Larry emerged from inside the lobby and opened the door just as Stuart stepped onto the maroon entrance rug.

"Welcome home, Stuart," Larry said. Stuart stopped just outside the door.

"Because I'm being badgered, I need to ask you again. Have you seen anyone in the building that you haven't recognized? Anyone new or suspicious visiting other tenants? Have any alarms been triggered, in my unit or any others?"

Larry smiled broadly and shook his head. "No, sir. Same old, same old here." Stuart nodded and looked back at Bailey. He was waving off the driver and hauling their bags up to the front door.

"Mr. Honeybourne," Larry said with a slight bow, "you better put those down. I'll lose my job if someone sees you carrying your own bag. Good to see you again, by the way. I hope your travels were uneventful."

Bailey bristled slightly, and then Stuart watched as the older man's demeanor quickly shifted into PR mode. He smiled, let out a sharp laugh, and nodded, followed by, "Yes, yes, please." He released the bags to Larry and puffed out his chest. "All was splendid." Then he glanced at Stuart. "We do need to get Mr. Mancini upstairs, though. He's not quite accustomed to the jet set," he said, clapping Stuart on the shoulder.

"Thank you, Larry," Stuart said. "Bailey, the bags will be up in a minute. Let's get upstairs."

Once in the elevator, Bailey stiffened again. "I'll call Parnell once we get inside. He'll want to know we've arrived." It was close to 10:00 p.m. in New York—three or four in the morning in Rome, Stuart guessed. He hadn't been gone long enough to think much of the time difference.

The elevator door opened into the darkened entryway of Stuart's apartment. He flipped the light switch and heard Bailey gasp.

His apartment had been ransacked. The framed artwork that had lined the entry walls was in pieces on the marble floor, littered among paper, clothing, and trash. Nearly every inch of visible flooring seemed covered with something.

"Oh, God no," Bailey muttered, shuffling forward into the hall.

Stuart was in shock. He hadn't moved since Bailey gasped. How did they know? How did they get in? Why didn't the alarm go off? His apartment wasn't accessible without the elevator key card. Only he and the front desk team had one. He looked at the alarm system pad and noticed it was unlit. It had been completely disarmed, or at least bypassed.

"Jesus Christ," he said, following Bailey into the main room. The furniture had been upended, and the upholstery of every piece had been sliced open and shredded. Stuart realized that the apartment was cold, and he felt a breeze. One of the main windows had a large oval cut from it.

"There," Stuart said, pointing to the window. Bailey scampered to the gaping hole and reached out to the glass. "Bailey. How did this happen? How did they know?"

Bailey shook his head, touching the edge of the hole. "Maybe … maybe it's a coincidence. Maybe it was just a cat burglar—a very *aggressive* cat burglar."

"That's ridiculous. Look at this place," he said, kicking at the debris.

Bailey spun around. "Where's the mirror?"

Stuart pointed to the powder room to his left. The door was slightly ajar and the light was on. Stuart approached the door and nudged it open with his knee. A lone nail protruded from the wallpaper, bent downward, where the mirror had hung. "It's …" he started to say, then saw the fragments of glass scattered across the floor. The frame of the mirror was cracked in half, face down in the corner. He took a step forward, the mirror shards snapping beneath the sole of his shoe, and carefully picked up the fractured frame. A large piece dangled from the frame and gave way, shattering on the floor.

"What is it?" Bailey called, now directly behind him in the doorway.

Stuart lifted the frame in front him and turned it around. The backing of the mirror, constructed of three oblong pieces of lightweight wood, was remarkably intact. Time and a combination of humidity and dryness had bleached the wood to a pale yellow. "There's nothing here," he said.

"May ... may I, Stuart?" Bailey said, squeezing into the modest bathroom. Stuart handed the now glassless frame to Bailey. He inspected the backing and carried it into the main room. Stuart turned off the light and followed.

"Is there a table ..." Bailey asked, pointing toward the archway leading out of the room, "maybe in the kitchen?"

"Yes, just around the corner."

Bailey strode into the kitchen, found the light switch, and disappeared around the corner. Stuart followed. The contents of his kitchen cabinets were similarly strewn across the countertops and scattered on the floor.

"Am I missing something?" Stuart said. Bailey was hunched over the kitchen table, the overhead lamp illuminating the dining table.

"I don't know," Bailey answered, still focused on the mirror's backing. "Do you mind if I dismantle the frame?"

Stuart laughed. "Hardly. It's already destroyed," he said, joined him at the table.

Bailey grunted and pulled at the sides of the frame. Bailey made the slightest tugs, gradually increasing the tension as he pried at the wood, but nothing moved.

"It's old, but apparently quite sturdy," Stuart said.

Bailey shook his head. "I'm not so sure," he said. He grunted and tugged harder. Nothing happened initially, and then Stuart heard a faint crack and the frame split in half. Stuart could see that the backing was actually made of two thin layers of wood. Bailey slid the layers apart, revealing a narrow space between the slats. A perfectly square parchment envelope slid from between the layers of the wooden backing. "Ahhh ..." Bailey said, turning to Stuart with a huge smile. "Take it."

Stuart pinched the envelope between his thumb and forefinger, then pulled it from the backing. Bailey set the frame remnants on the table.

"Holy mother, Bailey. What the hell is it?"

Bailey's hand inched forward then snatched the envelope from Stuart's hand. Stuart stared at him, perplexed.

"This … doesn't belong to you. At least not right now, Stuart. I need you to understand." Stuart glared then shook his head.

"Thank you," Bailey whispered.

Stuart left the table and ran his hands through his hair. "Bailey, I *want* to understand. Truly, I do. But … I mean, look at what's happened. Look at my home! It's destroyed. I've run away from my job, for the first time ever. I … I don't think I know how to make myself understand."

"Stuart," Bailey called. Stuart turned around to face him. "We've got to protect this," he said, holding up the envelope. "We need to take it to Parnell." He walked toward Stuart, out of the kitchen table light. "Talk to your man out front. Have them arrange to clean up the damage. We'll take care of the cost."

"I don't give a damn about the cost, Bailey. I need to know where this is going—what we're doing."

Bailey sighed. "I know, I know. Talk to Larry first. Pull together a new set of clothes and meet me at my hotel—The Carlyle. I'll arrange for a room for you. And I'll contact Parnell. We'll plan our next step once I reach him."

Stuart turned around and walked out of the kitchen. "How long are we planning to be gone this time, Bailey? I've got to talk to my office. What do I need to pack? Jesus, this is frustrating."

"You'll figure it out, Stuart. Meet me at my hotel. I'll show myself out."

Bailey left Stuart to finish packing and arrange for a cleaning and repair service through Larry. Stuart's initial report of the break-in sent Larry into a tailspin. He swore on every living and dead relative that he knew every single person who'd passed through the building's doors. Stuart pleaded with Larry to understand that he wasn't placing blame— that the burglars had obviously repelled or climbed the building from the outside. Larry finally regained his composure and contacted building management. He promised to secure contractors to clean and complete the necessary repairs. Back upstairs, Stuart threw a variety of clothes into the largest suitcase he owned. Packing raised his frustration levels. He felt helpless in the fragmented chaos. And yet he felt equally helpless in stopping himself. It was irrational. No one was forcing him to leave. No one was threatening him, yet he felt compelled by something he couldn't identify. He didn't seem to have any choice.

Before he called Larry for a cab, he dialed Heath's work number and left him a voicemail. He told Heath he was planning on taking a second week off and would call him later the next day to discuss details. He hung up, ashamed that he had no idea what the details were or what they'd be the following day.

## CHAPTER

# FIFTEEN

The Marrakesh airport was a circus. Ramadan was less than a week away, and it seemed the transplanted relatives of every resident of Morocco were landing in Marrakesh. Stuart exited the jetway into a sea of locals and southern Europeans. Machine-gun-toting guards loomed every fifty feet. They tracked the Anglos, including Stuart, as he fought his way through the initial crowd surfaced near a gift shop. Overhead signs, scripted in Arabic, French, and—in a few cases—English, directed him toward baggage claim. He stole a glance at his watch. It was 5:30. He was scheduled to meet Parnell at their hotel, La Mamounia, in an hour. Before then, he needed to exchange money, find his luggage, and track down a taxi. Although the baggage sign had been encouraging, he wasn't confident he would arrive on time.

Stuart and Parnell had a flight scheduled the following day into Addis Ababa, the capital of Ethiopia. Bailey was carrying the envelope found in the mirror and was to meet them in the capital. Both men were thrilled and anxious about the discovery in Stuart's apartment. Stuart found himself swept up in this newfound enthusiasm. He learned during the flight to Morocco that prior to the discovery of the envelope, Bailey and

Parnell hadn't been absolutely certain of what Helmut's captors were seeking. Their assumptions had been solely driven by the nature of the captors' demands and Helmut's encrypted messages.

Bailey had shared most, but Stuart suspected not all, of what had transpired in Rome with the captors' representative. The man they had met with at the Hassler also professed not to know what his superiors were seeking; only that, according to them, Helmut and his colleagues had access to the information they demanded. The meeting at the Hassler had ended with an agreement to reconvene in Rome the following week. The representative assured Bailey and Parnell that Helmut would remain alive as long as they met the commitment to attend the follow-up meeting. The man had also strongly implied that Helmut's well-being would rapidly decline if they attended the second meeting empty-handed.

Bailey had also shared that Parnell was struggling with disclosing anything to Helmut's captors, regardless of their demands and the potential consequences. The assassins had slaughtered Malcolm without attempting to negotiate. It seemed unlikely that Helmut would be spared even if their demands were met. Helmut was nearly seventy, with grown children, a wife twenty years his junior who stood to inherit millions, and only a few months from retirement. Aside from familial love, there was little of value or motivation that would justify a fair exchange. Parnell, Bailey had said, felt the best strategy was to reveal a forged substitute of the contents of the envelope and, he hoped, save Helmut's life.

When Bailey had called Stuart from The Carlyle to inform him they were traveling to Africa, Stuart hung up on him. He'd nearly chucked the phone through the hole the burglars had left in his window. Africa? Morocco, specifically? What happened to Rome? How was traveling to an entirely different continent going to save Helmut? Bailey had called back, ignoring the hang up, and explained that he'd reached Parnell in Rome and they had decided, together, to open the envelope. Given its contents,

Bailey said they were compelled to travel to Africa. They would split up, with Parnell heading to Marrakesh ahead of Stuart, and Bailey would fly directly to Ethiopia. Despite Stuart's angry pleas, Bailey had refused to disclose the contents of the envelope to him. "It's for your protection," was Bailey's standing reply. Eight hours later, they were back at JFK airport preparing to board their respective flights.

As Stuart snaked his way through the Marrakesh airport, he located a currency exchange window. He waited behind an angry German man who was struggling to get a cash advance on his credit card. The man eventually left with a wad of local bills, muttering a stream of German profanity. Stuart changed one hundred dollars and turned his focus to retrieving his bags.

Stuart fell in with the current of bodies flowing toward the baggage claim. The airport boasted a 1950's institutional interior design scheme— glossy off-white tile covered the walls, their shine muted by layers of dust, oil, and neglect, scuffed white linoleum rippled under foot, topped by a low, intermittently water-stained suspended ceiling. The heavy scent of spice, dust, stale sweat, and smoke hung in the air.

The pace of the parade began to slow, and Stuart realized they were butting up against the baggage claim area. The number of armed guards seemed to have multiplied, but most were gathered in groups of two or three, talking, smoking, and generally ignoring their surroundings. Stuart saw a Royal Air Maroc sign and an arrow attached to a supporting column. He followed the arrow and ended up in front of a stationary, empty luggage belt. A young American couple he recognized from his flight were standing nearby, so he assumed he'd made it to the right place.

Twenty minutes later, the belt began to move. By that time, he was coated in sweat. Breathing was hard. An invisible tide of noxious fumes blew in from the adjacent exits, supplanting the oxygen. Just before panic set in, Stuart identified his bag. He snatched it from the belt and pushed his way out the doors and into the Marrakesh afternoon chaos.

An enthusiastic teenaged airport aide pointed Stuart to the nearest taxi stand. Within a few minutes he was safely in a cab on his way to the hotel.

La Mamounia was a surreal, exotic oasis; the antithesis of the dingy Marrakesh Menara Airport, perched a few hundred yards from the ancient walled souk of Marrakesh. Several neighboring buildings shared the unfortunate design scheme exhibited by the city's airport, sharing the broad, dust-laden road that bordered the front of the hotel. Bikes, donkey-driven carts, fume-belching, European cars, and dilapidated trucks formed a steady flow of traffic in front of the resort.

Parnell had arrived late the previous evening. Bailey had shared earlier that while Marrakesh didn't have a formal chapter of The Kilimanjaro Club, there was a seasonal unsanctioned offshoot that operated deep within the souk. Parnell was going to arrange for a meeting that evening with one of the local members so they could gather recommendations on how to plot their next moves. While nothing had been promised, Stuart was confident that Parnell and Bailey would disclose the contents of the envelope soon. That secret, however, was unlikely to be shared with him before they arrived in Addis Ababa.

Stuart was surprised the staff of the hotel, while immersed in an ornate, authentic West African environment, had been westernized through some form of training. In fact, the man who checked him into his room wore a nametag that listed his home city as Toronto below his name, Pierre. Pierre delivered a well-rehearsed and evocative spiel about the hotel and its amenities. He verified that Parnell had checked in but no messages had been left. The bellman, a towering Moroccan with a gracious smile and shimmering green eyes greeted Stuart, picked up his suitcase, and motioned for Stuart to follow.

The moment the hotel room door closed behind the bellman, the phone in Stuart's room rang. He heard the chime echo from the bathroom and saw the handset situated next to the commode. Convenient. He picked up the receiver and said, "Hello?"

"Stuart, so good to hear your voice. Parnell Sumner here."

Stuart smiled, a bit astonished by how relieved he was to hear from Parnell, too. "Hello, Parnell. I made it."

"Indeed you did! Splendid accommodations, don't you agree? La Mamounia is a favorite of Bailey's—mine as well. I know he's quite jealous that he's missing this leg of the trip. Neither of us have spent much time in Addis Ababa, so we're booked at the Hilton. It should be reliable, but nothing like this palace."

"It's stunning," Stuart said. The sudden lack of activity and anxiety left a void that was giving way to exhaustion. Three trans-Atlantic flights within a week had sapped his energy. He took a deep breath and said, "So, what's our plan this evening? I need to keep moving. I actually slept some on the plane, but I'm fading fast."

Parnell laughed. "Perfectly understandable. Well, we have an appointment, dinner actually, with an old friend who owns a restaurant in the souk. It's adjacent to the club annex, I suppose you'd call it. He's expecting us in about an hour, so we'll need to leave in about thirty minutes."

Stuart agreed and decided a shower would wake him up. He unpacked what he needed for the next day and headed back into the bathroom.

Stuart met Parnell at the front desk as planned. The shower had successfully revived him, although he craved an iced coffee, or anything cold and caffeinated. Parnell's greeting was predictably stiff, aside from the gratitude his eyes revealed. He shook Stuart's hand firmly, kept his lips tight, then let his smile break through, slapping him on the shoulder. "Let's go, old boy. Into the souk." He led Stuart onto the street where a lively tour group and several locals—mostly men in long, robe-like garments—had gathered near the entrance.

Parnell intercepted a doorman and engaged in brief conversation. A moment later, the doorman escorted one of the robed men to Parnell, appeared to make an introduction, and accepted a tip from Parnell. Parnell turned to Stuart and waved him over.

"This is Abu," Parnell said. The man, a stout middle-aged Moroccan with a saucer-sized mat of wild hair sprouting from his pate, bowed and nodded.

"Bonjour," Abu said.

"French is widely spoken here," Parnell said, as if to apologize for Abu. "Abu's English is stronger than he's willing to admit, so he slips into French as a matter of comfort. For your benefit, he said he'd try to remember to speak English, but that we shouldn't depend upon it."

Parnell turned to Abu and rattled off something in French. Abu's eyes widened and he smiled, nodding repeatedly. He waved them onward and said, "Follow me."

Abu escorted them to a battered sedan parked across the street from the hotel. As they crossed, Parnell turned to Stuart and said, "It turns out that Abu also works for Said, our friend. He's trustworthy and loyal. The souk can be, frankly, confusing, and, at times, dangerous. Confusing for the tourists, dangerous for others. I'm counting on Said to help us with the next step of our venture. His assistance will be critical."

"So, you've worked with Said before?" Stuart asked.

Parnell shook his head. "Worked, no. Socialized, often. I see him every time I come to Marrakesh, but we've never conducted business together." They reached the car, and Abu opened the rear door for them. "I can explain more when we arrive."

Abu smiled and bowed, closing the door behind them.

The short drive to the souk was harrowing. Abu's gentle nature vanished. He seemed to be possessed by a deranged off-road racer. The journey was a continuous string of horns, sudden braking, jackrabbit starts, and harsh turns. Traffic clotted from every direction. Random roundabouts sprang from the craggy streets, stagnating all movement. Abu squeezed the car into any potential space that opened between other vehicles, curbs, structures, and pedestrians. The five-minute drive felt like an hour of torment. Stuart spotted a towering, sinuous stone wall through the car's rock-pecked windshield that stretched as far as he could see. A high arched opening, threaded with vividly colored banners and flags, came into view as the crowd and traffic dissipated.

Parnell pointed to the passageway. "That's it, the souk." Abu swerved to the side of the road and pulled into a partially vacant lot. Several other cars, a few small-scale panel vans, and a line of bikes and scooters were scattered across the dirt lot. A man dressed similarly to Abu waved them into the lot. Abu followed the man's direction and parked off to the side, away from the other vehicles.

"We walk from here," Abu said.

After surviving the dash through the traffic to cross the street, Abu motioned for Stuart to walk with him. "There is much excitement today, Mr. Stuart. Ramadan comes. You know of Ramadan?"

Stuart nodded and forced a grin. He'd certainly heard of the sacred Muslim holiday, but knew nothing other than it was important to the Muslim religion.

Abu shifted back into French, speaking directly to Parnell.

"He says it's too bad we won't be here for the first night. His family has a big celebration. You know of the fasting, right, Stuart? During Ramadan, the Muslims don't eat until sundown. And then, at least from my experience, they eat very well."

"Oui!" Abu said, nodding and smiling.

Abu led them into the streams of people who poured in and out of the souk entrance. Men and women—Stuart assumed many to be vendors or suppliers—hauled baskets and crates of food, linens, pottery, and other goods on their heads and shoulders. Others, carrying smaller baskets, were apparently local shoppers. Finally, there were the tourists. Most had an escort like Abu, and juggled a mix of cameras, guidebooks, and Western snacks. Stuart felt the temperature rise as the crowd density increased. The same scent of dust, sweat, spice, and smoke that had permeated the airport now accompanied the souk's heat, reminding Stuart of Manhattan's unique subway odor.

"It is not too long to walk," Abu yelled, waving them forward. Stuart locked eyes with Parnell, who was actually grinning.

"I love Marrakesh," Parnell said, slapping Stuart on the back again. "It's my Disneyland."

Stuart wasn't quite sure how to handle the new "cheery" Parnell. As dry and unemotional as Parnell typically behaved, there had been something comfortable about his composure and predictability. Frankly, this sudden change was unnerving, especially amongst the chaos of the souk. The bartering, bantering, arms and hands flapping, bodies, carts, and baskets darting, made the busy sidewalks and streets of Manhattan seem dull. Suddenly, Stuart heard a sharp electrical bray directly behind him. He stumbled and turned to see three teenage boys stacked on a sagging, battered Honda scooter, weaving their way through the crowds. A hand grabbed his wrist, and he instinctively tried to pull away. Abu's face sprang from the crowd, his huge, Cheshire-Cat grin, startling Stuart. "Come! Don't get lost," he yelled, laughing, and he tugged Stuart deeper into the throng.

Parnell was several yards in front of them, somehow successfully shopping the merchandise at one of the unending succession of booths while evading the neighboring vendors and customers.

"He is a good barterer," Abu yelled, nodding toward Parnell. "Shop with him. He always finds you a good deal. More than me!" Despite the sense of claustrophobia Stuart felt, Abu's manner and comfort within the souk managed to calm him.

They continued to shuffle and squeeze past an endless array of fluttering awnings and teeming storefronts, each operated by at least one highly enthusiastic marketer. Most were men, but there were also a fair number of women working the shoppers. Finally, Abu rose up on his toes and yelled, "Parnell," and then he whistled when Parnell failed to turn around. Parnell whirled and acknowledged Abu with a nod. Abu rose up again, jabbed a hand above the mob and pointed to the left. Between Parnell and Abu, amidst two stalls, was a narrow alleyway. Parnell dodged his way into the opening. Abu turned to Stuart, nodded in the direction of the passage and pulled him out of the press.

"I nearly missed it, Abu. I was lost in the wares," Parnell said. The foreign, misplaced smile had returned to his face.

"That is not a problem. I think we made our exit just in time. I'm afraid Mr. Mancini does not share your excitement for the souk."

"Now that's not entirely true," Stuart said. He felt a blush rise from his neck. "It was just a new experience, that's all. I'm still trying to recover from the jet lag."

"Ah, yes, jet lag. The perfect excuse for everything," Abu said, thumping Stuart on the shoulder. "Let's go. Said will be anxious to see you."

Although the alley was empty, it was equally as claustrophobic as the market. The walls stretched two or three stories high and, at its widest, was less than three feet across. The sun had begun to set and the alley was draped in shadow. Windows and doorways, scattered along the way, cast filtered cones of light through the thick air. The ubiquitous scent of spice and oil, products of various dinner preparations, intensified, hanging in the still air.

Abu led them along the narrowing walkway that abruptly opened into a spacious courtyard. The intricate tile work Stuart had noticed throughout the hotel was mirrored in the intimate square. A round fountain, brimming with water, occupied the center of the area. A broad, tiled staircase tumbled into the square on the fair side, leading to a brightly lit, three-story structure. A veranda wrapped around the second and third stories. Spirited voices and music echoed off the tile. The aroma of roasting meats and vegetables wafted from the top of the staircase.

"Wow," Stuart whispered, closing his eyes.

"Oh, yes, Mr. Mancini. It's worth the journey. Please," Abu said, motioning toward the staircase. "Let's not keep Said waiting."

A small ceramic sign hung above the right-hand banister. Golden Arabic calligraphy danced across the deep red background. Parnell said, "Raghba. It's Arabic for 'desire.'" His smile was still there. Stuart realized he'd have to get accustomed to Parnell's giddiness. Perhaps it was simply a result of the old Brit becoming comfortable with Stuart's presence.

They reached an intricately carved wooden dais at the top of the staircase. As they approached the podium, a young Moroccan woman with shimmering ink-black hair rolling over her shoulders turned to them.

She smiled and said, "Bon soir." She nodded to Abu separately.

"Good evening, miss," said Parnell. "We're here to see Said."

"Of course," she said, switching to English effortlessly. Just then, a tall, immaculately dressed man appeared behind the hostess. He whispered to her, and she darted away.

"Mr. Parnell," the man said, walking around the podium and opening his arms. Parnell stepped toward the man. The man formed a fist and tapped at his chest. Parnell mirrored the gesture and then they exchanged a warm hug. The man pushed Parnell away and gripped his shoulders. "It's been too long, no? How long? More than a year?"

Parnell laughed, patting the man on his side. "I'm afraid so, Said. Nearly a year and a half, I believe." The man shrugged and smiled.

"Abu, thank you so much for bringing my friends this evening," Said said. Abu nodded and touched his chest. The man returned the gesture and deftly passed something to Abu.

"I will meet you after your meal," Abu said to Parnell. He bowed, took a step backward, and glided down the steps.

"Said Musi, may I introduce you to Stuart Mancini. He's the grandson of Malcolm Buckley." Parnell turned to Stuart and said, "Stuart, Mr. Said Musi, a great friend and extremely hospitable ally of ours."

Said stepped forward, gripped Stuart's hand, and grasped his forearm with his left hand. "It's my pleasure. Please, my condolences on the loss of your grandfather. He was a great man."

Stuart pursed his lips and nodded. "Thank you. It's my pleasure to meet you, too."

"Come," Said announced, as if he were speaking to an entire audience. "We'll dine in one of the private rooms tonight." He motioned for them to follow as he led them along the perimeter of the dining room. Stuart hadn't noticed the interior of the restaurant. It was packed with guests. The soaring walls rose to a ceiling draped with silken fabric dyed various shades of orange, yellow, and red. Several full-scale murals adorned the largest walls, and an assortment of carved wood, hammered copper, and brass artifacts hung among the others.

They left the main dining room and entered an open-air hallway that extended the length of the building. A series of doors lined the opposite side of the hall, each guarded by large doormen in traditional Moroccan garb. Said led them to the last door. The doorman opened the door and stepped aside.

"Parnell, you remember my private room, no?" The door opened into a short hall. The walls were painted a rich red, trimmed in gold. Candle-laden sconces jutted from both sides of the hall. Ahead, Stuart spotted a heavily cushioned banquette and a low table. The service staff—two men and a woman—stood at ease at the far side of the room. Faint strains of exotic music, subtle string instruments, emanated from hidden speakers.

Said spun once they were all in the room and said, "Please, sit, sit. Make yourselves comfortable." Stuart followed Parnell's lead and sat at one end of the banquette. The seat and table were barely a foot off of the floor. Stuart's knees popped as he crouched, and he shifted his weight to find a comfortable position. Said waved at the service team and they sprang into action. A man and woman brought forward a bowl of fruit and a basket of breads. The other man began taking drink orders.

Said squeezed past Parnell and sat between him and Stuart. Once he was situated, the staff disappeared.

"So," he said, dropping his voice several decibels from his earlier volume, "you're headed to Ethiopia." He looked first at Parnell, then to Stuart, nodding slightly.

Parnell pulled a slice of bread from the basket and tore it in half. "We're running a bit blind right now, but, yes, Bailey and I agreed that Ethiopia is the appropriate destination."

Said looked back to Stuart again, apparently seeking affirmation. Stuart remained still.

"Have you been to Ethiopia, Parnell? Recently?" Said was suddenly all business. The man's face had grown stern.

Parnell continued to chew and shook his head. He swallowed and said, "No, in fact, it's been at least twenty years."

"And Bailey?"

"The same."

Said looked at Stuart again. While Parnell's joviality had subsided since their arrival, Said's shift in demeanor was gnawing at him. Stuart paused, then, assuming Said was silently asking him the same question, shook his head.

"Ah," Said said, slapping his thighs and appearing to loosen up. "Tell me then, why Ethiopia? What makes it, as you say, an 'appropriate destination?'"

Parnell cleared his throat and leaned forward. "We are obliged to protect and validate this … secret that Malcolm has entrusted us with.

And while we, meaning Bailey and I, have a fairly keen understanding of the information he was protecting, we don't know much more other than he regularly visited Addis Ababa. Once we connect with Bailey and fully analyze the contents of the envelope we've retrieved, we're confident the right local contact can assist us with our subsequent actions."

Said looked at Parnell for a moment, then erupted into laughter. "That's it? That's all you have, you old spy man? You're making this trip without having any idea where Malcolm might have intended you to go? How do you even know it's worth seeking?"

Stuart felt compelled to reply. "He was murdered, as you probably know." Stuart shot a quick glance to Parnell to see if he had a reaction to this disclosure. Parnell seemed unfazed. "And now there's a second person at risk. There's been a kidnapping. The captive is a—"

"He's another member of our club, Said," Parnell finished. "He's been able to communicate with us via code. He's the one who ultimately directed us to Malcolm's envelope. It was hidden in an artifact at Stuart's home."

"I see," Said said. He stroked his short beard and frowned. "But I'm still confused. What was in this envelope?"

Parnell looked at Stuart and sighed. "Information. Directions, to be precise. I am of the mind that we should seek some local expertise in order to decipher the contents and make our move. Bailey, on the other hand, sees too much information, at least at this point, as a liability."

"And you, Stuart?"

Stuart shrugged. "This is way out of my league, I'm afraid. My instinct is with Parnell. I don't like acting without available information. At the same time, I've never been involved with anything remotely close to this. I have to follow their lead," he said, gesturing to Parnell.

Said looked at Stuart, studying his eyes, and attempted a laugh. "Yes, yes." He turned back to Parnell. "Parnell, old friend, you don't have to tell me what you're chasing. But I must believe that you have a very good idea of what Malcolm was hiding, no?"

The female server entered the room and silently delivered the drinks. Parnell thanked her and took a long drink of an off-dry white wine.

"I do. I certainly do." He cleared his throat and took another sip. "Bailey and I arrived at the same hunch even before we found the envelope. Our cursory review of its contents confirmed our hypothesis. Malcolm was careful in his message not to specifically pinpoint Ethiopia, purposefully of course, but let's just say we're fairly confident. If, somehow, Ethiopia is wrong, then we're lost."

Said nodded.

"Said, you know more than any of us about the mysteries this amazing continent shields from us. I imagine just by saying 'Ethiopia' you may have an idea what we're seeking."

Said smiled and reached out, grasping Parnell between the shoulder and neck. "I could venture a sufficient guess, yes. But," he said, "there is no need to discuss the specifics. I simply wanted to be sure you were confident in your strategy."

"I would have thought you had more faith in me, Said. I'm hurt," Parnell said, smirking.

Said tilted his head. "Ah, but I'm surprised by things every day. I'm never happy if I'm comfortable, you see? It's best to confirm rather than assume." He looked back at Stuart and smirked, as if he was still withholding judgment.

The service team reappeared with three massive tagines. In a flourish, they lifted the lids from the hand-painted ceramic pots simultaneously. Aromatic steam swirled from the mounds of meat and vegetables resting on the plates before them.

"Allah be praised," Said said and picked up one of the servicing dishes and passed it to Stuart.

"So," Said said, "you leave tomorrow. Is that correct?"

"Yes," Stuart said. "Just after noon."

"We land in the capital tomorrow afternoon and hope to reach our hotel and rendezvous with Bailey by four."

Said began serving himself, nodding as he contemplated this information. "I know of a few men in the city who would be quite willing and capable of helping you. As you might imagine, they can be expensive. Highly skilled, and expensive."

"I hate to admit this," Parnell began, "but given our situation, money is no object. Safety and trust are our utmost concern."

"As I expected. I would guess that you're not planning to stay in the city. At least not long."

"No. We'll be in the city that first night, perhaps two," Parnell said. "I think we can expect to head deeper into the mountains."

"Good. Then the man I'll refer to you is Desta, an Amhara whose family has been in Addis Ababa for many generations. I would trust him with my daughter's life." Said pulled a business card and pen from inside his jacket and began scrawling on the card. "He's an assistant professor of anthropology at Addis Ababa University. His office is in the main social sciences building. He's quite well known. Simply ask for him when you arrive at the school. I'm afraid I don't have a telephone number for him. I'm not sure he even has a telephone. But you'll find him. I'll get a message to him tonight, or by morning. He'll be expeccting you." He handed the card to Parnell.

"Thank you, Said. Truly, we'd be lost without you. You know, I'm quite familiar with Desta. We met years ago," Parnell said, resting a hand on Said's shoulder. "I'm looking forward to seeing him again."

Said nodded and began to eat. As they were finishing the main course, the music suddenly transitioned to a louder, more recognizable Middle Eastern melody. Said, pointed to the ceiling. "George Abdo, 'King of the Belly Dance!'" Just then, a striking Moroccan woman swept into the room from the hallway. Stuart hadn't even noticed that the outer door had opened. She was draped in layers of sheer veils and seemed to levitate across the stone floor.

"Look at your friend Stuart," Said said, jabbing Parnell. Stuart noticed Parnell's smile had returned. He wondered if the entertainment was what actually made Marrakesh his "Disneyland." Parnell looked over to Stuart and raised his eyebrows repeatedly. "This is your first belly dance?"

Stuart nodded, thinking the closest thing to a belly dance he'd seen was Barbara Eden on *I Dream of Jeannie* and a handful of disastrous bachelor parties, including Heath's. After turning his attention back to the dancer, Stuart began to feel the allure of her movements. While she was well beyond attractive, the combination of music, the sweep of the colors, and passion revealed for her craft were what drew him in. She spent the first few minutes floating between Parnell and Said, almost oblivious to their presence. The music picked up and she spun away from the table and lost herself in a rapid twirl. The tempo abated and she subtly drifted toward Stuart. He looked up saw her eyes were locked onto his. No matter how complex the move, her eyes never strayed. The tempo gradually intensified, along with her movements. Her nostrils flexing with her fervor. She threw her head back, finally breaking her gaze, then dipped forward and reestablished her connection with him. Abruptly, the music stopped, as did she, with a sharp clap above her head.

Stuart simply stared. There was silence, then Said clapped him on the back. "Wonderful, no, Mr. Stuart? Have you seen anything like her?"

Stuart blinked and looked at Said. He had no idea what to say. He felt drugged. Finally, he shook his head and looked back to the girl, but she had vanished.

Parnell ordered another drink and launched into a discussion with Said about the souk merchants. Stuart leaned back into the banquette, which was like being swallowed by an enormous feather pillow. The dancer's accompaniment had been replaced with more modern African instrumental music. He couldn't shake the image of the dancer. The intensity of her stare, the mesmerizing rhythm, the shielded, delicate, seduction of her hands carving the air. She'd created an instant obsession.

He sat up and turned toward Said, pretending to listen. But instead, he replayed, as best he could, the dancer's performance. Her beauty and grace overshadowed anything as base and cheap as erotica, yet he couldn't deny the sensuality of the experience. He sighed and attempted to join Parnell and Said in conversation.

Said seemed to sense the shift in his attention. "So, look who's back," he said to Stuart, smacking him on the knee.

Said turned back to Parnell and continued talking about their plans the next morning. From the sound of it, Said was going to take Parnell into the souk for a final visit before they left for the airport.

"Stuart, do you want to join us? You didn't get much of a taste this afternoon. What do you say?" Parnell asked.

Stuart suddenly felt the weight of the jet lag, the souk, and the dinner. Nothing sounded better than collapsing into bed.

"You know, I think I'll have to pass. As much as I'd like to see the souk again, especially with you as our guide, Said, I think I need to get some rest. Addis Ababa is, what, seven or eight thousand feet above sea level? I live in Manhattan. Sea level. What's the altitude here, Said?"

He frowned and said, "Five hundred meters?" shaking his head.

"Exactly. Still hardly at elevation. I don't want to slow everyone down."

Said laughed. "You're half the age of these old bastards. And you are fit. I can see. But that's okay. Get your rest, young man. We'll be back in time to get you to the airport."

Stuart agreed and allowed the banquette to swallow him up again. For a few minutes, he fought to keep his eyes open, fought to find something in the men's conversation to keep him engaged, but it was fruitless. He drifted off, dreaming of the beautiful dancer and his first day in the desert.

# CHAPTER
# SIXTEEN

The maze of the souk was bewildering. The flood of humanity, beast, adobe, and merchandise tumbled over one another, erasing his past and obliterating his target. Every few moments he would hear the music, seeping in between the bark of the sellers and the bartering chants, the quickening of the tempo, the bass swelling, the ring of the finger cymbals. And then he would see her, or at least some glimpse of her. A wrist, a finger, the unveiled eyes, burrowing into his own. He darted down a barren alley, beyond the turmoil and the chaos. The air and noise had been vacuumed from his senses. In front of him, barely thirty feet way, he saw the corner of a veil disappear to the right. He ran, his eyes locked on the spot where the faint yellow fabric had winked at him. The tempo returned, the beat thumping, so loud and intense it seemed to lose the rhythm. He spun around the corner where he knew she'd disappeared and stopped, skidding on the loose gravel underfoot. There she stood, frozen, arms thrown above her head, a leg thrust forward, the web of veils drifting down around her in slow motion, and her mahogany eyes still locked upon him.

Silence. No motion.

Then the pounding and the loss of air.

Suddenly, a blinding flash of white light shattered the scene. He heard himself suck in a massive gasp of air, like a drowning man finally breaking the surface. The glare dissipated into reality. He was propped up on both hands, thrust above his pillow, dented with the imprint of his face. Nothing looked familiar, nothing smelled familiar. A second of panic struck. Where was he? What day was it?

The pounding returned and he realized it was someone knocking. The hotel. He was in Marrakesh. Who on earth was pounding on his door? Was it *his* door?

He rolled out of bed, steadied himself, and stumbled to the door. He blinked before peering through the peephole, willing his eyes to focus. He blinked and saw Abu about to resume pounding.

"Hold it, hold it, hold it," he said, coughing. He found the security latch and pulled the door open.

"Mr. Mancini! Oh, praise Allah. You are here!" Abu backed up and turned toward the hall. "Mr. Musi, I have Mr. Mancini."

Stuart followed Abu's call and saw Said bounding toward them.

"Stuart, have you seen Parnell this morning? Do you know where he is?"

Stuart jabbed a hand into his hair and tried to act coherent. "No, no, of course not. Abu woke me up. I—I was completely out of it. What's wrong?"

"He was supposed to meet me downstairs for breakfast over half an hour ago. He never arrived. I waited, thinking he might be moving a little slowly this morning, then I began to get worried." Said backed up and pointed to the room next to Stuart's. "This is his room. Next to yours." The door was open. "I know many of the employees here. I spoke with one of the managers and convinced him to let me in. He's gone, Stuart. Parnell's gone."

Stuart rubbed at his eyes quickly and pushed open Parnell's door. He stepped into the room and surveyed the interior. Parnell's suitcase was open and it appeared to be undisturbed on the luggage rack. One of the beds had the sheets pulled back and had been slept in. He stepped to the desk to see if any other personal effects had been left, but there was nothing. No wallet, no passport, no briefcase or cell phone.

He darted back to the bathroom. Parnell's dopp kit was next to one of the sinks, propped open. Said had followed Stuart into the room. The Moroccan looked ill.

"Stuart, I'm frightened."

"Are you sure he didn't get your plans mixed up? Did he go for a walk this morning and lose his way? Nothing seems out of place other than Parnell not being here." Stuart said. Then he pushed past Said and out of the room. He grabbed the sleeve of the employee who was talking quietly to Abu.

"What about security cameras? Isn't there a camera in this hall or this floor? What about the lobby?"

"Yes, sir, we have cameras. But it may take some time to review the tape."

Said walked out into the hallway. He still looked as if he was about to throw up. "Stuart, I don't know what is happening here, but I'm concerned about your safety. Nabil, please take Mr. Mancini to the front office. We need to check the cameras. Tell Mr. Chafani I've asked you to do this." Said turned to Stuart. "We need to get you to the airport as soon as possible. I'll arrange for a car to drive us. In the meantime, you go with Nabil. Mr. Chafani is the General Manager here. We're old friends. He will help us."

"Mr. Mancini, I'll gather your belongings and bring them to the front desk," Abu said, bowing.

"That's okay, Abu, I can—"

"No!" Said said, stepping toward Stuart and holding a hand up. "No, you will go with Nabil. You may not be safe here."

"But, Said, if Parnell is truly … missing, then I can't leave. I can't abandon him."

"No, you must leave at once. Find Bailey. Now go with Nabil. Abu will take care of your things."

Stuart stared at Said for a moment and realized he wasn't going to give in.

"Okay, Nabil, let's go. Said, I still have …" He looked at his watch, "nearly four hours until my flight."

"Believe it or not, you'll be safer at the airport. I'll be with you. We'll make sure you get onto the plane safely. I will deal with Parnell's disappearance."

Nabil motioned for Stuart to follow him. Stuart sighed, threw his hands up, and followed Nabil.

The sudden drama over Parnell's absence was frustrating. Okay, so Parnell was late in meeting Said. Did anyone check the pool? Maybe he was hungover and thought a dip in the pool might revive him. Had he indeed gone for a walk? They hadn't really checked the grounds. He could be anywhere. Now he was being rushed to the airport without Parnell, without knowing whether they were all overreacting.

The front office of the hotel was rife with activity. At least a dozen employees, including bellmen, front desk clerks, and cashiers, shot between the handful of desks situated in the room. Nabil caught the attention of a middle-aged man in a dark suit—likely a manager. Nabil said something in French to the man who looked at Stuart, scowling. Then Nabil said, "Said Musi." The man's face went blank. He blinked, sucked in a breath and nodded, closing his eyes. He turned and picked up the telephone receiver, punched four numbers and waited. He looked Stuart up and down while waiting for an answer. Stuart made out "Yousef" and "Said" and that was it. The manager spoke rapidly in Arabic, scrutinizing Stuart the entire time. He paused for a few beats, completely motionless. Finally, he made a sharp noise and hung up the phone. The man looked at Nabil and motioned them forward.

"Come," Nabil said. They followed the manager down a hallway and through the last door on the right. The room was lit by the flicker of an array of small monitors that covered one wall. Two men sat in front of the monitors. Each had what looked like a small mixing board and a joystick laid out in front of them. The men barely registered the arrival of the three intruders.

The manager leaned over to the nearest security guard and whispered something. The security guard leaned back and looked at Stuart. The guard looked back at the manager, nodded, and said something in Arabic to his partner.

"Okay," the manager said. "Please forgive me. I'm Yousef El Zhar. I'm the front office manager. As you can imagine, this is an unusual request, yet I understand there's some concern about your companion. Can you tell me your room number?"

Stuart went blank, then suddenly remembered it. He recited the number and the first security guard nodded. The guard went to work on the board, typing on a keyboard sunken into the desktop and flipping several switches on the large board. The guard watched the monitor just above his head and pointed. In the awkwardly angled black and white washed-out picture, Stuart recognized the hall. The fisheye lens distorted the perspective and depth of the picture. The date and time appeared in the upper right-hand corner. The digital tag read 2:33 a.m. The guard said something to Yousef. Yousef turned to Stuart. "When did you last see your friend?"

Stuart shrugged. "Well, close to midnight, I suppose? I was exhausted. I was barely conscious." Yousef pursed his lips and motioned for the guard to speed up the film. They watched the video flicker past; every few seconds a single person would appear in the frame and the guard would stop the video. None of the people on the screen were Parnell.

The guard continued to scan through the video. Stuart watched the clock skip through the hours. Another person appeared on screen, but it was a female housekeeper. When the clock hit 4:00 a.m. there was more movement. The guard stopped the tape and began playing it at the proper speed. A door in the hallway was open. It was nearly impossible to tell which room it might be. The perspective and the position of the camera blurred the room numbers. A casually dressed man stepped back into the hallway and looked to his left and right, appearing to be checking for anyone else in the area. The video was time-lapsed, like most security videos, so the picture jumped. A second person stepped into the hallway behind the first man. A third person followed and appeared to shut the door. The first and third men split for a brief moment, exposing the man between them. It was Parnell.

"That's him. Stop the tape! That's him," Stuart shouted.

The guard followed Stuart's command and froze the picture. Yousef leaned forward and squinted into the screen. "Parnell Sumner? Your friend is Parnell Sumner?" he repeated, standing up and looking at Stuart.

"Yes, of course. Play the tape again. I want to see what they did with him."

Yousef turned his body to face Stuart. "I can tell you what they did with him. They followed him out of the hotel and into a waiting car. I saw them myself. Look," he said pointing to an adjacent screen. "It was just after five o'clock. I was at the front desk and saw Mr. Sumner walk through the lobby alone. He nodded to me and I said, 'Good morning.' Those two men, they followed him, but didn't seem to be escorting him. Then I watched Mr. Sumner walk out the front door, down the steps, and then get into a car—a van. The two men followed. They ignored me. They were talking to each other. I didn't think much of it until I saw them get in the van after Parnell."

"You saw this? You … you know Parnell?"

"Of course. He's stayed with us many, many times. He loves Marrakesh. Surely he told you so. He tells everyone."

Stuart looked back at the video just in time to see the trio leave the frame. The time in the corner showed 5:07 a.m.

"The other men. Did you recognize them?"

Yousef shook his head, frowning. "No."

"What about the van?"

"It was a simple white van. A shuttle, or similar to one. It was the same type of van that our guests take to the airport."

Stuart heard a commotion in the hallway. Voices were raised then the door burst open. Said and Abu stood in the doorway. Two or three others stood behind them.

"Stuart, he's gone. One of the bellmen saw him leave early this morning."

"I know. We just saw it on tape, and Yousef saw him leave, too. They went in a van."

"Come on," Said said, waving him forward. "We have your bags. We must go to the airport."

Less than an hour later, Said was ushering Stuart to the Royal Air Maroc counter. At first the agent refused to talk to Said and would only allow Stuart to speak on his own behalf. She took Stuart's passport, confirmed his ticket, and began to check his bag and print his boarding pass. Said's frustration grew. He whispered to Stuart to step back. As he did so, Said went to work. At first, he could only hear Said whispering in Arabic. Finally, the agent began responding, whispering as well. Said reached into his jacket pocket and either gave or showed the agent something. Neither Said nor the agent spoke. Instead, Stuart heard the keyboard again.

"Mr. Mancini?" the agent called, looking around Said and smiling.

Stuart stepped forward. The agent held out a paper folder.

"This is your boarding pass and baggage tag. As an Executive Class traveler, you also have access to our VIP Lounge. You'll find it just beyond the nearest security gate," she said, finishing with a glance toward Said. "And this is your gate pass, Mr. Musi," she added and handed a folder to Said.

Said thanked the gate agent and guided Stuart toward security.

"What was that all about?"

"You have nearly two hours until your flight leaves. I don't want you sitting alone in the open here. We're much safer in the VIP lounge; plus, you'll enjoy the seating in business class. This pass allows me to accompany you through security."

They arrived at security, still guarded again by the armed military, and passed through without incident, continuing toward the VIP lounge.

"Remember, when you land in Addis Ababa, don't rent one of the blue taxis. They are not trustworthy. Look for NTO—they'll provide you with a car and driver at a reasonable rate. Also, you must change your hotel reservation. I'll make a reservation for you under my name at the Sheraton. It will be safer and easy for Bailey to find you."

Said's paranoia had become contagious. Stuart viewed nearly everyone as a potential captor or worse. Said, despite his connections with Morocco, and apparently throughout Northern Africa, was unable to draw a clear connection between what was known of Helmut's captors and Parnell's disappearance. The men on the security tape were impossible to identify. Stuart remembered one having closely cropped hair, like the man Bailey and Parnell had met in Rome. Said seemed surprised that a radical group based in eastern Europe would risk an abduction in Morocco. When Stuart pressed him on it, Said faltered. Perhaps it had more to do with pride. Regardless, Stuart felt exposed. Simply flying to another country, another completely unfamiliar environment, didn't seem to be the safest solution. Yes, he was concerned about Bailey, especially since he knew Bailey possessed the envelope, the item Helmut's captives sought. It felt like a trap.

The wait to board the plane was uneventful. The glass of wine Stuart ordered in the VIP Lounge did little to take the edge off. If anything, he felt more hyper-aware and uneasy than he had when they'd arrived. Said escorted Stuart to the gate, acting like a melodramatic henchman, and nearly pushed him into the crowd that was filing onto the plane.

"Go, go. Get on and get settled as quickly as possible," Said urged, continuing to nudge Stuart in the back.

"Said, I'm fine. I've got plenty of time."

"Call when you get to the hotel. I want to know that you've arrived safely. And Bailey, too, okay?"

Stuart nodded and fell into the crowd that had been drawn into the open jetway.

# CHAPTER

# SEVENTEEN

When Stuart spotted the Sheraton sign as the taxi pulled off Taitu Street, he felt an unexpected sense of security and familiarity. He didn't think he missed the States that much, especially considering he'd only been gone a few days, but the recognition brought about predictability. Even though he didn't frequent Sheratons often, he found himself yearning for a setting that offered comfort and, ultimately, safety. Just as Said had promised.

According to the original itineraries, Bailey should have arrived early that morning. Stuart felt an ice ball in his gut when he imagined telling Bailey about Parnell's disappearance. Stuart had considered calling Bailey from the airport after landing in Addis Ababa, but realized that the brief notice wouldn't provide much value. His procrastination also delayed having to deal with Bailey's reaction.

The taxi pulled inside the arching porte cochère, and a uniformed doorman pulled Stuart's door open just as the car came to a stop. Stuart stepped out, nodded to the doorman, and met the driver at the rear of the car. A bellman appeared at his side and offered to take his suitcase. Stuart stared at the bag a moment and the bellman said, "Please, sir. I'll bring it to your room." Stuart agreed, paid the driver, and stepped onto the sidewalk.

The hotel was magnificent. It could have been plucked from Paris or London and planted on top of an African mesa. A field of elegant fountains sprang from the rectangular pools centered at the hotel's entrance. Emerald green canopies dotted the façade, lit by concealed lamps that accented the pale gold stone. He allowed himself a couple of deep breaths, wondering if he truly felt the sudden change in altitude, and entered the hotel lobby.

There was a fair amount of activity both at the front desk and in the various sitting areas that comprised the lobby. Stuart started for the front desk when he heard, "Stuart!" from behind him. He closed his eyes before turning.

"Stuart!" Bailey called again. He was seated in a leather club chair near a corner of the lobby. As Stuart swerved and approached Bailey, he could tell the older man suspected something. Bailey's smile was tight as he rose from the chair.

"So, can you tell me what's happened?" He motioned to their surroundings. "I received a message when I landed at the airport that we had changed hotels. And …" he said, scanning the lobby. "Where's Parnell?"

Stuart exhaled. "Bailey, please sit down." Both men sat, and Stuart leaned forward, elbows resting on this thighs. "Parnell was kidnapped this morning." Bailey's face went slack, his mouth falling open.

"Sometime early this morning, around 5:00 a.m.," Stuart continued. "We saw it on the hotel security tape. Two men, dressed like those in Helmut's video. They took him in a van. We know nothing more than that."

"Good God," Bailey said. "This is madness! Not only am I deeply concerned about Helmut's and Parnell's well-being, but I'm also worried these people are accumulating a dangerous amount of information—now through both Parnell and Helmut." He paused and then said, "I suppose the change in venue was necessary, but I doubt we'll remain undiscovered for long. I have to assume that both of us were followed from the airport. We've got to be vigilant about each move we make."

Bailey sat back in his chair and scrutinized the lobby.

"Stuart, as I think about it, I'm not sure we can stay here. You and Parnell have just proven that hotels, even the most luxurious, are far from safe." He paused a moment. "Perhaps … perhaps if we speak to the general manager, we might be able to negotiate the services of a security guard, at least for the evening."

Stuart considered Bailey's suggestion. All sense of comfort he felt upon arrival had evaporated. "Even so. Would they be trustworthy? Couldn't they be bought off?"

Bailey nodded, frowning. "Yes, yes, quite, I'm afraid."

"Do you have your … belongings, you know, with you?"

Bailey nodded again and patted his lapel. "It may not be the safest place, but at least I know where it is."

"What if we choose to stay in public, at least as long as possible? There must be a bar here."

"Oh, several," Bailey said.

"We could find a quiet table, review the document in more detail when it seems appropriate or safe, and then map out our strategy."

Bailey harrumphed and looked down. Stuart watched him grip the thick leather arms of the chair.

"Oh," Stuart said, startling Bailey, "I almost forgot. Said gave me the name of a contact. The person we need to see here in Ethiopia." Stuart dug into his breast pocket and pulled out the business card he'd taken from Parnell's hotel desk. He held it up to Bailey. The old man shot forward and snatched it from Stuart's fingers.

"God damn it, Stuart," he hissed. "Please be careful." Bailey leaned back again, still palming the card and ignoring Stuart. As he continued to look away, he said, "This came directly from Said?"

"Right," Stuart said. "He told us both about the contact. He's a professor at the university. Anthropology. Said said he works in the main building and that he's well known. According to Said, we should have no trouble finding him."

Bailey made no attempt to acknowledge Stuart's comment. Instead, he leaned back and rubbed his eyes, saying, "Is it ... Desta?" Bailey returned from his feigned stretch and appeared bored.

Stuart began to follow Bailey's lead and spoke into his hand. "Yes. You know him?"

Bailey gave a quick, sharp nod, grinning. "Oh, yes. Desta is excellent. A brilliant man. Parnell and I met him ages ago." Bailey sat up, seemed to ponder something for a moment, then said, "Now, let's visit the bar, shall we?"

A small commotion erupted inside the main doors of the lobby as they stood. A gathering of what appeared to be native Ethiopians were greeting each other. The men and women all looked to be in their twenties, perhaps university students, and appeared dressed for a celebration.

Bailey stood and helped Stuart to his feet. "Follow me. Pretend we're on holiday," he whispered as Stuart stood.

Bailey strode toward the center of the lobby and approached a man wearing a hotel uniform. "Good evening!" Bailey said. "Pardon me, sir, but where can two weary travelers find a cold pint to quench our thirst? We want to toast our first day of holiday." The employee forced a smile and seemed a bit stunned by Bailey's approach.

"You know," Bailey said, mimicking hoisting a pint. "A bar? A pub?"

The man jolted and said, "Oh! The Office Bar." He turned and pointed toward a broad entryway near the rear of the lobby. "It is down that hallway."

"Excellent," Bailey said. "Come, Charles, to the Office Bar," he added, motioning in the direction the man had pointed.

The Office Bar, not unlike the club in Manhattan, was paneled floor to ceiling in dark wood. A small number of patrons were scattered along the bar and at the quiet tables. A melody from a solo piano, apparently piped in, heightened the atmosphere and made the bar seem more active than it actually was. Bailey pointed to a table near the back. No one would be within fifteen feet of them. The dim lighting barely reached the table, but a flickering candle provided them enough light to see one another.

As they settled in, Bailey said, "This isn't ideal, but I think we'll be relatively secure for now. We can always retreat to one of our rooms later." Bailey produced the card he'd snatched from Stuart and held it near the candle. "Yes, Desta," he continued, looking up at Stuart. "A little man. Always cheerful. Always surprising you with a new perspective. He'll be invaluable."

"Bailey," Stuart said, "I need to ask you again, especially now that Parnell is no longer with us. How do we get out of this? What are we looking for? What are we running *from*?"

The bartender appeared in Stuart's peripheral vision and approached their table. He said something that neither Bailey nor Stuart understood.

"We're English," Bailey said, smiling.

"That's not a problem, sir. I was sharing an Amharic greeting, 'Dena ideru,' Good evening," the bartender said.

"Wonderful," Stuart said. "I'd like a glass of cabernet."

"I'll have the same," Bailey said. "Oh, just bring us the whole bottle." The bartender grinned, offered something else in Amharic, and left.

Bailey reached into his jacket, then froze. He scanned the small number of guests in the bar and then eased the envelope from his breast pocket. He placed it on the table as if it were about to shatter. He tapped the envelope with his middle finger.

"This," he said, "I believe, is the key to a mystery, a myth, that's been a part of many cultures for hundreds, probably thousands, of years."

"Okay," Stuart said, stretching the word out.

Bailey sighed loudly. "Your grandfather spent much of his … *free* time, accompanying many fellow explorers, Parnell and I included, on our various follies. In many cases, we were hoping to track down some rumored antiquity or treasure. In far fewer cases, we were helping someone in need, in trouble; and on even rarer occasions, we had the opportunity to embark upon truly wondrous journeys. Malcolm, at some point, became infatuated with one particular myth. Obsessed, is probably a more precise description. He was relentless."

"What was it?"

"Stuart, I'm sure you are familiar with the legend of Ponce de León?"

Stuart paused, unsure of what Bailey was alluding to. "Of course. You mean the fountain of youth. But," he said, stopping, then stifling a laugh. "Are you serious? This is about the fountain of youth?"

Bailey simply glared at Stuart.

"But we're in the middle of Africa, Bailey, not … Florida. And besides, the Ponce de León story has been tracked to exhaustion, hasn't it? No one believes in it anymore."

Bailey smiled and touched Stuart's forearm. "Yes, yes, I know. Ponce de León is just one of the characters among many myths purporting a fountain of youth, a spring of eternal life, eternal health. This," he said, tapping the envelope again, "is *not* the story of Ponce de León."

"But … are you sure? You've read the contents, right?"

Bailey nodded. "Yes. It's what we suspected, Parnell and I …" he said trailing off.

"I think I need to see it, Bailey. Another set of eyes, right? Plus, we've got Helmut and Parnell to think about. I need to know exactly what these people are looking for."

"They—these people—are obviously seeking something extremely valuable, my friend. And this certainly fits that bill," he said, lightly shielding the envelope with one hand.

"So," Stuart said. "Will you share it?"

Bailey stood the envelope up on end and tapped it on the table.

"Do you understand the implications of this? I mean, truly?"

"You mean the fountain of youth?" Stuart said, still struggling not to laugh. He stopped when he saw the look on Bailey's face.

"Parnell and I have taken a great many precautions to protect you from the things you may not want nor need to know. We may chase many dreams, many myths, Stuart, but there's often a tremendous amount of truth in things that men will kill for. If Malcolm found the fountain of youth, and if it's a cure-all, a promise of eternal, or at least greatly prolonged, life, then it's truly priceless."

Stuart stopped himself from arguing. Again, he was baffled at how he'd been swept into this debacle. It would be one thing to chase through Africa looking for the tomb of some mythical pharaoh or a lost treasure, but magic? It was ludicrous. Even as a child he'd never gravitated to the typical Disney fairy tales and films that his classmates did. Instead, he devoured nonfiction, books on the First and Second World Wars, starting in the second grade. By the fourth grade, he was reading college level texts by Carl Sagan, Einstein, and John Keynes. Fiction, in his mind, was foolishness. He was overwhelmed by the wonder and intrigue in the factual, scientific world. And yet, while he found it easy to rest on the factual past that he'd built his entire life upon, he again felt the pull of this other world that Bailey and Parnell—and now new acquaintances—were opening up for him. A part of his psyche was pleading for him to board the next flight back to New York, while a fresh, opposing desire was taunting him to escape the known, the safe, comfortable existence, and actually live for once.

"Stuart, I know this sounds preposterous. It's one of the reasons we protect the club so diligently. Some of what we dabble in is, for many, completely inexplicable."

It was as if Bailey were reading his thoughts.

"Parnell and I decided to wait as long as possible to disclose the contents of this envelope so that you'd have one last opportunity to ... to walk away." He paused and looked up at Stuart.

"It's a bit late for that now, isn't it?"

"No. Not entirely. As I said, the information in here is cryptic on purpose. Although we're technically speculating, I'd stake my life on its intent. But even if our speculation is correct, the entire ... answer ... secret, may not be here," he said, tapping the envelope again. "This could simply be a significant clue."

"Well, I appreciate you thinking of my options. I have to tell you, there are times when I want to hop on the next flight to New York. I've left my employer hanging, right in the middle of a monumental transaction. It's the entire future of the founders and the partners. Me included."

"I'm well aware of that, Stuart. Believe me. There's a flight back to the States tomorrow morning at 10:15. I've checked. Seats are still available. You can go home and focus on your business, if you'd like. And," he said smiling, "you retain your membership. It isn't all so bad, is it?"

The bartender returned to their table with a pair of wine glasses and a bottle of red wine. Stuart noticed the face of an old man, whose head was wrapped in a loose turban, graced the bottle's label, along with Omar Khayyam in elegant script. Bailey glanced at the bottle and nodded. As the bartender struggled to cut the cap and open the bottle, Bailey continued, whispering.

"It's all set up for you, remember? Malcolm arranged for your full membership to be taken care of financially. Your dues, your monthly minimums, everything. It's all been arranged."

Stuart squinted at him and Bailey laughed as the bartender filled their glasses. "We spoke of it on your first visit, but of course you wouldn't remember. It's in your documents."

"Is this the million dollars that Prima told me about?"

Bailey nodded. "That's exactly it. Malcolm made that payment, well, his estate did, as well as established a trust set up to take care of the other costs."

"Okay," Stuart said, shaking his head. "That night's still a blank."

"My boy," Bailey said, slapping the table. "Let's drink to our health, to our safety, at least for today. And to the well-being of our dear friends." He slid a glass toward Stuart and took his own up in a toast.

"Salute!" he said and took a long drink from the glass. Stuart hesitated, then followed Bailey's lead.

After a few quiet moments, Stuart said, "Please, let me see it." He swirled the wine in his glass without looking up at Bailey.

"Hmmm," Bailey answered. "You haven't given it as much thought as I would have hoped."

Stuart tilted his head to one side and stuck his bottom lip out slightly. "I'm here, aren't I? I mean, I've been following two veritable strangers across the globe for the past week. I can't see much value in turning back now."

Bailey laughed quietly and took a sip of wine. "Very well. Yes, you can open it. Once we finish the wine."

"Okay," Stuart said, laughing with him.

"But I think that once you do so, we need to agree upon a more aggressive approach." Bailey's voice was suddenly solemn. "We may very well need to get the board involved. They should be made aware of what's happening to Helmut and Parnell. I think there's a suspicion about the motive behind your grandfather's murder, but … alone it was probably viewed as an unfortunate result of Malcolm's obsession."

"How do we do that? Get in touch with the board?"

"It just takes a phone call, at least to get started."

"And then what?"

"Well," Bailey said, sighing loudly, "that's my concern. It does get a bit complicated. I can't say that the board enjoys convening, unless it's in Barbados or Bali for a supposed working holiday. In fact, I can't remember the last time they had to be brought together for something like this. Certainly a decade or more."

They sat quietly and attempted to enjoy the wine and the atmosphere. A few additional guests had trickled in, most sitting at the bar, finally giving the bartender something useful to do.

"You know, I have to say you're holding up rather well," Stuart said.

"Hmm?" Bailey answered, not quite paying attention.

"About Parnell. God knows what he's having to deal with."

Bailey groaned. "A bad, old habit, I suppose. Too many years in crime work. My natural tendency is to … go numb, one might say. I have to admit, however, I'm very worried. He's not a young man anymore, you know? He's a tough old bastard, but still, not exactly a spring chicken."

The bartender made his way to their table again to check on them. He offered some appetizers and they settled on a plate of cheese and meats. Another server appeared with their food almost immediately.

"I'm having second thoughts about this place," Bailey said. He was carefully placing a slice of white cheese on a thin wheat cracker.

"What's wrong?" Stuart asked. He tried to scan the room without seeming obvious. "Do you see someone?"

"No, no. I mean about our baggage here," he said, nudging the envelope. "While I agree that we need to finalize our approach, I'm wrestling with doing so here in full view. We may need to retire to one of our rooms."

Stuart surveyed the bar again. No one seemed to be the least bit interested in them. The patrons were either individual guests deeply contemplating their beverages or couples engaged in focused discussion.

"I think we're fine here. Just be casual. No one will see."

Bailey nodded slightly and slid the envelope closer. Instead of discussing the contents of the envelope, he began to spontaneously recount a cricket match he'd seen the previous summer in India. It took Stuart a moment to understand Bailey's rationale, but then he fell into step, nodding and verbally affirming Bailey's comments as he seemed to absently open the envelope. When Bailey pulled the contents free, Stuart tried to appear disinterested and took a long drink of wine. He stared out the entrance of the bar into the hall and said, "So?"

Bailey was unfolding the papers from the envelope and smoothing them out on the cocktail table.

"Can you tell me what it says?"

Bailey didn't respond. Stuart fought to keep his eyes away from the paper and ended up fondling his wine glass.

"It's a bit of a jumble. I have to tell you I was disappointed at first. We have a mixture of a rather poorly drawn map and, from what I can tell, vague, handwritten directions," Bailey said, scanning the documents. "I can't say I truly expected a trumpeting declaration, but it will take some time to determine if there's enough information here to guide us to what we suspect."

"What do you mean when you say, 'guide us to what we suspect?' Are you implying that we seek out this fountain?"

Bailey didn't respond immediately, but cleared his throat and fingered his cocktail napkin. "Yes. I think we need to do everything in our power to protect Malcolm's discovery."

"And how do we do that?"

"I haven't figured that out yet, but we can't very well protect something we can't find. If we can … drain it, I suppose. Secure it. Stop anyone we can from finding it, then I think that shall be our charge."

Stuart set his glass down and stole a glance at the papers. The candle-light did little to help him. He caught a glimpse of an illustration and could see lettering, but nothing was clear.

"I'm going to the men's room. I'll be back in a moment." Stuart stood and smoothed out his trousers. Bailey looked up, seeming a bit alarmed. Stuart winked at him and walked toward the bar. The bartender pointed him out into the hallway.

Before stepping into the men's room, Stuart pulled out his cell phone. He powered it on and was thrilled to see three service bars. The roaming reminder was showing, and the surcharge from Ethiopia would probably be astounding. He selected his work voicemail number and retreated against the wall. The automated voice told him he had seven new messages.

The first two were solicitors. The third was from Heath.

"Hey, Stuart. It's Heath. It is … uh, Wednesday afternoon. I think you're still in Rome, but I'm not sure. Anyway, just wanted to see if you had any news on Helmut. We've still had nothing here. The board has suspended everything, which I guess is expected. Disappointing, but … let me know how you're doing, okay? Ciao."

The next message was also from Health. "Hey, Stuart. It's Thursday morning. Say, you need to know that we just heard from Helmut's wife. He's … well, according to her he's been kidnapped. I know … it's insane. She spoke with Kensington, so I got this second hand, but from what I gather, there's a significant amount of intrigue behind it all. She claims he's out of the country and that Interpol and, shit, the French or Italian authorities are involved. I can't remember. Anyway, it's got everyone all wound up. I think I told you not to worry about checking messages, but I actually hope you are. Give me a call."

The next two messages were hang-ups. The last was from Olivia.

"Stuart, it's Olivia. Heath said he's left a couple of messages for you. If you get this, please call him. He's worried. And frankly, I am, too. If I don't hear from you by tomorrow … it's Thursday evening here in New York, if I don't hear from you, I'll try your cell. I'm trying not to, but … I think it's important."

Stuart looked at his watch. It was just after seven local time. That meant it was probably midday on Friday in New York. He contemplated calling Heath now, but didn't want to worry Bailey. He used the restroom and returned to the bar. As he approached the table, Bailey was folding up the pages and sliding them into his jacket. Stuart settled back into his chair and reached for his wine glass.

"Any more luck?"

Bailey paused a beat and then said, "It's all deliberately vague. While Ethiopia isn't mentioned explicitly, nor the fountain, the name Simien, along with a few other hints, is noted."

"Simien?"

Bailey nodded. "The Simien Mountains are a beautiful and treacherous part of Ethiopia. I'm fairly certain the fountain, or the 'goal' as it's referred to in the letter, lies somewhere within those mountains."

"Have you ever been there?"

"No," Bailey said, shaking his head and swallowing a gulp of wine. "They lie in the northern part of the country, a good ways from here. We'll definitely need Desta, and probably at least a half dozen other men. That is, if they're willing to help."

"If? I thought you just said we had to do everything we could to protect it."

"Well, that's true, but—"

"But … what are our choices? Are we better off preserving this map, keeping it somewhere safe, at least while we try to determine what the situation is with Parnell and Helmut?"

"Stuart, we don't have the luxury of time here. May I remind you," Bailey said, getting agitated, "there's been one murder, at least that we know of, and now two kidnappings. Plus the ransacking of your apartment. These men are not content just waiting for us to lead them to … to what they're seeking."

"Okay, so from what you've shared, this fountain is hidden in some Ethiopian mountains. It's not like we can move it."

"Not the fountain itself, no. At least I don't believe so."

"Then what?"

Bailey cleared his throat and glared at Stuart. "It's not the fountain, but its contents we're interested in preserving. None of us are comfortable with its contents falling into the wrong hands. As I suggested, our best approach may be, frankly, to do our best to drain it."

Stuart scoffed and fell back into his chair. "I don't know, Bailey. This just seems …"

Stuart closed his eyes and tried to process their predicament. What value would he add in such an expedition? His trekking experience was essentially limited to walking across Central Park on a warm spring afternoon. Was he just putting himself, as well as Parnell and Helmut, at greater risk? Plus, he needed to get in touch with Heath. It was unlikely that there would be any urgent reason for him to return to work. In fact, his absence might be welcome during the hiatus. Either way, he needed to talk to Heath before committing to another week or ten days away from the office.

"Do you …" he started, "have any idea how much time we are talking? How long this journey would take? How much … content is there?"

Bailey laughed. "I have no way of knowing. I would have to assume that we could drive a good ways in and then hike the remainder. Even so, I would estimate at least seven, eight days. And that's if we bypass the board and find enough help to assist us."

"I thought the board was just a phone call." Stuart said.

"Yes, well, that's assuming we find some way of getting everyone together quickly, and that they agree with our strategy."

"Okay, I see. But just what *is* our strategy?"

"That, my friend," Bailey said, taking another sip, "is where I'm strug-gling. We're supposed to be back in Rome within the next couple of days."

# CHAPTER

# EIGHTEEN

Parnell's first conscious notion was of intense thirst. His tongue felt as if it had been melded to the roof of his mouth, sealed into place by his cheeks. He tried to pry his eyes open but found they were gummed shut. A faint slice of light crept through as he forced his left then right eye open. Next came the headache. Searing pain, like frozen steel slicing through his forehead, reverberated behind the wave of blurred light. Nothing was in focus. An intense smell of mildew and something rancid flooded his sinuses. He heard a voice whispering in Italian.

"Oh, ho, look who's now awake," the voice said, switching to English. Another voice responded in Italian.

Parnell forced his eyes fully open and waited as the room swam into focus. He could only make out bulky shadowed shapes. He opened his mouth and tried to talk, but nothing escaped. He heard both men laugh. He managed a painful swallow and tried to clear his throat.

"Please, water, something … to drink," he croaked.

A hand, and then an arm, emerged from the shadows holding a soda can. Instinctively, Parnell tried to reach for the can, then he realized he was bound. The men laughed again. The one with the soda raised the can to Parnell's lips and tilted it forward. Parnell sucked down a couple gulps of the warm carbonated liquid, the fizzing burn aggravating the sting in his arid throat.

"Go," one man said. "We should tell him our friend is awake." The second man grunted, and Parnell sensed movement off to his right.

As his eyes continued to adjust to the darkness, Parnell perceived the hazy shape of the man who remained in the room. A faint light glowed behind his captor, casting a halo of pale light through the room. He blinked a few times, details fading in, and he could see that the walls were earthen. He assumed they were in a cellar or basement.

"The boss, he may cut you loose. If you play nice." The man stifled a laugh. Parnell licked his lips hoping for another sip of soda.

Muffled voices came from somewhere behind him. He craned his neck, looking for the source, but saw nothing but darkness. A moment later he heard the *click* of a door opening.

"Mr. Sumner," he heard a new voice—higher pitched and with a Germanic accent. Both men came into view on his right. "I'm so glad to see that you're ready to join us. The other lamp," he said to one of the other men. "Turn it on. I can't see a damn thing." A slightly brighter light snapped on near the door.

"Better, but not much," he said. "Mr. Sumner. Do you know why we've asked you to join us here? Hmm?"

Parnell tightened his lips and shook his head.

"Oh, come now. Let's not be difficult. You're well aware that we've been … *working*, shall we say, with your colleague, Mr. Rhinegold. Sadly, that hasn't gone so well. I'm afraid we encountered similar results with Malcolm Buckley. But that you're aware of, correct?"

Parnell focused on the man's voice. The accent was definitely German—Bavarian—but something seemed contrived, as if the man was mimicking the accent. Of course, he could have been German from birth but spent time elsewhere. Parnell knew many club members whose international living experiences had transformed their unique accents into amalgamations of multiple inflections. Rather than speak, Parnell grunted again.

"What, cat has your tongue? Isn't that the proper saying?" the man said, finishing with a laugh. "Really, each of you are making this much more difficult than necessary. I'm merely looking for, when it comes down to it, coordinates. That's all I require. The rest will be up to me, right?"

"I don't know what you're talking about," Parnell said.

"Oh, come now, Parnell. We've been watching your movements these past weeks. London, New York, Rome, Morocco, a ticket to Addis Ababa. Do you expect me to believe that this is some sort of pleasure trip around the globe?"

Parnell remained silent.

"And your new companion? Mr. Mancini? I suppose it's merely a coincidence that he is, was, Buckley's grandson?"

Parnell grunted again.

"I understand your trepidation, Parnell. Certainly I do. I know how close you and Honeybourne were with Malcolm. He was a ... unique man. Stubborn, certainly, but a renegade. A maverick of sorts, right? And fiercely loyal. I know. A shame that his loyalty, his stubbornness, killed him. He had no sense of cooperation, which I frankly found disappointing. Thaddeus had set such high expectations."

Parnell closed his eyes and tried to force the image of Malcolm's lifeless body from his mind. He and Bailey had been called to the morgue in London for the identification. Malcolm's face was so swollen they had difficultly confirming a positive identification. Both lips, he remembered, were thicker than farmer's thumbs.

"I ... don't know ... what you need," Parnell said.

"Of course not. The trip to Ethiopia was part of your philanthropic endeavors, right? Red Cross? Doctors Without Borders? Something like that, right?"

Parnell sensed movement accompanying the silence that followed. Finally, a hand, wielding a syringe, crept into the light.

"Do you know what this is, Parnell? Surely you do. It's that old staple of the club, Scopolamine."

Parnell felt his heart begin to race. Despite the darkness, he could see how much of the drug the syringe held. It was easily double the dose he'd used with membership candidates.

"I'm happy to give you one final opportunity to cooperate without the assistance of the drug. As you know, at higher dosages it's difficult to predict the … damage that can be done. We're not known to be as careful here. We live with our mistakes."

"That'll do you no good," Parnell said.

"We're willing to take that chance. What do we have to lose?" the voice said. "I'll give you one opportunity to answer before we take this step, though. Can you help us find what we're looking for?"

Parnell exhaled. "I … I don't know. I don't know what it is you are looking for. When we met with your colleague in Rome, he refused to share any details. How … how can I give you what you want if you don't tell me *what* you want?"

There was laughter from both men. The syringe disappeared into the shadows. Parnell heard movement. Then he could hear the men whispering again in Italian. Parnell waited, trying to determine how much he would be forced to reveal. The drug would wipe out any opportunity he would have to shield his limited knowledge. He had the same strong inclination as Bailey about the contents of the envelope, what Malcolm had found, and what these men were seeking. There would be no way to hide. Was he better off revealing what he knew now, without the drug, so that he could maintain some degree of control? He might spare his own life and perhaps that of Helmut. Assuming Helmut was still alive.

"Mr. Sumner. I respect your request, but surely you realize our apprehension. What we seek is invaluable. If this knowledge were to spread, the opportunity to achieve our goal would be greatly diminished. The competition for this treasure would be intense—in fact, it already is—and we likely would not be triumphant."

Parnell nodded.

"Here's what I know to be true. Malcolm Buckley dedicated years of his life to seeking a legendary treasure. We have reason to believe that he was eventually successful. We also know he spent a great deal of time in Ethiopia while he followed his obsession. He visited other parts of the world—China, Brazil, Tasmania—but he always returned to Ethiopia." The man paused, either awaiting a reaction or determining if he should share more.

"Is that helpful?" he continued.

Parnell again weighed his options. There was little he could confirm other than their suspicions. This group was well informed. Helmut probably knew as much, maybe more if Malcolm shared exactly what he'd found. Parnell doubted that Malcolm had given Helmut anything more than that. Of course, there was the real likelihood that once he shared what he knew, his captors would quickly dispose of him. As he contemplated this possible outcome, he realized the captors had reneged on the deal they had made in Rome. They had given him and Bailey a week to return with information. In the meantime, they had sent a team to ransack Stuart's apartment *and* kidnap him.

"Help me … help me understand how this is supposed to work?" Parnell asked. "You're asking me the same questions your colleague asked of us in Rome. We didn't have the answers. He told us we had a week to return with information or Helmut would be sacrificed. The week hasn't elapsed and yet you've taken at least two extreme actions in order to gain this information before we had an opportunity to follow up. What's my motivation to help? How do I know that Helmut is even alive? You killed Malcolm. You've lied to me. Why should I cooperate?"

The men laughed again. The hand with the syringe emerged into the lamplight again.

"We're a motivated team, Mr. Sumner. We're not patient. We'll take every action we feel necessary to locate our target. I don't recall making any promise or guarantee that we would suspend our search while we waited for you to return. Am I correct?"

"It was strongly implied," Parnell said. "Is Helmut still alive?"

There was laughter. "Oh, Helmut is … alive. We've kept that promise. That *was* our commitment, right?"

Parnell shook his head.

"Well, I see we have no alternative other than to move forward with our initial plan," the man said, waving the syringe. He said something in Italian to his partner. Parnell could see the shadows shift and the second man passed in front of one of the lamps. The man with the syringe stepped forward. Parnell could make out some of the features of the man's face. He had cropped dark hair and a gaunt face. Two hands grabbed Parnell's shoulders and pinned him back against the chair. Parnell watched the syringe plunge into his right bicep, right through his shirt. He flinched at the pinch and subsequent flaming sting that resulted from the injection.

"There. We'll give you a moment to enjoy the initial effects of the drug, Parnell. Then we'll continue our discussion. Capisce?"

# CHAPTER

# NINETEEN

The next morning, Stuart and Bailey were up, showered, and dressed by 5:30 a.m. After dining the previous evening at the hotel's Italian restaurant, Stagioni, Bailey suggested they ask the front desk if a suite was available in exchange for the two individual rooms they had booked. They were moved into a spacious junior suite. Stuart was initially hesitant to share accommodations with the older gentleman but soon realized the anxiety he'd suffered about their safety would be greatly mitigated by knowing they were together. He didn't want a repeat of the prior day's morning—waking to pandemonium and an absent travel partner. Parnell had been more than a partner; he'd been their leader.

During dinner at Stagioni, where Bailey had soaked up most of a bottle of Barolo and a monstrous plate of tagliatelle, Stuart had begun to probe into Parnell's fascination with Morocco and its souks. Bailey became more melancholy as he contemplated the question. He explained to Stuart that Parnell had been married for over twenty years before his wife passed away. They had honeymooned in Morocco, spending most of their time in Casablanca and Marrakesh, but also driving east of the cities through the Atlas Mountains and their quaint, faux-Alpine villages. Parnell and his wife had gone on to celebrate each five years of their marriage in Morocco. Catherine, his wife, had been immediately captivated by the bartering and energy of the souk. Much of their home in England was furnished with Moroccan rugs, intricate woodwork, and handmade furniture. During their visit to celebrate their twentieth anniversary, Catherine proposed a pact that they would each promise to return as often as possible, should one of them pass away, to celebrate their love for the country. A few months later, Catherine died unexpectedly. She'd been gone over thirty years now, and Parnell had religiously made at least one trip every year since her passing.

Bailey's explanation had made Stuart feel more at ease with Parnell's strange enthusiasm and disconcerting smiles. He was embarrassed that he hadn't asked Parnell directly. Bailey went on to explain that a few years prior, Parnell had confessed that during his return trips to Morocco, he began to sense—then, later, actually see—Catherine as he roamed the souk. Parnell had stopped short of calling her a ghost, but it was something more than an emotionally conjured spirit. Although Stuart was somewhat surprised that Parnell, a man seemingly grounded in logic and veracity, privately held this belief in ghosts, he regretted his aversion to Parnell's humanity. The man remained deeply and devoutly in love with his wife.

Summerfield's, the hotel's main cafe, opened at 6:30 a.m. In the meantime, Stuart brewed a pot of Ethiopian coffee in the room, and both men sat on the veranda overlooking the massive pool area. The sun rose behind them, bathing the pool water and the surrounding hills in a silver mist. Their plan was to take a cab to the university as early as possible and seek out Desta. Bailey felt certain the veteran scholar could help them hire a team for their journey into the Simien range. They would need to do some shopping, too, since neither had packed for a mountain trek.

"I've been rethinking my comment about involving the club's board," Bailey said.

"Why? I thought you said this had gotten out of hand?"

Bailey sipped his coffee and nodded. "Oh, indeed. It *has* gotten out of hand. But I'm worried about timing. These Italians, if that's truly who they are, are not interested in playing by rules or respecting our position. They've promised not to harm—kill—Helmut if we choose to give them what they want by Sunday. In the meantime, they've deployed a team in New York to break into your apartment, and they nabbed Parnell in Marrakesh. They're not counting on us to deliver. My fear is that Helmut will be easily sacrificed and Parnell will be next. Honestly, I have doubts that Helmut is still alive. They tested us in Rome, and I think they realized we didn't have, or wouldn't share, what they wanted. They may see Helmut as worthless now."

"If they think we can't help them, why kidnap Parnell?"

"Plan B. I'm sure they believe one of us, or the combination of us, can lead them to the fountain. They're monitoring our every move. They have to know that you and I returned to New York, and we know they followed you to Marrakesh. I also have to assume they had someone follow me— and now you—here. The fact that we didn't return directly to Rome has them thinking that we're doing damage control."

"So, we screwed up is what you're saying," Stuart said. He was beginning to get scared and frustrated again. Scared because he could likely become collateral damage in this group's efforts to find a ludicrous fountain of youth and frustrated because he found himself following two retired adventurers around the world who, despite their supposed expertise, weren't demonstrating that they could deal with something this deadly.

"Thus, I've been rethinking our strategy. This might be a good time to call upon a colleague I have at Interpol."

"Interpol? But I thought you didn't want to involve the authorities? I thought the secrecy of the club was at stake?"

"Stuart, a growing number of lives *are* at stake, including yours and mine. If I were to get the club presidents—our board—involved it might take the better part of a week to gather them together for this sort of intervention. We don't have that luxury. Plus, I think they'd agree with my current notion."

"Okay, then," Stuart said, sighing. "Who is this contact at Interpol? Can they be trusted?"

Bailey stared out at the pool and remained silent.

"Bailey?"

"Rupert Honeybourne."

"Honey—"

"Yes. He's my son. He's something of a special agent. Extremely well connected and well respected. I've been in awe of what he's accomplished in his career."

"For God's sake, Bailey, why haven't you involved him sooner? We're trying to play James Bond, and your son's a bigwig in the police force?"

Bailey looked at Stuart. "Don't you understand the conflict of interest? I could easily end his career with a misstep. I can't do that to him."

"Okay, okay, I understand that, but if you're in danger, don't you think he would want to know? Don't you think your own son would want to intervene?"

"Stuart, he has nearly twenty years with law enforcement, both with Scotland Yard and with Interpol. Neither of us wishes to jeopardize his tenure. This isn't necessarily new territory. We've discussed it in the past. He's well aware of the club. He knows what our endeavors are. And we've mutually agreed not to cross paths."

"But now you're considering it, right?" Stuart said.

Bailey looked over at Stuart, silent, and then turned back to focus on the view again. He took a sip of coffee and cleared his throat.

"Parnell Sumner is … is invaluable to me. I owe him my life, literally. A debt I've incurred on more than one occasion. I can't sit back knowing that there's some solution, some approach, that I could take, but that I'm now avoiding, that would bring him to safety. So, yes, I have to play all of my cards now. And if that means involving Rupert, then so be it. Parnell is his unofficial godfather. We're not Catholic, but that was the title Rupert anointed Parnell with ages ago when he was a boy. He … would understand."

Stuart avoided the topic throughout breakfast. He was unsure if Bailey planned on seeking out Desta or if he intended on them leaving Ethiopia immediately. After settling the bill, Stuart finally spoke up.

"I need your help, Bailey. I'm out of my league. What are we doing? Are you calling Rupert? Are we meeting with Desta? Do we still need to find the fountain?"

Bailey stopped. They were just outside the entrance to the restaurant.

"All the above. I believe it's what Parnell would do. You have to understand, Stuart," Bailey said. He pulled him away from the entrance. "The Kilimanjaro Club was predicated on … on quests such as this. If Malcolm indeed located the legendary fountain of youth, or something even remotely similar, then we owe it to all of our fellow members to seek out what Malcolm died for. Do you … do you have any idea what's been sacrificed in the name of adventure, in the spirit of exploration? Do you understand that our passion is not only for the individual pursuit of the improbable, but also for the betterment of mankind?"

Stuart stifled a laugh. "Mankind? Come on, Bailey. You're talking about a rich man's—a *very* rich man's—extravagant country club. Instead of chasing highly compressed rubber balls around manicured grass, you chase myths and legends around the globe, relishing the opportunity to brag and gloat about your triumphs to your cohorts. Don't try to sell it as something more."

Bailey stepped back and regarded Stuart from the waist up. "You're an ignorant, ungrateful …" Bailey stopped and shook his head. He shuffled in a tight circle and, after taking a deep breath, said, "Our members … our members include some of the most highly regarded scientific explorers on the planet. Their expeditions and discoveries are published in nearly every issue of *National Geographic*, the *American Journal of Archeology*, and *Cultural Anthropology*, just to name a few. We're not simply amateur hunters, traipsing through swamps and jungles, waiting for natives to pluck leeches from our skin each night. The original fraternity, which has grown to include many amazing women, like Prima, mind you, recognizes both the value and the protection that our exclusivity has afforded. I realize you've had but a few days to try to absorb all this, but for God's sake, put aside your own pomposity and trust what we've accomplished."

By this time Bailey had advanced on Stuart and was jabbing a bulbous index finger into his lapel. Bailey's face had gone deep red, and a thin layer of perspiration had begun to bead across his hairline.

Stuart sighed and placed his palms on Bailey's lapels. "Okay, okay. You're right. I … I don't understand all of this. I don't get it, and I apologize for slighting you and what the club stands for. You've got to understand. I'm a friggin' CFO. I count beans, right? I sit at a desk. I give presentations. I conduct meetings. I analyze the rational. I scrutinize things that balance, add up, make sense, stand up to audit, align with regulations, okay? When some stranger pops into my life and tells me I'm about to embark on a search for the fountain of youth, it violates everything I've committed myself to. It … it doesn't compute."

Bailey stepped back. An older Caucasian couple approaching the restaurant podium was staring at them. Bailey sighed and slumped.

"I'm sorry, Stuart. Please forgive me. I was out of line. I—"

"No, don't *you* apologize. This, to me, feels like an insane time. I have to admit, I'm programmed to being in control, to accurately predict and respond. Being here," he said, motioning to their surroundings, "is as far from predictable as I can get. And you know what, Bailey? As much as it's making me crazy, there's an evolving part of me that's loving it. I keep reminding myself that I'm here of my own volition. I could hop into a cab at any time, head to the airport, and fly home. Nothing, no one, is stopping me. But I'm here, right? I'm here, waiting for you to tell me what's next. It's an adventure, just like it's supposed to be, right? It's what the club is all about."

Bailey stared into Stuart's eyes for a few seconds, then seemed to soften. He reached out with both hands and grasped Stuart by the upper arms. "It is, Stuart. It is. It's what drives us to save Helmut and Parnell, as well as seek out the fountain."

"Desta, then?" Stuart asked.

"Yes, Desta." Bailey said, smiling and then looking at his watch. "He should be in his office by now. Let's go."

The school of Social Sciences at Addis Ababa University was crowned by an imposing three-story building boasting a distinctive, early 1970's design. Massive, white, curvilinear ribs stretched from the ground to the roofline, interspersed with expansive windows, each masked in an intricate, boxy pattern of framing. The campus was buzzing with students and faculty dashing between buildings. The grounds of the university were a stark contrast to the ravaged neighborhoods they traveled passed from the hotel. It was as if small pockets of property, like that which held the Sheraton and now the university, had been plucked from eastern Europe and planted in the midst of a society struggling to survive. The disparity between what Stuart had seen in Manhattan's most dilapidated areas and the poverty the Ethiopian population endured was disheartening.

The taxi dropped Stuart and Bailey at the entrance of the Social Sciences building. Inside, Bailey stopped at the main desk and inquired about Desta. The young woman behind the desk erupted in a vibrant smile when Bailey spoke Desta's name.

"Oh, yes, Professor Desta's office is in this building," she said in clear, clipped English.

"I'm afraid we've arrived somewhat unannounced. Would it be possible to ring him and see if he's available? My name is Bailey Honeybourne."

The woman nodded and said, "Yes, of course, Mr. Honeybourne." She picked up the receiver and punched a few numbers on the broad console. Bailey stepped from the desk and nodded for Stuart to join him.

"I believe I've hit upon a slightly different approach," he said to Stuart.

"You mean with Desta? Is something wrong?"

"No, I'm thinking of both Rupert and Desta. And our deadline."

"Okay," Stuart said slowly.

"Excuse me, Mr. Honeybourne? The professor will be down in a moment. He's asked that you make yourselves comfortable in the meantime." She pointed toward a small seating area adjacent to the desk.

"Thank you, miss," Bailey trumpeted and led Stuart to the sofa.

"Depending upon Desta's reaction, I think … I think we should split up."

"Split up? Are you mad? I've already lost Parnell on this trip. You can't possibly expect me to continue this alone."

"First of all, you wouldn't be alone. I wouldn't abandon you if I didn't feel you were to be well looked after. If Desta feels he can assist in the expedition, then I think your role should be to assist with the trip. Stuart, I'm … God, I'm *well* over sixty years old now. I'm not conditioned," he said, cradling his belly, "to trek through mountains with any level of acceptable speed. I'm the slowest of snails. Paint dries faster than I move, especially at these altitudes."

"But—"

"And I'll return to Rome. I'll have Rupert meet me. I can call upon Prima to coordinate some of the resources I believe he'll require. We'll meet up with the captors again and see what we can gain from them."

Stuart grunted and shook his head. "I really don't know about this, Bailey. I'm already way out of my element. An adventurous day for me is skipping the subway. Really, how am I going to help Desta?"

"Frankly, you'll pay him. That'll be one of your more important responsibilities, at least in his mind. You'll need to look at yourself as a tourist of sorts who's hired a highly competent, and I imagine, high-priced, guide and staff."

Stuart looked around the lobby of the building, watching the flow of students merge up the stairwells, conducting casual conversations and impromptu meetings in the various nooks and alcoves, and plunging headward into their studies.

"You haven't even spoken to Rupert yet. What if he declines? What if—"

"He won't, Stuart. He's my son. He might be unhappy, but he won't say no," Bailey muttered.

"Bailey Honeybourne!" Stuart and Bailey turned to see a slight man dressed in linen pants and a flowing cotton shirt. His skin was a rich red-black that glistened in the natural light of the building lobby. He was mostly bald with tiny ears, crowned by thin patches of grey hair pinned back against his skull. He reached out to Bailey as he stood and warmly embraced him.

"My God, Bailey, it's been a long, long time, and you look wonderful."

"Yes, yes," Bailey replied appearing to blush. "It *has* been very long—"

"At least fifteen years, perhaps twenty? How can that be? You were—"

"Old even then, I'm afraid, dear Desta. It seems I've always been old."

Desta released Bailey and clapped him on the shoulder.

"This," Bailey said indicating Stuart, "is Stuart Mancini. His grandfather was Malcolm Buckley."

Desta regarded Stuart with a sympathetic tilt of the head. "I was so sorry to hear of Malcolm's passing. He was a frequent visitor and a generous benefactor of the university. All of which I am sure you know."

"Actually, I didn't," Stuart replied. "I'm … we didn't have much contact. Bailey's been trying to catch me up on all of his passions."

Desta laughed and reached forward to shake Stuart's hand. "Your grandfather was a unique man. So … what's the right word?" he said, looking to Bailey. "Committed, I suppose. Once he set his mind to something, he was relentless. Yes, that's it, *relentless*."

Stuart stepped back, unsure of how to respond. No matter what Bailey or Parnell attempted to share about his grandfather, it was like trying to bond with an alien entity. There remained fleeting, almost imaginary, memories of a towering, gaunt man with a distinct nose and slightly disheveled hair in formal dress, but these brief visions were jumbled. He'd been so young. His mother's frequent ranting had conjured a ghost, a banshee, of a man who deserved nothing more than to be disparaged and discounted at the slightest provocation. None of this jived with the flood of accolades he'd heard over the past week.

"Come," Desta said, sweeping an arm. "Let's go to my office. We'll be able to talk more freely."

Desta walked them up two flights of stairs and down a long, linoleum paved hallway. The climb sapped Bailey and Stuart's breath. Every fifteen feet or so, a pair of doors sprang from either side of the hall. Each door was plastered with announcements, sign-up sheets, and grade postings. It was surprisingly, and comfortably, equivalent to Stuart's memories of his own undergraduate studies. As he stopped in front of a door that was similarly adorned, Desta apologized for the long walk. He led them into his office and closed the door behind them. Desta's office contained three chairs, an old, wooden swivel desk chair and two metal folding chairs pushed against the window.

Bailey and Stuart sat in the metal chairs while Desta leaned against his desk and folded his arms.

"So, as I'm sure you know, Said Musi contacted me yesterday and *warned* me of your visit. He said 'warn,' not me. I was genuinely excited to hear you were coming. He was discreet, as always, but I have learned to interpret his tone well over the years. He was quite worried, and I gather rightly so. Am I correct?"

Bailey glanced quickly at Stuart and cleared his throat. "Yes, Desta. There's definitely cause for concern. And we are still trying to determine how best to respond to our situation."

"Where is Parnell Sumner? Said mentioned that he'd traveled to Marrakesh," Desta said. He was stern, the congeniality that had flowed through his voice now nonexistent.

"We … don't know," Bailey responded, glancing at Stuart. "That's become a significant part of our problem. He's been abducted, Desta. We have no idea where he may be. Morocco … Italy, likely. But we've no proof."

Desta stared at the floor and shook his head slowly. "That's bad, my friend. We've lost Malcolm; Helmut Rhinegold, I understand, is also at great risk; and now … now Parnell. Said did mention that he thought you were looking to go into the Simien Mountains. In my humble opinion, I do not think we should be planning an expedition into the Simien. No matter how well we might know the area." He looked up. "Have you contacted your board?"

"That was my initial reaction, but I've had to rethink that approach. Desta, getting the board together could take days, even weeks, and there's no guarantee we'd end up with an actionable decision."

"So what do you plan to do?" Desta said.

"I've decided to call my son, Rupert. You may remember his role at Interpol. He can assist with the kidnappings. Concurrently, I was hoping I could contract you to gather a team and take Stuart with you."

"Bailey, I understand if you can't answer my next question. But you must know that your response will determine how much I can do to assist."

"I understand," Bailey answered.

"What's your purpose for traveling into the Simien Mountains when your friends are being held elsewhere?"

"Desta, you said you knew Malcolm Buckley well, right? He spent considerable time here in Ethiopia, and expressly in the Simien area. Do you have any idea why?"

Desta smiled and nodded. "I ..." Desta laughed quietly. "I am aware of his motives, yes. I know he was seeking a ... place, a mythical place."

"Well," Bailey said, sighing, "we have reason to believe he was successful, as do the men who have kidnapped our colleagues. I don't think there's anything we can do to secure his discovery, but I do believe we can ... say, *extract* a significant portion before it's discovered by others. And perhaps prevent their discovery of its location."

Desta stared at Bailey for what seemed like a full minute before speaking. "I can't say I'm confident about either strategy. I don't know enough about Helmut and Parnell's capture, but this group you're dealing with seems efficient, organized, and radical. To execute two international kidnappings flawlessly is impressive. And trekking into the mountains ..." Desta trailed off, turning his gaze out the window. "So, it's true. Malcolm found it."

"Yes," Bailey said, shooting a glance at Stuart. Stuart wrestled to stay put. An uncomfortable level of tension seemed to be building between the two men. He was unsure if it was because they'd caught Desta off guard or if something more ominous was at stake.

"That doesn't make it easier, Bailey. Do you know ... does it ... does it follow the legend?"

Bailey stalled, toying with his mustache. "I have every reason to believe it does. I'm not at liberty to provide specifics, but I'd wager nearly everything I own that it's truly a fountain of youth."

"Okay. And you confident that your son can be effective? You have an Italian group masterminding these attacks, correct? A kidnapping, we can assume, in the U.S., another in Morocco, and a murder in London to boot?"

"We're assuming they're Italian, but frankly, we don't know," Bailey said. "Rupert's position puts him in regular contact with the Interpol Response Teams. I know he can garner the support he needs if I ask."

"And you believe engaging Interpol is the proper approach?" Desta said.

Bailey nodded. "I do. We could have three murders, one of which would essentially end my life, at least as I know it today."

Desta seemed to process this information. He rocked gently and looked to Stuart.

"We'll be followed," he said.

"Perhaps," Bailey said. "Certainly, I will be, but that may be preferable. I believe you could assemble a team without drawing any additional attention. We could make it look like Stuart here has disappeared. At least initially. It would give you an ample head start. Perhaps enough to elude anyone who might be planning to follow."

Desta returned his gaze to the floor. The three of them sat in silence until Desta finally moved.

"You must have been followed here, Bailey. These people will continue to monitor your movements very closely. You're asking me to take on a tremendous risk. Not just for me or Stuart, but for anyone else we bring with us. I'm not sure I can justify putting that many people in harm's way."

"You shouldn't feel obligated, Desta. That wasn't my intent. I wanted to give you the opportunity to be a part of this, in addition to the customary fee that such an outing would require. Certainly, if you aren't comfortable leading the expedition, I understand. This is not a recreational endeavor."

Stuart shared the same doubts Desta voiced. Stuart acknowledged the escape hatch of fleeing to the airport and flying back across the Atlantic. He could flip the switch back to everything he left behind in

New York—the safety, routine, familiarity, success—all secure within his apartment and his life at D'Artagnan. Was there truly any reason to risk everything he'd achieved over the past two decades?

His thoughts returned to his mother and the loyalty he felt to her. If she was lucid, would she tear into him, berating the mere consideration of connecting himself with Malcolm? Or would she spring that look, that glare, accompanied by a muted hiss, that routinely accompanied her dissatisfaction. Or would something else surface? Some repressed memory of her father before she rejected him. Would the hint of her father's passion, the exposure of some dormant trove of emotion, reignite the love she once held for this man? He would never know.

"I will tell you what I agree with, Bailey. I agree you should leave. It's too dangerous for you in Ethiopia, or Africa for that matter. There must be someone downstairs, in the car park, waiting for you to leave. You'll need Rupert to mobilize a sufficient force to meet you in Rome, if that's where you're going." Desta said, finishing with a look to Stuart.

"You, on the other hand," Desta continued, offering a smile to Stuart and softening his tone, "I know I can assist. It's just the question of whether I can manage an approach that doesn't seem foolhardy."

"Is it safe for me to call Rupert from here?" Bailey asked. Desta nodded. "Right, then if I may have a moment alone, I'll contact Rupert and arrange for my return. I assume you or someone on your staff can recommend a taxi service to drive me to the airport?"

"What about your things at the hotel? Do you want me to get them for you?" Stuart asked.

"You won't be returning to the Sheraton," Desta said. "I don't see how either of you can return safely. We can arrange for your belongings to be brought to my office. I have an acquaintance who works at the hotel."

Bailey waved a hand toward Desta. "There's nothing of value. A change of clothes and toiletries. Stuart, what about you?"

Stuart tried to remember what he'd brought with him. More than one change of clothes, but nothing irreplaceable. He instinctively tapped his front pocket. His cell phone was still with him. He had his passport and wallet in his breast pocket.

"No, I suppose not. Certainly nothing worth risking my life for."

"Oh, we'll have plenty for that," Desta said, flashing a grin that hit Stuart like a gut punch.

Desta motioned for Stuart to leave the office to Bailey. They stepped into the hall where foot traffic had increased. Students and staff were crowding the hallway, ducking in and out of doors.

"Office hours for many of my colleagues," Desta said. "May I ask you," Desta continued. He spoke just loud enough for Stuart to hear him. "Is this what *you* want? Are you prepared for what Bailey has proposed?"

Stuart paused. "I really don't know. I've been mindlessly following Bailey and Parnell for the better part of a week. I feel like I haven't made a decision of my own since we left New York—which isn't accurate. Part of me is saying go home. Another says this is what my life will be about, something that feels like destiny, at least for the very near future. As you've noticed, I'm not in any way prepared for what I've leapt into." He raised his hands in the air. "I mean, look at me. I'm a lost Wall Street executive chasing down ..." He lowered his voice and continued, "chasing down ... improbable myths. Trying ... trying to, what? Reconnect with my grandfather? Why?"

Desta regarded Stuart with a focused, stern look. He raised a thin forefinger to his top lip. "I appreciate your honesty. Especially since we've just met. But I see your dilemma. Come," he said, motioning to a short row of metal chairs a few feet from his office door. "Let's sit while we wait for Bailey."

Desta turned in his chair to face Stuart and touched him on the forearm. "Tell me, Stuart Mancini, what kind of work do you do?"

Stuart squirmed a bit and sat up stiffly in his chair. "I work for a boutique investment firm in Manhattan."

"Ah," Desta said, nodding and smiling. "Like the Michael Douglas character, yes?"

"No, not quite. I'm more of a back-office guy. I manage the firm's finance and accounting functions, make sure our books balance, make sure we have the money available to do the things we do for our customers."

"I see. So, forgive me, I don't know New York well. I've visited on two occasions, but didn't see much beyond *A Chorus Line* and the Empire State Building. Is there an opportunity for you to get out of the city? Do you have places to hike, to climb?"

Stuart laughed. "My version of hiking is limited to taking the stairs when the elevators are crowded or foregoing the subway on a nice day. I run daily, or at least I did before meeting him," he added, jabbing a thumb toward Desta's office.

Desta grinned at Stuart's attempt at humor, but his eyes held their intensity. "The reason I ask is that our mountains are treacherous. Granted, we're not scaling the Himalayas, but this will also not be a simple weekend backpacking trip. If I decide to do this, if we do this together, we'll have, I hope, a team of six to ten men and women accompanying us. We may hike and climb up to fifteen miles a day, more if necessary. We'll be sleeping on the ground or in tents, eating what we can carry, dealing with the elements … evading stalkers. Do you understand? It will be unlike anything, I imagine, you've ever done."

Stuart understood Desta was testing him, trying to scare him into backing out. Desta had been practical, but far from enthusiastic, about Bailey's news and ensuing plan. He wasn't certain as to what was causing Desta's apprehension. Was it the physical challenge of the expedition? The uncertainty of finding the fountain? The fact that there were, frankly, killers looking for the same thing—killers who were only one step behind them?

"What do *you* think? Do you think I can do it?" Stuart asked, as much to Desta as himself.

"Well," Desta said, easing back from Stuart, "you appear fit, able, relatively young. Those are all positive things. What I see, though, can't predict how your mind will respond to long days of rigorous climbing. When was the last time you spent the night outside of a bed?"

Cub Scouts, Stuart thought, but he didn't say it out loud. His one and only camping experience had been in the third grade. His Cub Scout den had spent two nights at the Blue Mountain Reservation in Westchester County. The trip occurred in late May, typically a comfortable time of the year. That spring, the weather had been wildly unpredictable, and the forecast was for rain and highs in the forties. Stuart's mother had insisted they purchase a new mummy-style sleeping bag. The model she chose had been tested at negative twenty degrees Fahrenheit. As it turned out, the rain turned mostly into fog and the temperatures hovered in the fifties the entire weekend. Stuart woke in the middle of the first night bathed in sweat. The humidity trapped within the tent paired with the sleeping bag's heat-retaining design created a miserable mini-sauna. The second night was a slight improvement, but Stuart stifled tears as he fought to sleep.

"It's been a while," Stuart said.

"I'm not surprised. Please understand I don't ask you these questions to build a case against going on this exploration. In the end, I'll do what Bailey needs. I'm unwilling, however, to foolishly contribute to a casualty, or worse. I can do this with or without you."

If he was being completely honest with himself, Stuart's wish would be to return to Italy with Bailey. There was no valid reason other than seeing Prima again. The thought hadn't occurred until Bailey told him of his plan to return to Rome. Stuart assumed he'd have the chance to go back—either with Bailey and Parnell or alone—and see her outside of this debacle. The temptation to go was strong now.

"I suppose I could go with Bailey to Rome, if you think I'd be a hindrance."

"Oh, I don't necessarily believe you will be a hindrance. I simply have nothing to base my confidence upon, you see? Had you told me that you spent a week each year camping in the Canadian Rockies or climbing in South America, I would have committed immediately. But, just look at your hands, Stuart. Your fingers are long, lean, unblemished, free of scars, calluses. The true mountain men, the ones who are accustomed to the things we'll see in the Simiens, have hands like stone. Rough, muscular, battle-worn. If I had felt such a thing in your initial handshake, we wouldn't be having this conversation."

The door behind Stuart clicked, and Bailey stepped into the hallway. He motioned them to come back into the office. Once inside, Bailey said, "Good news. I reached Rupert in his office just now. He's ... he's hesitant and none too pleased about the situation we've found ourselves in. But," Bailey continued, taking in a deep breath and rocking back on his heels, "he is willing to help. He's booking a flight into Rome as we speak. I'll meet him there either this evening or tomorrow morning. I've arranged my flight for this afternoon."

Desta looked at Stuart and clenched his jaw. "I've been talking with Stuart about what to expect should he decide to embark on this trip."

"What do you mean, 'should he decide?' I thought—"

"Bailey, you've pulled this poor soul out of the modern world and plunged him into a completely foreign land. He's faced with spending a week or more trudging through some of the highest mountains on the continent. He needs to understand what's at stake, what he'll be risking."

Bailey looked at Stuart and scrunched his face. The contempt was glaring.

"It's all right, Bailey," Stuart said, pausing. "I'm going." It felt like the appropriate, instinctive response. Bailey's shoulders fell an inch or two as he sighed.

"Right, then," Bailey said, slapping Stuart on the shoulder, "about that car, Desta. I'll need get to the airport as soon as possible. Are you still confident you can keep Stuart under wraps?"

"You should know better than to question my capabilities, Bailey Honeybourne."

Bailey puffed up again, for a moment, then let out a laugh and shook his head.

"Give me a moment to call downstairs. Bailey, you'll take the freight elevator at the end of the hall down to the basement. There'll be someone there to meet you and walk you to the loading dock. Your car will be there," Desta said. He lifted the receiver, dialed, then delivered a few brief instructions in Amharic.

"Stuart," Desta said after hanging up the phone. "I think it would be best if you stayed with me this evening. I'll have my car brought to the dock as well. You'll need to ride in the rear and stay hidden. I typically leave around 4:30. It's important for me to demonstrate a consistent schedule. We'll plan our trip this evening and get started in the morning, by noon at the latest."

"Desta, I don't know quite how to thank you," Bailey said. He walked to the slight man and gripped his shoulders. "You're putting yourself at great risk for our benefit."

Desta patted Bailey on the shoulder. "This is why I'm a part of the club, old man. I live for this, no matter what the risk." He smiled, his ebony eyes disappearing within the deep creases of his face. "Let's get you to Rome."

# CHAPTER

# TWENTY

A mélange of apparitional images swam before Parnell's eyes. He heard muted voices and objects and furniture being moved. He fought to focus on the manifestations that clouded before him. The voices and the movement suddenly stopped. Somewhere the light grew dimmer, greying out his vision. He realized he was lying flat on his back. The only movement he could muster was breathing. His arms and legs were leaden. Something—a face—like a smeared mask, came into view. As he began to identify details, something dark and soft covered his eyes.

"Hello, Parnell," a familiar voice called. Parnell struggled to place the voice, but his brain continued to misfire. He tried to croak a reply but nothing came out. "Ah, you're thirsty," the voice said. The accent—it had a European tinge. Helmut. Parnell squirmed and attempted to speak again. "Here, drink from this," Helmut said. Parnell felt a plastic tube against his lips. He pulled it into his mouth and drew deeply. Ice-cold water saturated his barren mouth and throat. He choked back a cough, but he continued to gulp. "Careful," he heard Helmut say. The tube slid from his lips.

"Helmut, it *is* you, isn't it?" Parnell said. The combination of hydration and the realization that he was with Helmut clarified his consciousness. "Are you okay? Where are we? I … I was afraid you were dead."

Helmut laughed. "No, I'm very well, my friend. Very well indeed."

"Good, good," Parnell said. "Why … why am I bound like this? Am I on a bed, some type of gurney? Can you free me?"

"Yes, they have you strapped to a gurney, rather tightly, too. I'm afraid I can't help you, though. Not right now."

Parnell scowled behind the draping that covered his face. "Why not? Are they watching? Is that it? They don't want you to help me?"

He heard Helmut sigh. "Something like that. How's your head feeling?"

Helmut's question brought back the throbbing Parnell had blocked out. It was a deep, pulsing pain that sprang from the base of his skull and rocketed over his scalp in searing bolts.

"Yes, God, it's brutal."

"I think they may have overdone it on the narcotics."

"What do you mean?" Parnell asked.

"What's the last thing you remember, Parnell?"

Parnell's first thought was of nothingness. It felt as if he'd spontaneously materialized without a history. As he concentrated, his efforts were hampered by the throbbing pain. There was Marrakesh. Right, dear Marrakesh. Stuart. Said. A dancer, that beautiful dancer. Something clicked into place. He remembered walking, petrified, through the lobby of La Mamounia toward a white van. He remembered stepping into the van, lowering his head, and being pulled into a seat between two hooded men. There was a flash of a plane, a small private jet. More men dressed in dark clothing, all hooded.

"Morocco, I suppose," Parnell said, finally.

"Hmmm, that sounds about right. Anything else?"

"A plane, right? I was flown here. Are we back in Rome, somewhere in Italy?"

"I'm afraid I can't answer that question for you, Parnell."

"But … *why*? Don't you know where we are?" His question was met with silence. "Helmut? Are you still there?"

"Yes."

"Please … take this hood off. Can you?"

Parnell heard a chair slide across the floor a short distance. Then he felt something warm, air, no, breath, against his neck.

"I thought for certain you'd be the one who held the key for us, Parnell." Helmut's raspy half whisper wafted across his earlobe.

"What do you mean?"

"It started off so well, our conversation last night. You were responding to the drug. You were confirming everything we'd imagined, right up to your destination in Ethiopia. But, then …" Helmut said, his voice growing louder. "You failed. You didn't have it, and I was astonished. I couldn't believe you entrusted that fool Bailey with Malcolm's secret."

"Helmut! You …" Parnell stopped. At first, he thought it was a trick, that one of the captors had been impersonating Helmut, but it was spot on. They'd all been duped. Helmut had lured them into this chase only to be led to the prize. Parnell was furious and embarrassed.

"It's okay, though, really. You told us where we could find Bailey and Mancini. We already had men in Addis Ababa, so it's been easy for us to deploy them. I would've preferred to skip this part of the puzzle and jump directly to the end, you know? All this kidnapping, murder, sneaking around—it's very messy and dangerous. But … we do what we must."

Parnell felt himself begin to hyperventilate, huffing into the cloth that wrapped his face, the moisture from his breath gluing the fabric to his lips and nostrils. He forced a sharp laugh. "You're wrong, Helmut. It's not in Addis Ababa. It's not anywhere near there. You—"

"Oh, come now, Parnell. It's much too late to play that game. What you don't remember is everything you told us under the influence of the drug. It was all true. I'm quite confident of that. Now …" Helmut said. Parnell heard the chair scrape the floor again. Helmut was moving away. "I'll leave you to rest."

"Wait, wait, Helmut!" Parnell screamed, thrashing beneath the thick straps that bound him to the gurney.

"You will be the one waiting, Parnell. I have a search to manage." Parnell heard a distant door creak open and slam shut. A second later, all traces of light disappeared.

# TWENTY-ONE

B ailey caught a private car at the Rome airport and departed for Trastevere shortly after sundown. The Mercedes floated along the narrow, cobbled side streets past the cafés and taverns as they began to fill. The car pulled into the Piazza di Santa Maria. A fair number of locals and tourists occupied the square and the outside patios of the neighboring restaurants. The car followed the perimeter and slowed as it approached the far corner. Bailey leaned forward and tapped the driver on the shoulder. The car glided to a stop.

A set of travertine steps led to the whitewashed double doors. The walk-up was three stories tall and illuminated by a nearby streetlamp and the various lights scattered throughout the square. A grid of dark windows graced the front of the building. Bailey remained seated and retrieved his cell phone. He punched in a number and listened as the phone rang until an older man's voice began speaking in Italian, followed by a sharp beep. Bailey punched the "1" button six times, ended the call, then peered out at the building. A few seconds later, a light came on in one of the third-floor windows. Bailey nodded to the driver who stepped out and headed to the rear of the car. Bailey opened his own door and met the driver to retrieve his briefcase. He climbed the steps casually and opened one of the towering doors. He stepped into darkness, closing the door behind him.

Laser-thin strips of external light seeped from the sides of the heavy curtains that shaded the two main front windows. The surrounding darkness swallowed any particle of light that attempted to escape the seams of the drapes. Bailey blinked, trying to force his eyes to dilate and acclimate to the murk. His other senses shifted into overdrive. He smelled the remnants of fresh bread, butter and onions, or perhaps scallions. Somewhere above he heard a lone cello's hum. Objects materialized within the shadows. He eventually spotted a staircase several feet in front of him. He took a breath and began climbing the steps.

"Welcome back," a female voice called out as he reached the first landing. It was Prima.

"Prima, it's good to hear your voice. Are we free to talk?" he said in a hushed voice.

"Yes, of course. I'm up on the second floor. I want to keep the lights at a minimum, just in case we happen to have a straggling follower."

Bailey nodded and continued up the stairs. As he reached the second-floor landing, Prima approached him and extend her hand. He caught it and swept it up to his lips for a light kiss. "I can't tell you how grateful I am of your hospitality. I would never—"

"Shush, Bailey," she said, tapping his chest with her fingertips. "I can't believe you even hesitated to ask. You should know you're always welcome in my home. Come, let's go upstairs. The light is already on and we can escape this darkness."

She led him into a broad casual sitting area on the third floor that stretched the width of her flat. The cello's thick murmur droned through the room, unobtrusive yet hauntingly real. Several large candles complemented the single lit lamp, radiating a delicate glow. Prima wore a dark velour sweat suit and silver ballet slippers. She motioned for Bailey to sit in one of the overstuffed sofas off to her right. The glass table in front of the sofa held a decanter of red wine. Two glasses, one full, one empty, sat next to the decanter. A pewter bowl with twin compartments held nuts and olives.

"My brother will drop your bag by within the next couple of hours. Your room is just down the hall. If you decide to turn in before he arrives, I'll make sure it's outside your door."

"You're too kind, Prima dear," Bailey said, sinking into the couch.

"Wine?" she asked, moving toward the decanter. "It's Montepulciano d'Abruzzo. Perhaps a bit heavy for the evening, but I can't get enough of it."

"Please," Bailey said. He leaned forward and watched her fill his glass. They cheered and drank. Prima dissolved into an ornately upholstered armchair and cupped her glass. While her tone and posture appeared relaxed, Bailey could sense the tension in her face. Slight furrows crept into her normally placid forehead and her jaw was set. She broke from his stare and absently sipped at her wine.

"What's the latest from Rupert?" she said.

"He's arriving later this evening. He's rented a room a few blocks away. We won't meet until early tomorrow morning. My thought was to have him meet me here. Is that wise?"

"Of course," Prima said, smiling. "As I told you on the phone, I've arranged for several associates to keep an eye on our building and the activity in the square."

"Well, I'm sure there was some attempt to follow me. I'm hoping our driver was evasive enough to throw them off. Based upon our current situation, we didn't take these recent events as seriously as we should have. Rupert really lashed into me, and rightly so. I'm thankful we have a strong relationship. If I were his sibling, say, rather than his father, he would likely allow this mess to teach me a lesson, regardless of the outcome." Bailey scooped up a handful of almonds and sat back into the couch.

"This is a beautiful location, Prima. This," he said motioning to the room, "the Piazza, all of it. Have you owned it long?"

"Oh," she said, unwinding her legs and leaning forward on her knees. "My father owns the building. He bought it back in the early 1970s as a rental property. We had a string of wonderful tenants. I think only three families in all up through the early nineties. Then, as papa got a bit older, he didn't want to have to deal with being a landlord, but he didn't want to sell it either. So now either the family uses it from time to time, or close friends who come to Rome to visit. It can be a nice getaway without going far."

"You're very fortunate. I'm not sure I could leave."

Prima laughed and said, "Well, you're welcome any time. I'd love to have you stay when things aren't so crazy. This area, Trastevere, is such an amazing part of the city. My favorite restaurants are all just a short walk from here."

"I should ask you," Bailey said. "Have there been any stories circulating at the club this week?"

"Surprisingly, no. But I can't imagine that will last. People still talk of Malcolm's death, and Helmut has always been popular with our members. The people he sees regularly are going to start to suspect something even if a rumor doesn't start. I have to admit, Bailey, I'm relieved, but also a bit frightened, that Rupert and Interpol are getting involved."

"It's not an official agency engagement," Bailey said, cutting her off. She raised a hand and took a sip of wine.

"I understand, but still. The more people who have knowledge of Helmut, and now Parnell, the more likely the club grapevine comes to life. It's a gossipy group."

"Yes, that's our nature, I'm afraid. It's all about the stories, right? Always has been. The fact that truth and rumor, myth and legend, are all intertwined and eventually inseparable is what fuels our membership."

Prima nodded and looked at the now empty nut and grape dish. "Oh, I'm such a poor hostess. Would you like something more to eat? The kitchen is downstairs. I'm sure we could pull together. Pasta? Some prosciutto and cheese?"

"No, no, Prima. You've already gone well beyond the call of duty. I'll likely have another spot of wine and then retire. I have much to share with Rupert tomorrow morning. I'm really hoping he can see something that we've missed."

"He's traveling alone, I assume?"

"Traveling, yes. But he told me he'd leverage at least one other agent stationed in Rome. I suppose it's unavoidable, but as you said, the more who know about this predicament, the more damage control we face."

Prima's gaze wandered beyond Bailey as she twirled her glass between her fingers. "If you can, let me know who Rupert decides to pull in. I've had contact with a few agents from Interpol over the years, and I'm afraid I haven't always been impressed, if you know what I mean."

"I can't think Rupert would protest, but I'm also confident that he'll be very selective. One, because this is off the books, and two, because of my involvement and that of the club. He's never sloppy, so this would be one time where I believe he'll be exceedingly careful."

"Good," she said, and then she stood and stretched. "Why don't I leave you here to finish your wine? Your room is the first door on the right. I'll crack the door and turn on a light for you." Bailey smiled and nodded, lifting his glass to her. She stepped into her slippers. "If there's anything you need, just let me know. My bedroom's on the second floor, right across from the top of the stairs."

"Oh, I should be just fine, Prima. You've been wonderful. Thank you again."

"Have a good night, Bailey." She walked over to him, leaned down, and kissed his forehead. "Oh, I nearly forgot. What of Stuart? Do you think he'll be safe in Addis Ababa? I'm a bit surprised that he's still caught up in this."

Bailey sighed. "He's a good man, just out of his element. But I do think he's catching on. I can tell there's something about this adventure of ours that's intriguing to him." Bailey laughed and continued. "I believe he'll be well looked after by Desta. He's fit, spry, a bit hard headed at times, I think, but all things that should suit him well. They have quite a trek ahead of them."

"They're being followed as well, right? Isn't the danger in some ways worse for him?"

Bailey nodded. "They'll be targeted until this group gets what they want. They're not going to give up on pursuing Malcolm's grandson. I'm sure they believe Stuart knows how to get them what they need. Ironically, his travels with Desta may fulfill that assumption. I know he's considered returning to New York, and I can't say I blame him. But he's chosen to stay on, so far. If nothing else, this has turned into an exceptional entrée into The Kilimanjaro Club."

She gave Bailey a look that said, "No one deserves *that* type of welcome," and said, "Good night, Bailey."

As she walked away, Bailey said, "I believe he'd be pleased to hear that you're concerned about him." Prima stopped, hesitated, and then looked over her shoulder at him. Bailey smiled and winked. Prima smirked, then turned and sauntered from the room, waving a hand over her head.

Bailey closed his eyes and absorbed on the music. He felt anxious but knew if he allowed himself to be overcome by the stress he'd never sleep and ultimately be a burden to his son. Rupert *had* ripped into him. At first Bailey couldn't tell if it was because Rupert was embarrassed to have to bail his father out, or if he was just frustrated to have to take the time to do so. Although they only spoke for a few minutes, it was Rupert's closing statement that hinted at his perspective.

"Dad," he'd said, "I'm worried about *you*. Very worried. You're too old for this. I … I don't want that telephone call. Not now. Not over something like this." Rupert hadn't been a cold, distant child growing up, but he struggled with his feelings the way many men did. Bailey knew Rupert's fear was genuine if it triggered such a comment.

There had been a time when Bailey was the one called in to rescue some poor sap who'd trundled into an unstable country or violated some sacred edifice. Dozens of such occasions. However, it had been years since he'd played the role of the hero. He knew Rupert was right, and Bailey *was* embarrassed—not for having to call in Rupert's help, but because he'd been so bold and bullheaded to think he and Parnell, dragging along an accountant, for God's sake, could foil an international kidnapping. Prima's concern for Stuart was well founded, too. Bailey had abandoned him in a desolate foreign land, with a band of strangers who were about drag him through an expedition like nothing he'd ever experienced. Then there was the very real threat that the entire party would be hunted as they plunged through the Ethiopian wilderness.

The music ended and Bailey stared at his glass. He had a swallow of wine remaining, which he dashed off in frustration. In the silence he thought of Parnell. It had taken all of his willpower to do anything but worry about the safety of his trusted friend. First, he hadn't wanted Stuart to find any additional cause for concern. Second, he wanted Prima to see him for the man he felt his reputation defined—steady, rugged, detached, committed, and unemotional. And finally, possibly most critical, he was afraid that if he allowed himself to dwell on Parnell's fate, he would crumble.

He took a deep breath, picked up the wine bottle and drained a final sip into his glass. He stood, taking in the room, wishing he were here on holiday, simply relaxing and thinking of how to spend the next leisurely day in this amazing city, rather than contemplating how his next mistake could end the lives of two dear friends and greatly endanger a new one.

# TWENTY-TWO

S tuart woke with a start and found a hand clamped across his face. Another hand shoved his shoulder back down and a voice quietly hushed him and whispered, "It's Desta." Stuart blinked, fighting for some difference between open and closed. Wherever he lay was completely devoid of light. His heart pounded as the grip on his mouth and shoulder released.

"As quietly as possible, get dressed and gather your bag. We're leaving *now*."

Stuart nodded in the dark and eased into a sitting position. As consciousness trickled into his being, he remembered where he was and what was happening. Desta had tucked him away in a secluded room in his sparse university apartment. Stuart's makeshift bed was wedged between boxes and below hanging clothes. His bag was beside the mattress, wedged into a corner.

"I'll be back in just a minute," Desta whispered. Stuart could feel him leave the room. A moment later, a faint light seeped into the room from Desta's bedroom. He could see just enough to slip on his socks and shoes. He carried a toiletry bag and his suitcase out of the room into the narrow hall. Desta padded out to meet him.

"Is there a sink I can use? I'd like to brush my teeth."

Desta smiled and nodded, guiding him toward an adjacent hall that had been transformed into a kitchen. A sink the size of a textbook split the counter. Stuart ran the water, splashed his face, and brushed his teeth. He realized that it might be some time before he had the luxury of running water again, no matter how basic Desta's facilities seemed. He wiped his face and mouth on his sleeve and looked at his watch. It read 3:47 a.m.

Five minutes later, Desta led them down the staircase of the dormitory into an underground parking area. A row of low-wattage ceiling lights failed to penetrate the deep shadows of the dank parking garage. Desta seemed to relax as they crossed the parking area.

"I've borrowed the keys to one of the university's vans. We'll drive it to a nearby building where we'll trade vehicles. One of my colleagues has lent me his sedan. We'll drive it up near the trail we'll be following."

"Just let me know what you want me to do," Stuart said. He felt his stomach growl. Desta had provided a modest dinner the night before, consisting of some variety of marinated meat and a few steamed potatoes and carrots. His body had burned through the food in the few hours he slept. It was probably his last substantial meal before they began their hike.

Desta led them to a van that looked like it had been built for hobbits. They stashed their gear, climbed in, and Desta fired up the engine. It sounded like a robust go-kart. Desta smiled and shrugged when Stuart glanced at him. They rolled of the garage and crept along the university streets. The only other vehicles Stuart noticed were on adjacent streets. They drove for a mile or so, entering an area that seemed to be half residential, half university. Desta parked in front of a one-story, barrack style building adjacent to a larger structure.

"This is it. That brown Toyota," Desta pointed toward the windshield. "That's what we'll be driving. I don't think anyone followed us, but we need to be careful. Close the van door quietly. We'll transfer the packs and supplies from the van to the car." Stuart flashed an "okay" sign at Desta and got out of the van.

Once they loaded the trunk of the Toyota, Desta slunk out of the area until they reached a major four lane road that headed north where the traffic picked up significantly. Mostly trucks and a number of small blue taxis. It was nearly 4:30 a.m.

Desta remained quiet until they reached the main thoroughfare. "We'll be driving for several hours. It will depend upon traffic. It can be highly unpredictable. One never knows when construction will occur, or a washout. A single accident can stop the flow of vehicles for hours. Let's hope our early start will limit any delays."

Stuart peered into the back seat and noticed a small pack.

"Is that yours?" he asked Desta.

"What?"

"This bag," he said, pulling it up onto his lap.

"No … be careful."

Stuart found a zipper and pulled it open across the bag. He pried open the bag and peered in.

"What is it?"

Stuart pulled out four bananas.

"Ah!" Desta said, smiling for the first time since they'd risen. "Kala took care of us."

As Desta drove the dimly lit highway, Stuart found himself continually turning around and looking out the back window.

"Don't worry," Desta said, glancing Stuart. "No one is following us—yet. I've been watching."

Stuart stared at Desta for a beat, then back out the rear window. There was just enough traffic to be unnerving. It was nearly impossible to tell if anyone was following them. There were always cars and trucks within a few hundred yards. As it turned out, many pulled off to the side or made turns down intersecting streets. Still, Stuart was convinced they were leading a group of terrorists into the wilderness.

"Even if there was someone following us, it's unlikely you'd be able to tell."

"What do you mean?" Stuart asked.

"From what Bailey described, these are well-trained professionals. I don't know much about kidnapping or committing crimes, but I do know that intelligent people rarely do stupid things. Following us so closely that we could tell we were being followed would be stupid."

Stuart gave one final look back and then turned around.

"You see that truck? A block or so in front of us?" Desta said.

Stuart leaned forward and squinted. There were three sets of taillights in front of them. Two sets appeared to be smaller and likely from cars. The third were wide set and higher off the ground. "Yes, I think so."

"If there was someone with an eye on us, I would guess that they would be in that truck."

"In front of us? How can they follow from in front?"

Desta laughed. "Obviously, they aren't following, just watching. If we were to stop or turn, they would stop and double back. But don't worry. I don't believe that's the case." As soon as Desta stopped speaking, Stuart saw the truck ease off to the right side of the road. A few moments later they passed the truck. The driver of the truck was stepping from the cab as they drove by. He wore a grey coverall and carried a notepad. He didn't even glance at their car as they continued on.

"Furniture salvage. They pick up large discarded items. Like I told you," Desta said, reaching out and tapping Stuart's forearm, "we're safe. As long as we continue to be careful, we will safely reach our destination."

Stuart sighed and settled into his seat. As they headed further north into the outskirts of the city, the traffic volume, the development, and the lighting dissipated. He stole a glance at Desta, who was grinning and seemed to be enjoying the quiet drive. Stuart turned to the window and allowed the sparse passing building façades and landscape fronts to blur into a kaleidoscope of muted reds, yellows, and greys. The distance between street lamps grew, splashing puddles of dim light across a single lane. Fatigue suddenly overtook Stuart. His eyelids fluttered shut, despite his efforts to stay coherent. They eventually left the city limits and drove in complete darkness. The car hit a pothole, startling Stuart awake. As he was about to give in to sleep again, a flash caught the corner of his eye. A light had reflected from some part of the sideview mirror. He sat up and looked behind them. Far back, a set of headlights trailed behind them.

"Desta," he said. "Desta, there's someone behind us."

Desta investigated the rearview mirror, then brought his eyes forward, and then peered back at the mirror again.

"It's nothing. This is road gets busy."

"At 6:00 a.m.? There's nothing out here. No one was following us that closely when we left town."

Desta shrugged. "I've been watching. Vendors go in and out of Addis Ababa every day. The smaller towns along the highway depend upon the markets in the city. It's probably just a truck that caught up with us. I haven't been driving the speed limit. Or they may have turned onto the road after we passed."

"I don't remember any intersections or roads connecting with this one—not since we left town."

Desta grunted and shifted in his seat. Stuart turned around and watched the headlights for a while. They seemed to keep their distance. Perhaps Desta was right.

"I know traffic is light, but this is a major thoroughfare. We're going to encounter other vehicles, even at this hour."

Stuart snorted, still struggling to stay awake. He let his eyes fall shut and tried to imagine the plan Desta had briefly sketched out for him.

From what Stuart could gather, a team of six to eight porters were set to meet them at designated spots along one of the secondary hiking paths through the mountains. He and Desta would start in the southeastern portion of the range. The remaining team pursued set coordinates along the trail and, according to Desta, were already making headway into the mountains. The drive to the trailhead would take up to six hours. From there, they would hike another two to three hours, depending upon their energy levels and the weather. By the end of the second day, perhaps earlier, they should meet up with the entire team. Desta estimated another day or so of hiking until they reached the spot highlighted on Malcolm's crude map. Desta seemed unfamiliar with the area the map appeared to indicate, and he was somewhat negative about how long they might be searching in the vicinity. "There won't be a large well-lit sign announcing Fountain of Youth you know," he had quipped. Then, of course, they'd have another two- to three-day hike on the return.

The backpacks Desta had secured for them were far from contemporary. They were similar to WWII backpacks—bulky duffles jerry-rigged to ride high upon the back. Empty bota bags—suede wineskins fashioned to hold water, or, more often, liquor—were crammed into the sides of each pack. Desta had equipped them with locally made grain bars, several bags of dry Ethiopian trail mix, canteens, small blankets, and, to Stuart's relief, a small water purifier. The boots Stuart wore were property of the university and were well worn and within a size of what Stuart normally wore. Barring significant rainfall or extreme temperatures, Stuart felt they would stand up to a five- or six-day hike, although he really had no experience to justify his outlook.

Stuart's daydreams floated into real dreams as he faded into sleep. The mountains he imagined melded into the streets of Soho, trees and shrubs became people, boulders became cars and trucks. A moment later he was walking through the revolving doors of his office building, nodding to the security staff, and waiting for the elevator to arrive. The door opened and he felt a sudden jolt. His eyes shot open and he felt the car bouncing along the dirt shoulder of the road. Desta was hunched over the steering wheel, gripping it like an old, near-sighted woman, groaning.

"What the hell's happening?"

Desta turned to him, a panicked grimace plastered across his face. "Something's hit us."

The car lurched forward again and back toward the road. Stuart spun in his seat and looked out the rear window. The car's taillights reflected off the cloud of dust they'd left behind. Something was behind them, shrouded in the billowing dirt. Then the car filled with blinding light. It was a mammoth truck, its bright lights flooding the car's interior.

"Faster, Desta! Step on the gas!" he screamed. Desta looked back at him again and then down at his feet.

"I … I am. I—" The truck rammed them again, nearly sending the sedan into a spin. Somehow Desta fought the car back onto the road and regained traction. He stomped on the accelerator and began to pull away from the truck.

"Stay on the goddamn road, Desta, whatever you do. I'm not sure they can stay with as long as you keep it on the road." Desta nodded and leaned in closer to the steering wheel. Stuart turned back and watched the truck's headlights. They were keeping pace, within twenty yards behind the car, wavering in an attempt to pick up speed.

"Can we lose them out here?"

"I don't know," Desta said, eyes locked on the road. "Perhaps … perhaps if we keep this speed up, we'll attract a police car."

"Do they actually patrol out here?"

"We can only hope."

The interior of the car began to grow brighter again. Stuart turned and realized the truck was gaining ground. It began flashing its high beams.

"Oh, God, Desta. They're right behind us."

Desta lean forward, throwing what weight he had onto the gas pedal. Nothing seemed to change. Then the truck fell back again momentarily. Stuart relaxed for a second, then realized the truck was prepping for a charge. The bright high beams blinded him as the truck lunged into the rear of the sedan. The small car slid to the right, and then fishtailed back to the left, settling in the middle of the highway. The truck drifted to the left and fell back several car lengths, then launched another charge. Stuart braced himself as the hood of the truck struck the left rear bumper of the car. The car jumped to the right and threatened to spin. Stuart heard a shriek of metal and turned to look out his window just as the truck's right headlight reflected off the sideview mirror. A split second later, the other headlight spun above them and erupted into a frantic spin. The truck was flipping out of control. Their car began bucking. Stuart gripped the dash and watched as the headlights whirled, illuminating the rough underbrush and rocky left-hand shoulder. Desta glanced into the rearview mirror and exhaled. He decelerated and brought the car back into the proper lane. Stuart spun back and watched the truck's lights flail through the darkness and then stop abruptly.

"Drive!" he said. "Just keep going."

Desta grunted and increased their speed as they settled back onto the pavement. Stuart continued to watch out the rear window, waiting for an explosion or fire, but saw nothing.

"What the hell was that?" he yelled.

Desta sat back in the seat and closed his eyes briefly. "It's worse than I imagined."

"Do you think there are others?"

"I don't know. Probably. If so, I imagine they're not far behind. Given what happened to their friends, I don't know if they'll try to engage us or simply follow us until we stop."

"What about the team that's meeting us? Are they being followed, too?"

Desta shook his head. "Highly unlikely. I contacted them through a third party … agents I suppose you would call them, in Gondor, near the mountains. They're responsible for recruiting a trustworthy group."

Stuart gave a final glance behind them and then collapsed into his seat. "How much longer?"

"It's eight hundred kilometers between Addis Ababa and Gondor. Our destination is an hour south of the city limit of Gondor. Barring any more attacks, we'll arrive at the trailhead by midday. Go ahead. Sleep, if you can. I'll wake you in two hours and let you drive."

Desta drew in a deep breath and exhaled through pursed lips. Stuart shifted in his seat and gazed out his side window, watching the shadows flicker past and fuse until he fell asleep.

He dreamed of Rome, and Prima.

# TWENTY-THREE

Parnell woke in complete darkness, drenched in sweat. His stomach cramped as he squirmed. The straps continued to pin him to the gurney. His eyes were sticky, the lids catching as he blinked, and his tongue felt like a discarded sponge. Hunger followed the thirst and consciousness. He had no idea how long he'd been strapped down. He remembered little after Helmut had left. They'd probably drugged him again, not to gain information, but to simply keep him quiet.

He put aside the hunger pangs and his parched mouth and thought of Bailey and Stuart. The incentive to meet his captors' demands would have escalated. Bailey was operating with bad information. He and Stuart still assumed Helmut was being held captive as well. Perhaps, like he had, they assumed that Helmut had already been killed. Depending on what day it was, their deadline may have passed. It was impossible to guess the current stakes.

His flittering thoughts were interrupted when a narrow line of light broke across the room, beneath the door. He heard footsteps, more than one person, and muted voices. The light flickered with shadows. The voices continued—gruff whispers growing argumentative—then silence. The door opened and the overhead light stunned him.

"Mr. Sumner. Top of the morning. Isn't that what they say?"

Parnell craned his neck to see who had entered the room. His eyes swam in clouds of refracted color as his pupils adjusted to the brightness. There were two men again; neither was Helmut. The first, and presumably the one who spoke, was short and slender, dressed in a tight-fitting dark turtleneck and jeans. The second man was taller and bulkier, his bald head reflected the light of the naked bulb.

"You must be very thirsty, and famished, I would suppose," the short man said. He stopped at the side of the gurney and peered into Parnell's face. Now able to focus, Parnell recognized him as the man he and Bailey had met at the Hotel Hassler. "It's a shame. I don't think we remembered to bring anything, did we?" he asked, turning to the taller man. The big man grunted, laughed, and shook his head.

"I'm so forgetful sometimes. Surely you understand, don't you Parnell? Such as," he said, raising a finger to his lips and gazing away, "today. Today is a special day, isn't it? It's the day you tell us about Malcolm's little secret. Remember our agreement? You and your friend, Bailey, the big man, were going to meet with me again today and share the information I was seeking. The problem is, you're not going to make that meeting. It's …" he said, looking at his watch. "Well, all I can say is that I believe you may already be quite tardy."

"What about Bailey?" Parnell said. "Isn't he waiting for you? Unless you've done something with him as well, he'll be there. I'm positive."

Both men laughed, and the smaller one put a hand on Parnell's forehead. "I suppose there's still a chance he'll show, but I'm doubtful he'll deliver what we need."

Parnell paused. "Surely you realize that we have no … no idea if Malcolm found anything. If you knew him, you'd …"

"Oh, we knew him, Mr. Sumner. That's exactly why we're pushing so hard for the map. We know it exists. Thaddeus—you know Thaddeus, yes? Thaddeus followed Malcolm's movements very closely."

Parnell forced a laugh. "Face it. Malcolm was a braggart, like all of us. Like Thaddeus, too. It's what made him such a figure in our club. Helmut knows that. At least half of what he uttered was pure rubbish; the other half, at best, was highly inflated."

The smaller man motioned to his partner. The taller man walked around behind Parnell to the other side of the gurney and began loosening the straps.

"I'm willing to try a different tactic, Parnell. In exchange for a bit of comfort, I'd like to question you again. Does that seem like a fair arrangement?"

Parnell looked at the smaller man and then shifted his gaze to the larger man, who had paused while loosening the strap across his thighs. He knew there was nothing new he could share. Yes, he could, under duress, admit that Bailey and Stuart had found a map. He may have already told them so. But he couldn't recall the details of the map, the supposed location of the fountain, or what Bailey's and Stuart's plans were at this point. This group knew as much, if not more, than he did.

"I'm … willing to talk, civilly, if we can."

The man grinned and clasped Parnell's upper arm. "Of course! We are nothing if not civil. Isn't that correct, Karl?"

The ogre, Karl, chuckled and removed the strap. A moment later Parnell was freed.

"I must apologize, Mr. Sumner. I gave you a false name when we met in Rome, but now, since we're being *civil*, I'll properly introduce myself. I'm Eckhard. Eckhard Haff." Eckhard extended his hand to Parnell who hesitated, then took it. The small man tugged on Parnell's arm and helped him sit up. The room swam before Parnell's eyes. He feared the hunger and thirst would cause him to pass out.

Eckhard seemed to sense Parnell's state and said, "Karl, please bring Mr. Sumner a glass of water, and a few biscuits."

Parnell leaned forward and closed his eyes, breathing deeply. He didn't want to keel over and plant his head on the dingy cement floor. A tap on his back brought him back. Karl handed him a glass of ice water and stood by with an oddly dainty plate of madeleines. Parnell grabbed the glass from Karl and took a large gulp. The water was frigid—painfully cold, yet unfathomably quenching. He half choked but continued to drink.

Eckhard laughed and pulled up a chair. "Please be careful. We don't want you to drown. At least not yet."

Karl smiled and exchanged the glass for the plate. Parnell grabbed two butter cookies and crammed them into his mouth. The sugar felt as if it were directly absorbed into his bloodstream. Energy, or the illusion of it, pulsed through his veins. Out of the corner of his eye, he saw Karl move behind Eckhard into the shadows.

"Better?" Eckhard asked. Parnell swallowed and snatched another cookie. He nodded and chewed. "Very well, then. Let's skip the formalities, shall we? The map. That's why we're here. You know Malcolm insinuated he'd found the legendary fountain of youth. Given what we've learned from him before he … left us, and what little we've been able to garner from other sources, including the travels of your colleagues, we're certain that Malcolm located the fountain in Ethiopia. Would you say that's accurate?"

Parnell slowed his chewing and looked at Karl. This was certainly not the first time they had posed this question to him. He had little choice but to tell the truth. If he contradicted anything he'd shared when he'd been drugged, they would probably kill him out of spite. He cleared his throat and said, "Yes, Bailey has gone to Ethiopia. That's where we believe the map directed us."

Eckhard brought his clasped hands to his lips. Parnell spotted a slight grin. "Yes, good. As you can imagine, though, we're struggling with the next critical question. *Where* exactly in Ethiopia did he make this discovery? It's not a small country, Parnell. We need a bit more assistance to accomplish our goal."

Parnell shook his head. "I don't know. Honestly. I never saw the map. Bailey retrieved it in New York. I haven't seen him since he left Rome."

He was met with silence. Eckhard didn't move. "Forgive me if I have difficulty believing your answer. Helmut shared the depth of your friendship with Bailey Honeybourne. You are inseparable. On such a critical, life-threatening mission you expect me to believe that he told you it was in Ethiopia but didn't tell you where?"

"We agreed to limit the details, for precisely this reason. If either of us were in a position to ... to disclose what we found, it would protect Malcolm's discovery."

Eckhard laughed. "Bullshit, Parnell. Bailey has the map. He knows the location, and he's probably enroute, if not already there, right? If and when we capture him, he'll have what we need. You're proving to be worthless in this situation." He sat up and turned back to Karl. "I'm disappointed, Karl. This hasn't gone well." Karl nodded and walked to the small counter by the front wall. He opened a cabinet door and rummaged through various containers.

Parnell took a shuddering deep breath. Whatever Karl was searching for was not going to result in anything pleasant. He attempted to return to his training, although it had taken place four decades earlier. Ironically, for all of the stress and anguish he endured as a naïve, gung-ho agent, he'd never found himself in a situation that required him to apply the various counter-interrogatory tactics that had been etched into his psyche. In the early days, the easy way out had always been a cyanide pill, a short-lived and ultimately wasteful response to severe examination. Survival, while protecting state secrets, was nearly unattainable. The interrogators assumed their subjects would end up dead. The key was to learn as much as possible before that foregone conclusion materialized. Regardless, there had to be something he could access that would help him now.

Karl closed the cabinets and turned toward Eckhard. He held up a bulky, beaten wrench-like tool, the steel catching the light.

Parnell let out a brief laugh. "Gentlemen, please, before we let this get out of hand." He sat up and focused his energy on appearing to relax. "I know Thaddeus and Helmut have told you quite a bit about The Kilimanjaro Club. You know the type of members we attract. Dreamers, wealthy underachievers who buy their way into adventure, frustrated multi-millionaires. Most often we ride the coattails of the men and women, the scientists, the archeologists, historians, and the … the anthropologists who have lain the groundwork. I … I'm well aware that Malcolm had a very serious obsession with the legend of the fountain of youth." He paused a moment and tried to gauge his captors' reactions. Both men were attentive, yet composed.

"You have no idea how much he invested, originally, in pursuing the myth in Florida. Sadly, most of the money Malcolm spent was wasted on hoaxes and scams. People recognized his obsession immediately. He couldn't bloody hide it, couldn't control it. And they burrowed into him. While I can't prove it, I'm highly skeptical of the information Bailey and Stuart Mancini found in Stuart's apartment. I'm certain Malcolm believed it to be valuable, but I think it was all a part of his pipe dream. It's really," he said, laughing again. "It's really a lark. It's what we do. We search out the mythical when such opportunities present themselves, but those efforts are overshadowed by the routine safaris, summits, and ocean crossings that pad our résumés." He shrugged and grinned. Neither Karl nor Eckhard reacted.

"So," Eckhard said finally, sitting back in the chair and balancing it on the back legs, "you expect us to believe this is just an elaborate fantasy of Malcolm's, correct?"

Parnell tilted his head to one side and popped his bottom lip out.

Eckhard shook his head and sat forward. The chair struck the cement floor with a crack. "Awfully elaborate, don't you think? Your story might seem plausible were it not for Helmut. He's a member, too, Parnell. Remember? He knew Malcolm nearly as long as you and Bailey. He has close relationships with dozens of other members. Do you think he would take the steps he has if this were all some elaborate charade? Some fabricated dream?" Eckhard paused to give Parnell a chance to respond, then nodded to Karl. In what seemed like unnatural speed, Karl snatched Parnell's right arm, twisted it behind his back, and pinned Parnell to the gurney face down. Karl's knee was wedged between Parnell's legs and clamped on the edge of his scrotum. Karl yanked on the pinned arm until a brief but audible pop shot from his shoulder. Parnell barked and buckled.

"I honestly can't say whether I remember you being a pianist, or entertaining any similar hobby, Parnell, but I think any proficiency you've gained may suffer here shortly."

Parnell felt Karl pry his right hand open and slide the tool up against his hand.

"Go," Eckhard said. An immediate searing pain flashed up his spine. He heard the crunch almost as an echo. It was detached yet distinctly connected to the unnamable sensation that set his hand aflame. Karl pulled up on his arm again and squeezed his hand. Parnell clenched his eyes shut as consciousness mercifully drifted away. The relief was short-lived. A hand came down on his left cheek, cracking against his skull, and thrusting him back into reality.

"You'll not pass out on me, you lying bastard! Otherwise, you'll awaken with far fewer than the nine fingers you now have," Eckhard screamed into his ear. Nausea swept through Parnell's abdomen. He could feel blood soaking the back of his shirt. Karl kept his right arm pinned behind him and pulled his left arm into the same position. He heard himself groan, but the sound seemed to emanate from above the ceiling. Eckhard leaned into the side of his face again and said, "I have one question for you and your boyfriend, Mr. Bailey Honeybourne." Eckhard was slobbering against his ear while Karl continued to maneuver his left arm. "In what year were you born? Think about it before you answer, Parnell. Think hard about your answer."

Parnell clamped his eyes shut and bit into his tongue. Just before consciousness escaped him, he thought he heard Eckhard say "Go" again.

# CHAPTER

# TWENTY-FOUR

Late one evening, in the spring of 1927, Walter Hightower sat in the Weapons Room of the Nairobi Kilimanjaro Club smoking his pipe and nursing a wine goblet half filled with twenty-five-year-old Glenmorangie scotch. Jelly Roll Morton was alone on the stage in the adjacent atrium playing the piano while a handful of couples took in the music, some dancing slowly, in and out of rhythm with Jelly's improvisations. Hightower took a short puff of his pipe and glanced at his watch. It was 3:30 a.m. He smiled, thinking back to the highlights of the evening. It had been one of the most, if not *the* most, memorable celebrations the club had hosted.

Earlier that evening, Charles Lindbergh, Charlie Chaplin, and F. Scott Fitzgerald had attended Jelly Roll's raucous after-dinner set. Peppered throughout the crowd were stage actresses and dancers from Paris, dignitaries from Germany, Italy, and Spain, plus a contingency of U.S. Senators set to embark upon a ten-day safari. Hightower was pleased that he'd thought to invite Hector Chavez, the club's unofficial photographer, to capture the evening's events. There would be a number of unforgettable candid photos that would soon join the scores of other framed pictures that adorned nearly every wall in the club.

The Weapons Room had quickly become Hightower's favorite. Partly because the size, décor, and ambiance often contrasted the frantic pace of the rest of the club, but also because Fitzgerald, Black, and Enright avoided the room for the same reasons Hightower preferred it. He could escape, alone, or with a guest or two, without having to contend with his partners' bothersome complaints and worries.

The room was roughly twenty feet square and tucked into a distant corner of the subterranean structure. Originally, the area had been slated to be the club's wine cellar. It was adjacent to the main bar and far enough from the stage, noise, and heat to sustain a proper storage environment. Enright, the team's self-appointed oenologist, believed his handpicked selections for the cellar would safely age within the room. During construction, however, the local excavating team had happened upon a natural offshoot of the main cave directly behind the bar area. While it had been smaller than Enright's original vision, the catacomb-like cavern proved irresistible, and Hightower swept in and claimed the former cellar for himself.

As construction crews continued working around him, Hightower fretted over how to put his signature on the room. He was fortunate that his remaining partners, Fitzgerald and Black, were social butterflies whose passions gravitated toward the bar, seating, and performance areas. Fitzgerald, especially, saw the opportunity to create the perfect, Africanized speakeasy, without the security burdens of hiding alcohol and meticulously managing guests. Hightower knew there would be times when guests of the club, typically celebrities, various political leaders, artists, and others would seek a less public area. He saw this as an opportunity to create both a VIP lounge for his guests and a semi-private getaway for himself.

Hightower produced dozens of crudely sketched drawings in an attempt to translate his desires into actionable layouts and design schemes, but he became frustrated once he realized it was impossible for him to transfer his vision onto paper. On a desperate whim, he arranged to have one of his younger cousins, Sheila, who lived in Nice, flown to Nairobi for a month to assist with the build-out.

After ten minutes in the space, she turned to Hightower and said, "Christ, Walter, haven't you got scores of old spears, axes, and what-have-you stashed away in your attic in Hyde Park? They'd be perfect here!" She spread her arms out, framing the far wall. "You could call it, I don't know, the War Room, or the Weapon Room." His response had been to swallow her in a bear hug and launch her from the dirt floor.

When construction on the entire club was nearing completion, the price tag surpassed the three-hundred-thousand-dollar mark. In finishing the project, the Kenyan craftsman had created one of the most striking and innovative structures within the country. It would be years before reliable electricity would reach the hidden masterpiece, so the owners relied heavily upon candlelight, several huge fireplaces, and the cave's naturally regulated temperature to create a hospitable environment. Fitzgerald was a car enthusiast, so instead of relying upon the existing rutted trails, he led the construction of a graded gravel road leading to the club that could accommodate modern vehicles without destroying their fragile suspensions.

Enright spent thousands of dollars shipping one hundred cases of French and Italian wines to the club. The wine cavern's steady temperature of fifty-eight degrees Fahrenheit replicated the traditional environment the prized bottles had thrived in throughout Europe.

All four club founders were quite fond of the music that permeated similar lounges in the world's major cities, but it was Black who led the creation of a hall that would welcome and accentuate the jazz greats who were dominating the scene. The raised stage provided enough space to accommodate a multi-piece band, yet blended with the intimate nature of the main room to give each table the sense they were experiencing a private concert. At the rear of the hall, a colossal ebony bar, backed by a seventy-foot, granite framed mirror, counterbalanced the attention drawn by the stage.

Aside from Hightower's Weapons Room, two other semi-private rooms branched from the main structure. The first, nearest the stage, was a formal dining room. The second was a reception chamber, laid out and furnished like a typical sitting room from an English estate, and a near replica of a similar room in Black's grandmother's manor in Kent.

Several years after the club's inauguration, each distinct area within the club had established a reputation, a purpose, that fit the unique, evolving desires of its members. One consistency was Hightower's regular presence in the Weapons Room. His visits almost always began at the bar, near the club's entrance, where he could watch and greet the evening's arrivals. On some nights, frankly during entire weeks, the flow of members might never surpass twenty. On others, the crush of bodies created a manic, suffocating, exhilarating mass of raucous conversation, sensuality, and frivolity. Regardless of the night's party level, Hightower eventually migrated to the Weapons Room; pipe in one hand, scotch in the other.

On one particular evening, Hightower had decided he would have his driver take him home once he finished an early nightcap. He had family arriving the next afternoon—his sister's children—and he anticipated Jelly Roll would play two or three more songs before ending his set. With a couple of swallows remaining, Hightower turned as he heard someone enter the room. An imposing man in uniform, a British airman, stepped into the room and stopped. He regarded the myriad spears, darts, knives, and shields that crowded the fabric draped walls, oblivious to Hightower's presence. Hightower watched as the man drifted toward the nearest wall and stroked a brightly painted mask.

"That's a Bantu celebratory mask," Hightower said. The man spun, crouching in self-defense. Hightower laughed and straightened in his chair.

"I didn't mean to startle you, man. Just thought you might have an interest in its origins."

The airman slumped for a moment then returned to an erect, militaristic pose. He smiled and blushed, lowering his gaze to the parquet floor.

"My apologies, sir. I didn't see you. I was struck by these … these beautiful instruments."

"They are quite remarkable, aren't they? It's taken years to amass them."

The airman looked at Hightower, his mouth dropping open in astonishment. "These belong to *you*?"

"Yes, yes," Hightower said. He stood and took a drink of scotch. "Walter Hightower. Proprietor of sorts, collector of native weaponry, scotch and tobacco enthusiast." He cradled his glass in his left arm and reached out to shake the airman's hand.

"I'm afraid I'm but a mere servant of her majesty. Malcolm Buckley, Corporal."

"Pleasure to have you with us this evening. What brings you to our humble establishment?"

"Well, I'm the guest of one of the gentlemen who insists on wearing out the dance floor, Terrance Black. I believe his uncle is one of the owners of this club, a partner of yours, I presume."

Hightower smiled and guided Malcolm to one of the chairs near his. "Please, have a seat. By the looks of things," he said, nodding toward the main room, "your friend may be a while."

Malcolm smirked, nodded, and sat.

"Can I get you something to drink, Corporal Buckley?" Hightower asked, raising his goblet.

"No, thank you, sir. I've had my fill this evening, and frankly I'm exhausted. I'll bloody pass out if I have another."

Hightower laughed and said, "I understand, Corporal."

"Please, call me Malcolm."

"Not much for the military formality, are we?"

Malcolm shook his head. "On the contrary, I have tremendous respect for the guard. But when I'm in a civilian environment I prefer a more civilian way."

"Fair enough, Malcolm, fair enough, but you're in uniform."

Malcolm looked down at his jacket and blushed. "It's all I know. I'm afraid I travel with a limited wardrobe."

"I take it you're on assignment here in Kenya, or at least Africa?"

"A mission of sorts," Malcolm said, his voice a notch lower than before.

"Anything you care to discuss? Or is that out of bounds?"

"It's classified, Mr. Hightower. I can share the basics, though. I'm actually here in search of my brother. He disappeared during an operation last month. Took off from an airbase outside of Cairo and never arrived in Nairobi. That's probably more than I should share, but ..."

Hightower raised his pipe in acknowledgment. "I'm sorry to hear that. I wish you luck."

"Thank you, I'll need all the luck I can manage to garner. There's certainly a limited amount of support from ... other sources."

Hightower raised his eyebrows. "Is that so? The Queen's not pulling her weight, eh? Left you in a bit of a lurch?"

Malcolm sighed and nodded. "I should be careful. I don't have the full story. I begged for the opportunity to find him. My superiors in England reluctantly granted me permission. This *mission,* as it were, is a meager attempt to placate me. I'm due back at the base next week. It's doubtful I'll make any headway in that time."

The two men sat quietly, allowing Jelly Roll's improvisations to bridge the silence. Hightower drained the last of his scotch and plopped his goblet on the table beside his chair.

"It's a shame you're under such time and … bureaucratic constraints. I imagine we have a number of members who would be both interested and capable of helping you launch a more successful search."

Malcolm looked at Hightower, somewhat astonished. "Really? I thought this club was for wild game hunters … mountain climbers, and the like. Seems a bit of a stretch to get chaps like that interested in tracking down a missing airman."

"You'd be surprised. A number of our men are veterans. They have a fierce loyalty to those they served with."

"Mr. Hightower, did you serve?"

Hightower laughed and drew on his pipe. "Yes, yes, of course, but only for the bare minimum. I struggle with … authority. Not with having it, mind you, but with following others who attempt to use it over me. I'm sure Her Majesty's Armed Forces were delighted to see me discharged."

Malcolm smiled. "I understand more than you realize."

"Well, young Mr. Buckley, if you find yourself free of her majesty's service one day and wish to explore our odd little fraternity, I'd be happy to entertain your curiosity."

"Thank you. I doubt I'll ever have that opportunity, but if I do, I'll definitely take you up on the offer." Malcolm paused, then asked, "Do you mind … can I inquire as to how one becomes a member of this club?"

"The Kilimanjaro Club? Well, I'll be the first to admit that it's completely subjective. There are three other founders in addition to me. We unabashedly handpick those we want to be a part of the club. Hardly fair, I suppose. But we're a selfish lot."

Malcolm nodded. "What do you look for? What tilts one's hand?"

"Fair question. We aim to stay true to the foundation of the club. We created The Kilimanjaro Club to join with other men who had an insatiable fascination with adventure, exploration, and … frankly, social endeavors."

"Something like The Explorers Club, is it? Or the Royal Geographic Society?"

Hightower scowled and shook his head, groaning. "Certainly *not* like those … buffoons. Now, don't misunderstand, Malcolm. There are some fine men in those organizations, but they're infinitely stodgier and conceited, and all about blood, often, right? I … *we* are interested in attracting a diverse, exhilarating, competitive collection of men who have a fondness for spirits, excellent music, decent food, and the geographical challenges offered by Mother Nature. And really, you need to be a decent chap. One has to be tolerable over a good pint."

"I gather it's rather expensive to become a member. Terence's uncle—Mr. Black—is loaded …" Malcolm stopped himself and blushed a bit. "Forgive me, I mean he's been wildly successful, and he's not made a secret of it."

Hightower laughed and said, "No need to apologize. You're correct. Our initiation fees are considered high against just about any standard, and the ongoing dues are rather steep as well."

"I'd imagine the cost of upkeep for such a place in the middle of Africa can be expensive," Malcolm said, motioning to his surroundings.

"I would categorize it as inconvenient. Still, for us, seeing this dream come to fruition has been invaluable. It's given each of us a chance to live a dream, create something we couldn't imagine in our typical, past lives."

Malcolm grinned, then turned his attention back to the weapons hanging from the walls. Hightower wondered if Malcolm, as he had, was speculating how many had been used to kill other men, either in battle or in cold blood. What stories were behind the swords, the masks, the crudely carved knives and shivs? Hightower always imagined Zulu warriors stepping from the walls, materializing in the dense air, grasping their long-lost spears, and recalling the death brought by each weapon. Malcolm turned away and frowned.

"Something wrong?" Hightower asked.

"Um, no, sir. Just … just drifting off, you know. My brother …" he said. "My brother would have liked this room, this club."

"Would have? You sound like a man who's surrendered. Surely that can't be the case. I'd be terribly disappointed."

Malcolm cleared his throat. "No, I didn't mean it that way."

Hightower wasn't convinced. Given what little time he'd been given, and the expanse of land between Cairo and Nairobi, it was a nearly impossible task. The plane could have gone down, if that's what truly happened, anywhere in the expanding cone that spread from the Egyptian airbase. It might be months, years before any progress was made.

"Buckley!" a voice called from the entryway. "Come hither, you drunken rat bastard. It's bloody time we left this …" Malcolm's colleague lurched into view, gripping the heavy wood doorframe. He swayed, jacket unbuttoned. The girl was nowhere in sight.

Malcolm looked up at Hightower and shrugged. "My apologies for the behavior of the captain. He tends to struggle with grain alcohol. He's been drinking vodka tonics all evening."

"Damn right, Buckley. Hey," the captain said, weaving around, "where'd the little lassie run off to? Buckley! Did you see her? Is she hiding in here?" The captain stumbled into the room, arms out.

"Perhaps we should take our leave," Malcolm said to Hightower. He stood and extended a hand. Hightower drew on his pipe, stood, and shook Malcolm's hand.

"Colonel Buckley, you're always welcome at The Kilimanjaro Club. I do hope I'll see you again."

Malcolm nodded then looked over at the captain, who was now inspecting a mask from two inches away. Malcolm shook his head and thanked Hightower again.

Hightower watched Malcolm guide the captain out of the Weapons

Room, whispering something about finding the woman he'd been dancing with. Hightower doubted he would ever see Malcolm again.

# CHAPTER
# TWENTY-FIVE

Stuart had been driving for three hours when Desta awoke and pointed to an oncoming sign. In English, beneath a slew of swirling characters, the sign read Gondor, 5 kilometers. For the first time since taking over the wheel, Stuart felt the throbbing tension in his lower back release. He rotated his head, savoring the soft popping that accompanied the stretch. They had driven without incident since losing whoever it was that had attempted to run them off the road outside of the capital. Although Stuart was looking forward to getting out of the car, he was having serious second thoughts about the hike they would be facing.

"We'll take a road on the left ahead. Just about a kilometer or two," Desta said. The compact man stretched in his seat and yawned loudly. "You drive well," he added, smiling.

"Believe it or not, it's been a while. I rarely drive in the city … New York. About once a month I drive up to visit my mother outside of Boston. Sometimes I fly, sometimes I take the train, but the drive is relaxing."

"What does your mother do in Boston? Does she work?"

"Oh, no. She's … she's not well. She's in a home, a hospital, really. She has some significant memory issues."

"Ah, Alzheimer's, correct?"

"Not exactly, although it isn't much different."

"I'm sorry to learn that, Stuart. It must be difficult. My own parents lived to be quite old, in their nineties, both of them. Somehow they both escaped the typical diseases that plague the elderly. They both died in their sleep, less than two weeks apart. No apparent reason. Their bodies just … gave up." Desta sat up quickly and jabbed a finger across the dash. "There it is, just past those scrub bushes. Do you see it?"

Stuart nodded and began breaking. He glanced in the rearview mirror—as he had repeatedly since he'd begun driving—and there was no one in sight. Stuart eased the car onto the narrow dirt road. Severe ruts, several inches deep, scarred the road. The path meandered westward toward a gap in the nearby foothills. Pathetic, withered trees, clinging to a smattering of wilted, dark green and grey leaves, broke from the dark earth along each side of the road. Stuart noticed that the bark on the trees was heavily weathered, like mummy skin.

"How far is the trail?" Stuart asked. The condition of the path was deteriorating. The car bucked and jumped as he braked and fought against the wavering ruts.

"The trailhead is about four kilometers farther, I believe."

Stuart glanced down at the car's clock. It was approaching 12:30 in the afternoon. He felt anxious about heading into the mountains in broad daylight. If they were concerned with escaping anyone who might be eager to follow, they weren't being very stealthy.

"I realize it's a bit late," Stuart finally managed, "but do you still think this is a good idea? Our driving out in the open like this? It sure makes it easy for someone to follow."

Desta seemed to consider Stuart's questions then shook his head and frowned. "After what we experienced leaving Addis Ababa, I have to assume there are others, but we don't have the luxury of worrying about them. If they are following, they don't appear to be close behind." He emphasized his point by stretching his neck and looking out all of the windows. "Do you see anyone? I don't."

"Okay, but they might be more discreet than the earlier group."

"Perhaps. I believe we'll be in a more advantageous position once we begin hiking. It'll be more difficult for them to track us effectively, at least without making themselves known."

Stuart realized he wasn't going to get anywhere trying to argue with the man. Besides, it wasn't as if they could simply turn around and pretend they were heading deeper into Gondor. They'd made their move and were better served continuing forward.

The dirt road became more overgrown with scrub and indigenous ground cover as they headed west. The foliage seemed to stabilize the surrounding earth and flattened the aggravating ruts. As they approached the base of the foothills and began to squeeze into the entrance of the valley, Stuart noticed the terrain continued to evolve. The reds, greens, and blues that sprang from the rain- and wind-carved rock became more vibrant. The midday sun had erased many of the shadows and was reflected off the thriving plant life and windswept stone. The road climbed as the walls of the pass slunk inward. Stuart spied a crest several hundred yards away, in between two larger groups of trees.

"This area is … it's very beautiful, Desta. I guess I didn't expect such vivid colors."

"Yes, the Simien Mountains are well known for their beauty, at least in this part of Africa. Tourism is still limited throughout Ethiopia. There remain many concerns, especially from the west. They remember the famines of the eighties and nineties. They think of Rwanda, which is near Ethiopia. They hear about Hutus and Tutsis and assume everyone here is driven to slaughter their neighbors with machetes. While I can't say we're perfectly stable, I feel there's less to fear. The crime rate in Ethiopia remains low. The vast majority of Ethiopians have tremendous respect for human life, and not just refraining from killing one another. It's a respect for one another's differences and similarities. What they call in the U.S., diversity, correct?"

Stuart laughed, "Yes, I suppose you're right." All of Wall Street was aware of its whiteness and its maleness. Even though D'Artagnan employed fewer than fifty people, the firm made a sincere effort to achieve the same levels of operational excellence that the massive investment banks purported to pursue. Stuart remembered a series of workshops where organizational development professionals hammered home the idea that everyone was different, regardless of how they looked, where they were born, where they went to school. D'Artagnan, like many other firms in Manhattan, sought out women and people of color. The reality was that the number of diverse individuals looking for Wall Street jobs fell significantly short of the opportunities in competing firms. Those who pursued a career in investment banking were often scooped up by Bear Stearns and Goldman Sachs. Having that experience on a résumé was a ticket anywhere, especially for a successful diversity candidate. At the same time, he had to admit that the firm's hiring practices hardly set them up to attract candidates who were different from the existing population. Heath, and the firm's other founders, had all graduated from top five business schools, and their hiring practices were typically limited to pursuing the offspring of fellow alumni, sons, daughters, nephews, nieces, and neighbors of the people they lived near, played golf with, or met in social circles. It was no surprise that the vast majority, if not all, were white. They hired the people they knew, and those people were often just like them. Stuart knew it was lame to use the partners' network as an excuse for the firm's lack of diversity, but it was the sad truth. They didn't take the time, nor employ the appropriate resources, to attract the limited number of diversity candidates interested in their line of work.

They crested the small incline and entered a breathtaking valley. Stuart stopped the car, and his mouth fell open. Across the visible horizon was an expanse of rock, trees, and greenery that unfolded like a mesmerizing impressionist painting. He felt they'd driven through a portal to some other planet. The foliage had thickened exponentially. Humidity seemed to seep through the car windows, basking them in warmth.

"Holy shit," Stuart muttered, unable to maintain his surprise.

"Not quite my sentiments," Desta said, laughing, "but I certainly understand. I love this country."

Desta instructed Stuart to drive a few hundred yards ahead and park the car in a small clearing to their right. By the time they reached the trailhead and unloaded their gear, it was long past one in the afternoon.

"Okay, so where do we go from here? Are there supposed to be other members of our team meeting us here?"

Desta shook his head. "No, no. We'll rendezvous with them further down the trail. They will have entered the area through another pass, north of us. We'll meet the final part of our group another couple of kilometers down the trail."

"Where do we camp?"

"It'll depend upon our progress." Desta looked up at the surrounding mountains. "The sun will set over those mountains in about four hours. If we make good time, we'll reach both groups. If not, one certainly, and then the other in the morning. If we're up and moving early tomorrow, and if we don't run into any unforeseen delays, we should reach our destination tomorrow evening."

Stuart wrestled with his backpack, loosening the cumbersome straps, wriggling beneath the pack weight and unfamiliar pressure points. Along with the provisions Desta had pulled together, their packs were loaded with a variety of empty wineskin-like bags, a few WWII-era canteens, and several smaller plastic containers. All told, both men were hauling over forty pounds each. Desta, in the meantime, was strapped into his pack and watching, amused, as Stuart gyrated.

"It'll never be comfortable," he said to Stuart. Stuart glared back at him and pulled at the two straps near his shoulders again. He released the straps and stood; arms flayed to the side as if he were fighting to keep his balance.

"Is this right?" Stuart asked as the pack leaned precariously to his left. Desta shook his head, walked to Stuart, and pulled the straps until the pack sat evenly on Stuart's upper back.

"There," Desta said, stepping back. "That should suit you for the first kilometer or so. Then you'll begin complaining of blisters, or bug bites, or …"

"Let's just go. You can criticize me later, when I'm moaning around the campfire, or whatever we will set up when we decide to stop."

"Very well," Desta said, hoisting his pack up onto his back again. "We're off." He led Stuart down a well-worn path that splayed from between two broad banks of bushes and weaved downward from the clearing.

The first hour of their hike was uneventful and, to Stuart's surprise, enthralling. The natural beauty of the Simien Mountains continued to fascinate him. The contour of the trail shifted continuously, as did the variation in foliage, rock, and wildlife. Many of the animals they encountered were small rodents, along with a variety of birds, and what Stuart believed were lizards or salamanders. The altitude caused him to struggle initially, but he eventually found a groove and breathing pattern that suited his body's needs.

Desta stopped at an outcropping that overlooked a corner of the valley below. Several large boulders created a natural sitting area and opened to the mountains' beauty in the early afternoon sunlight. Desta pulled out a couple of water bottles and gestured for Stuart to do the same. Stuart hopped up on one of the smaller boulders, wrestled himself out of the backpack and found, surprisingly, a Snickers bar and a water bottle. His feet and calves throbbed and tingled as he relieved them from the weight.

"How are you feeling?" Desta said.

"Good. I'm still a little short of breath, especially when we're climbing, but I'm getting accustomed to the thinner air."

"Excellent. It doesn't get any easier. We have …" he said and paused, looking toward the path they would continue on, "another hour, probably two, before we meet up with the first group. Do you see that gap up ahead?" Desta pointed to another pass that split the perimeter of the mountains. "They should be coming through that pass. I've asked them to bring more food and water for us. Once we reach them, we'll hike for at least another hour, perhaps longer. It'll depend upon where the sun is and where we are on the trail."

"I'm assuming we shouldn't continue in the dark," Stuart said.

Desta nodded as he swallowed. "The danger is more often mis-stepping and injuring an ankle. Plus, you're not a seasoned trekker, Mr. Mancini. Bailey asked me to take care of you."

Stuart laughed and felt a blush coming on.

"Look!" Desta said. He pointed to a spot on the mountain up above them. At first Stuart saw nothing but rock and the scrub brush that peppered the mountainside. Then he saw movement. A pack of animals—monkeys it appeared—scampered down the craggy terrain. From a distance they looked like baboons. "Gelada. Last minute grazing before the sun begins to set."

As Stuart focused in on the troop, he estimated there were at least fifty monkeys traveling together.

"That's a huge group. Is that normal? Are they running from something?"

"No, I doubt it. I've seen packs of two, three hundred. I have friends who claim they've seen over five hundred together."

"Are they …"

"No, no. They typically keep to themselves. You don't want to interfere with their feeding, though. They can be feisty." Desta began packing his water and putting on his pack. "We should continue. The others are probably waiting for us."

Stuart finished his candy bar and took a last swig of water. He felt a tinge of pride as he managed to put his backpack on alone. At least it felt like it was situated correctly, and Desta didn't attempt to adjust it for him.

Their path continued to weave between flatter, open prairies and steep, rock-riddled spaces that were nearly impassable. At times the path disappeared, yet Desta forged on, climbing over sharply carved boulders and between substantial bushes and trees. They worked their way deeper into the valley, dropping a few hundred feet in altitude and decreasing the gap between the late afternoon sun and the surrounding mountain peaks.

Desta stopped at one point and waited for Stuart to catch up. He pointed to the hillside again. Less than fifty feet away stood a lone deer or gazelle. Large sickle-shaped horns protruded from the animal's bearded head. The horns reminded Stuart of American mountain goats except they were unfurled.

"That's an ibex. One of my favorite creatures. Something about them reminds me of old wise men," Desta whispered. "There aren't many in this area."

They watched the ibex for a moment longer, and then it bolted behind a cluster of rocks.

"You should know, too, that there are leopards and wolves in the mountains."

"Leopards and wolves? Do we have any way of protecting ourselves?"

"Yes," Desta said, patting his pack. "But we won't need it. They rarely attack humans. There's enough other wildlife in the mountains to keep them satisfied. I wanted you to know in case we see one."

A line of clouds materialized to the west, cloaking the late day sun and dropping the temperature several degrees. The layer of sweat that had coated his body evaporated and left Stuart chilled. His hiking boots were holding up well, but he could feel blisters threatening to form on the backs of his ankles and the balls of his feet. Desta had said they had an hour or more to walk until they met up with their colleagues. By Stuart's watch they'd surpassed the ninety-minute mark. Nearly an hour had passed since the last time he saw Desta check his map.

They climbed a slight incline that bent hard to the right, craning over a rocky overhang. Desta stopped as they rounded the curve and Stuart joined him.

"There," Desta said, pointing farther down the trail. Approximately half a mile away, Stuart saw a thin pillar of grey smoke rising into the still afternoon air. "I assume that's our welcoming crew."

Stuart was relieved that their camp was close but was concerned about the signaling of the smoke.

"Is that safe? The smoke? Are we attracting anyone?"

Desta paused, nodded his head slightly, and said, "I think the risk is small. The Simiens attract hikers and campers from across the globe. Besides, we'll need a fire this evening for cooking and heat. It's good that they have it started." He waved Stuart on, and they continued down the gradual decline that led toward the smoke.

Knowing that rest, food, and sleep—he hoped—weren't far, Stuart pushed forward during this last segment of the hike. Rockets of pain spiraled up his calves, exploding in his thighs and lower back. He knew he needed to preserve his drinking water, but his parched mouth sucked energy from him with each breath, each step. Desta's typical lead of five to ten yards stretched to twenty as they met a compact grouping of stunted trees. Desta turned to look for Stuart as he reached the outer edge of the trees and stopped.

"You've done well, Stuart. I realize it must be difficult, not being accustomed to this type of activity. Don't feel badly."

Stuart smiled and thanked Desta, then followed the indefatigable Ethiopian into the shadowed foliage. Stuart kept a close watch along the edges of the trail as they moved deeper into the trees. His emerging fear was that a snake or lizard—poisonous of course—would strike at him when he was crawling distance from camp. A moment later, Desta stopped. Stuart heard his gasp.

"What? What is it?"

"My God," was Desta's answer. Stuart could see they were on the verge of a clearing. He could smell the campfire smoke. As he approached Desta, he peered into the clearing but then noticed Desta's attention was directed on the trail in front of them. A yard beyond Desta's feet was a severed human forearm. Fresh blood coagulated with the dust of the trail. Stuart felt a rush of vertigo and stepped back awkwardly.

"What the hell …"

Desta's trance broke, and he crouched, scanning the area around the clearing. The campfire was fifty feet away, just off to their left, following the gradual arc of the trail. Stuart tried to tear his gaze from the limb, not yet comprehending what he'd seen. Desta stood upright and motioned for Stuart to stay put, then crept into the clearing. Stuart's eyes drifted across the meadow. He began to identify bodies, packs, and clothing scattered throughout the camp. His stomach cramped as their reality hit him. Then he heard a moan, then another, and he sprinted past Desta.

# CHAPTER

# TWENTY-SIX

Bailey and Rupert arranged to meet for breakfast at Ristorante Cipresso, a block and a half south of the piazza, early the next morning. A steady rush of Roman commuters scurried through the streets and created a sufficient buffer for their conversation. Bailey smothered Rupert in a hug as the younger man arrived at the table. He met Bailey's broad smile with a tight grin, apparently repressing the delight he felt in seeing his father. Bailey clapped Rupert on the back and grabbed him by the shoulders before releasing him to sit.

They ordered coffee and a basket of breakfast rolls, taking a moment to appreciate their reunion and absorb the activity around them.

Finally, Rupert said, "I have a feeling I should have opted for something stronger than coffee this morning. Perhaps a mimosa, or a vodka."

Bailey laughed and leaned over to clasp Rupert's forearm. He shook it playfully and sat back in his chair.

"I know I'm trying to make light of this ... conundrum you've concocted, father, but I'm still very, *very* worried. This situation is grim. These aren't bloody West End toughs you're dealing with. The research I've gathered is disturbing."

Bailey remained silent as the waiter delivered their coffee and rolls. He tended to his coffee and sipped it before glancing up at Rupert.

"Don't think I'm diminishing the severity of our situation, Rupert. I, too, am extremely concerned, and embarrassed. A good friend of mine is dead, another has been held captive for over a week, and now Parnell's life is at risk. And, mind you, I've dragged an innocent man into all of this, and now he's with a stranger in an unfamiliar wilderness. All for—"

"All for what? Have you decided if you can tell me what this is all about yet? You know, it might be helpful."

Bailey snorted and stirred his coffee again. "I know you don't believe me, but I don't see how it's relevant, Rupert. The fact is there's a radical group, likely based here in Italy, that's aggressively forcing our … *my* hand in sharing information I'm not prepared to share. It's blackmail. It's illegal, and it's dangerous."

"I've watched the video a dozen times. While it's nearly impossible to pinpoint where the captors were filmed, I was able to get one of our experts to review it late last night. She's relatively confident it was filmed in Italy. The tile layout behind Helmut is indicative of a style that was popular about fifty years ago in many Italian institutions. If you watch it again, you'll see what she pointed out. There's a thin decorative line of tile with a light blue design that runs about waist high across the wall. She said she's seen similar designs in France and Turkey, but they're not as common. When you add in your meeting here in Rome, it seems doubtful they would be operating from another country."

"Okay, so we've confirmed—"

"Ah! Not confirmed, simply narrowed down."

"Right," Bailey said, "So we're safe to assume that Helmut, and probably Parnell now, are being held in Italy. Quite possibly nearby."

Rupert shook his head. "Assumptions are dangerous. She didn't go beyond favoring Italy. They could be anywhere—Milan, Florence, Naples, some smaller town anywhere within a couple of hours from Rome. And none of that is a guarantee."

"Rupert, we can't canvas all of Italy, let alone Turkey or … or France. There's no time," Bailey said. He needed to remain calm. He didn't want to commandeer their efforts. "Do you have a recommendation? We're set for our meeting this evening. What can we expect to accomplish before that?"

Rupert avoided eye contact and seemed to watch the stream of people moving past the restaurant. He turned his focus to the pastries, selected a small, fruit-filled roll and looked back to the street. He took two small bites, chewing methodically, as if he were dining alone and daydreaming about what he might do for the remainder of the day.

"Rupert, I understand that you're angry, and that I've possibly put your position in jeopardy, but I need your help. I need your guidance."

Rupert exhaled and looked at the ground. "I'm not angry, and frankly, I've not given any thought to whether your actions or my involvement are threatening my job. Father, I …" His voice began to crack, and he covered his face in his hands. "I can't stand the thought of you putting yourself in danger at … at your age. Why now? You've proven so much to all of us. These men, they killed Malcolm Buckley. They've kidnapped, and likely tortured, perhaps even killed, two other men, including your closest friend. Good God, Father, you're over one hun—"

"Rupert!" Bailey barked. A few diners close to them glanced up at his outburst. Bailey leaned over and whispered, "Rupert, I've invited this situation. It's how I've always lived my life. It's not me that I worry about; it's my colleagues, and it's Stuart, a man I didn't know whom I've willingly thrust into jeopardy. You, of all people, should know that if my last days on this earth are spent swept up in some unbelievable adventure that I'd be perishing in all my glory. This is not about keeping me safe. Get a grip, man! Now, can you and your brethren help me, or do I need to find more capable resources?"

An unruly group of American tourists swarmed the front of the restaurant, drowning out the nearby conversation and street noise. A local tour guide waved a tiny American flag extended from a fiberglass rod. Bailey's frustration was interrupted by a middle-aged married couple in the group, bickering and attempting to pull the lens cover off their digital camera. The tour guide was yelping in broken English about the piazza they were facing. Rupert looked at his father for a moment and then erupted into laughter. Bailey sputtered and began laughing, too.

"Forgive me. I'm glad to be here, truly. We can help. I want to help."

"So, help."

Rupert launched into a description of the team of colleagues he'd gathered within the city over the past twenty-four hours. One agent was based in Rome, and the other two were forensic experts in London who were dissecting the original video and the remaining details Bailey had supplied. Rupert expected an update before midday and was cautiously optimistic about their chances of narrowing down a location.

"My meeting with the captors is at seven this evening. Do you think I'll need to keep that meeting? And if I do, what will I have to offer? How can I stall them?"

"It's too early. I know, I know. Your meeting is less than twelve hours away. Nothing seems early, but I believe you'll either be able to skip the meeting or … or meet your commitment with enough new information to put you in a position to barter."

"Barter? What will I possibly barter with? Parnell's life? Helmut?"

Rupert shook his head. "No, knowledge. If we're unable to locate their holding place before the meeting, you'll know enough to make them worried. That'll be your chip. It'll buy you enough time for us to finish the job."

"And what if they fail, this team of yours? Or what if they determine that they shot this video in … in … I don't know, Iceland. Then what?"

"Dad, let's try to remain rational. There's a ninety percent chance, probably higher, that they're in continental Europe. I'd wager greater than seventy-five percent that they're in Italy. We'll find them. Don't worry. I'll make it happen."

Bailey shook his head and tossed his napkin on the table. "Cocky," he said under his breath.

"I beg your pardon?"

Bailey glared at Rupert. His face warmed as he felt a surge of anger, then he chortled. "I remember … I remember feeling cocky like you. Like I could tackle anything. It felt good. It feels good, doesn't it? To feel invincible, unbeatable."

"I'm not being overconfident, Father. This is what I do. This is what I'm paid for, remember? And I'm not alone. I've got incredible resources behind me."

Bailey leaned across the table and grabbed his son's hand. "I trust you, Rupert. I know what you're capable of. I need you to have that same confidence in me. Do you understand? Now, tell me, how are we going to nail these bloody bastards?"

# CHAPTER

# TWENTY-SEVEN

Four men had made the trip into the Simien Mountains from the northern town of Mek'ele. Three were veterans of the Ethiopian National Defense Force. The fourth was a lifelong civilian who had previously worked in the service of one of the nation's more prominent organized crime leaders. According to Desta, the former gangster had turned snitch in the 1990s and was living undercover. His former specialty, Desta shared, was "extermination with common kitchen elements." It was this man's left arm the two men had encountered upon entering the ravaged camp.

The youngest of the veterans, a cartographer, was slumped behind a pod of jagged boulders on the far side of the open space. After overtaking Desta into the clearing, and a split second after he heard and felt the automatic gunfire spray through the dirt, Stuart had somersaulted behind the rock and landed next to the dead navigator. The gunfire stopped as he hit the ground. The crack from the firearm echoed across the surrounding cliffs and faded. Stuart had landed awkwardly on his right side but remained still as he listened. Once the echoes ceased, there was only silence.

Stuart focused on the dead man next to him and saw a pistol—something that looked like it belonged in a museum—lying near the man's head. Stuart slid lower and reached for the gun.

The pistol was cumbersome and splattered with gore. As Stuart hefted the weapon, he realized it was the first time he'd ever held a gun. He had no idea how to tell if it was loaded or if the safety was engaged.

To his left, near where he assumed Desta had hidden, he heard voices. A moment later gunfire erupted again. Stuart flattened himself against the dirt and inched around one of the boulders that shielded him. At first, he didn't spot any movement. The remnants of the campfire—a ring of rocks surrounded smoldering tree branches and larger chunks of wood—were several feet in front of him. Just beyond the fire, near an outcropping of stout bushes, he saw a body. As he focused, he could see the man was wounded, still breathing. A makeshift bandage fashioned from torn fabric wrapped the man's upper right arm. The man moved erratically, jerking, and reacting to sounds and movement both real and perhaps imagined. Stuart couldn't tell if the man was armed at first, but then he saw him drag a rifle from the nearby bushes. Stuart's gut, and nothing more, told him that this man was part of the party Desta had coordinated. He wasn't the enemy.

A voice called again, and Stuart recognized it as Desta's. The man Stuart had spotted reacted to the call but motioned a hand toward the ground as if he were trying to quiet Desta. The gunfire erupted again. Stuart watched the injured man dive for cover.

A shadow fell across the clearing as the sun dipped behind the ridge across the valley, cloaked by a thick bank of clouds. The blur of twilight smeared the edges of anything further than a dozen yards beyond the boulders shielding Stuart. In the silence, he raised the pistol to his face and examined the machined detail of the barrel, the trigger, and the butt. He wiped the bloody grip on a pant leg. His greatest fear was having to fire the weapon at another human being and, instead of hitting his target, watching the hammer kick back, in slow motion, into his forehead, the shattering echo of the shot splintering his eardrums. *God, let Desta do this*, he thought.

As he raised his head, a rapid staccato split the air. Instinctively, Stuart flattened out on the dirt and clamped his eyes shut. The gunfire continued for several eternal seconds. When the gunfire ceased, he waited for the reverb to complete its bounce off the surrounding canyon. As slowly as he could, he lifted his head from the ground and opened his eyes. The wounded man had pulled back into the shrubbery, crouching. He was still alive, but motionless, his attention glued to something in the distance.

Stuart eased forward, creeping around the edge of the furthest boulder, craning his neck to see what the man was staring at. As his line of sight passed into the eastern part of the clearing, he saw the edge of the forest he'd exited with Desta. He took a breath, absorbing the still landscape, when from his far left he noticed something stir. Suddenly, Desta sprang into the clearing, screaming and firing a massive machine gun. The weapon erupted, shattering the brief silence.

"No, no, no!" Stuart screamed. He leaped from behind the boulder and was suddenly on his feet, racing after the crazed man. Desta was blanketing the forest and hillside in bullets, aiming at everything. Desta skidded to a stop, feet splayed, the gun hugged to this right hip, the stock kicking wildly as he screamed and swung the barrel randomly across the horizon. A moment before Stuart reached him, the gun fell silent. Desta continued to scream, flinging the gun back and forth. Stuart tackled Desta and rolled toward the edge of the trees. They lay together, in clear view, only a foot or two from disappearing into the low shrubs on the perimeter.

As they lay together, both men nearing hyperventilation, the surrounding air was silent. The ricochet of the gun had faded as quickly as it had erupted. Stuart clenched Desta, his hands clamped onto his forearms, nearly suffocating the frail Ethiopian.

"Stop," Desta said between gasps. "Let me go, you fool. Release me."

Stuart relaxed his grip and rolled back onto the dirt. Neither man moved as they waited for a counterattack.

"Did you see who you were shooting at?" Stuart asked.

Desta shook his head, twisting his body up onto one elbow. "I thought they might be firing from just above the trees," he whispered.

"Do you know the man back there? The one you ran past?"

Desta glanced back. He wasn't visible from their position. The ground sloped upward a few feet between them and where the man was hiding. "I've met him before, but I can't remember his name. He's with us. We can trust him. Especially after we saved him."

They waited for what seemed like several minutes, remaining quiet. Nothing happened.

"Now what? Do you think they're still up there?"

"No," Desta said. "I believe there was only one left. I have a feeling he's dead. I can't tell you why, other than the silence. I just feel it."

Stuart sighed loudly and pulled his legs up into his body. "You're out of ammunition, right? Empty?"

Desta dug into his pocket and pulled out an eight-inch magazine. He waved it at Stuart with a grin.

"Can you reload? I …" Stuart started, his mind racing. The rush of adrenaline that racked his system was intoxicating. "I can sprint back to those boulders while you cover me. I think it's our best chance of seeing who might be left."

Desta paused, looking deeply into Stuart's eyes, then pried the empty magazine from the rifle and replaced it with the new one. "Go on three," Desta said. "One, two …"

Stuart jumped up and ran, eyes clenched shut for the first few yards, toward the boulders he'd originally hidden behind. He heard Desta's gun blasting behind him. Adrenaline rocketed through Stuart's legs as they pumped him forward. He was upon the rocks in an instant and launched himself over the boulders, landing beyond the corpse he'd encountered earlier. He rolled several times before slamming against a stunted palm tree. He curled into a ball and hid his head behind his fists. Gasping, he closed his eyes and tried to calm himself. Aside from the impact of his dive and the few scrapes that strung across his skin, he felt whole. No one had fired at him during his dash across the clearing.

"Stuart!" he heard Desta call. "Stuart, are you safe?"

"Yeah! Yes, I'm fine!" he called back. Stuart uncurled and breathed deeply. He rolled onto his back and stared up into the deepening twilight.

"Stuart," he heard from beside him. He opened his eyes and saw Desta standing over him, dangling the machine gun from his right hand. "I think we're safe."

Stuart sat up and looped his arms around his knees. He buried his face between his legs, sucking in a few more breaths.

"It's okay, Stuart. It's okay. Take your time. "

Stuart raised his head and blinked. "Let's check on the others. This man," he said, pointing at the body in front of him. "I think he's dead."

Desta turned and nodded. "There should have been four, if they went by our original plans. I'm not sure where the other two are."

Stuart struggled to his feet and staggered. He crouched—a new instinct—and then realized that no one was shooting at him.

"You check that side," Desta said, pointing toward the trailhead they'd emerged from across the clearing. "I'll check on the other one. I believe he's called Hakim." Desta turned and headed toward the row of bushes opposite the campfire.

Stuart crept forward, still leery of who might be watching, waiting for an opportune time to open fire again. Somewhat satisfied by the lack of retaliation, he hurried to the trailhead. As he reached the edge of the trail, he saw a foot protruding from a large bush off to his right. He stopped, feeling his heart race again, a swell of nausea rising in his belly. He stepped forward and saw the leg and torso protruding from the branches. Stuart grabbed the ankle. There was no response. He kneeled and pulled back the outer branches of the bush. He could now see the man's head, dangling from his shredded neck. Both man's arms had been severed from just above the elbow.

"Des …" he started to say, then realized there was nothing he could share that would matter.

Stuart and Desta sat near the makeshift fire pit, taking turns tending to a fledgling fire. The two remaining members of their party were wrapped in blankets, leaning against a log they had rolled from the woods. Hakim and Kaleb were both bordering on shock but hadn't sustained any significant wounds. Hakim was the man Stuart had seen from behind the boulders. The machete cut on his arm was superficial and had stopped bleeding. Kaleb had somehow fled the camp as the attack began and hid fifty yards down the slope from the campsite. Although both men were relatively fluent in English, they slid into their native tongue, Tigrinya, when speaking with Desta.

Hakim had witnessed most of the attack and appeared to be recovering from the shock. He explained that he and his three colleagues had arrived about three hours earlier. They had started a fire and were hoping Desta and Stuart would arrive in time to cook an evening meal.

As they had begun to pull their belongings from their packs, sniper fire rang out from high ground. Negasi, the man who had lost his arms, had dashed into the trees. That was the last any had seen of him. Manu, the man who died behind the boulders, was hard of hearing and didn't realize they were being fired upon until he was first hit in the shoulder. Hakim had already sought cover in the bushes when he saw Manu react to the initial shot. Manu had scrambled toward the rocks, hurdling the shortest one, but gunfire caught him in midair, shredding his back.

Desta had urged Stuart to search the grounds above the clearing with him to ensure they had eliminated their enemies, but Stuart resisted. Although he didn't mention it to Desta, seeing Manu and Negasi's dead bodies had shaken him. The last person he knew who had died had been his father, and he'd certainly not been allowed to see the body before the cremation. There had been something both artificial and conversely ultra-realistic about the dead men's bodies that stuck in his mind. Even though there was a chance they would stumble upon the bodies of the people who had tried to kill them—something that should have been comforting—Stuart dreaded the thought of encountering another corpse.

Hakim emerged from the blankets to help Desta cook dinner. He unwrapped a few ounces of raw meat and placed them on the cooking grate they'd brought. Desta worked on a pot of rice, adding a handful of spices he'd pulled from his backpack. Kaleb continued to sip from a canteen, still silent, stunned by the attack. He cleared his throat and began speaking in English.

"These men are monsters you seek," he said to Desta. "They came from nowhere, shooting, without warning. What if we had been common men simply living in the mountains?"

Desta stirred the pot and nodded. "They'll stop at nothing, that much is obvious. I feel terrible for bringing you into this. I didn't expect this level of aggression."

Kaleb raised a hand and waved at Desta. "Please don't misunderstand. I don't regret our decision to join you. You told us there would be a risk. I … I didn't expect this type of … enemy."

Hakim spoke up. "We expected to hide, to be invisible. We failed."

"What about the others?" Kaleb asked. "Do you think they've been targeted?"

Desta shrugged, checking the rice. "I have no way of knowing, Kaleb. They'll obviously be much deeper in the mountains when we reach our rendezvous point, but ... I don't know. A part of me hopes they've heard the gunfire. But these mountains can be tricky. They can cloak, absorb the echoes. We seem to be much more closely followed than I anticipated."

The four men sat in silence as Desta portioned the rice into small wooden bowls that Kaleb supplied. Hakim turned the meat with a stick he'd found.

"Mr. Desta," Kaleb said, peering into his rice bowl, "I told your agent, when he contacted me to come today, that I didn't need to know what we were seeking ... or protecting during this trip. At that time I was only interested in providing my services. He was clear. This would be dangerous. But now I need to know, especially now that two of our friends have died. What are we looking for? Why are we here?"

Desta picked up a stick lying near the fire pit and poked at the kindling beneath their pot.

"The treasure of Herodotus," he said quietly.

Kaleb leaned forward and turned his head. "Hero ... *Herodotus*? The ... the Greek? But ..."

"The fountain," Hakim said, reaching out to Kaleb. "He's talking about the fountain of youth, right? Isn't that the legend?"

Kaleb appeared shocked, then began laughing. "We're chasing a *legend*?" His laughter quickly faded and he jabbed a finger toward Desta. "We were told this was a dangerous job. *We* were warned, but I trusted that we were seeking something of value, something worthy. Instead ... instead you have caused the murder of two innocent men! Yes, you've done so, Desta!" Kaleb was standing now, illuminated by the flames, and pointing repeatedly at Desta. "You ... you are ... a disgrace! A fool! No, no, *I* am the fool. We're the fools, Hakim and I, and ... and Manu and Negasi. We are ..." He staggered backward and began to slump. Hakim stood to catch him, but he sat hard on the ground, a halo of dust rising around him.

Stuart stood and said, "Kaleb, you can't blame Desta for this. He's only following my instructions. My friends and I, we're the ones who asked him to lead us here. If you're angry, and I know you're angry, you need to be angry with me."

Kaleb looked up at Stuart with incredible pity. Hakim extended a hand to Kaleb, urging him to take it so he could help him up. Kaleb waved Hakim off and scampered to his feet.

Hakim turned to Stuart and said, "There's a bond of trust that the men of our country have. When one man tells another that he needs help, he doesn't ask why. He trusts the request is … worthy, important … noble, otherwise the request would never occur. This … this is what Desta asked of us, plus the others, I'm assuming, right, Desta?" Desta didn't respond but stared into Hakim's eyes. "I am right," Hakim continued. "Desta needed our help. We offered to do what we could. Not why. Not why me, why us. We said, 'Tell us when and where, and what to bring.' And now half of us are dead. Pointlessly murdered."

No one spoke for several minutes. Desta continued to poke at the fire. Stuart sat down and stared into the flames. Eventually, Stuart spoke again.

"You should be upset … angry. It seems a waste. But you need to know what's driven us to this point. My grandfather was murdered over this *legend*. Murdered by the people who have now kidnapped two of our friends. We don't know if either of them is alive. Neither of them has the information their captors are seeking. We have it," he said, pointing to himself and Desta. "They don't have it. Yes, they know where I am, that we're looking in Ethiopia now. But the exact location can't be gained from our friends. My grandfather refused give it to these monsters. So they killed him. Just like they killed your friends. This is not about a legend. I can't believe that it is. Something is out there. Something of value. Is it a true fountain of youth? I don't know. But these people we're fighting are convinced of its value, its powers. And something tells me that we can't allow them access to it. We must find it and stop them from doing the same. Now, you can either choose to help us or leave.

I understand if you want to go, but you need to know why Desta and I will continue."

Hakim and Kaleb looked at each other, neither saying anything. Finally, Hakim made a slight motion with his head. Kaleb nodded in response and turned to Stuart.

"We'll stay with you tonight. It's too dark, too dangerous for us to return now. In the morning, we'll make our decision."

"Thank you," Desta said, finally looking up from the fire. Stuart saw for the first time that tears were running down the man's gaunt cheeks.

# CHAPTER

# TWENTY-EIGHT

The throbbing was punctuated by a sharp, burning pinch that mirrored his pulse. The exhaustion, dehydration, and loss of blood left him wavering between consciousness and an elusive semi-comatose state. From what he could tell, he'd been wedged into a vacant mop closet. A hard plastic tray numbed his rear and his heels were squeezed against a narrow ledge. They had bound his ankles with either tape or synthetic cord. He couldn't tell. His feet tingled as the circulation sputtered through his calves. His wrists were cuffed behind him. Plastic riot cuffs, if he guessed right.

They've left me here to die, he thought. No food. No water. No light. Rudimentary first aid applied to his ravaged hands. Neither Eckhard nor Karl had spoken to him after the second amputation. They blindfolded him and bound him, knocking him into walls along the way, and dragged him into a hallway. There had been a brief elevator ride, then the arrival at the closet. That part was blurry. By then, the shock had kicked in and he was about to pass out. He hadn't been able to provide anything of value to them, and now he was worthless collateral damage. There was no need to keep any witnesses alive. Parnell would have made the same choice had he been in their shoes.

He assumed they were holed up in a vacant institutional building, perhaps a school or hospital. The walls of his initial holding room were standard white porcelain tile. Similar tile seemed to be on the walls of the closet. It was cool beneath his thinning hair and against the base of his neck. He was probably in a sub-basement—a hospital morgue perhaps—far enough underground and away from the main floors that if he managed to scream or, he imagined, decomposed, no one would take notice. Foul odors of mildew, organic decay, and general rot permeated the closet.

Over the past hour he'd begun to distance himself from the pain of the cramps and his wounds by focusing on Bailey and Stuart. He didn't believe in telepathy or the ability to project signals or emotions mentally, but he'd exhausted every other avenue. If there was some possibility that his brain waves, his deepest emotions, could escape this derelict building, he had to hope that they would reach someone.

Thinking of Bailey brought about memories of their exploits together. Together they routinely prioritized the social aspect of their expeditions over risk and potential danger. Despite their strategy, they occasionally found themselves in unexpected, treacherous predicaments. Those scares—often short lived and resolved more easily than many outsiders would have believed—made the post-conflict celebrations that much more festive. Years ago, Malcolm had introduced Parnell and Bailey to his favorite scotch, Glenmorangie, a luscious single malt whisky distilled in the Highlands of Scotland. Bailey had proclaimed it as their traditional celebratory libation ever since.

Confined in the dark, Parnell evoked the herbal-citrus aroma of that first sip. Long after the trip's adrenaline rush had cleansed his veins, the scotch swept away any lingering fears or apprehension that remained after their experience. It made them immortal.

Immortality. Horribly ironic that their quest for immortality had expedited his own death. Honestly, it was more embarrassing than ironic. He and Bailey had been charged to protect Malcolm's discovery, not hoard it. And by committing themselves to this quest, sadly his last, they had lost themselves in a challenge far greater than they would have ever imagined.

An early memory of Malcolm, perhaps of the first time he'd met the man, slipped into his mind. They were at the Nairobi club. Parnell and Bailey were in Kenya for a hunt with three Swiss members. It was to be their first African safari.

They'd settled at the bar early that evening, planning to dine before the activity in the club escalated. The safari was scheduled to depart at five the next morning. From what he could remember, there were only a few other members present at the club. Then a lone man had descended the large spiral staircase that emerged from the upper entry room. He was taller than average—a shade over six feet—wiry, fit, and apparently in his late thirties or early forties. Short cropped black hair, lightly speckled with grey, swirled over his narrow pate. The man scanned the lifeless room and frowned, then took a seat at the bar a few stools from where Parnell and Bailey sat. Parnell had watched the entire entrance while Bailey had been contemplating who in their party would get off the first kill the following day. The man seemed oblivious to Parnell and Bailey. Hector, the afternoon bartender, had nodded at the man and poured a rocks glass nearly full of scotch. Parnell caught the label: Glenmorangie.

After taking two carefully drawn sips, the man glanced over at Parnell and winked. "My day has just begun," he'd said, raising his glass to Parnell.

Parnell had taken the opportunity to introduce himself. "Parnell Sumner," he said, sliding from his stool. He approached the newcomer, extending a hand. The man set his glass down, pursed his lips, and shook Parnell's hand with a crushing grip. It subsided nearly as quickly as it had started.

"Malcolm Buckley, degenerate, scoundrel, roustabout, and just about any other derogatory name you can attach to a man."

Parnell laughed and leaned against the bar. "I'm afraid I'm nowhere near that colorful. Merely a member of MI6."

"Oh, ho!" Parnell's new acquaintance chirped, leaning back and nodding. "I'd better keep my distance from you then, officer."

Parnell was confused. "I'm sorry ..."

"Oh, it's nothing. Just having a laugh. I take it you're a member? One of our newer colleagues, eh?"

"Well, yes. My friend and fellow traveler here, Bailey Honeybourne," Parnell said, stepping back and gesturing toward Bailey. "We joined back in London at the start of the year. This is our first trip to Africa."

"Brilliant!" Malcolm said, raising his glass again. "Hats off to you and welcome to The Kilimanjaro Club."

Bailey hoisted his drink and joined the two men. He shook Malcolm's hand and introduced himself.

"Another member of the Queen's finest, I presume?" Malcolm asked.

"That's debatable, but yes. This old toad has to put up with me at work, as well."

Malcolm seemed a bit shocked and impressed. "Excellent. I've always envied the agents within your organization. Amazing work you do. I'm sure the stories are tremendous."

Bailey blushed and chuckled, failing to counter with a clever response.

"No need for modesty, Honeybourne ... Honeybourne? You know, your name is familiar," Malcolm said, raising a finger to his chin and gazing at the ceiling. "Have you been with the agency long?"

"Nearly fifteen years."

Malcolm smiled and nodded. "You may not remember, but I think you and I may have crossed paths early in your career with MI6."

Bailey squinted and shook his head. "I'm afraid I don't recall. Are you certain it was me?"

Malcolm laughed. "Certain? Of course not. I trust my memory less than I trust the Germans. Oddly enough, though, names tend to stick for me. I rarely connect them with the appropriate person, but the name itself is usually embedded somewhere up here," he said, jabbing a finger at his temple.

"By my estimate, you've been a member of the club for some time, is that correct?" Bailey asked.

Malcolm nodded, swallowing his scotch. "I stumbled upon the place years ago while I was in the military. It's suited my personality much better than the rigor and staunch of the armed forces. I love the hunt, the unknown lurking behind the next outcropping of trees, within the cave beyond, lying in the jungle." Malcolm's face shifted as he spoke. He gestured to paint what he described.

Parnell laughed nervously and said, "I must admit to having the same fascination, yet my fear is based upon the fact that I've never ventured much further in the wilderness than a casual stroll through the moors."

Malcolm continued to drink, nodding again. "It's not unusual. You recognize it in yourself first," he said, punching himself in the sternum. "It's an itch you have to scratch. It draws you here, or to India, or the Orient. Maybe Australia. Beautiful place, Australia. At any rate, it's who you are, right? You feel as if you have no choice."

Parnell turned to Bailey and nodded.

"What brings you to Nairobi now?" Bailey asked.

"I was on a dig in Egypt. Spent eight weeks in the middle of the desert. Bit of a wild goose chase, though. Lionel Farnsworth convinced me that one of the ancient pharaohs had established an oasis several miles south of Luxor. A little-known legend had led him to believe that this old man had stashed half his fortune in several modest stone huts in the middle of this wasteland. Turns out, the buildings existed, and Farnsworth uncovered dozens of urns, all in excellent condition and certainly of some value, but nothing remarkable. Nearly burned the skin off my neck and back helping him and his cronies burrow through endless mounds of sand."

"Sounds a bit disappointing," Parnell said.

Malcolm shrugged. "Yes, but one can never know, right? We did have a bit of excitement. There was a wandering group of locals—Bedouin, you know—who were none too happy with our little invasion. Thankfully, they were armed only with arrows and spears. Farnsworth can be a frustrating old bastard at times, but he's almost always accompanied by a hoard of well-armed henchmen. They finally chased the marauders off."

"Are all of your escapades so fruitful?" Bailey asked. Parnell shot him a glance, concerned about insulting Malcolm. Instead, Malcolm laughed.

"My goal is that they end up more memorable, and with me alive. No matter the value of those vases, I can't say losing two months of my life in that sandy hell was time well spent. It's certainly not a story I'll be sharing on a Friday night."

"Story Night, right?" Parnell said.

"Of course," Malcolm sputtered. "I don't know how they've been handling it up there in London, but Friday nights are reserved for establishing rank in the Nairobi club. It's heated, intense. There are better than two dozen highly competent, well-traveled scholars who commit themselves to one-upping the lad who spun the last greatest adventure."

"It appears London is a bit behind. There have been a number Friday nights when we haven't had a single member share a story."

Malcolm grimaced and finished his drink. "Pathetic, really." He waved a hand toward Bailey. "I'm not saying you're at fault. I blame Black. He's been responsible for the development of the London club since it opened. It's an embarrassment to hear that such a critical function of the club has faded to something inconsequential."

Bailey's face reddened, from either anger or embarrassment. "Mr. Buckley, I assure you there is nothing about the London club that should cause you or anyone embarrassment. Our members are on equal footing with those from any other club, including this one," he said, jabbing his index finger toward the ground.

"Pipe down, Barton."

"It's Bailey."

"Right, Bailey. No matter. Just pipe down. I'm not accusing you of anything. But I do believe it's important for our members, no matter where they hail from, to understand the full history of this organization and the reason we created it."

Bailey sucked in a deep breath and said, "My apologies, Mr. Buckley. I'm a prideful mug. I can get a bit defensive when pushed against a wall."

"We've felt honored since the initial invitation to represent the club, Malcolm," Parnell added. "We're both a bit in awe of being in the original location, preparing for our first true safari."

Malcolm nodded and regarded both men. "Right. Very good. I'm happy to hear it. You'll have to forgive me. I had high hopes for this Luxor endeavor and frankly haven't forgiven Farnsworth for letting me down. Not that it was his fault, but, like I said, I had high hopes."

"Tell us about the Friday Stories, Mr. Buckley. The tales you've witnessed here," Bailey offered, hoping a change of subject might calm the man as well as his own nerves.

"Ah," Malcolm said, smiling and looking down at the bar. "You know, originally they didn't occur on Friday nights alone. They happened whenever someone returned from an expedition. We had a smaller membership then, perhaps twenty or thirty. There were often more guests present at that time as well. Everyone from wives, mistresses, celebrities, dignitaries, the wealthy. They all ended up in the club at one time or another during a visit to Kenya. Once or twice a month someone would return, unscheduled of course, stumble back to the club, order up a stiff drink, and gather everyone here in the dining room to share his story.

"It became competitive quite rapidly. I credit Simon Hodges with triggering the official competition that ensued. He left Nairobi in September of 1928 with two gentlemen he'd served with in the armed forces and a dozen local men to explore the Congo River Basin. They expected to be gone six weeks, hunt a bit, take a few photographs, test themselves against the elements, you know. It was Simon's first venture into Africa, like the two of you. He wasn't looking for anything legendary, but his story became more than legend.

While Malcolm recounted the story, groups of other people, men mostly, began to file into the club. Some appeared to have just come in from a hunt, dusty, sun- and wind-burned, and still full of energy. Others were dressed more formally, ties and jackets. The few women who were accompanying the men wore what were best described as party dresses— flashy and flirty.

"Nine weeks after departing, Simon returned. Both of his colleagues were dead. Eight of the original twelve Kenyans returned with Simon, but three more died shortly thereafter. Although he concocted a brilliant tale to skirt the truth, frankly, the expedition had become lost about midway into the trek. Their camp was attacked by what Simon described as a 'sandstorm of lionesses.' That assault took the lives of his friends. The next day, the survivors unanimously elected to turn back. As horrible as the attack had been, the subsequent two weeks were hell on earth for Simon and his team. He spoke uninterrupted for nearly two hours that night, layering disaster upon disaster, unbelievable triumph upon triumph, leading to his miraculous return to Nairobi.

"The following evening, Enright, one of the founders, unearthed a gaudy, tarnished football cup that someone had shipped down to the club. He mounted it on a discarded piece of mahogany and dubbed it the Kilimanjaro Cup, presenting it to Simon for his incredible story of survival. From that point forward, the cup traveled to the explorer who experienced, and recounted, the most impressive adventure. As one might imagine, it was the recounting, the skill at storytelling, as much as the actual adventure, that determined the cup holder. Imagination and a convenient absence of witnesses often contributed to the best Friday Stories.

"Word of the club and our competition soon made it back to Britain. The Nairobi Kilimanjaro Club quickly became a destination for more men who had something to prove, something to brag about. Within a year or so we had so many members and adventurers, both professional and others purely amateur, vying for an opportunity to not only tell their story on a Friday evening, but to leech the cup from the poor sap who'd most recently won it."

Bailey and Parnell were silent for a while. Finally, Bailey said, "As you might imagine, events are somewhat tamer in London."

"I have no doubt," Malcolm said, poorly veiling his contempt.

"Out of curiosity, Malcolm, who currently holds the cup?"

"Today? It resides permanently up there," he said. He pointed to a large, glass shielded alcove situated ten feet above the floor on the wall behind the bar. A thin strip of parchment framed in brass beneath the glass had been carefully hand scripted. It read K. Edmunds.

"Kenneth Edmunds won the cup ... two months ago? Wonderful trip up the Nile. Unbelievable experiences. It's his second time to win it, you know."

"But the cup stays here?"

"Right. It's never left."

The bartender approached the group, carrying the bottle of scotch, and filled Malcolm's glass. Malcolm thanked the bartender and ordered two scotches for his new friends. They toasted Africa—Malcolm's suggestion—and drank in silence. In an adjacent room, a Victrola fired up a Benny Goodman record.

"I must admit, Malcolm, I'm very much looking forward to our safari this week, but I am afraid we'll not return with stories that are competitive for a Friday evening," Parnell said.

"One never knows, Mr. Sumner. One never knows." Parnell smiled, impressed that the man had remembered his surname.

"I suppose that's true," Bailey added. "It's a bit like our calls back on the job, right Parnell? What one believes will be a routine pub brawl turns into a hostage situation or a triple murder."

"Well, gentlemen, I do hope your expedition is successful and free of unnecessary drama. But I imagine that you'll find your way into a Friday Stories competition if you continue to frequent this location."

Parnell and Bailey exchanged a glance, and followed with sips of their scotch.

# CHAPTER

# TWENTY-NINE

Rupert guided the rented Mercedes toward the outskirts of La Pisana, a district west of central Rome, maneuvering through the late evening traffic, puffing through his nostrils, and ignoring his father's babbling. Over the past twelve hours, Rupert and his team had scoured the city and its surrounding boroughs hoping to locate the holding place of Helmut and, ideally, Parnell. Rupert had just received a phone call from an agent who'd been assigned three potential locations—two in La Pisana and one in Corviale. The site in Corviale had been razed two months earlier and remained an unsightly mound of concrete, wood, and rubbish. The first location in La Pisana was still standing but was amid renovation. From what the agent could discern, it was scheduled to reopen later in the year as a dormitory for a neighboring college. The last site, the location Rupert and Bailey were approaching, looked more than promising. It had been a multi-story mental hospital up until six months earlier. It had been vacant since closing and was relatively secure. The research analyst confirmed that the building continued three floors underground. A potentially ideal location for a group of rebels to operate without drawing attention from anyone above ground.

"Rupert, I understand we are in a—"

"Shut up, Father. I'm sorry, but just shut up. You know how these situations can change," Rupert said, darting into oncoming traffic to overtake a weaving city bus. "I'm not interested in arriving thirty seconds too late."

"Neither am I, Rupert. But I would like to arrive upright, rather than on a gurney."

Rupert glared at his father. He stepped on the accelerator and sped past a line of cars.

"We'll have two other agents meeting us at the hospital. There's a car park within two blocks as well as space on the street. We'll park nearby and go on foot."

"Don't you think they'll be watching for us? They'll have to be on guard with me missing the meeting." Bailey and Rupert had argued throughout the morning about whether Bailey should attend the evening's follow-up meeting. Rupert was convinced the captors would either attempt to kidnap his father, just as they had Parnell, and continue to gather people who might have some or all the information they sought. Bailey feared his absence from the meeting would guarantee Parnell's death. He assumed Helmut was already dead.

"I'm inclined to believe what Hennings shared with me. She's fairly certain she recognized one of the men in the first video of Helmut. If he's who she thinks he is, then there are fewer than eight or ten people at the hospital. My instinct tells me fewer. This faction is an obscure political sect hell-bent upon eternal life. It's an odd enough agenda that they don't attract the stereotypical sociopath."

Rupert finally slowed to within fifteen kilometers per hour of the posted speed limit and began to check the cross streets. They traveled a few more blocks then coasted through a right turn. Rupert cut the lights and allowed the car to roll to a stop, avoiding the brake and illuminating the lights.

"Remember, if anything, *anything*, out of the ordinary occurs, call the carabinieri. Once you get them moving, call me. The alley across from the hospital should be sufficiently dark to keep you hidden. And If I don't return in thirty minutes, call the carabinieri. Right?"

Bailey nodded.

"Look, I know you want to go in, Dad, but it doesn't make sense. We need to be quick and nimble. If we're in the right location, this will be a surgical attack. I can't be lugging you up and down staircases while dodging bullets, or worse."

"Just take care of Parnell, if you find him. He'd expect me to be there."

Rupert smirked. "He might, but given the choice, I think he would favor younger, more agile, Interpol agents to unfathomably old retired bobbies. Don't worry, Dad. I'll do everything I can to get both Helmut and Parnell out of that place safely."

"Assuming they're even in there …"

"Yes, yes, of course. This could be a dead end. We won't know until we get in. But I'm trying to be optimistic. It looks good. Are you ready?"

Bailey nodded again and yanked on his jacket lapels.

"Good, then as we discussed, get out and walk up to that alley," Rupert said, pointing to an opening on the opposite side of the street about thirty yards beyond them. "I'll wait about five minutes and then head to the rendezvous point behind the hospital. Look at your watch. Remember, after thirty minutes, call."

The rain that had fallen throughout the day had subsided after sundown. Bailey was relieved he wouldn't be fighting the elements along with his nerves. Rupert eased the car down the narrow street, lights still out, and disappeared around the next corner. The alleyway appeared uncluttered from the street. Bailey was anxious about encountering a contingency of homeless Italians or local hoodlums. As he reached the alley, he confirmed it was vacant. Nothing, not even a dumpster, obstructed the damp pavement that stretched to an adjacent street. The streetlamps at the far end of the alley reflected off the scattered puddles that had collected. Bailey paused at the mouth of the alley, glanced to his right and left and, not seeing anyone, lit into the shadows. He noted the time from the glow-in-the-dark hands of his wrist watch and leaned against the brick wall.

Bailey Honeybourne had learned to doubt his gut instinct just as frequently as he followed it. This particular night his instinct told him that Parnell and Helmut were caged somewhere within the bowels of the vacant mental hospital. Something about the thought of being trapped in a medical facility that had been left to rot made him momentarily queasy. Germs, disease, discarded bodily fluids, all left to their own devices after sanitation practices skittered out with the staff.

It had been two decades since Bailey had participated in anything remotely akin to a stakeout. As he realized this bit of trivia, he felt his pulse jump. He fumbled in his coat pockets absently, realizing he was missing a key element of his past stakeouts. A firearm. He carried nothing but a fragile pocket watch, an heirloom from his father that might raise a nasty welt if properly wielded, but no match for anything that qualified as a weapon.

To pass the time, he tried to imagine the steps Rupert and his fellow agents were taking. Assuming no one other than Parnell, Helmut, and a few guardians occupied the old building, there was little that would impede Rupert from entering the hospital. Once inside, however, the stakes would escalate. Any electricity in the building would be generator driven. They would have to maneuver through the dark, searching floor after floor, above and below ground, hoping to stumble upon the holding area or the captors.

Then there was the distinct possibility, regardless of Bailey's unreliable intuition, that his friends were being held in some completely different building, or worse, dead and discarded elsewhere. There was no guarantee they were even in Rome, or Italy for that matter. Yes, the existing evidence overwhelmingly pointed to Rome and its surrounding locales, but truly, how many white porcelain tiled empty medical facilities dotted the European continent? Dozens? It was a huge leap.

A car turned the nearby corner, following the same path Rupert had driven earlier. It appeared to be an older Fiat. One headlight glowed dim. Bailey felt his heart leap in his chest again as he pressed back into the shadows. Shortly after passing the alley, the car stopped. The headlights shut off but the car continued running. Bailey reached into his back pocket and pulled out his cell phone. The driver's door opened, and a man leaped from the car. Bailey stepped back deeper into the alley, unsure of his next move. The man sprinted to the curb on Bailey's side of the street and bolted past the alley. Bailey exhaled as he saw the man was carrying a large white bag. Delivery driver. A waft of garlic and olive oil followed the man down the sidewalk. Bailey put the cell phone back into his pocket and sighed.

He looked at his watch again and realized that only five minutes had passed.

# CHAPTER

# THIRTY

Rupert parked the rental car on the street two blocks east of the hospital. He waited several minutes before easing out of the passenger door and stepping onto the sidewalk. The street was eerily vacant.

The team had agreed to meet at the main loading dock at the rear of the building. Hennings had pulled the hospital's architectural plans from an Italian government archive and confirmed that the highest concentration of potential entrances was near the loading dock. Rupert carried a thirty-seven-piece professional lock-pick set. His colleagues, Anand and Lexi, would be armed and carrying additional tools. While they didn't expect the captors would leave the building unsecured, Rupert was wagering that their adversaries didn't have the time nor resources to install sophisticated locks and security in the vacant hospital.

As he was about to cross the street toward the building, a sedan swung around the far corner of the hospital, skidding slightly on the damp pavement, and accelerated toward the intersection. Rupert froze, and then he ducked behind a parked car. The sedan sped past, gaining speed, and drove through the red light at the next block. Rupert stood and watched the car continue down the street. He looked back toward the corner where the car had emerged, waiting to see if the police or another car had followed the sedan. After a few seconds, he was satisfied no one else was coming and continued to the rendezvous point.

The rear of the hospital was surprisingly free of debris and litter. Rupert had anticipated a heap of discarded medical supplies and equipment. Instead, he found a lone dumpster near the dock, The sparse street lighting kept the dock cloaked in shadow. A handful of lit windows from adjacent buildings provided a faint glow across the back of the hospital. At first, Rupert assumed he was ahead of Anand and Lexi. When he passed the dumpster, though, Anand emerged from the deeper shadows and nodded. Lexi followed. Both were dressed in black.

"What's our status?" Rupert asked.

"There are two doors on either side of the dock. Both are locked, but you should be able to pick them quickly," Anand said.

"The two garage doors are locked as well, but they'll be too loud. I think they would lead us to roughly the same place as the side doors," Lexi added.

Rupert motioned for them to step out of the light.

"Have you heard or seen anything? Any sign we're in the right location?"

"No," Lexi said. "If they're keeping these men in the basement, or a sub-basement, we wouldn't hear anything. These buildings are layered in brick, cement, and steel."

"I have night goggles for each of us," Anand said, reaching into a canvas backpack and pulling out the equipment. He handed Rupert and Lexi each a pair of goggles. "We can't risk flashlights. I'm sure they use interior light as little as possible, especially at night. Any sign of activity would draw the authorities."

Rupert pulled on the night goggles and activated the system. It took him a moment to adjust to the green cast of his surroundings. Anand and Lexi looked like zombie clones of their real-life selves. Subtle details of the back dock came into view. Steps leading to the higher level of the dock opened to a broad expanse of cement. Rupert could see the two doors Anand had mentioned, as well as the larger loading doors.

"Hennings said the layout of the basement and first sub-basement are nearly identical. The second sub-basement has fewer rooms and appears to be more mechanical. Any feeling on which floor they might favor?" Rupert asked.

"I don't think they'll be in a mechanical area," Lexi said, adjusting her goggles. "Too open and too many potential items that could be used against them. A regular office or lab-type room would be my guess, likely on the first underground level. What do you think, Anand?"

"It depends on what's actually in the second sub-basement. There may be a few isolated rooms, sanitation or engineering offices they could use as holding cells—perhaps a morgue, as well. We'll have to go methodically through each area."

"Then let's go," Rupert said. He pulled the lock-pick set from his back pocket and headed up the steps toward the nearest door.

It took less than sixty seconds for Rupert to bypass the door's lock. Months of inactivity left the hinges tight, and they squealed as he pushed the door open.

"Jesus," Lexi whispered. "Be careful."

Rupert nodded and waved her off. "We'll keep it open."

The night goggles picked up the reflected light from the building's tiled walls. The trio made their way into the main hallway, passing what Rupert assumed were shipping/receiving offices. Anand motioned for them to wait before heading further. He held a hand to his ear, encouraging his colleagues to listen. After a few moments, Rupert shook his head and pointed down the longer end of the hall.

Aside from a healthy legion of rats, there was no activity on the main floor. And, from what Rupert could see, nothing indicated any recent inhabitants. They congregated at the central stairwell and whispered about their next steps.

"I don't know, Rupert. It looks like this may be a dead end," Anand said.

Lexi nodded and added, "I expected some sign that someone had been here, but I haven't seen a thing, have you?"

Rupert shook his head. "They may not use this entrance. We've got to check out the lower levels. There's still a chance those men are here."

"Okay, I get that," Lexi said. "I just feel like this place is dead."

"Wait 'til we get to the morgue," Anand said, smiling. Rupert pushed at him and led them down the staircase.

While there didn't seem to be any indication the captors or their hostages had been in the area recently, Rupert realized he hadn't run through any cobwebs. It didn't necessarily mean anything. It was just a common occurrence in vacant buildings. Perhaps the old hospital was too empty even for spiders to find anything of value.

They reached the first sub-basement and stopped. The air was decidedly heavier and dank on this floor. The infrared light was scarce, diminishing the utility of their goggles. The main hallway on this floor was narrower than the first floor. Rupert, who rarely felt claustrophobic, couldn't shake the feeling of impending collapse around him.

"Should we split up?" Lexi asked.

"Why?" Anand said.

Lexi shrugged. "Cover ground faster. It's worse down here. I don't think we'll find what we're looking for."

"No," Rupert said. "Let's stay together. On the outside chance we do encounter someone, I don't want to leave anyone stranded. Remember, these maniacs have killed at least one innocent man already. A ninety-five-year-old man, at that."

Lexi agreed and Rupert led them down the hall. There was a junction several yards in front of them. Rupert stopped and pointed right, then continued forward.

"I don't think there's any reason to go this slow," Lexi said, pressing a hand on Rupert's back. They turned the corner and stopped.

At the end of the passage, seventy-five feet ahead, was a thin strip of light emanating from beneath a door.

# CHAPTER

# THIRTY-ONE

The first direct rays of sunlight hit the campsite just before seven o'clock the following morning. Stuart dozed, facing east, and woke the moment light spread across his forehead. He was wrapped in a thin blanket that felt like a flimsy woven sieve. He was surprised he'd been able to slip into unconsciousness given the temperature. He remembered hearing once that it was impossible to freeze to death in your sleep. If that was true, he was sure he had tested that theory.

From the looks of the ashen logs within the circle of stones, the flames had died out hours earlier. Stuart wedged an elbow beneath his ribcage and sat up. Desta, Hakim, and Kaleb were spaced around the stone ring, all asleep and draped in similar paper-thin blankets. Hakim was on his back, snoring. Kaleb's long, incredibly thin bare feet sprouted from the bottom of his frayed cotton slacks. Desta was curled in the fetal position, his head propped upon one of the smooth rocks surrounding the fire pit.

Stuart stood and attempted to stretch. His calves locked immediately, on the verge of a dual charley horse. He shrunk back down and took two deep breaths. The tension in his legs faded. Dehydration. The altitude and lack of water, piled on top of five-plus hours of mountainous hiking, had shredded his legs.

He dug a canteen from his backpack and gulped. The water was still frigid and gave him a sudden brain freeze, a feeling that sparked a memory of giant blue margaritas at a hole-in-the-wall Mexican restaurant near Battery Park. That world was light-years away now, buried on the other side of the wormhole that had sucked him from an ordinary reality into the living pages of *National Geographic*. Stuart found what looked like a candy bar and tore open the package. Consciousness and water had tripped his hunger into instant overdrive. He chomped the bar in half and gnawed it, bits of carob dropping from his lips. As the contents turned to the equivalent of sand and mud in his mouth, Stuart stopped chewing and grabbed the canteen.

"So, what do you think of our energy bars?" Stuart heard from behind him. He turned and saw Desta sitting up, wrapped in a blanket.

Stuart shook his head and forced himself to swallow. "Particle board? Drywall? Kitty litter?"

Desta laughed and leaned over. "They're high in fiber. Very nutritious. We're working on the flavor. It's somewhat secondary around here."

Their brief discussion roused Hakim and Kaleb, both of whom were now writhing on the dirt, yawning and groaning.

Desta watched the two men greet the day. Once Hakim made eye contact, he asked, "Have you made a decision? Are you continuing on with us?"

Hakim blinked and widened his eyes. He met Kaleb's stare, then turned to Desta. "We are going with you."

"Excellent!" Desta said, slapping his thighs. "You must understand that I do not, for one moment, take your allegiance for granted. I have no words," he added, then paused, "no words to express the grief I feel for the loss of your friends." He hesitated again as both men seemed to shrink at the reminder of the previous day's massacre. "So, let's keep moving. We have no idea who may be following up on yesterday's attack. Stuart and I fought off a truck loaded with these men just outside of Addis Ababa. Perhaps the group you encountered yesterday was all they had left. We can't count on it, though."

Hakim and Kaleb agreed and set to gathering their belongings and folding their blankets.

"I wish I had something more palatable for you, Stuart," Desta said as he fanned out a handful of similar bars.

"Don't worry," Stuart said. "I forced the one down. I'll be fine, but I wish we had some coffee."

Desta shrugged and put the bars back into his pack. "Next time."

The foursome finished packing and rejoined the trail, heading deeper into the canyon. Desta spent the first mile talking them through the remainder of the day. The second group of travelers was scheduled to meet them adjacent to the next pass that led inward from the eastern foothills. Stuart could see a portion of the cleft in the hill near the horizon. Desta estimated they'd reach the rendezvous point by mid-afternoon. Depending upon how everyone felt, they would either camp a second night near the meeting area or, if time and energy permitted, they would continue on to their destination. Doing so would mean hiking for close to two hours after sundown and into the night, an alternative neither Kaleb nor Hakim seemed enthusiastic about.

As the sun rose in the cloudless sky, the negligible breeze ceased. There was little humidity, but the ground seemed to reflect the intensifying heat of the sun. The temperature had rocketed since dawn. For the first time, Stuart worried about having enough water for the return trip. Sweat matted his shirt along the center of his back and saturated his brow. He watched the three Ethiopians trudge ahead of him. From what he could tell, none of them were perspiring.

The complexity of the landscape deepened as they dropped in altitude. A greater variety of plant life—spiky, mutant palm trees, and sagebrush-like bushes—grew in larger clumps along the jagged rock fissures lining their route. From time to time throughout the hike, Desta pulled the map from his pocket, paused the group as he surveyed the immediate area as well as the peaks surrounding the valley, then he'd fold the map, jam it back into his pocket, and wave them on. The man never spoke while he navigated. Hakim and Kaleb paid no attention to the elaborate pantomime, but Stuart couldn't take his eyes off of Desta. Surely there was something he could learn from watching him integrate into their surroundings, glance at the paper intermittently, then veer them onto a slightly different course, often through untrodden dirt, rock, and plant fields.

When the sun approached its peak, Desta guided his followers to a stone outcropping perched at the top of a steep decline. "Lunch," he announced, freeing himself from his backpack and foraging through its contents. Hakim and Kaleb had been silent most of the morning. Stuart heard them talking to one another at times, hushed and in their native language. The anger and betrayal they had exhibited the night before had somehow completely disappeared. If Desta asked them all to leap off the next cliff, he wouldn't have been surprised to see the two men bounce off the ledge without missing a step. Trust. Unwavering loyalty. Traits that were now rare among business leaders in the States. It was equally shocking and refreshing.

"How do you gauge our progress?" Stuart finally asked Desta. Stuart had pulled another sawdust bar from his pack and glared at it, looking for a way to delay the inevitable.

Desta glanced up at the sun then back to the ground. "We'll need to spend another night before we reach it." He shook his head, more a signal of disappointment to himself than anything else. "I was too optimistic. Even with good weather like this, our pace is too slow."

"That's probably my fault," Stuart said.

Desta shrugged and said, "Maybe." He seemed to be mulling Stuart's admission over in his mind. "I believe it has more to do with my hope that we could reach our goal and be out of the mountains within four days. I see now that my optimism was unfounded."

"What do you plan to do once we find this fountain, Desta?" Kaleb asked. His tone of voice hinged between contempt and sincerity. Desta looked up and seemed to register Kaleb's intent.

"I don't know. Not now. But I will. Once we arrive."

Kaleb regarded Desta for a few seconds then nodded, appearing to accept the man's nonanswer.

"The good news is we should make the next camp before sunset. We'll need adequate rest. Tomorrow will be … it will be a significant day. And then there will be the return trip. As you've noticed, we're heading deeper into this canyon. We'll be climbing on the way back. It's much slower. Much more difficult," he added, looking directly at Stuart.

Stuart refocused on his bar, peeling the paper way from the block of dust-colored meal and grain.

Their break lasted less than fifteen minutes. Desta checked everyone's food and water supplies, then launched the next leg of their descent. Although Desta seemed satisfied with their provisions, his earlier comment raised a concern for Stuart. If the trek out of the canyon was that much more difficult, wouldn't they need more food and water? Sure, all four men were being careful about rationing their provisions, but by Stuart's estimation they'd consumed close to half of their rations and hadn't reached the halfway point of their journey.

They hiked another quarter mile before the trees and surrounding shrubbery noticeably thickened. Stuart realized Desta was leading them into a veritable forest.

"Desta? Is this typical of the canyon? All of these trees? This forest?"

"Yes," he answered, not looking back at Stuart. "There's a fair amount of rain and moisture that concentrates in the deeper segments of the canyon. Plus, with the lower altitude, we find more varieties of foliage."

Stuart hadn't noticed anything remotely similar to a trail since early in the morning, but as the number of trees increased, he noticed Desta had guided them to a well-traveled path that plunged into the valley. The thickening canopy that obscured the brilliant sky dropped the temperature a few degrees. Conversely, Stuart felt the humidity climb in the denser woodlands.

The consistent descent made the day's journey a bit easier, but Stuart sensed fatigue testing his lower legs. Shin splints, an ailment he hadn't experienced since his high school cross-country days. Wildlife, vermin scattering as they happened upon marginal hiding places, momentarily broke the monotony of the hike and distracted him from the pain. Stuart's foremost concern was the condition of their meeting place. He dreaded the thought of their enemies already overtaking their new colleagues, effectively ending their endeavor. Desta, Hakim, and Kaleb appeared to share none of his concern. They continued forward, apparently confident that their nemesis and its minions had exhausted their resources.

As the afternoon stuttered forward, the sun faded toward the western mountain ridge. He hoped Desta would either recognize the location of their next meeting point, or determine that the troop needed to stop and rest. Each time they rounded a blind curve, Stuart yearned for an ideal clearing or a small welcoming party. After the sun fell behind a line of clouds, just above the mountainous horizon, he gave in.

"Desta," he asked finally. "How much longer today? When do we meet up with the next group?"

Desta grunted without turning toward Stuart.

"Really, how much longer?"

Desta groaned and said, "Less than thirty minutes. Be patient."

Stuart began to respond but glimpsed Hakim shooting him a disap-proving glare. He huffed and continued forward.

As it turned out, Desta's prediction came true. Within twenty minutes they arrived at another clearing, similar to the location where they'd spent the previous evening. This time, however, no one, neither dead nor alive, awaited them. Desta circled the area, kicking at the dirt absently with his hands on his hips. He looked to the darkening sky and scowled, then ordered the group to gather wood and stone to construct another fire pit.

"How many are we expecting?" Stuart finally asked.

Desta stopped unpacking his bag and looked off into the distance. "I asked for three more people to meet us, but I can't promise that's what we'll find. I expected them to be ahead of us and settling camp by this time, but I was obviously wrong. It's also possible that no one followed through. Let's just hope that if they did decide to meet us, that they haven't run into any trouble."

Hakim and Kaleb barely spoke as the foursome attempted to settle into camp. Stuart wasn't sure if their silence was the result of a renewed aggravation with their destination, a concern about the well-being of their future comrades, or simple fatigue.

"So, you said we'd reach our destination tomorrow if we spend an additional night in the mountains," Stuart said. "How early do you think we'll reach it tomorrow? Before midday? Early afternoon?"

Desta shook his head without looking up. "Before noon. As I said, if we had made better time, we could have pushed it."

Hakim and Stuart decided to search the area for additional firewood. Desta and Kaleb focused on rounding up a few more rocks to enclose their fire pit. Hakim surprised Stuart by striking up a conversation as they tramped along the edge of the forest.

"How do you find America? Is that where you were born?"

"It's my home. I used to think I would never live anywhere else, but

I've had a chance to see more of other countries in the past week or so than I imagined."

"But were you born there? Your accent. It's more like English … England, right?"

Stuart smiled. "Yes, I can't seem to shake it. My mother is English. She …" he began. Then the realization that life was continuing on without him in Manhattan hit him again, and in Massachusetts, at his mother's retirement home. It seemed like weeks since he last thought about, or checked in with, his office. He hadn't bothered to look at his cell phone since they left Addis Ababa. While he doubted cell coverage existed anywhere near their location, he had to admit that the financial world was the furthest thing from his mind. His mother, similarly, had slipped from his mind. That, he admitted, wasn't as rare. His thoughts of her were typically concentrated on the weekends or on a Thursday night before he traveled up to Boston to see her. He'd been experiencing a guilty, invigorating selfishness; one that didn't include his work, his boss, or his mother, one that had saturated his existence over the past … how many days? He honestly couldn't remember.

"I was born in the U.S. My mother and I spent a lot of time together. I grew up with her accent, listening to her, learning how to speak. It … it shaped me, I guess you could say."

Hakim nodded, seeming to understand, but said nothing. Stuart took this as a clue to ask about Hakim's background. They had stumbled into an area rich with fallen branches and sections of dead bushes. Both men filled their arms quickly.

"Do you live near the mountains?"

"Not too far. About twenty kilometers from the pass Kaleb and I entered through."

"Do you have family? A wife?"

Hakim shook his head and focused his attention on the ground.

"I'm sorry, I …" Stuart stared.

"No, no, you shouldn't apologize. There is a lot of loss in our country. Too much loss. I'm just like everyone else. I'm only twenty-eight years old. My parents have been dead for over ten years. I had six brothers and two sisters. Now I have only one brother remaining. I … I never married. But once," he said, turning to Stuart and smiling broadly, "I was so close. But …" he added, shrugging with an armload of kindling, "she didn't make it."

"I'm sorry, Hakim."

"Thank you, but again you have nothing to be sorry for. We lose those we love to so many different, senseless reasons. It could never be a stranger's fault. What of your family? Are you married?"

Stuart laughed. "Oh, no. I work. A lot. It's my life, I suppose. It's what I enjoy. It's what I'm good at. It's … comfortable."

"But certainly you have women to meet, right? In New York City? There are millions of beautiful women. All shapes, all sizes, all colors, right?"

Stuart laughed again. "Yes, yes, I suppose there are. I end up spending all of my time on other things."

"Work?" Hakim asked.

"Yes. Work," Stuart said. For the first time since he could remember, that answer was embarrassing, silly. Hakim hadn't been the first to ask him such questions. It happened during every business event or dinner he'd attended. The small talk, the excruciating part of any business interaction for Stuart, always gravitated quickly from the weather, or the Yankees, or the Giants, or the Rangers, to family. Stuart had eventually developed a twisted pleasure in watching his clients pause, uncomfortable, when he told them he wasn't married, wasn't seeing anyone special, had no children. They would look as if anticipating the punch line, then, when Stuart either just stared back at them or drove a fork back into his Cobb salad, they would often blush and look for something to occupy their hands. Now, his answers seemed not only cruel and unprofessional, but sad and empty.

"I think we've gathered enough," Hakim said. Stuart looked at him. Hakim had twigs and shards of log stacked up under his chin. Stuart agreed and they made their way back to camp, dropping a few sticks along the way.

When they arrived back at the campsite, Desta and Kaleb were sitting cross-legged on the ground near the circle of stones they had completed.

Stuart walked over to Desta and looked at the other men. "So, are we ready?" he asked.

"I'm concerned," Desta said, staring into the dirt.

"About the others?"

Desta nodded.

"There's nothing here that indicates they had the same encounter we did," Kaleb said.

"You mean to say there's no evidence in this very spot, but they are over an hour late, Kaleb. They could've been intercepted at any point along the trail. Perhaps never even started their journey."

Hakim stood, hands on his hips, and stared into the sky. The bank of clouds that had gathered near the setting sun thickened. Hakim scanned the sea of navy blue for a moment and said, "No vultures."

Desta sniffed and tossed a pebble into the fire pit. "I'm finished worrying for now. Let's finish setting up camp. Kaleb, there are matches in my backpack."

Stuart located his pack and fished out a package of crackers and what looked like beef jerky. He pulled out a canteen, grabbed his blanket, and returned to the fire pit. Kaleb and Hakim repositioned the firewood, then lit several smaller branches to act as kindling.

As smoke billowed from beneath the stack of sticks, a piercing bird-call came from somewhere above them. Desta froze and shushed the group. The call came again. This time Stuart could tell it came from their elevation or further up the slope from the clearing. Then Desta mimicked the call perfectly. Stuart gawked at him. Desta had his hands cupped over his mouth and was crouched as if to pounce. The call came back, twice, quickly this time. Desta made a single call and took a tentative step forward.

A second later something burst from the edge of the clearing toward Desta. At first Stuart thought it was a gazelle. It was tan, thin and fast; a blur of fur. Then Desta's high-pitched laugh split the air. Stuart stepped around the fire pit and saw Desta embracing the gazelle, except now he could see that it wasn't an animal, but another human being. A woman. Desta lifted her off the ground and spun her.

"Kaleb! Hakim! Stuart! Come! Come here," Desta yelled, setting the girl down and waving them forward. "This is my Aisha, my daughter!"

The three men converged upon Desta and the young woman. As Stuart stepped from the smoke and came closer, he was struck by her beauty. She was slightly taller than her father and solid, carved by sinewy muscle.

Desta stepped back and said, "But … why—"

"When I heard you needed help, I knew I had to come," Aisha said. "Besides, I've been bored."

"But I didn't intend for you—" Desta protested.

"It's okay, Father," Aisha said, placing a hand on his shoulder. "I need to be here with you."

Desta hugged Aisha, then made introductions. As he led her toward the firepit, Desta asked Aisha about the rest of her group.

"They're coming. I left them with our packs so I could come ahead. I'm sorry we're so late. We had a flat tire on the way to the mountains."

"I must tell you that I was so worried. Kaleb and Hakim, they were attacked at their camp yesterday." He paused, "Two men died."

Aisha retracted and raised a hand to her mouth. "Died? What? Who attacked them?"

"It's the same group that kidnapped Stuart's friends. I told you they were looking for something here in the mountains. They are obviously quite serious."

"But, Father, what is driving these people to kill? This is crazy!"

"You may not be pleased with the answer," Kaleb said, looking down.

"What is it? Why wouldn't I be pleased?"

Desta took Aisha's arm and rested his other hand on her shoulder. "They're after an old myth from this area. A legend."

"What legend? Is it something real?"

"I have to believe it is, Aisha. In fact, I know it is. I think Stuart believes so, too. Isn't that right?"

Stuart didn't move. He wasn't exactly sure how to respond. This was the first time Desta had made a definitive statement about the fountain. No one had asked him directly what his feelings were about this search. He was simply following directions.

"My grandfather was murdered, Aisha. Now two of my friends have been kidnapped. The group that's doing this is obsessed with something my grandfather kept hidden. A map. A map of this area."

Aisha stared at Stuart for a moment, then looked back at her father. "It can't be … the fountain? That silly fountain of youth?"

Desta looked down and nodded.

Aisha started to move and then halted. She took a deep breath and backed away from Desta. "Okay, okay. I understand, I suppose. I … I *am* having difficulty understanding why we're all out here risking out lives, but I … I will help. Father," she said, stepping back to him, "if you feel this is legitimate, then I'm with you."

Desta hugged Aisha but she was slow to return the gesture.

Shortly after, Aisha was joined by the two men she had traveled with,

Grima and Lebna. The new members of the group surprised Desta and his team by packing a lavish assortment of provisions. Both of Aisha's colleagues were young, towering athletic wonders, male versions of Aisha. The pack Lebna unloaded had towered over his head and weighed, from Stuart's estimate, over fifty pounds. Grima tossed off a similar pack that must have pushed forty pounds.

The remaining daylight disappeared behind the western ridge as the fire settled into a steady roar. Aisha took on the role of hostess, nearly skipping among the men, passing out trail mix, dried meats, and torn pieces of bread. None of the six spoke much while they ate, allowing the sharp snap of the fire to punctuate the calming silence. Stuart watched Desta and Aisha make sporadic eye contact. There was a cautious acknowledgement of trust mixed with concern and sincere doubt. Grima and Lebna hadn't reacted to the disclosure of their intended destination. They listened to Aisha's announcement, seemed to ponder the information, then went about unpacking. Stuart assumed that both men, being at least a decade younger than himself, Kaleb, and Hakim, saw the pursuit of a myth as just another challenge they could easily overcome—the naïve invincibility of the young.

Once the food had been consumed, Desta addressed the group to share the next day's journey. Aisha had shifted closer to her father as they ate and seemed more comfortable and accepting of their charge.

"While I'm extremely happy that Aisha and her friends arrived at this spot without encountering any hindrance, this lack of incident also has me worried."

"Desta, you've been worried since you arrived at camp last night," Kaleb said.

"And with good reason, Kaleb. You witnessed what happened. You survived. I can't believe that we won't see more from this group."

"We need to leave early. Before sunrise, if possible," Aisha added.

"Yes. And in order to ensure we do so, we need to keep a reliable watch. We have, I estimate, between seven and eight hours before we should plan to break camp. Seven hours of rest at most. I propose we take one-hour shifts. Minimize the amount of time any one of us has to be awake and aware, and maximize the amount of rest we get."

"How long do you think we'll have tomorrow? How far to the fountain?" Grima asked.

Desta sighed. "I can't be exact, but my hope is that it'll take us no more than five hours."

"Then what do we do?" Lebna asked. No one answered. "Is there a plan? How long will we need to stay? Are we simply guarding the location?"

Stuart decided to speak. "Assuming we find this fountain, I believe we first need to drain as much of its … contents as possible, right, Desta? We have empty containers to use." Desta nodded, focused on the fire. "Once we've done so, then I assume we'll need to determine whether the site needs to be defended, destroyed, or … or …"

"Hidden," Desta added. The older man looked into the fire for a few seconds and then nodded. "It's difficult to say. We'll need to determine that this fountain is … is functional. We'll make that determination after we arrive."

"These people who are seeking the fountain. The madmen who are killing to find it. Don't we have an obligation to stop them no matter the cost? I understand that we may not be able to disable the fountain. But we can't allow it to fall into the wrong hands," Kaleb said.

The group nodded together but no one spoke.

"Stuart, you take the first shift. It'll be your choice who takes over for you, and so on for each of us. Agreed?"

They all agreed and then went about arranging their sleeping areas. Stuart watched them all, wondering if they would still be together twenty-four hours from now.

# CHAPTER

# THIRTY-TWO

Thirty-three minutes after Rupert dropped him off in the alley, Bailey dialed his son's cell phone number. The four minutes leading up to the end of that first half hour had been excruciating. An intermittent procession of cars, bicycles, taxis, and pedestrians, including several joggers, provided a maddening number of false alarms. Bailey knew, too, that he couldn't call exactly at the thirty-minute mark. Rupert, if he and his colleagues had been successful, would explode if Bailey called when they were on their way back to pick him up. So, he had to decide just how much time was appropriate. He settled on three minutes. While they had calibrated their watches within thirty seconds of one another, the extra couple minutes seemed to be a forgivable time frame.

Bailey listened to the phone ring once, twice, and three times without Rupert picking up, then he heard a distinct click. "You've reached the cellular phone of …"

"Damn," Bailey cursed. He ended the call and shoved the phone back into his pocket. He resumed tapping his foot and breathing loudly. He counted to a hundred, slowly, then pulled his phone back out and punched redial. Rupert's voicemail message picked up again.

"Bloody Christ!" Bailey yelled and stomped out of the alley and onto the sidewalk. Bailey had promised to call the carabinieri if he didn't hear from Rupert within a half hour, but he wasn't prepared to involve the authorities just yet. He could get to the abandoned hospital within five minutes and detect if something significant had gone awry.

Bailey took several steps down the sidewalk and saw the hospital across the street at the next block. Streetlamps cast a pale glow across the stone façade, reflecting off the darkened windows, but no light came from within the building. He crossed the street before reaching the corner and slowed to a casual walk as he approached the crosswalk leading to the main entrance of the hospital. Ahead on his left, three quarters of a block away, he spotted a wide alleyway. He knew it must be a service entrance or loading dock.

The alley was dark and vacant. He stepped into the passageway, careful not to make noise or cast an unnecessary shadow. The loading area appeared to be roughly fifty feet ahead. He assumed this was the location Rupert and the other agents chose to enter. As he reached the end of the alley, the murky loading dock opened up before him. Random streaks of light reflected off segments of the building and concrete but were little help in distinguishing details. The large bay doors came into view first, then the standard doors adjacent to the dock. He followed the drive to the set of steps on the right side of the dock and followed them toward the doors. The first door across from the steps was locked. He crossed in front of the bay doors and found the second side door. He turned the handle and it opened, squeaking.

As he inched the door open, he suddenly regretted his decision to follow Rupert. While he'd reached the hospital in under five minutes, he was alone and, frankly, much too old to attempt to rescue a team of highly trained government agents. Even during his heyday, a rescue or intervention such as this, especially solo, was beyond his typical means.

He'd been trained. He'd trained others. He'd delivered executive briefings on similar incidents, but the truth was, he was just that—a mentor, a coach, a liaison, not an executor.

Bailey fingered the phone in his pocket and considered stepping back into the alleyway and calling the carabinieri. If the team was truly in trouble, the authorities might arrive in time to intervene. He closed his eyes and attempted to meditate on the decision. His brief moment of peace was shattered by a muffled scream and several muted gunshots. On instinct, Bailey shoved the door open, and ran into the building, blind.

The darkness in the hall was nearly absolute. Bailey thrust his right hand out in front of him as he edged forward, blinking, willing his eyes to adjust. Another burst of automatic gunfire and yelling shattered his focus. A step later his hands collided with the cold tile and he skidded to a stop just before headbutting the wall. He peered to his right, where the shots and screams had emanated from, and saw the wide institutional hallway unfold into shadow. Doors alternated down the hall. A hidden, muted source of light defined only minimal detail.

"Rupert!" he called out. The moment the name jumped from his lips he regretted the impulse. A door halfway down the hall opened and a silhouette stumbled across his path. Bailey crouched and inched forward.

"Who …"

"Bailey?" he heard a familiar voice call. A German accent.

"Helmut? Good God, man, is that you?" Bailey said, rushing forward. Helmut was crumpled on the floor, wedged against the wall.

"Yes, yes. Thank God you're here."

Bailey found Helmut and knelt beside him. "Are you injured? Did they hurt you?"

Helmut groaned. Bailey grabbed Helmut's shoulders and squared them against the wall. The man's left shoulder was drenched.

"You're bleeding. You've been shot. Who was it?"

Helmut coughed and attempted to steady himself, pushing against the floor.

"I think … I think I'll be okay. They hit the fleshy part of my shoulder. Hurts like bloody hell, but …"

"Just take it easy, old man," Bailey said. More voices, shouting, echoed down the hall again. Two shots rang out. Helmut struggled to stabilize his upper body, flinching. He jammed a hand into his jacket pocket.

"It's okay, Helmut. Can you stand? We've got to get outside."

Helmut seemed to ignore Bailey, peering back down the hall toward the source of the conflict. He shook his head and then yanked his hand out of his pocket, jamming something cold into Bailey's throat. His left arm was pinned to the floor.

Bailey jerked back, falling onto his rear. In an instant, Helmut was upon him, forcing the object deeper into his Adam's apple. At first, Bailey thought it was a knife and he waited for the flood of blood to drown him. Then he realized the pain was intense pressure. Helmut had a gun barrel rammed against his throat.

"Helmut! Get off, get off!" He grabbed Helmut's elbow with his free arm.

"Shut up or I'll pull the trigger," Helmut hissed, pushing harder on Bailey's throat.

As Bailey gulped for air, he tried to piece together what was happening. Was Helmut confused? After days of abuse and torture, was he delirious, simply reacting to an opportunity to escape?

"Helmut, God damn it! It's me, Bailey Honeybourne. We're here to help you." Helmut eased off the pressure but continued looking down the hall. The yelling and gunshots were uninterrupted now, echoing through the ceramic halls.

Helmut looked back into Bailey's eyes. "I know who you are, you old bastard. Now shut up and listen to me."

300

The gun barrel plunged deeper into his throat again and Bailey choked. Helmut leaned forward, his nose bouncing off of Bailey's. Bailey could smell wine on the German's breath.

"You're going to stand up once I move off you. Then you'll go through the door behind me. Do you understand? If you make one noise, one quick movement, the gun goes off. Okay? I'll blow your thieving brains all over the wall."

Bailey nodded and suddenly understood. Helmut had set a trap, and they had fallen into it without a hitch. Helmut had never been kidnapped. His mind leaped to Parnell. If Helmut had killed Malcolm and was apparently prepared to kill him, then what had happened to Parnell? His partner only knew that he and Stuart were headed to Ethiopia. Parnell had never seen the map. He had no other valuable information to give to Helmut.

Helmut eased his weight off Bailey and pulled him upright by the lapels. Bailey struggled to gain his balance without alarming Helmut. Meanwhile, the firing and screaming came closer.

"Get up," Helmut hollered. He yanked Bailey again and the old man landed hard on his knees.

"Go! Go! Go! Go!" Bailey heard from the far end of the hallway. He turned as Helmut was jerking him onto his feet. A massive shape rolled into the hallway and headed their way. It took a second, but Bailey recognized Rupert's voice just as the figure halted.

"Take another step, Honeybourne, and the old man dies," Helmut said.

Bailey heard Rupert's colleagues whispering. "Shut up!" he heard Rupert say.

"Helmut, just let him go. This is it. It's over. You're all alone. Your friends are dead. Just let him go," Rupert said.

Helmut laughed. It sounded sick and scared, alien. He tugged Bailey in front of him and slid the barrel to Bailey's temple. Helmut pulled them back a step.

"I'm going to walk out of here, and you're not going to move. One flinch and I'll fire. I don't care."

Helmut pulled them back a few more steps until they were even with the junction to the main hall.

A shot rang out and Bailey collapsed. An intense burning pain, like a smelted iron spear skewering his brain, flashed across his vision. Then there was silence, and he was in a dream. A quiet, empty meadow. Alone.

# THIRTY-THREE

The chill of the night air brought him back to full consciousness. That and the sense of floating, which he soon realized was because Anand and Lexi were carrying him onto the loading dock of the hospital. He identified a figure in front of them sprinting across the darkened concrete. A moment later, as they stopped at the top of the steps, he heard a crash in the alley.

"Sit down, Mr. Honeybourne," Anand said, urging his shoulder down. Reality came rushing back at him. Rupert was chasing Helmut. The crash must have been their collision. Rupert would have caught the older man within twenty yards.

"No, no. Let me go," Bailey said, trying to pull from Anand's grip.

"We can't," Lexi said. "You're hurt. An ambulance is coming. Please, sit and let Rupert handle it. Anand," Lexi said, looking up at her partner, "make sure he's taken care of that last man. I'll go inside for Parnell."

"Parnell's inside? Is he … is he okay?" Bailey asked. Lexi caught Bailey as he attempted to stand and eased him back onto the cement.

"He's alive, Mr. Honeybourne. That's all we know. Now sit down and let me bring him out here."

Bailey fought for a moment and then relented. He swung his legs over the edge of the dock and turned to watch Lexi disappear through the rear door.

Anand jogged back to Bailey, switching his cell phone off. "Don't move. I know Lexi told you the same thing. I'm going after Rupert."

Before Bailey could respond, Anand dashed into the alley, erupting into huge strides.

By the time Anand was out of sight, Lexi had pushed through the door. Bailey could see a body draped over her shoulder as she shuffled onto the dock. Bailey rolled up onto his feet and fought to stand as Lexi swung around toward him.

"Look out," she said, easing Parnell down onto the pavement. "Can you stand?" she asked Parnell. Lexi had him suspended under his arms. Bailey rushed around behind Parnell and grasped him around the waist. "Careful," Lexi warned, steadying Parnell. "He's barely conscious. I'm not sure what he's been through. He's covered in dried blood and what little he's said hasn't made sense."

"Let's sit him down," Bailey said. He stepped back and, with Lexi maintaining a hold on Parnell's upper body, eased him into a sitting position on the dock. Bailey sat with him, keeping an arm around Parnell's shoulders.

"Parnell. Parnell Sumner. We've medical help on the way. Can you hear me? Do you know where you are?" Lexi asked.

Parnell's eyes fluttered open, and he stared at his outstretched legs. He didn't appear to acknowledge either Bailey or Lexi. A mottled cone of light fell across Parnell's lap. His tattered clothes were matted with splattered gore, dirt, and hair. For the first time, Bailey's gaze fell upon Parnell's hands. They were wrapped in heavily soiled, boxing-glove-sized rags. Flies and gnats swarmed around the blackened bandages.

"Good God, Parnell," Bailey said, reaching for Parnell's right hand. Parnell flinched but allowed Bailey to cradle it. "No ..." Bailey whispered. A siren's howl began bouncing off the building walls.

"Dad! Dad!" Bailey heard from the alley. Rupert ran into the light. He was waving toward the dock. "Dad! Can you come here? Come quickly!"

Bailey looked at Lexi who nodded back at him. He tromped down the cement stairs and waddled as quickly as he could toward Rupert. Rupert met him on the incline of the dock drive.

"What is it?" he asked his son.

"This man. He's asking for you." Rupert pulled Bailey into the alley and toward the street. A pair of small dumpsters were bunched on the left side of the alley. A few oil drum shaped objects dotted the other side.

"Are you talking about Helmut? What does he want?"

"He won't say. He just keeps saying, 'Get Bailey.' He's badly wounded. I don't think he'll survive."

On the far side of the dumpsters Bailey saw Anand kneeling over a dark shape.

As Bailey approached, he said, "Rupert, that's Helmut Rhinegold, the man who accosted me inside. The man you shot." Bailey sighed, then added, "It was a set up. Helmut was a damn red herring."

Rupert looked at his father for a moment, shook his head, and knelt next to Helmut. Anand stood and backed away. Light fell across the alley wall, onto Helmut's head and chest. He was bleeding from at least three different spots. Helmut's chest was heaving and his eyes were closed. Bailey dropped onto his knees and leaned into Helmut's face.

"Helmut? Helmut. It's Bailey again."

Helmut's eyes shot open and he coughed. Blood-streaked spittle shot from his mouth and splattered his chin. Bailey could see Helmut's eyes register recognition. A weak smile spread across Helmut's face.

"Mancini," Helmut said.

"Stuart? Yes, what of him?"

Helmut nodded and licked his lips. Blood spread across his lower lip. "He's dead."

"What?" Bailey grabbed Helmut's shoulders and shook him.

Helmut's head flopped and smacked against the brick. A coughing fit followed. He tilted Helmut's head up into the light. Blood rushed from his grinning mouth.

"The Simien Mountains," Helmut whispered. It sounded like he was talking through a sponge. "We ... have people ... waiting for them. By now ... they've found them. He must be dead." Helmut smiled again and Bailey released him. Helmut fell back onto the pavement and groaned.

Bailey closed his eyes and tried to simultaneously push Helmut's claim out of his mind and analyze whether it could possibly be true.

"We ... had them followed. Three groups. Ready ... to intercept them. Follow and ... intercept."

"No," Bailey muttered.

He heard Helmut begin to heave. Then he realized Helmut was laughing, or at least attempting to laugh. The coughing started again, followed by a deep groan.

"Bailey?" Helmut moaned when he caught a breath.

Bailey didn't respond.

"Did you keep a copy of the map?"

Bailey stood and looked away.

The heaving started again. The sound was unsettling, like listening to someone drown.

"You old ... fool. Always ... always make copies. And ... and you call yourself ... an adventurer."

Anand stepped up beside Bailey, pulled out a revolver with a huge silencer and fired it into Helmut's forehead. Helmut lurched upward and slammed back into the pavement. Anand pocketed the gun as the ambulance pulled into the alley behind them, bathing the area in colored strobes, the siren shrieking at an unbearable level, then silencing.

# CHAPTER

# THIRTY-FOUR

Prima wore a simple, elegant black dress, open at the sleeves, a classic neckline that teetered along the border between sophisticated and provocative. She glided across the room carrying two goblets of red wine, looking like a runway model, drifting in slow motion. She lowered her head almost imperceptibly, but the result was stunning and the message was clear. She slowed in front of him and raised a glass up to his face. It was the most graceful gesture he could ever remember seeing. He took the glass from her. Prima's mouth fell open in a half smile. He could see the thin white arch of her teeth and the tip of her tongue. Was she about to say something?

"Stuart," he heard. But it wasn't Prima's voice. The wine, the vision, rapidly disintegrated into grey. "Stuart! Wake up!"

Smoke and the smell of something sweet, rancid. As Desta's face came into view, he realized it was Desta's breath.

"What … what time is it?"

"I'm not sure. Close to five. Perhaps a bit later." Desta paused as Stuart propped himself up on an elbow. "We have to go. This is a big day."

Stuart closed his eyes and exhaled loudly. For a moment he hoped the dream would return. What was Prima about to say to him?

"Good morning, Stuart," he heard Kaleb call. Stuart raised his free hand, eyes closing, and murmured a response. He was definitely still in the middle of Ethiopia.

Just like the previous day, the sun rose and illuminated a perfect, cloudless, pastel blue sky. The low humidity coupled with the growing warmth of the sun's morning rays seemed to energize everyone. Desta's daughter had smuggled coffee into their camp. Stuart chugged two large cups, scalding the roof of his mouth, but he didn't care. The caffeine flowing through his system made him feel invincible.

Within fifteen minutes the group was on its way. Desta had been studying the tattered map, lit by a small flashlight. He gazed up, scanning various points on the pale horizon, the peaks and valleys defining their surroundings, and directed them deeper into the canyon.

"We'll reach our destination within four hours, possibly much sooner," Desta announced as they fell in behind him.

"And then what?" Aisha asked, her tone half teasing, half serious.

Desta shrugged and took a few steps before saying, "We shall see what this fountain is all about, I suppose." Kaleb and Hakim shared a look. Kaleb shook his head, but continued on.

As dawn unfolded, the landscape continued to morph into a denser, jungle-like environment. The rocky, arid land they had traveled through the two previous days had given way to heavier, almost foreign, vegetation. Walls of twisted, deeply barked trees sprang from a dank clay foundation that slid beneath their boots. The air smelled like an old tent.

Aisha dropped back from Desta's side to walk with Stuart. She smiled and tucked a wily strand of hair behind her ear.

"Aren't you scared?" she asked, continuing to smile. Stuart stared back at her, surprised both by her question as well as the fact that she was actually interested in talking to him.

"Well, I don't know, really. I've tried not to dwell on it."

She scowled at his answer and made a puffing sound. "So, this is normal hiking in America? Every campsite filled with dead bodies? Murder, capture, torture lurking around every corner?"

Stuart realized how inane his answer had sounded; even though, to a large degree, it was true. Allowing himself to be led across the globe by virtual strangers, happening upon dead bodies, mesmerized by belly dancers, sleeping in the open air. The sheer novelty of these experiences overshadowed any fear he might normally realize and, frankly, relieved him of his mundane responsibilities. Something that hadn't happened in decades.

"I'm sorry. No, I mean, yes, I … I am scared. I … I just haven't acknowledged it. I'm trying to focus only on what we're doing next," he said. She gave a quick nod, focusing her gaze on the ground. "I suppose it's different for you. It's … difficult to explain."

"It's okay," Aisha said, looking back up at him. "I can't imagine spending my life living in a huge foreign city, and you can't imagine having grown up in … this," she said, motioning to their surroundings.

"I haven't talked to my boss now for … for days now. Maybe before I met Bailey and Parnell …"

"Who are Bailey and Parnell?"

"Friends. New friends. They know your father. That's why he's with me. They're members of a … oh, never mind. It's complicated, and a little embarrassing."

"Tell me, Stuart," she said, leaning into him. "Are they Americans, too?"

"No, English, at least by birth. I'm not entirely sure they even have a true home. They seem to jump from city to city, country to country."

"I'm sorry. I interrupted you. You were saying something about your work," Aisha said.

Stuart laughed. "Just thinking out loud. It's sad, I suppose, that before this last week I hadn't gone more than twenty-four hours—probably really no more than twelve—without talking to someone from my firm. It's all I did."

The trail steadily grew more treacherous and technical. Aisha stepped in front of Stuart. Walking side by side had been unpractical. Grima and Lebna brought up the rear while Desta, Kaleb, and Hakim each worked to clear as much of the path as possible.

"Do you miss it? The city?" Aisha called over her shoulder.

Stuart shrugged and said, "Yes and no. I'm out of my routine now, so in some ways the change is welcome. Other times, like when I'm trying to fall asleep with a sharp rock stuck in my ribs, I ache to be at home in my own bed." He laughed. "I'm sure that must sound comforting. Here you are, helping your father with some stranger who's searching for a mythical fountain of youth, going at it like it's second nature, and you're left dealing with a glorified accountant who's homesick."

Aisha didn't respond at first. She continued on, ducking a few branches, and then said, "I don't expect you, or any of these men, to protect me, if that's what you mean."

"No, no, I just meant—"

"It's okay," she said, turning to him with a slight smile. "We're here to protect *you*. You know that, don't you?"

Stuart realized that, no, he hadn't thought of it that way. He saw Desta's planning as a way of putting together an expedition. They had a destination in mind. They needed help from others, to carry supplies, help with camp, and … and all the other things Stuart tried to imagine Desta had to consider before accepting Bailey's proposal.

"So, I don't understand why you're here, then. I mean, I realize your father, indirectly, asked you, but, aside from that, why would you do this?"

Aisha walked in silence again, and then said, "In my life, I believe opportunities come to us. Sometimes we seek them out, but more often our own actions, our own passions and interests, bring us in contact with all kinds of challenges. This, to me, is just another unexpected challenge that has happened because of my relationship with my father, and your relationship with your friends." She paused again and said, "And of course, there is the pay." Stuart could hear the smile in her voice.

Stuart noticed the surrounding foliage begin to brighten and, a few yards later, he followed Aisha out of the jungle and into the open. Desta, Kaleb, and Hakim waited for them on a barren rock shelf. Stuart's attention was torn from staring at the men to gazing at the vista that unfolded to his right. They stood on the edge of a miniature Grand Canyon. Except to Stuart, it looked exactly like the Grand Canyon since he'd only seen pictures of the actual western marvel. The land dropped off vertically for a least a hundred feet. Across the valley, a mirroring stone wall, blotched with outcroppings, patches of shrubs and brush, glowed in the sunlight. Grima and Lebna walked up behind Stuart.

"Quite beautiful, isn't it?" Lebna said.

"It's been a long time since I've been here," Aisha said, leaning over to peer into the canyon.

"You've *been* here?" Stuart asked.

Aisha nodded. Desta moved over to her side and slid his arm around her waist.

"We hiked regularly when Aisha was a little girl. She raved about it. We couldn't come here enough. Her mother and I learned of this trail from an old family friend. We almost gave up before we found this shelf. But we'd been promised a life-altering experience by this friend, so we continued on. The first time we came, we spent three entire days right here."

Aisha nodded again and hugged her father.

"Why did you need the map?" Stuart asked.

"I didn't, not really, at least not up until now. We're headed down into this canyon. I've never attempted this segment of the trail. When we visited before, we never wanted to leave this area. I wanted to be sure the map was taking us to the trail that led into this canyon."

The group of seven gathered and reveled in the array of colors, shapes, and patterns that erupted as light and shadows shifted across the valley wall.

"From here we repel," Desta said, as much to the valley as to his colleagues.

"Repel?" Stuart muttered. Aside from a brief, embarrassing experience bounding down the collapsed high school bleachers back in New Jersey, Stuart had never encountered climbing equipment. Now, his Ethiopian guide expected him to toss himself over the side of a cliff that dove into rock and spiny brush.

"We're good at this," Aisha said from beside him. She placed a hand on his shoulder for a brief moment then moved to her father.

Grima and Lebna unshouldered their packs and began extracting bundles of thick, multi-colored rope. Hakim walked back toward the edge of the forest and lassoed one of the larger trees near them.

Stuart approached Desta and said, "I'm not sure I'm really prepared for this Desta. I apologize but …"

"Oh, enough, Stuart," Desta said. "We're only going down about fifty meters. There's a broad ledge at that point with a substantial path that'll take us down into the valley." "Okay," Stuart said, stretching out the word and peering over the precipice. "But … how do we get back up? I mean, once we're ready to return?"

Desta laughed and clapped Stuart on the back. "Not to worry, my friend. We'll help you."

By the time Stuart turned around, Grima and Lebna had secured two ropes to the tree Hakim had selected. Grima had diverted one rope to the side via a boulder the size of an armchair to split the two ropes. Aisha passed out gloves to everyone.

"Aisha, I think you and Hakim should go first. You're the lightest. Then Stuart. He'll need a bit of help at both ends. Then Lebna, then Kaleb, and last, me."

Aisha put her hands on her hips and glared at her father. "Really? You're planning to come down last?"

"Of course. Why not?"

Aisha looked down at the dirt and shook her head.

"Come now, let's get to it. I don't want to finish that trail in the dark."

Stuart silently agreed with Desta's declaration. He continued to sneak glances over the edge of the cliff. There did seem to be an outcropping or shelf far below them, but from this height it hardly seemed like something they could land and hike upon.

Aisha and Hakim clipped into their gear and followed the ropes toward the edge. They tugged alternatively and nodded toward Desta.

"Just be patient," Desta said, focusing his attention on his daughter.

"Don't worry, Father," she replied, smiling sideways. "Ready?" she asked Hakim. The gangly young man nodded, though Stuart thought he saw a look of utter terror flash across Hakim's face.

"See you below," Aisha said, and hopped over the ledge. Hakim glanced up at Kaleb and followed Aisha's lead. Desta stepped forward and placed a hand on Aisha's rope. Kaleb followed suit and guided Hakim's tether.

Stuart watched the ropes twitch between Desta's and Kaleb's hands and the rocky ledge. The rope skipped rhythmically for a long minute or two, then slackened.

Stuart heard Aisha call up to her father. Desta and Kaleb walked to the edge, looked down, then simultaneously began yanking the rope up to the top. When both ropes had been retrieved, Desta brought a harness over to Stuart.

"Are you ready?" he asked Stuart, an unsettling smile crinkling his face.

Stuart thought for a brief moment, knowing that the question was meant to be rhetorical, but still, he had to ask himself, was he ready?

"Raise your arms," Desta ordered. Stuart cooperated and Desta fastened the harness around Stuart's waist and over his shoulders. When he was finished, he tugged roughly at the connection points and stepped back.

"Put on your gloves," Desta said, "It's a short drop. Nothing to be afraid of. There are no obstacles. No outcroppings or sharp rocks. Five or six repels and you'll be with Aisha and Hakim. Lean back, as if you're sitting, or about to sit. Let gravity take you in an arc. Cushion your landing with your knees. Then spring back into another repel. Now, go."

Kaleb waited at the edge, back toward the abyss, rope firmly gripped in both hands. He smiled and nodded as Stuart made his way to the rim. He turned and faced Desta.

"Here," Desta said, handing the rope to Stuart. "Both hands. See Kaleb? Just like him. Pull it now. It's tight. Don't take too big of a leap off the edge. The next couple can be bigger. The first will simply get you started."

Stuart tugged on the rope and looked over at Kaleb. Kaleb smiled again and hopped backward over the edge. Desta reached forward with a single finger and prodded Stuart in the sternum. Stuart took a deep breath, squeezed the rope, squatted, and sprang backwards.

The fall felt like slow motion, and the rope and gravity sucked him back into the canyon wall smoothly. He stuck his feet out, spreading them just broader than his shoulders, and cushioned his landing by springing his knees inward. He looked to his left and saw that Kaleb was already twenty or thirty feet below him. He leaned back and pushed off again. The second repel almost felt natural, despite his racing pulse. He hit the wall fifteen feet further down, paused, and sprang back again. This time he went a bit beyond where he'd intended. His feet caught the wall just before his upper body ratcheted past the balance point. The near miss vacuumed the air from his lungs. He steadied himself, looked down to his left again, and saw Kaleb at the bottom, standing next to Aisha and Hakim, less than thirty feet below. He took another deep breath and executed two clean repels to land at the bottom.

"Bravo!" he heard Desta call from above him. He looked up and saw the little man waving at him over the ledge. Stuart waved, embarrassed, and began to unhitch the harness.

Kaleb had sent his rope and harness up to Desta already. Within two minutes, Desta landed with the group.

"We'll leave the ropes here," Desta ordered. "We should be back soon, I hope." The team shouldered their packs and began the trail descent further into the canyon.

# CHAPTER

# THIRTY-FIVE

The emergency room was a chaotic mess. Scores of carabinieri, physicians, nurses, representatives from the Rome Interpol office, and the press packed the once tranquil waiting room. A group of administrators hovered around the automatic doors, forcing back camera crews. Rupert managed to break away from the Interpol brass long enough to accompany Bailey into an empty emergency room stall and yank the curtain closed.

"Dad, I need you to wipe your mind clean. Do you understand? You don't remember a thing, okay?"

Bailey nodded and sat back on the gurney. The intensity of the last ten minutes at the abandoned hospital had traumatized him. He wasn't sure if it was just the result of exhaustion, a sensory overload, or something more concerning. There was no time to worry about himself, though.

Rupert leaned forward to whisper something else to his father when the curtain shot open. A harsh looking man, clad in a near black charcoal suit, white shirt, and red silk tie, stepped into the stall and stood directly behind Rupert.

"Honeybourne. I want to talk to you now," the man snapped. He jabbed an elongated index finger toward the floor and kept it there, motionless, as Rupert backed away from Bailey.

"Yes, sir."

"I assume this is your father, Bailey Honeybourne?"

"Yes, yes, it is, sir. I—"

"Stop. Don't say another word. Before you make the mistake of uttering some form of nonsense that somehow further obliterates your career with Interpol, I want to remind you of the specific circumstances we are dealing with this evening."

It was clear from the man's accent that he was British. Bailey knew this wasn't going to be in Rupert's favor. While Interpol was an international agency, embarrassing his home nation was just about the last thing he would want to do.

"First, we have five—do you hear me—five fatalities. All shot dead. All found in or near the hospital where you were found by the local authorities. Second, you were accompanied by two other Interpol operatives who were on a completely different assignment. Third, you've been given no authority to operate in Italy. You, in fact, are on holiday. Fourth, one of the dead men is apparently a very wealthy U.S. citizen who's been reported missing for the past week. And fifth—I cannot believe there's actually a fifth—but this man, Helmut Rhinegold, from initial reports, was shot dead in the alley. Lying down. Unarmed."

Bailey watched Rupert fight to maintain his composure preserve some degree of dignity. It was difficult to watch.

"Sir, if I may," Bailey began. Both the Interpol commander and Rupert glared at him.

"I wasn't speaking to you, Mr. Honeybourne," the commander said.

"Yes, I understand, but I think it's—"

"Dad, please. Shut up. You—"

The Interpol commander flashed back to Rupert and stepped directly in front of him. He leaned down until his face was less than an inch from Rupert's.

"Don't make me add 'disrespecting a superior' to the litany of grievances I'm prepared to file."

Rupert stepped back, leaning into the curtain, and pushed a hand through his hair.

"I understand, sir. I—"

"Stop, Honeybourne, and listen to me. I want both of you out of here. Do you understand? There's an exit behind the last stall in the emergency room. I don't want anyone here who can allude to the slightest hint of what happened tonight. Am I clear?"

Rupert tilted his head, as if he'd misheard the man. "But—"

"Now," the commander said. He turned to Bailey and asked, "Do you need medical attention or can you leave?"

"I'm … I'm just a little disoriented, but—" Bailey started to say.

"Good, then get moving." The commander turned to Rupert and added, "Anand and Lexi have already left. The press are tangled up with the police at the moment. Rupert, you will monitor your cell phone until I call. You will make yourself available immediately. Do you understand?"

Rupert nodded.

"We don't have much time. Find someplace safe to stay for the time being, someplace convenient."

Rupert looked at his father. Bailey said, "We have a place."

"Good. Now get the hell out of here and don't talk to a soul. Rupert, I'll call within the hour. Understood?" The man pushed past Rupert and parted the curtain. "There's the exit. Now go."

Rupert grabbed Bailey's coat sleeve and pulled him out of the stall toward the exit. He marched his father toward the back of the room and through the door beneath the exit sign. As they started down the stairwell, Bailey began to speak but Rupert hushed him. They followed the stairs down four flights and then came to the bottom landing. There were two doors, one on either side of the landing. Bailey assumed one led outside and the other back into the hospital.

"We are not going back in, Dad. It's too risky."

"I know. Find a taxi to take us to Prima's. That bloody twit will still be able to reach you in Trastevere."

Rupert scowled and stared at the floor.

"What's the matter?" Bailey asked.

Rupert shook his head slowly. "I don't know, Dad. I'm not sure we can trust this Prima. It's not as if things have gone particularly well since you and Parnell connected with her."

"Rupert, you must be joking. We've known Prima for years. She's the general manager of the Rome chapter. We've known her father, her family, for over … two decades."

"And how long have you known Helmut?"

Bailey snorted and turned away from his son. He wasn't accustomed to this level of mistrust anymore. It was one of the things that eventually drove him from the MI6. Each case he'd worked on involved a morphing cast of liars, conmen, and undercover internal affairs officers, desperate, career-obsessed narcissists who would co-opt any available opportunity to trounce a fellow agent in the dust. It was a hostile culture that had germinated in the early 1970s and took firm hold by the end of the decade. The loyal, honorable, humble, committed agency he'd been so proud to be a part of had been wiped from the island and replaced by an organization that thrived on fear, coercion, and manipulation. On July 16, 1975, Bailey walked into his superior's office at 7:30 a.m. sharp, presented him with a one-line resignation/retirement announcement, and had his office emptied by 8:15 that morning.

The catharsis, the indescribable elation, he'd felt striding to the underground station—a tattered box, originally intended for London's finest hand soap that now held the few personal items he'd retained from his office, balanced upon his shoulder—was something he'd never have predicted. It was the most joyous moment he'd experience in his thirty-plus years at the agency.

Recently, that once eternal feeling of security and freedom had shattered. The revelation of Malcolm's murder, Helmut's supposed kidnapping, Parnell's kidnapping, and ultimately Helmut's shocking betrayal. It had all piled upon him. And this time he couldn't quit.

Bailey stopped circling and approached Rupert.

"You're right. Everything I felt I could trust has been destroyed as of late. And I don't have a shred of information that will convince you that Prima is trustworthy. Nothing other than the fact that there's been nothing she's ever done, nothing her family has ever done, that would cause me to question her loyalty or integrity."

Rupert looked up slowly and just stared.

"Let me propose something. What's the likelihood that she has any awareness of what happened tonight? If she's not involved, if she's trustworthy, then I believe she'll be completely unaware of what we've experienced. If, on the other hand, she says something like, 'Oh, I heard what happened. Are you okay?'" Bailey mimicked in a very poorly executed impression of Prima.

His falsetto made Rupert smile, something he couldn't remember seeing for some time.

"It's rather weak," he said. "The press is here. Some form of story must be hitting the news. But I suppose it's worth a try. If she truly is on our side, then we might be able to leverage some of her local contacts."

"Leverage?" Bailey asked.

"We're not finished here, Dad. This was just one loose end. One big loose end. We need to find Stuart before it's too late. And we'll need help doing so."

The exterior exit door led them into a small side parking lot.

"There's an entrance around this side of the building," Rupert said, pointing toward the corner of the hospital.

A short walk brought them to the main visitor entrance to the hospital. Within a few minutes, they contacted a taxi dispatcher. While they waited, they debated calling Prima ahead of time. Ultimately, they convinced themselves that a surprise visit would more accurately test Prima's devotion.

After they piled into the cab, Bailey realized how war-torn they must look and smell. Rupert had flakes of tile and drywall matted into his hair. A spray of dark spots shone across Rupert's chest when the taxi door opened. Blood. The entire ordeal had caused him to sweat heavily and now, sitting, Bailey could feel his shirt plastered against his back and weighted down by his sports jacket.

The taxi pulled out onto the main thoroughfare and blended in with the light traffic.

"Rupert, I'm so—"

"Stop, Dad," Rupert said, holding a hand up but not looking at his father. "I told you before. I'm not angry. I was concerned. After tonight's cluster … after tonight's *disaster*, I'm exceptionally concerned."

"But your career, Rupert. This could create significant problems."

Rupert dismissed his father's comment with a comically French "pffft."

"Christoff's a harmless bastard. He loves this rubbish. Gives him a chance to feel superior. Spout off at his underlings."

"But, Rupert, men were killed tonight. You heard him. He was genuinely pissed."

"Right, and you know what else gets him genuinely pissed? Poorly pressed trousers. Arsenal losses. Unattractive … his words, mind you, unattractive page-three women. He reacts the same to all of those and more."

Bailey pondered Rupert's explanation as they headed toward central Rome. On top of everything he was worried about Parnell. He'd never looked so frail, so old. They had admitted him into intensive care while he was semi-comatose. Bailey had overheard one of the Interpol agents translate for Christoff. "He's lost a lot of blood. A lot." An idea popped into his head. Perhaps Prima could visit Parnell and provide a report. He just hoped the initial drama around the evening's events would blow over quickly. It wasn't likely, but it was something to hope for.

"I'll call Christoff once we get settled at Prima's. I can coerce him into giving me a status report on Parnell. I know you're worried."

Bailey nodded and grinned. He was both relieved and a bit embarrassed that his son could read him so well. A result of the combination of too many years away from the force and the thorough training his son had received.

"What's our contingency plan?" Bailey asked.

"For tonight?" Rupert paused and looked out the taxi window. "If she's not home when we get there, we go across the square for a late dinner. Keep an eye on her front stoop."

"There's a private inn a few blocks from her apartment. I overnighted there a few years back, I believe."

"Good," Rupert said. "The more I think about it, my concern about Prima may be misplaced. Regardless, we need to plan for a potential escape."

"I suppose it's necessary. I have to tell you, Rupert, I'm not sure I'm prepared for another betrayal. I'm utterly exhausted. I'm accustomed to operating with people I can trust, on my own terms, and at my own pace."

Bailey jumped slightly when he felt something brush against his hand. He looked down and was surprised again to see his son's hand wrapped around his own spotted, dried-leather skin. Bailey peered through the windshield as the taxi pulled into Piazza di Santa Maria. It was after ten o'clock and a fair number of people were loitering throughout the plaza. The taxi had to maneuver through the pockets of pedestrians. What appeared to be a group of musicians and dancers were streaming away from the fountain. The entertainers were dressed in vibrant, festooned costumes; reds, greens, purples, almost renaissance clothing.

"I think I would have preferred to spend our evening here, Dad," Rupert said, his eyes following the crowd as the taxi stopped in front of Prima's building.

Bailey exited the car and saw light coming from two of Prima's windows. Rupert paid the driver and joined Bailey after the car pulled away.

"Well, it looks like she's home," Rupert said. "Let's work out a quick system in case either of us feels that she's not to be trusted. If I have a bad feeling, I'll tell you I need to call London. If you're concerned, ask me to check on Parnell, okay?"

Bailey continued to wrestle with the possibility that Prima could also be a turncoat. "Fine. I still want you to call Christoff about Parnell."

"I will. I will. Just use it as a code phrase, okay? If we don't feel safe, I'll still make the call and we'll tell her he's ordered us back to the hospital, or Interpol. Either way we'll be able to escape with an alibi."

"What if she asks to come along?"

Rupert thought for a moment, then shook his head. "She won't. Not if she's involved. Let's get moving."

Bailey rang the bell twice, but no one answered. Finally, Rupert rapped on the door with his knuckles. Still quiet. Then Bailey thought he heard a voice and another light came on within the apartment. The door opened and Prima stood before them in a black silk robe, a wine glass in one hand. She seemed stunned to see them.

"Bailey. Rupert. You're back. Is … are you okay?"

"Yes, my dear. We are just fine. We were hoping we could impose upon you again. Just for one night," Bailey said.

"Oh … please, come in, come in," she said, backing away from the door. The two men stepped in and she closed the door behind them.

"I'm sorry it's late. You're sure we haven't come at an inopportune time?" Rupert asked. Bailey had to admit she seemed a bit flustered. They had probably interrupted a date, or something more. He wasn't aware of Prima having any serious romantic relationship, but that didn't mean she was above taking care of herself.

Prima laughed and shoved a hand through her wild, thick dark hair. "No. There's nothing to interrupt. Don't worry. I was upstairs watching *Breakfast at Tiffany's*, one of my favorites. Once a month or so I open a bottle of decent wine, curl up in bed, and watch love stories. Typical woman, I know." She stepped back into the foyer. "Please, have a seat in the living room," she said, motioning them into a sitting room adjacent to the foyer. She flipped a light switch and illuminated a quaint and immaculate sitting room. Three formal chairs surrounded an octagon shaped table. As they walked into the room she said, "Oh my God, what happened to you? You're … Rupert, is that blood?"

Bailey had forgotten about their appearance.

Rupert caught his reflection in the framed mirror that ran across the wall. "Bloody hell. I'm sorry, Prima. We're disgusting."

"Are you hurt?" she asked Bailey.

"Just a bit frazzled, I'm afraid," he answered.

"Here, let's go to the kitchen so we can clean you both up," she said, directing them back into the hall. When they reached the kitchen, she flipped on the lights and asked, "Was this the result of your meeting, Bailey? Did—"

Bailey looked at Rupert. "No. I … we decided I shouldn't go. Instead, well, we were sidetracked a bit."

She set her glass on the kitchen table, approached Rupert, and plucked a piece of debris from his hair. "What do you mean, sidetracked?" she said, then looked at Rupert's shirt. "That is blood, isn't it? I—"

"Yes, but not mine," Rupert said, stepping back. Bailey pulled a chair from the kitchen table and sat. Rupert followed suit. Prima gaped at them, hands on her hips.

"Which one of you is going to tell me what's going on?" she demanded. Bailey noticed color rushing into her cheeks. "Is it Stuart? Did something happen to him?"

Rupert shot Bailey another look.

"Oh, my God," she said, covering her mouth. "It is Stuart, isn't it?" she said to Bailey. Prima knelt beside his chair and grasped his forearm.

"Actually," Bailey said, watching Rupert carefully. "It's not Stuart. We've had no word from him."

"Oh, grazie Dio," she said, standing. "Then, what is it?" Bailey noticed the relief that seemed to rush to her face.

"Sit," Rupert said, gesturing toward an empty chair between the two men.

"Do I need to call someone? Bailey," she said, leaning toward him. "Do you need me to contact the Board?"

"No, Prima," Bailey said.

"At least not yet," Rupert added. It appeared Rupert had made a quick judgment about Prima's innocence. "The good news, Prima, is that we were able to rescue Parnell."

"Is he okay? Where is he?"

"He's in intensive care at … what's the name, Rupert? Hospital Di Nancy?" Bailey said. Prima finally sat, clasping her robe near her neck.

"Surrounded by an army of Interpol officers," Rupert added.

Rupert spent the next half hour recounting the events that had taken place at the abandoned mental hospital, most of which Bailey hadn't been aware of. They had stumbled upon Parnell, cowering, delirious, and wrecked in a broom closet. Their discovery triggered the firefight Bailey had interrupted. By Rupert's count, there were at least four men, in addition to Helmut, holed up in the hospital. It had been chaos. Little or no light. Screams. Gunfire. Rupert said he was still stunned that the four of them had escaped with nothing more than bruises.

"Helmut Rhinegold was behind all of this? He killed Malcolm? He kidnapped Parnell? And now he's trying to kill or at least intercept Stuart?" Prima said. She leaned forward and put her head in her hands. Thin threads of muscle popped from her forearms.

"It's true. And I'm horrified," Bailey said. "I can't believe neither Parnell nor I suspected Helmut."

"But why would you?" she asked. "He'd been friends with Malcolm for years, as well as with both of you. Stuart, too. Even now, knowing what you know, is there something that you think you should have noticed that would have tipped you off to his treachery?"

Bailey drew his gaze to the floor and sighed. Prima's question was the one he'd been fighting to avoid. He feared there would be at least one past experience he'd recall that would force him to admit that Helmut shouldn't have been trusted. The sting of the betrayal was too fresh. He wasn't prepared to magnify the guilt he'd already accumulated.

Prima had her chin cradled in her hands, elbow on the table. Her swirling deep green eyes dug into his soul. Rather than answering, he sighed and shook his head.

"Well, of course you can stay here," Prima said, sounding exasperated. "But, tell me Rupert, why are you here? Why aren't you at the hospital with Parnell? And, for God's sake, who's taking care of Stuart?"

"It's complicated," Rupert answered. "My intervention ... the involvement of multiple Interpol offices, all ... freelance, I suppose you could say, has caused problems."

"Not to mention four or five deaths," Bailey said.

"Dad, that's not helpful. I did this for you, remember? This nightmare was brought on by you and your bizarre friends!" Rupert had sprung forward and was shouting to the point where spittle flew from his mouth. Bailey blinked and tried to process Rupert's outburst. While he knew Rupert was often tightly wound, his son rarely showed any range of emotion. Anger was habitually communicated via silence. Happiness, well, happiness was silence, too, but without the intense vibe.

"You're right, that was uncalled for. I apologize," Bailey said.

Rupert sat back in his chair, causing the legs to screech on the floor, and covered his face with his hands. After a few breaths, he leaned his head back, staring at the ceiling. "No, no, Dad. I'm sorry. I'm just …"

"We were asked to leave, Prima. Rupert's superior was orchestrating, or at least attempting to orchestrate, the bedlam in the Emergency Room. Rupert was correct. Press, agents, and medical staff were all swarming the area. Christoff, his commander, was furious, and, frankly, we were easy targets. Anand and Lexi, Rupert's colleagues, had already left. Do you remember, Rupert?"

Rupert brought his head forward and nodded.

"I realize I keep coming back to this, but what of Stuart? He's down in Ethiopia with a professor, right?"

"Yes," Bailey said, nodding, "Desta. An old acquaintance, someone we met years ago through Malcolm. From what we know, though, he's both entirely trustworthy and competent. If all goes as planned, they should be back in Addis Ababa within four or five days."

"*Days?*" Prima said, "That's an eternity." She folded her arms across her chest and frowned.

"I'll tell you what concerns me, Dad. I'm worried that we've cut the head off of this beast and the arms and legs are still flailing away down in Africa. I can't believe Helmut doesn't have a crew sniffing right behind

Desta and Stuart. They don't know to stop."

Just then Rupert's cell phone chimed. He dug it from his jacket pocket, glanced at the screen, looked up at Bailey, and pointed toward the hallway. He stood and hurried from the room. "Honeybourne," Bailey heard him say as he entered the hall.

There was an uneasy moment between Bailey and Prima after Rupert left. Bailey coughed to fill the void and Prima shifted in her chair. Finally, she said, "Do you think I'm being silly? Worrying so much about Stuart?"

Bailey smiled and shook his head. "Of course not, my dear. We're all worried. I'm certain he's a resourceful man, but the Ethiopian highlands are a world away from the concrete streets of New York City. I don't believe the poor boy has ever spent a night out of doors. At least not until the last couple of evenings."

Prima smirked and appeared to relax. She retrieved her wine glass from across the table and finished the last swallow.

"I honestly don't know what's come over me. I only spent a few hours with him but I feel both … responsible and … and concerned. I don't know," she said, shaking her head. Her hair fell across her cheeks.

"At the very least, you'll end up good friends," Bailey said.

"Bailey Honeybourne, if you knew how many good male friends I've had over the years, you'd be either embarrassed or highly skeptical. One more is the last thing I need."

Bailey was about to respond when Rupert walked quickly back into the sitting room.

"That was Christoff. We need to return to the hospital, Dad."

"What's happened?" Bailey said, standing.

"I'm afraid it's Parnell. They … they think he's gone into cardiac arrest."

# CHAPTER

# THIRTY-SIX

The lack of vegetation, absence of direct sunlight, and the stagnant air transformed the valley into a completely different ecosystem. The narrow rock chasm they'd dropped into had widened as they hiked north. Well beyond their current position, Stuart sighted trees returning, shouldered by a variety of bushes. He couldn't judge how far they had traveled or how much further they had to go. Stuart's quads and shins burned with each step. When they began their descent into the canyon. he'd looked forward to the downhill hike, but learned within the first fifteen minutes that the steep decline would wreck his legs. Only Kaleb trailed him, but purely as a safety net. Kaleb was well over six feet tall and Stuart's meager strides were beginning to frustrate the Ethiopian. Kaleb didn't complain though, but the regular scuffing of his boots along the trail sounded more like a non-verbal grievance than a fatigue-driven motion.

Not only was their progress difficult to measure, but Desta's confidence in their exact whereabouts appeared to have faded since they plunged over the edge of the cliff. The professor had held the group up at least a half dozen times, more so recently as they penetrated the rocky floor of the canyon, pulling out the battered map, referencing his compass, gazing across their diminishing surroundings, and then moving them on their way again. Stuart had refrained from posing any direct questions to Desta during these interludes, but he silently vowed that when they stopped again, he was going to flat out confront Desta. Something didn't feel right.

Stuart noticed that the pain in his lower legs began to subside. There were no longer nails being driven into his shins, now it was simply the steady thwack of a ball-peen hammer against his tibia. As the trail leveled out, they drew closer to the clump of trees he'd seen earlier. The vegetation thickened all around them and "trail" had become a relative term. Desta, Hakim, and Aisha drew razor-sharp machetes at the base of the valley and began slashing at the imposing plant life. Stuart wondered when the last expedition had passed this way and who had been a part of that group. Malcolm? Bailey, even?

From what Stuart could determine, their course had unfolded in a north-northwesterly direction since repelling into the canyon. Now, a few dozen feet ahead, the path veered directly west. Desta and Aisha halted at the dogleg and waited for the remainder of the group to catch up.

When Stuart and Kaleb arrived, they turned their attention to Desta.

"I must admit," Desta began, "I was certain we'd be there by now, but … I have misjudged our route."

"What does *that* mean?" Stuart pressed. Desta seemed irritated by Stuart's question.

"Well, Stuart, it means that in all likelihood our map wasn't drawn to scale."

"Or it means you misread the map and we're lost," Stuart added. Something triggered a dormant emotion. A dull, painful electricity balled within his chest. His patience had evaporated.

"I understand you're tired, Stuart. We all, I assume, feel the same. I can only follow the map."

"But are you? Are we really headed in the right direction? Do you think we'll actually find it? And if we do, can we get back?"

Desta's attempt at diplomacy faded. He dropped his hands to his sides and took a step toward Stuart.

"Need I remind you, sir, that we've all undertaken this journey because of you and your friends. If I understand correctly, this map we're using is your property. I can only follow what's been documented on it. Now either you can help us reach this destination or you can be a burden. Which do you wish to be?"

Stuart realized he'd lost the initial battle with his emotions and was embarrassed by his outburst. The fatigue of the hike, the radical change in environment, his lack of control, all contributed to his faltering attitude. He stared at Desta. A good four or five inches shorter than he was, easily twenty years older, forty pounds lighter, and he was diligently pursuing this fountain, while Stuart was pouting about … everything.

"You're exactly right, Desta. I'm sorry. I've … I've just about reached my limit. This is so … foreign to me, literally. Corpses, mountain climbing, sleeping outdoors—I really don't know how to function like this."

For the first time since he'd encountered Bailey and Parnell in the Oak Room of the Palace Hotel, he felt completely alone. Consciously or not, everyone else in the group had gradually gravitated toward Desta, and Stuart stood alone.

"We can turn back, if you'd like," Desta said.

"No, no, that's not what I want. Not at all," Stuart said.

"Then what is it?" Aisha asked. She stepped in front of her father and poked her head toward Stuart.

Stuart shifted his weight between his feet, then simply collapsed on the dirt. He threw his hands up and said, "I'm not sure I can answer that, at least not right now. I'm … I'm on this trek to find something my estranged grandfather found years ago. I … I've been following orders, following

Bailey and Parnell. For whatever reason, I trust them and I feel like this is something I need to pursue. But I ..." He didn't know what else to say. He hadn't thought through his motivation clearly enough to answer the same questions for himself.

"You said *estranged* grandfather. What does that mean?" Desta asked.

"Estranged, separated, distanced, I guess. My mother severed all ties with him when I was very young. I ... I really never knew the man," Stuart said.

"I understood Malcolm Buckley was your grandfather, Stuart, but I wasn't aware you didn't have a relationship with him. This ... is somewhat disturbing," Desta answered.

Stuart nodded and stared at the path beneath him. "It was always a mystery to me. He didn't exist in my life. Not until these two odd men confronted me in Manhattan."

Aisha threw her hands in the air and stormed away from the group, muttering in her native language. Kaleb, Hakim, Grima, and Lebna exchanged glances and then averted their eyes from both Desta and Stewart.

"Look, everyone. I realize all of you have risked a tremendous amount, sacrificed ... friends, all to help me. I'm deeply grateful. It's just that I ... I can't explain something that I'm just coming to grips with myself."

Aisha made her way back and zeroed in on Stuart, a long thin index finger boring toward his face. She began to speak when Kaleb stepped forward and intercepted her. He caught her upper arms, absorbing her momentum, and gracefully redirected her.

"Aisha, I believe I can help you," Kaleb said. She glared at him for a moment, then spat out another foreign word, kicking at the ground.

"Stuart," Kaleb said, "many of us have very close, intricate families in Ethiopia. We tend to have what others may see as intimate interest and knowledge of each other's activities. Even the, what's the phrase—black sheep, the outcast—right? Those who operate on the fringe of a family, nearly everything they're involved with makes it back to the family. We know what they're up to as much as those who remain close.

"I have several older siblings. Three are men, and two are my sisters. My brother, Rafa, the second oldest, was the outcast of our family, except that he actually managed to detach from us. None of us ever understood what drove his dreams, but he ran away just before his thirteenth birthday. In many cases, those who run away end up with distant family or friends. They latch onto something that will at least keep them afloat, but they really don't get far. But not Rafa. We waited weeks, months, thinking we'd hear from an aunt or uncle, a distant friend, that Rafa had settled somewhere within the country, perhaps only a few kilometers away. But that word never came."

The cadence and intensity of Kaleb's voice shifted as he spoke. Aisha stopped pacing and eased into a lotus position next to Grima.

"A year passed and we feared the worst. This was when the entire world knew our country because of the intense famine. Death was all too common—a given. A thirteen-year-old on his own, away from family and friends, in a time when the most basic nourishment was nonexistent, it was impossible to think of him surviving.

"My mother, she was the last to give up. When the second year passed, she finally resigned herself. Honestly, we hoped some form of proof would arrive so that she, so that all of us, could let Rafa go. We were never so lucky.

"I was seven when he disappeared. Through my own good fortune, I was able to enroll in university after my eighteenth birthday. I completed my first year and did quite well. My efforts earned me an opportunity to study abroad, in Paris. Somehow all of my family pulled together enough money to help keep me alive for that year. My scholarship took care of tuition, books, and one round trip ticket."

Kaleb's eyes began to gloss over. He rubbed at them with his fingers and cleared his throat.

"I struggled at first in Paris. I knew French well enough, but I'd never been to such a city. And I felt like everywhere I looked I saw people who were different than me. Even those I assumed were from Africa. They weren't dressed like me. They fit in, where I did not.

"One afternoon I was eating a simple lunch in Jardin des Tuileries, not far from the Louvre. It's a popular place, lots of people, but for some reason I was always comfortable there. So, I'm sitting on the lawn, eating a piece of bread and some cheese, when I feel, then hear someone behind me.

"'No much like Soloka, is it?'" the voice said.

"At first I didn't move. I thought I heard the voice of my father. And at that point he'd been dead over five years. The bread, I remember it sitting on my tongue. I was afraid to turn around because I thought I'd imagined the voice and I would see no one there. Then, I'd be sad and frightened. I wondered if I was losing my mind.

"I forced myself to swallow, and I turned around, so slowly I didn't think I'd ever see behind me. The first things I saw were two immaculate black shoes capped by thin dress slacks. I followed the legs up to a jacket, a glaringly white shirt, a dark tie, and then my father's face.

"'Father?' I started to say, but I couldn't get it out. The man, my father, burst into laughter. I scrambled to my feet and nearly fell backward. I stepped on the remainder of my bread and slipped.

"'No, you silly boy, I'm not your father. It is I, Rafa. Your long-lost brother? Has it been so long that you do not remember me?'"

Grima smiled and nodded at Aisha. Kaleb cleared his throat and scribbled in the dirt again.

"I was in utter shock for … for I don't know how long. Finally, he stepped forward and embraced me. It took me several seconds to move and return the gesture. I had no idea how or what to feel. Rafa's disappearance had caused so much strife, pain, fighting, everything negative, within our family, yet all the while we kept this hope that he might return.

"You see, Stuart, Aisha, I was faced with this opportunity to find out what my brother had been doing for so long. Find out what we were eventually forbidden to discuss. And yet I could still see the pain on my mother's face. Each day. I know she never forgot."

Aisha listened intently as Kaleb told his story. Stuart thought he saw some of the tension draining from her face.

"He took me in immediately, even though I was ambivalent at first. I think I was probably a lot like what Stuart has been describing. I accepted my brother's invitations to see the city, to meet his friends, learn of his life in France, but I was following him blindly."

Kaleb turned to Stuart and said, "I realize I'm making an assumption that I understand your personal feelings, but there are many things that remind me of my own situation. It was the strangest time for me. Part of me wanted to run away, curse him, hurt him the way he'd hurt each of us; and another part of me wanted to drink in everything that he'd experienced over the past decade. And I didn't feel like I had any way to properly express either emotion."

No one said a thing for what felt like several minutes. Finally, Aisha stepped forward and hugged Kaleb. He patted her on the head playfully and she squirmed away, slapping at him. Then she approached Stuart, this time without the accusatory finger.

"I don't know how much of what Kaleb shared with us is true for you, Stuart, but I realize that I ... overreacted. And I realize this is all probably something much larger than you, or your grandfather. Please, accept my apology and, I hope, also accept my viewpoint." She took another step forward and spread her arms. Stuart stuttered, took a half step forward, and accepted her embrace.

The shroud of cloud cover that had floated across the early afternoon sky dissipated, unleashing a shower of sunbeams that peppered the surrounding jungle. The moment the sunlight hit, the tranquility was split by an explosion of sound, detritus, and dust. Stuart felt something spray across his face just before he dove to the ground. There was a chorus of screams, punctuated by someone yelling, "Roll! Roll! Roll!" Stuart clamped his eyes shut and rolled, burying himself beneath a nearby bush. The noise, automatic gunfire, continued in staccato bursts. From where he lay, he could see two bodies lying still in the dust. He caught movement across the path from him, but he couldn't identify the source.

More shouting, unintelligible, came from his right. Some other language. The shouting came closer and suddenly he saw an array of legs streak into his field of vision and stop. The barrel of a gun hovered over the two motionless bodies. Fire spit from the barrel as the gun pumped countless rounds into figures. One attacker approached the perimeter of the branches that concealed him. Someone spoke, then gunfire ripped through the foliage around him. The others—perhaps four in total—joined the shooter who fired in Stuart's direction. Another scream erupted from down the path. Stuart caught another person— Aisha?—sprinting into view. The assailants bellowed, punctuated by a blast of gunfire.

"Run!" Stuart heard someone else yell. He hesitated and then barreled into the open path, springing to his feet and tearing blindly after the shape in front of him. He ducked, batting away branches randomly, fighting to stay upright on the precarious jungle floor. Stuart glanced up for a flash and realized Desta was leading him. He could sense someone else behind him, but he didn't dare turn around.

"Keep running!" Stuart heard Aisha call from behind him. She had to be on his heels. Hearing her voice energized him, and he plunged forward, chasing Desta as they dove deeper into the thickening woods. His thighs screamed, burning, and his lungs fought to deliver the oxygen he consumed. He continued windmilling through the underbrush—a bizarre vision of Snow White flashing through his mind as she spun through the haunted forest, deeply barked trees grasping at her cape, her ankles. His right foot hit something immobile and he went airborne. There was the briefest of moments, without sound, as he waited to collide with something sharp, something painful. Instead, his momentum carried him into something forgiving. When he settled, he opened his eyes and saw Desta above him. A second later Aisha slid beside him.

"We can't stop," she yelled at her father.

Desta shushed her.

"But, Father ..."

He pointed over her shoulder. Silence. He shook his head, then extended a hand to help Stuart stand. Aside from a faint breeze rolling through the higher tree branches, they heard nothing. Desta raised a finger, keeping them still. They waited what felt like for ten or fifteen minutes. Somehow satisfied, Desta nodded first to Aisha, then to Stuart, and circled them away from the scene of the attack.

Desta sliced through the heavier underbrush with his machete. Aisha was emptyhanded. Stuart grappled with his footing as they edged down a steepening slope, dodging slick rock, tangled floor vines, and decaying plant life. The incline leveled out, and several yards later Stuart followed Desta into an opening.

Stuart leaned over, hands on his knees, and steadied his breath. His quads and lower back threatened to seize. He stood up straight, stretching, hands balled into his lower back, as Aisha emerged behind him. He exhaled forcefully, then realized what lay before him.

The barren oval clearing extended at least a hundred feet in front of him. The plethora of fauna they had just stepped from had been eradicated. A massive rocky outcropping, thrusting upward at least two stories, shot from the desolate soil. The stone didn't match the rusty hue that underscored the Simien landscape. Instead, radiant purple, deep green, and a vibrant, pulsing blue refracted the sunlight that blanketed the clearing.

"What is this?" Stuart muttered.

"I think," Desta said, stepping forward, "this is it."

# CHAPTER

# THIRTY-SEVEN

Prima's driving through the streets of Trastevere and western Rome was nearly as harrowing as the night's earlier events. Rupert was crammed into the back seat of the Mercedes Coupe, and Bailey clung to the dash, having moved his seat forward to accommodate Rupert's legs. Prima gunned the accelerator through the tight, often cobblestoned, corners, downshifting aggressively, pumping the brake, and nearly red-lining the engine. She whipped the car out to Via Gregorio VII, weaving through traffic and speeding toward Ospedale San Carlo di Nancy. Although Bailey hadn't timed their earlier trip between the hospital and Prima's flat, he knew she'd cut their travel time in half.

They ducked behind an ambulance pulling away from the Emergency Room entrance and stopped with a screech before the automatic doors. Bailey tumbled from the passenger seat and turned to pull his son from the rear. As soon as Rupert had both feet on the ground, Prima punched the accelerator, slamming the door shut with her momentum, and shot from the porte cochère. Rupert jogged ahead of Bailey, sliding through the doors as they reopened, and pushed his way through a group of patients waiting at the reception desk. Bailey paused, sucking a deep breath, and hobbled after his son.

"The nurse says he's in something called custodial intensive care. She won't even tell me what floor or wing he's in," Rupert said as he returned to Bailey. "I'm calling Christoff." He hit a button on his phone and waited.

"Yes, we're in the Emergency Room waiting area. No, I have no idea where you are. Okay. Okay." Rupert was quiet. He looked into his father's eyes for a moment, then Bailey heard a voice from the cell phone. "Got it." He ended the call and turned, calling, "It's this way," over his shoulder as he strode down the hall. Bailey attempted to jog after him.

"Signore! No cell phone!" a nurse called out as they passed the main desk.

As they reached a bank of elevators, Rupert sprinted ahead and caught the door of one car that was headed up. "Hurry!" he yelled at Bailey, waving him into the elevator. A group of doctors yelled at Rupert in Italian. Bailey bolted into the elevator, the doors closing behind him, and faced the three glaring doctors. He smiled, shrugged, and turned around.

"He's on the seventh floor, room 722. Christoff will be there." The doctors got off on five, each muttering what was surely an Italian curse as they exited. A moment later, they arrived at the seventh floor.

Christoff was pacing outside the elevator. He pointed at Rupert and ordered, "Follow me." There was no recognition of Bailey.

Christoff led them along one arm of the wing and rounded a corner. Bailey identified several uniformed and plainclothes officers hovering in the hallway beyond them. They drew the group's attention as they approached and parted. Christoff stopped outside of room 722 and caught Rupert on the chest with an open hand.

"He's not conscious. At least he hasn't been for the past half hour. I'll only allow you a few minutes," Christoff said, finally making eye contact with Bailey. "After you see him, I want to see both of you. I have a conference room reserved on another floor. I'll meet you out here in five minutes."

Rupert thanked him and allowed Bailey to enter the room ahead of him.

Two nurses were stationed at Parnell's bed. It was a private suite. One nurse was on the near side of the gurney, obstructing Bailey's view of his friend. The other nurse was monitoring the bank of machines on the far corner of the room. The nurse standing at the bedside turned as they entered and held up a hand. Rupert halted and caught his father's jacket sleeve. Bailey skidded to a stop. The nurse turned back, finished what she was doing, then backed away from the bed, motioning for them to approach.

The person beneath the bed sheets was heavily masked. A thin stocking covered the top of the head. It was impossible to recognize who was lying in front of them. Bailey stepped to the bed rail and examined Parnell's face. Emerging bruises, smudges of grotesque yellow and reddened purple, contrasted with the nearly translucent skin that delicately draped his facial bones. A number of scattered open wounds, glistening with antiseptic, peppered the left side of his face. Bailey finally allowed himself to listen for the electronic echo of Parnell's pulse emitting from one of the bedside machines. He looked up at the first nurse and asked, "How is he?" The nurse looked alarmed and shot a glance to her partner.

"He's stabilizing," the other nurse said. "He had … cardiac, uh, arrest, yes? That is correct English?"

"Yes," Rupert said, joining Bailey at the bed rail.

"The doctors were with him. We …" she started, then pantomimed the shocking pads. "Yes? You understand?"

Bailey nodded and the nurse smiled.

"Yes, and he … he came back." She moved forward and ran the tip of her finger across the thin strip of exposed skin on his forehead.

"Is there anything else you can tell us?"

The nurse sighed and gazed over the faint hump of Parnell's body under the sheet. "Dehydration. Loss of blood. Infection … in his hands," she said, gesturing toward Parnell's right arm. It was heavily bandaged and lying on top of the sheets.

"Has he been conscious, awake?" Bailey asked.

The nurse shrugged and said, "Yes and no. He opened his eyes, make noise, but he has not said anything I understand."

Bailey looked at the face, the body seemingly disintegrating beneath the stark white linens, and tried to force himself to recognize one of his oldest friends. He recalled the countless colleagues he'd seen fallen over the decades. It had been a dozen years since he'd watched anyone this close to him die. It was one of the things he thought he'd escaped when he left the force. It was surreal and frustratingly sad to watch Parnell deteriorate. There should be wry quips streaming from his lips, the subtlest of looks, grins, twitches of the cheek. Instead, he beheld a poorly crafted mummification of his friend.

"We'll leave you for a few moments," the nurse finally said. She said something in Italian to her partner and they slipped from the room.

Rupert joined Bailey and placed a hand on his father's. Bailey appreciated Rupert's demonstration of support, of love, but continued to focus on Parnell's face and his breathing.

"You know, Dad, there's a good chance he'll pull out of this. He's a tough old bastard, just like you."

Bailey nodded, savoring the contact with Rupert's grip.

"I want to see a sign. Something that gives me some sense of hope," Bailey said as much to Rupert as to Parnell.

"You know, they say that patients in comas, people who are unconscious, can hear what doctors, friends, family members are saying while they're out of touch. Tell him what you're thinking. It may make a difference."

Bailey exhaled and shrunk a bit. Aside from the incessant, but reassuring bleep of the pulse monitor, the room remained completely still and silent. Bailey took another deep breath.

"Look here, Parnell. We've been scampering all across half the globe these past few weeks, and we still have work to do. You can't leave me now. You can't leave Stuart. God knows I feel horrible about stranding him with Desta in that bloody jungle. We've got one more trip to Africa to go, Parnell. I need you there with me. To reel in Stuart, to … avenge, to some degree, Malcolm's senseless murder. Hold on, old man."

Bailey felt Rupert squeeze his hand again and release it. Rupert backed away from the bed and left the room.

"God damn, you, Parnell Sumner. I'll be back here every day until I see your blasted crooked teeth and smell your rancid tea breath again. Then I'll drag your pathetic living corpse down to Kenya and have Gavin pour us an unending stream of scotch until your wounds pickle. Do you hear me? Do you understand, you filthy twit?"

"Excuse me, sir?" he heard from behind him. He recognized the nurse's strained English. "Please, he needs rest. Please come out now."

Bailey raised a hand to touch Parnell's arm, resting beneath the sheets, but pulled back at the last minute. He had an irrational fear that contact would negate his command for Parnell to recover. Bailey took a step backward, turned, and shuffled from the room.

The crowd outside of Parnell's room hadn't dissipated. If anything, it had grown over the past several minutes. A few of the men regarded him as he exited, but quickly returned to their conversations. Bailey peered down the hallway to his left and found Rupert talking to Christoff. He yanked on his jacket sleeves and walked toward his son.

Rupert was facing Bailey's direction while Christoff leaned into Rupert's face, a shaking finger raised up to his nose. Bailey could hear Christoff hissing. Rupert broke his focus on Christoff and met his father's gaze. Bailey heard Christoff pause, tilt his head, and spin around.

"We'll continue this later," Christoff spat and stormed past Bailey, ignoring him.

"It doesn't appear that he's put this evening's incidents behind him, eh?" Bailey said. Rupert's face was flushed. He looked away and shook his head.

"He's embarrassed. That's all he's truly concerned with. How this makes him look."

"So it's considered bad form to break up an international extortion operation, solve a murder, and a kidnapping? All in one fell swoop? I must say the standards of excellence at Interpol have risen far beyond what I was accustomed to."

"Dad, you know what the problem is. We … *I* did this on my own, out of proper jurisdiction, without consent. I involved and endangered two other agents, also working without consent. He claims he's been fielding calls from Raymond Kendall all evening."

"The Secretary General? Right, and he's unhappy about these accomplishments as well?"

"Again, I did this outside of protocol. You're not that daft, Dad."

"I know, I know. I remember all too well how management reacts when anything extraordinary occurs that they weren't informed about," Bailey said.

"Exactly. The local bureau chief has apparently been tearing into Christoff about us acting alone. I put him in a difficult position. If Christoff tried to admit he knew of our actions, he'd piss off the chief because he'd failed to escalate. If he said he was unaware, then it looks like Christoff doesn't have control of his operatives. He's been avoiding any disclosure, and he's still extremely pissed and embarrassed."

The two stood quietly for a moment. Bailey knew there was little he could do to buffer the situation. Rupert was right. He'd acted independently, wrangled in Lexi and Anand, and ended up with several dead perpetrators. At best, there would be a significant internal investigation that would end in a reprimand, something formal in Rupert's personnel file. It might not have any immediate impact but could certainly stall or halt his professional development. At worst, termination.

"Does he want us to leave?" Bailey asked.

Rupert shook his head. "No, in fact, he doesn't want me out of his sight for the time being. I'm not so sure how he feels about you."

"Me?"

"He knows about The Kilimanjaro Club. He … he knows a few members." Rupert paused. "He's not a fan."

Bailey raised his eyebrows and rocked back on his heels.

"He feels there's 'a lawlessness that permeates the membership.' His words. It's difficult to argue with him given where we are tonight."

Bailey chewed on Christoff's slight. Not everything fit into the neat little boxes that the police and legislators attempted to create and maintain. In fact, the most significant efforts, the invisible fabric that protected everything from individual citizens up through entire nations, often succeeded only because they operated outside of established law and practice. To criticize the club because its members often followed similar paths when executing their expeditions seemed little more than petty jealousy. Men like Christoff pursued roles that gave them power and authority over highly structured organizations. Confronting those who ultimately achieved more by defying prescriptive protocol was akin to a blatant taunt. It sent them into a tizzy.

"Bullocks, Rupert. He's pissed because, ultimately, you'll be responsible for cracking this case."

"Dad, there was no case. This will never see the light of day."

"Helmut's disappearance was eventually reported in the *New York Times*, the *London Times*, and Lord knows what other papers. His death will generate the same level of press. People will want to know the story, and it'll point back to you."

Rupert stared at this father for a few seconds and then nodded. "I suppose you're right."

"Of course I'm right, God damn it, I'm your bloody father."

Rupert laughed and leaned back against the tiled wall.

"Perhaps that's my angle with him," Rupert said.

"Beg pardon?"

"Christoff. He's worried about the wrong thing. I can turn this in his favor. Make the press think he was behind it all. He could be cast as the hero."

Bailey smiled broadly, both because of pride and relief.

"Wait here a moment," Rupert said, and dashed after Christoff.

"How's Parnell?" Bailey heard from behind him. He smiled and turned. Prima was there, keys in hand and slightly out of breath.

Bailey regarded her, then hugged her tightly. "He's … well, he's alive. Unconscious. I'm not sure what else we could expect."

"Really?" she asked, pushing him away.

"He's been through a buzz saw, but he's somewhat stable, so they said. Looks a bit like … like a wraith, frankly."

Prima grasped his arm. "I'm sorry, Bailey. It must be so difficult."

He forced a weak laugh and shoved his hands into his pants pockets. "If he recovers, which I damn well expect him to, I'll get him back to normal. He'll regret ever wandering away from his proper guardians."

"And …" she said, tilting her head, "if he doesn't?"

It was something few people would have asked at a time like this, but it was what intrigued and enamored him with Prima. Fifty years earlier and he would have tried to work his charm. Not that he would have been even remotely successful. It had only worked for him once, but that didn't stop him from an attempt every few years.

"We've talked more of our demise than is healthy, I suppose. He'd be happy to pass on after such a stint. Kidnapped, tortured, hidden away. Who could ask for anything more mischievous? It would surely top any exit I have in front of me."

Prima hugged him again. "Do you and Rupert want to come back with me? Or would you rather stay here?"

"I think I'll check in on Parnell again, assuming the nurses will allow it. Then see what Rupert wants. His boss is none too pleased, I'm afraid. Rupert may be stuck here for the evening."

"Then let's figure that out," she said. Prima slid her arm beneath his and led him down the hall toward the tall, agitated man outside of Parnell's room.

# CHAPTER

# THIRTY-EIGHT

Desta and Stuart skirted the perimeter of the stone structure, mesmerized by the subtle crystalline glimmer that flickered from every minute crevice.

"Dad!" Aisha yelled. "Dad, what are you doing? We've got to go back. We left them behind. Grima, Lebna ... the others ..." Her voice climbed to a shriek, yet Desta seemed mesmerized, unable to acknowledge her cries.

"Desta, she may be right ..." Stuart said. He understood what exactly Desta was experiencing. The magnetism of the fragmented light was hypnotic. Once he looked away, he had to look back.

"Okay, dear ... just ... one minute."

"No!" She leaped forward and nearly tackled Desta. He stumbled against one of the spires, caught his balance, and steadied himself. Aisha wrapped her arms around him and pulled him away from the rock. Stuart kept his eyes locked onto Desta, fighting the draw of the stone. Aisha spun her father away from the rocks and grabbed Stuart.

"Aisha," Stuart said. "Do you really think it's safe? I ... I saw at least one ... one body."

"Look, you selfish rat," she growled at Stuart. "Those men risked their lives to get you here. I am not going to let you simply abandon them. Now let's move." She yanked Stuart's arm and marched him into the forest. Desta stumbled after them into the shadows.

"We have no weapons," Desta whispered. "We'll walk into a massacre."

"Shhh," she said. "I have your machete," she said, holding up the huge knife. Desta had dropped it near the rock formation. "Whoever attacked us is probably gone."

"We don't know that," Stuart said.

"Listen. We can't just leave them. We have to bring them back here. And we left our packs. We need them, too."

Stuart glanced at Desta. The old man didn't react at first, but then nodded. Aisha grunted and plunged forward. She wielded the machete expertly, slicing through the ubiquitous ferns and vines. She worked her way into a rhythm for a several yards, then froze. She held a hand up behind her. Stuart and Desta obeyed. Aisha crouched and crept forward, keeping one hand behind her and the other, holding the machete, pointed forward. She stopped again. There was no movement, no sound, no breeze, then she bolted, screaming wildly, and disappeared behind a barrier of branches. Desta sprinted after her, screaming her name.

Stuart hesitated, terrified of what to do. Aisha's and Desta's screams blended. A brief, deafening sputter of gunfire rang through the trees, then another scream. Stuart closed his eyes and waited. He heard a voice. Aisha. He opened his eyes, thrust his hands forward, and charged through the smothering plant life. The screams and gunfire had stopped. He pushed through the thinning vegetation and popped from the jungle into a familiar setting.

Aisha and Desta stood in the middle of four motionless bodies. Stuart swept his gaze across the group. He recognized Hakim, Grima, and Lebna. Only Lebna was moving. The fourth body was clad in make-shift camouflage. It didn't have a head.

"Stuart, come here," Aisha said, waving him forward. She bent over Hakim and felt for a pulse. "They're all still alive, but just barely. We need to move quickly. You take Hakim. I'll take Lebna, he's smaller. Dad, can you carry Grima?" Desta nodded without hesitation.

Aisha stood and pointed to their packs. "First, we get these men out. Then we'll worry about the packs. Pick someone and hurry. Kaleb is still out there."

Stuart had never carried another human being. He remembered reading that a lifeless or immobile body was extremely cumbersome and difficult to maneuver. He dragged his pack over to Hakim and crouched. Blood soaked through Hakim's shirt and jacket. Hakim made a disturbing whistling sound as Stuart slid a hand beneath him and pulled him into a sitting position. Stuart kneeled further and wedged his shoulder into Hakim's abdomen. The man's ribcage felt like a thick woven basket. Stuart staggered, pushing upward, grasping at Hakim's clothes. Hakim cried out as Stuart replanted his feet to gain leverage. He pumped his legs, sliding Hakim over the center of his shoulder, and stood. Aisha and Desta had already taken Lebna and Grima out of the jungle.

When he emerged into the clearing, Lebna and Grima were laying in the shade of the rock. He lurched toward the men and eased Hakim down beside Lebna. Stuart dropped to his knees, his heart thudding in his chest.

"Stuart," Aisha called. She was hauling one of the packs out of the trees. "Help me."

"Where's Desta?" he said, huffing.

"Searching for Kaleb," she answered, swinging her pack near the wounded men. She unzipped a pocket and pulled out a roll of gauze and a soft plastic packet. She laid the items on Lebna's chest and ripped open his left sleeve. His arm was a bloody mess. A steady burble of blood pulsed from Lebna's left bicep, just above the interior of his elbow. Aisha grabbed the packet, ripped it open with her teeth, and squirted a stream into the wound. Lebna didn't react. If he hadn't seen the blood pumping from the wound, Stuart would have assumed Lebna was dead.

"Check the others. Tally the wounds, then let me know where we need to start."

Stuart scrambled to Grima and Hakim. Both men were breathing, but Hakim's breath was hitching. His entire abdomen, past his waist, was soaked in blood. Stuart inched forward and began unbuttoning Hakim's shirt. He flinched as he pulled the shirt open. Hakim's stomach was peppered with black holes. Stuart glanced at Hakim's face just as he began coughing up blood.

"Aisha," Stuart said. "He's … Hakim's bleeding from the mouth. It's really bad."

"No shit," she said. "Give me a moment." She finished wrapping a bandage around Lebna's arm, tied it off, and scooted toward Stuart. "Get him," she said, nodding toward Grima. Stuart nodded and shifted around to Grima's side.

Grima appeared to be relatively unscathed. Stuart scanned him from the head down to his legs but didn't see any obvious wounds. Grima's eyes were open but he stared blankly into the sky past Stuart.

"Grima," Stuart whispered. He grabbed Grima's chin and pulled his face toward his own. Grima's eyes were flat. Then he saw the blood pooling behind Grima's right ear. He leaned down and lifted Grima's head off the dirt. His thin hair was matted with blood. "This doesn't look good either." He shifted his weight and felt something damp on his foot. He looked down and saw another large pool of blood. Then he realized the problem. Grima's left foot was spun in the wrong direction. "Aisha …"

Grima bucked upward, nearly knocking Stuart backward. A guttural moan erupted from Grima's throat and his eyes bulged. He convulsed, snapping into the fetal position for a second, then shooting back into a rigid line. Aisha jumped up and shoved Stuart aside. She grabbed a stick from beyond Grima's head and shoved it between his teeth.

"Get my bag, Stuart! Now!" she yelled at him. He reached past Hakim, snatched her backpack, and swung it toward her. She caught it and brought it to her side. "Hold his arms. Get up over his head and hold him down." Stuart straddled Grima's head and grabbed at his thrashing arms. He snagged both wrists and pinned them to the dirt. Aisha muttered something under her breath and tossed the bag aside. She peeled a tablet from a square of foil and jammed it between Grima's teeth. The pools of blood beneath his head and at his ankle grew. "Hold him!" she yelled again.

"Wait! Wait!" Stuart heard from behind him. Desta ran from the jungle with his pack and slid in beside Stuart. He yanked a flask from his pack and thrust it toward Grima's lips. Stuart released one of Grima's arms and slid to the side.

"Dad, he's con— "

"No, make him drink this," Desta said, tilting the canteen so that a small trickle of thick purple liquid oozed onto Grima's teeth and lips. "Drink, damn you," he whispered. Desta poured another measure into Grima's mouth, and Aisha pulled his chin up so that he was facing directly upward.

"What is that?" Stuart said.

"Drink, Grima, drink!" Desta wailed. He swept the excess liquid that ran down Grima's cheek into the man's mouth.

Suddenly, Grima's tongue slid from between his teeth and licked at his lips. There was a pause, then he licked again, pulling his lips in and sucking at the purple ooze.

"Good, good," Desta whispered, rising. Beads of perspiration gathered along Grima's forehead as his skin darkened. Then the bucking started again. Grima's slender body bowed upward, balancing for a moment, then crashed back to the ground. His entire body flexed violently, then relented, then flexed again. The bucking stopped, but Grima's arms and legs began to spasm. Then he fell still.

"Dad," Aisha said. She leaned over Grima and clasped his face in her hands. Almost immediately she pulled them away. "He's burning up!"

Desta didn't move. He looked at Stuart and then his daughter. "It's okay. That's a good sign. He'll cool down quickly."

Aisha hesitated, then returned the back of her hand to Grima's cheek. "You're right. He's still warm but not hot." Stuart watched Grima's face relax. The tension that had forced the man's body into such rigidity melted away. Grima's chest rose as he pulled in a deep breath.

"Quick, Aisha. Over here," Desta said, crouching over Lebna. Aisha knelt over Lebna and squeezed his cheeks, attempting to pop his lips open. They relented and she slid an index finger between his teeth.

"Go," she said. Desta raised the flask to Lebna's lips and squeezed a runny glob into his mouth. His tongue darted at this lips, eyes still closed, and then his body jerked to the side in a vicious spasm. The tremors continued as he rolled on his side. Desta motioned for Aisha to back away. The seizure grew more violent, Lebna's arms and legs thrashing, at times at impossible angles, snapping sounds cracking the air.

"Dad, something's wrong."

"Wait," Desta whispered, his brow furrowed. As quickly as the spasms had started, they subsided. Lebna let out a low groan and rolled onto his back.

"It seems unpredictable, Aisha. I … I think he'll be okay. Let him be. Now," he said. pointing to Hakim. "Help me with him." Aisha stood and Lebna screeched. Aisha and Stuart recoiled. Lebna arched off the ground, as if he'd been electrocuted, his neck craning, veins thrusting from his neck, the back of his head supporting his entire upper body, then he fell back flat. There was an instant of silence and then Lebna's mouth shot open. A thick jet of blood and mucus rocketed from his lips. Aisha lunged toward him but Desta waved her off. The gore continued to spray from his mouth. Lebna's hands and forearms swelled rapidly.

"Get back, oh God," Desta said. Lebna shuddered again, and blood splattered across Grima and Hakim. Lebna thrashed from side to side, the blood finally subsiding, then he fell still. A second later his left hand twitched.

"What the hell happened?" Stuart said. Desta was several feet back from them now.

"I-I'm not sure," Desta answered quietly. "It may be an allergy, a … a reaction. It may be …"

Aisha was at Lebna's side now, cradling his head and placing a hand on his neck. "Oh, no," she whispered, rocking him slowly.

"What is that, Desta? What did you give them?" Stuart asked.

Desta raised the small canteen and said, "It's what the fountain produces. It's … a healing agent."

"What the hell kind of healing agent kills someone, Desta?"

Stuart joined Aisha and slid Lebna's wrist into his hand. There was no pulse.

"How did you get it?" Stuart said, looking up at Desta. "You found it? The fountain?"

"It's hidden within this rock," Desta said. "When I realized the extent of their injuries, I … I went inside. I wasn't looking for Kaleb. I was looking for this," he added, raising the flask.

"But what happened?" Stuart asked.

The old man turned away from them. "I've never heard of this happening, but … I suppose … I mean, I haven't seen it administered more than half a dozen times." He turned back to face them. "The initial convulsions," he said, waving toward Grima, "the brief, intense body heat. The rapid recovery. That's what I've seen before. Aisha, I'm so sorry, so sorry. I don't know what else to say."

"We need to take care of Hakim," Stuart said to Aisha. She rocked Lebna a moment longer and then rested his head gently on the dirt.

"What if the same thing happens?" Aisha asked. She was looking at Stuart, not her father.

Stuart shook his head. "He'll die if we don't do anything." Aisha stared at Lebna's distorted face and slid around to Hakim. He was still breathing, but it remained shallow. Stuart waved Desta over and then moved to the other side of Hakim. Every square inch of his clothing seemed to be awash in blood. Hakim's hands shook.

"Quickly, he's going into shock," Aisha told her father. Desta followed the same basic ritual. Hakim's mouth had fallen open and easily took the substance. Aisha and Stuart shifted away from Hakim, waiting for the fluid to take effect.

First, Hakim's eyes shot open. Instead of the bucking that the others exhibited, his body began to vibrate. An audible hum rose from Hakim's lips. His mouth fell open and the hum transformed into an alien warble rattling from deep within his chest. The wail was broken by a series of grunts, his legs kicking up each time. Stuart watched his open mouth, waiting for the groans to give way to the fountain of gore. Instead, Hakim began to perspire. Aisha moved in and caressed Hakim's forehead. The vibrating subsided as she gauged his temperature. She glared at her father.

"Red hot," she said. "It seems to be working." Hakim exhaled, like an exaggerated sigh of relief, and softened. Grima began to stir, returning to consciousness. Stuart stepped around Lebna and crouched beside Grima.

"Grima? Are you okay? Can you hear me?" Stuart asked.

Grima's eyes floated toward Stuart's voice. He looked terrified but managed a nod.

"Good, good. Just rest. We'll get you some water. Are you thirsty?" Grima nodded again. Stuart looked down at Grima's mangled left ankle. "Does it hurt?" Grima wrinkled his forehead and shook his head.

While Grima and Hakim rested, Desta and Stuart moved Lebna's body near the jungle and draped one of Aisha's spare shirts over his face. They didn't discuss what to do with his body.

"We need to find Kaleb," Aisha said. It was more of an order than a suggestion.

"I don't know, Aisha. I'm worried about going back right now. We have no idea where he might be or if he's even alive," Desta answered.

"We've got a bloody decent idea where he is," she yelled, pointing to the jungle. "Right back in there! If he's dead, we'll find his body. If he's alive, then he's hurt, and he's not gone far. I'm not leaving without looking."

"No one said anything about leaving," Desta said.

The sun dipped behind a mountain range out of their view, and a grey-green shadow swallowed the upper edges of the rocks that flanked them. Stuart realized they were going to spend at least one additional night outside, and a heaviness settled in his gut.

"We've got to go now," Aisha said. "It'll be too dark if we wait."

Desta scanned the tops of the surrounding trees as if there were a hidden escape hatch tucked away that would spring them from the valley. "Okay," he said, sighing. "You're right. Stuart, you go with Aisha. Take the machete. When it gets dark, you come back. I'll set up camp and tend to our friends."

Aisha grabbed her pack and rifled through it. After some digging, she pulled out a small, sheathed knife and tossed it to Stuart. "I'll take the machete. Let's go."

Three steps into the jungle and nearly all light disappeared.

"Don't worry. This isn't dark. You'll adjust in a minute. When it's truly dark, you'll know. You won't see a thing."

She led them back through the area they had cut through earlier and back to the small clearing where they'd rescued the others.

"Do you think he's still around here? Would he have tried to go back?"

Aisha shook her head. "I have no idea. It depends upon his injuries.

He could be hiding, just waiting for confirmation that it's safe to come out or head home." She placed her hands on her hips, the machete handle dangling from her fingers by a thin, rough rope. "Let's search the perimeter of.this area. Don't wander too deep into the jungle." She pointed to her right and they began their search.

He wasn't sure if the natural light was fading faster than he'd expected or if this section of the jungle was simply denser, but they were in near total darkness just outside the clearing. Aisha reached back and grabbed Stuart's hand.

"Okay, so this is pretty dark," she said. They trudged a few steps, and she began to call Kaleb's name quietly. Stuart checked their distance from the clearing as often as he could. In most places it was impossible to tell if they were anywhere near the open area.

As they completed a full circle, at least as far as Stuart could tell, he began to call Kaleb's name as well. A few seconds later Aisha stopped. "Shhh," she said, squeezing his hand. The steady background hum of insects, birds, shimmering leaves, hissed across Stuart's ears. "There," Aisha said, gripping him tighter. He couldn't hear anything but the random activity surrounding them, then he heard it. A low, fluttering moan on their left. Aisha jerked him forward and plunged into darkness. "Kaleb!" she screamed, darting from side to side. Stuart lost the moaning and focused on maintaining his balance and dodging the invisible branches that lashed at his face and neck.

The light had completely abandoned this part of the jungle, and the terrain was growing more uneven. Aisha's grip on Stuart's hand slipped as they clambered over the rocks and through the invisible crevices. He stumbled to his right, lost Aisha's hand, and crashed onto his knees. Something sharp punctured his shin, eliciting a cry.

"Stuart!" Aisha called. He took a breath and began to reply when he felt a hand grab his forearm.

CHAPTER

# THIRTY-NINE

The evening of April 29, 1938 was a historical night for the Nairobi Kilimanjaro Club. First, it was a Friday, so it was a story night. Second, the Duke of St. Albans, Osborne Beauclerk, a dear friend of Walter Hightower's, had arranged to celebrate the thirtieth birthday of his son, Charles, at the club in Kenya. Finally, two warring exploratory parties, one led by Wilfred Wainright, and the second by Malcolm Buckley, had returned to Nairobi earlier the night before. Both planned to present their stories that evening.

As with any production of this magnitude, Hightower's plans didn't unfold flawlessly. His partners, Black, Fitzgerald, and Enright, bristled at Hightower's efforts to sensationalize the club. Their word-of-mouth marketing approach had suitably seeded the membership of the Nairobi club and generated a high demand for additional clubs across the globe. Efforts to maintain secrecy remained paramount, and the strict privacy of the club fed its mystique. Still, Hightower's attempts to insert the Nairobi club into the headlines of the society pages in New York, London, Los Angeles, and Paris soured on his partners. And while they did nothing to derail Hightower's objectives, they passively boycotted the event by not attending nor assisting in any manner.

Entertainment started at 8:00 p.m., and dinner was to be served at 8:45, with the Friday Stories scheduled to begin at 10:30. Just before dinner, Hightower's adrenaline high tapered off. Neither Wainright nor Buckley had made an appearance. The energy throughout the club, however, was unprecedented. Hightower estimated that even if the story-tellers failed to materialize, the event would still be considered a rousing success based solely on the remaining guests' fervor.

A moment before the first course exited the kitchen, Wilfred Wainright appeared at the top of the circular steps. The attendees erupted into wild applause as Wainright waltzed around the perimeter of the tables, waving and shaking hands as he encountered various club members and other familiar faces. The Wainright table was situated on the far side of stage right, and Hightower intercepted Wilfred halfway through this parade and escorted him to his seat.

As the applause and greetings died down—the quartet had stopped once they'd been drowned out—there was an awkward silence. Attention fell back to the staircase where, it seemed, most assumed Malcolm Buckley would follow. But after it became clear that no one was following Wilfred, the music started up again and the party stuttered back into action.

Hightower snuck back to the main bar and watched from afar. Hector, the head bartender, appeared at his side and delivered a generous pour of scotch.

"Thank you, Hector. So," Hightower said, without making eye contact, "what do you think of our little gathering thus far?"

"Frankly, sir, I'm worried about Mr. Buckley. By all accounts, he was back in Nairobi yesterday evening."

"Yes, yes, I know. I'm not worried about him, at least not from a health standpoint. But I am disappointed that he seems to be snubbing our invitation at the last minute."

"If I may say, Mr. Hightower, that's exactly what has me concerned. I can't imagine why Mr. Buckley would miss an evening like this. Regardless of how competitive both expeditions have been."

"Agreed," Hightower said. He sipped his scotch and decided to approach Wainright's party. Hightower circled the table, extending greetings to each guest before stepping behind Wainright.

"Wilfred, my good man, I must say, you look extremely well rested given what we can only guess was one of your most harrowing adventures."

Wainright, a somewhat curmudgeonly man, even though he was barely forty, waved off Hightower's comment and cradled his glass of Burgundy.

"What did you do to scare off Malcolm Buckley?" he said, hoping to bait Wainright into an actual conversation. "I can't imagine he's going to allow you to soak up the spotlight this evening."

Wainright took another swig of wine and cleared his throat. "I understand he's gone back to London."

"What?" Hightower said.

"Is that true?" Eliot Blair asked from across the table. "He's deserted us on this very special evening? The guest of honor, er," Blair said, attempting to correct himself, "I mean, one of the guests of honor? Rather rude, don't you say, Hightower?"

"I'm just pulling your chain, man," Wainright said. "I have no idea where he is. Likely that he's learned what my team and I will be sharing this evening and decided to take ill."

Hightower was angry with himself for reacting so strongly to Wainright's jest and at Wainright for acting like an ungracious snob, not that he should have expected more civil behavior. He fumbled through an awkward exit and headed back to the bar.

The remainder of dinner went as planned, and while Hightower was diligent about visiting each table, he did so fighting off the distraction of

Buckley's no-show. Hightower had no concerns about the grandiosity of Wainright's story. Wilfred was better known for his extravagant lies than he was for his actual accomplishments, which themselves were legendary. This was a man who had scaled Eiger, navigated over a thousand miles of both the Nile and the Amazon, sailed to the South Pole, and hiked the Great Wall of China. What Hightower craved, however, was the pure competition, the tension, the injection of testosterone, almost visible in the room when competing members went up against each other on a given Friday night. Wainright's presentation was guaranteed to be entertaining, but for Hightower, it would be anticlimactic.

By the time Wainright was scheduled to present, the combination of dancing and alcohol had whipped the guests into a genuine frenzy. Herding everyone back to their seats for Wainright's presentation took the concerted effort of the entire staff.

The service staff dimmed the lights, and Hightower regained the stage.

"Ladies, gentlemen, esteemed guests, most honorable members of The Kilimanjaro Club, welcome ... welcome to the Friday Stories." To his delight, the audience erupted. He waved them down and thanked them for their enthusiasm.

"As you know, we had anticipated a ... *friendly* rivalry of sorts, a gentlemanly bout of escapades, between Wilfred Wainright and Malcolm Buckley, but, alas, it appears Mr. Wainright has once again frightened off a formidable foe, not unlike the pride of rabid lionesses you fought off single-handedly back in '35, right Wilfred?"

Wainright, who remained seated at his table, failed to react to Hightower's tease, but the audience appreciated the humor.

"But before we hear from Wilfred, we have a bit of tradition to take care of, don't we fellow members?"

The service staff appeared from about the perimeter, each server carrying a cocktail tray laden with shot glasses.

"For those of you who haven't had the pleasure of joining us for our Friday Stories, you are being served a dram of Italy's most mediocre grappa. It was this modest beverage that my partners and I toasted with upon the creation of this very club nearly twenty years ago." One of the servers swept past Hightower and handed him a shot glass.

"Gentlemen, honored guests," he said, raising his glass.

"Tukio!" the attending members shouted at him.

"Tukio," Hightower repeated, then toasted the audience. Shouts of glee, disgust, screams, and laughter followed the downing of the grappa.

"Horrible, isn't it?" Hightower said, laughing. "Ah, but memorable. Now, let's make way for our keynote speaker this evening, Wilfred Arthur Wainright, voyager extraordinaire." The audience erupted again as Hightower backed away from the microphone and Wainright rose from his chair.

Wainright waved one of the servers up to the stage as he took his place behind the microphone and ordered another drink. He toyed with the microphone, cleared his throat, and began speaking.

"Contrary to popular belief, the result of our recent expedition didn't include the elimination of Malcolm Buckley." Scattered, uncomfortable laughter rippled through the room. "Frankly, I have no idea why Malcolm didn't bother to show this evening. But," he said, clearing his throat again, "that's not why I'm here tonight." A burst of piercing feedback split the air as Wainright fumbled with the microphone.

The server arrived at the front of the stage with his martini, and Wainright accepted it without acknowledgment.

"At some point last year, I had a conversation with a fellow club member, Nicholas Browne, who told me of a group of albino gorillas reportedly living in a highly secluded area of the Congo. I had never heard of such an animal and, after hearing Nicholas's tales, questioned the validity of the legend. After all, each of us—members that is—have been witness to truly unbelievable accounts of encounters with unicorns, Loch Ness Monsters, wild ape men, and so on. But, not long after hearing Browne's tale, I heard a similar recounting from one of the elders of the Luo tribe. This tribesman, Jomo, unprompted, related a nearly identical story. After a bit of investigation, I realized this legend was relatively well known, yet no one I encountered had ever observed the beasts first hand. In fact, the tale was always a third- or fourth-hand story. Something struck me about these independent, yet highly consistent, legends. I felt compelled to investigate myself."

Wainright went on to tell the story of his quest for the albino gorillas. True to form, his story featured a series of more and more miraculous and unbelievable trials and ordeals. He purportedly left Nairobi with two zoologists from Oxford and fifteen guides from Kenya and the Congo. Three of the guides were killed when they stumbled upon a rare nest of black mamba. Shortly thereafter, they were attacked by what Wainright categorized as "an undocumented tribe of violent cannibals" who were committed to stocking their food stores with the flesh of Wainright's crew. Finally, before ever stepping foot in the Congo, his team traversed an expanse of grassland saturated with enormous attacking bees.

By this time Wilfred had polished off the martini and waved down another server for a refill. Wainright's mastery was in his ability to transform from a grumpy, smug intellectual into a hypnotic storyteller. He painted vibrant, detailed landscapes, layered intricate smells, sounds, and textures into his address. From Hightower's vantage, the entire room was literally on the edge of their seats waiting to hear Wainright's tale unfold.

Both zoologists carried sophisticated photography equipment to capture images of the gorillas. Secretly, Wainright admitted, he hoped they might have the opportunity to capture a juvenile specimen for the London Zoo. He'd coerced one zoologist to bring an ample supply of tranquilizers, reportedly to fend off lions or hippopotamuses, but he anticipated the drugs would also allow him to snare an albino gorilla of his own.

"After thirteen days in the trenches, plodding through endless fields of marshland, swamp, incredibly dense jungle, so dark in midday that we carried torches to penetrate the gloom, we fell upon a highlands meadow that looked as if it had been transported from a spring day outside of Edinburgh. Painfully blue sky, not a trace of clouds, a blanket of foliage caressing the undulations of the hillsides. We stopped, unable to move on, stunned by the magnificence of the area. After some indeterminable time, I saw movement off to my left, two or three hundred feet away. The grasses swayed as some significant being moved slowly through them. Then, an arm, a hand, cloaked in ivory white fur, sprouted from the grass, followed by a face, a countenance that seemed both warmly familiar and frighteningly alien. A snowy primate, decidedly not human, and yet so identifiable.

"I couldn't move. None of us breathed. Every member of the team was frozen. As if on cue, the grass began to move in a wave across the landscape before us, and two, four, a dozen, *two* dozen, beautiful, alabaster white gorillas emerged. It was if they had been expecting us. Watching, waiting, knowing that I, and my crew of loyal travelers, would stumble from the jungle to witness their beauty. Their delicate, docile manner brought me to tears."

A murmur of gasps and amazement swept through the club's audience. Wainright took a large gulp of gin and continued.

"I have to admit, as a lifelong hunter and admirer of the world's wildlife, I struggled with what to do next. A part of me, a primal part of me, felt compelled to arm myself and bring down the nearest adult as the rarest of trophies. And yet another, honorable, subservient part of me understood the wonder of this find, the unique, unadulterated existence of this band. I knew, once I meditated on this fact, that I could do nothing but order the shooting ... of photographs of these wondrous beings."

Wainright paused for another sip and the audience began to applaud. Before he could wave them off, the entire room was standing. He waved harder, clearly frustrated, and the group quieted and returned to their seats.

"In a fairy tale world this would have been the end of the tale. Alas, it is not. We spent the remainder of the afternoon photographing and, eventually, tentatively interacting with the gorillas. I say tentatively only because both parties, ours and that of the gorillas, never appeared comfortable with either's existence. We made contact, examined one another's skin, hair, scent. More in awe than anything else. Regardless of what others had professed to me of these extraordinary mammals, I had no doubt that this was this group's first encounter with human beings. Our fascination was mutual. They truly appeared just as curious and amused by our odd manner—our clothing, our faces, our tools—as we did with them. It is an afternoon I will never forget."

This time the room remained silent, awaiting Wainright's next encounter, his next discovery. From far in the rear of the room a sole pair of hands began clapping slowly.

"Bravo! Bravo, Wilfred!" called a voice. Hightower, who had settled into an empty seat at a table near Wainright's, recognized the voice immediately.

Malcolm Buckley had returned.

Malcolm continued ahead, his hands raised in front of his face, clapping methodically. Wainright, in mid-sip, squinted and leaned forward, lips pursed as the liquor cascaded off the back of his palate. Every head in the audience turned toward Malcolm. A ripple of hushed voices shuddered through the room.

"The Lost Band of Albino Gorillas. You must be extremely proud, as well you should be," Malcolm continued, advancing upon the stage. "How often do we have an opportunity to either prove or disprove such a legend?"

Hightower was shocked, elated, and frightened. His original plan had come to fruition, yet he had hoped the two competitors would retain some degree of decorum. Malcolm Buckley, it seemed, was bent on disruption and embarrassment. Wainright hadn't moved since Malcolm slipped into the dim light. His mouth hung open, and his hand dropped his drink to his side, a thin dribble of gin oozing down the side of his glass.

"Truly, Wilfred, I'm not jesting. You deserve kudos for surviving the obstacles you described, and more so, I would argue, for proving the existence of the albino gorilla. I, for one, am most anxious to see the results of your photography." Malcolm ascended the steps of the stage and landed beside Wainright, who had yet to move or acknowledge Malcolm's presence. As Malcolm reached out to clasp an arm around Wainright's shoulder, Wilfred sprang to life and jumped aside, as if Malcolm had shocked him.

"Malcolm, really, this is quite unusual, unacceptable, to be rather frank. You, of all people, appreciate the club's protocol. If you're to take part in the Friday Stories, you need to be present at the point the stories are initiated, when the motto's recanted." Wainright's complaint was an embarrassment to those who knew him well. He was defensive, sophomoric in his defiance of Malcolm's presence.

Malcolm laughed at Wainright's dismay. "Wilfred, please, dear man, get a hold of yourself." He advanced on Wainright and hugged him again. "I'm not the least bit facetious. I am in true awe of your accomplishments. I'm here merely to honor your achievement and publicly announce my ... my forfeiture."

"Forfeiture?" Wainright sputtered. The remainder of his drink spilled upon the worn stage floor.

"Yes, yes, old man. I ... well, I had a life-changing expedition into Ethiopia, truly. But, when one attempts to portray something so personal, to do so at the expense of our guests is ..." he said, sweeping an acknowledgement to the crowd. "It's simply inappropriate. No, you and those fascinating, fascinating primates. You deserve the recognition this evening. Nothing could be more appropriate for such a celebration."

Wainright, somewhere during Malcolm's diatribe, appeared to regain his composure, as if considering whether to accept Malcolm's suspicious compliments. He righted his glass, albeit nearly empty, and stepped forward.

"Well, then, very well. Yes, yes, I … I appreciate your sentiments. But Malcolm, can't we count on you to share *something* of your journeys with us? Surely there must be some tidbit you can relay that will allow us to understand what you have encountered."

Malcolm smiled and hugged Wainright from the side again and shook his head. "No, no, no, my worthy adversary. It's not suitable for this environment, and, to some I would wager, quite dull. I'm ecstatic to be back in Nairobi, savoring a massive tumbler of Glenmorangie," he said, saluting the audience with his drink. "Listening to your story, taking in the music, the frivolity of Mr. Beauclerk's celebration—congratulations on mimicking adulthood!" he added, toasting the room again. Laughter erupted from several tables, and Hightower could hear Charles bark out some incomprehensible slur.

Wainright appeared to relax and allowed himself to smile.

"Wilfred, everyone here is well aware of the rivalry we've maintained. I'll be the first to admit that the mere thought of going up against you often fueled my motivation to live through the most amazing stories I could … concoct. But tonight … tonight is your night, in all honesty. Please, embrace and celebrate it. You deserve this!" Malcolm raised his glass, this time to toast Wainright, took a deep drink, and shouted to the room, "To Wainright!" In unison, perfectly on cue, the entire room shouted back, "To Wainright!" each raising their glasses and cheering.

Hightower broke from his trance and trotted to the stage to mitigate any ramifications of Malcolm's unprecedented forfeiture. Malcolm was about to raise a second toast when Hightower bounded onto the stage.

"Well, well," he said, splitting the two adversaries and raising his arms. "What a truly amazing evening, everyone. Wilfred, I am at a loss for words. Your discovery of this lost society of albino gorillas. Extraordinary, really. I can't think of another Friday Story quite like it."

Wainright backed away from Hightower and returned his glare to Malcolm.

"Uh," Hightower muttered, concerned that the men might still come to blows. "Malcolm! Please, I do understand, and I think we all can appreciate, your gracious forfeiture to Wilfred here, but, as Wilfred asked, could we impose upon you to at least give us a hint at the results of your expedition?"

Malcolm looked at the floor in front of him, smiled, and shook his head, hands clasped behind his back. "Oh, no. Not tonight. Tonight is Wilfred's night. Let's allow him to celebrate his most amazing accomplishments."

Hightower grinned at Malcolm, then spun toward Wainright, extending his hand.

Wainright jumped back, as if spooked, then turned and started to march off stage when Hightower snagged his jacket sleeve. While he'd been worried about the evening possibly disintegrating into a drunken brawl, he was now thoroughly offended at Wainright's contempt.

"Wilfred," Hightower growled, spinning the taller man toward him. "Shake … my … hand," he said, grabbing Wainright's right hand and clinching it. Wainright returned the grip and gritted his teeth.

"Let go, you embarrassing charlatan. I'm leaving."

Meanwhile, Malcolm was waving to the dining room and striding down the front stage steps. Hightower released Wainright with a slight shove and turned as Malcolm disappeared into the crowd. Nearly everyone in the dining room appeared to have left their seats and were either talking excitedly or crowding toward the two adventurers. Hightower stood alone on the stage watching the evening continue without him.

By midnight, everyone in the club had forgotten about Malcolm's ironic upstaging of Wainright's presentation. Although Wainright gloated over winning the competition, most of the post award chatter focused on Malcolm. What had he found? What had seemingly caused his notorious ego to be supplanted by uncharacteristic humility and deference? Hightower had hovered at Wainright's table far too long in an attempt to calm Wainright's temper. While his presence did seem to defuse a sliver of Wainright's anger, it didn't stop the old explorer from barking insults between gulps of gin.

"Bloody clown! What kind of guttersnipe saunters into an event such as this and tosses off some derisive mumbo-jumbo about celebrating my achievements? As if he didn't care, didn't just spend a fortnight tramping through Ethiopia. What a pompous … turd." His last comment generated embarrassed guffaws, and one of the ladies at his table coughed white wine through her nose.

Hightower was surprised to find Malcolm at the far end of the bar, talking to a retired member of Parliament who had recently joined the club. He flagged down the bartender, ordered a port, and walked up behind Malcolm.

"I do recommend the Amazon. Mind you, it's a grueling trip. The mosquitoes are the size of sparrows and the food … well, the nearest sophisticated metropolis is on Curaçao. You won't see anything recognizable for weeks," Malcolm was telling the man.

"Malcolm, Mr. Harding, please pardon my interruption," Hightower said, clapping Malcolm on the shoulder.

"Mr. Hightower," Harding said. He grabbed Hightower's hand and shook it with both of his. "I want to thank you again for inviting me to this wonderful celebration."

"You're quite welcome, Bradford, but you know, as a member, you are welcome, and I dare say expected, to join us for these significant events."

"Oh, I will, I will," Harding said, still shaking Hightower's hand. Hightower pulled way, forcing a laugh, and turned his attention to Malcolm.

"Malcolm, may I have a word with you in private?" Hightower asked.

"Yes, of course, Walter," Malcolm said. "I hope you'll pardon us, Bradford."

Harding blushed, profusely thanked Malcolm for his time, and staggered along the bar toward an open stool.

"Hightower, I do hope you're not going to lecture me on the proper etiquette for Friday Stories again," Malcolm said. He raised his scotch and took a healthy drink.

"No, I can't say I have any real issue with what happened this evening. Just look at this place," Hightower said, motioning to the dance floor. "Can you recall ever seeing this many people having such a fine time?"

Malcolm gazed at the room and smirked, "No, I suppose not. I assumed, though, that Wainright had sent you over to chastise me for my behavior."

"Oh, he's right pissed. And while I can't say I necessarily blame him, I am having difficulty identifying any real offense. I'm curious, though. What happened during your expedition? What would cause you to … to simply show up and concede to Wainright? Anyone but Wainright."

Malcolm laughed and polished off his drink.

"All I can tell you, Hightower, is that it was a most unexpected discovery. Our trip was rather rudimentary, at first. I planned to complete some detailed mapping of the Simien Mountain range and look into a few local legends, but really didn't expect to return with anything of true substance. The whole ordeal with Wainright was an afterthought, really. I wanted him to run off thinking that I was pursuing some unfathomable treasure.

I wanted him to worry night and day about what I might return with. And to a great degree it worked. It made this evening that much more enjoyable."

"All right, I can understand you wanting to tease Wainright, but Malcolm, there's something else you're not sharing. You're so … I don't know, almost melancholy. Not like you one bit."

"I stumbled upon something completely unexpected, Hightower. Something I would have never imagined in my wildest dreams. And, you see, it transcends any petty argument I have with someone as shallow and pithy as Wainright. I guess I'm basking in the pleasure of my discovery. I don't know if that explains what you're seeing, but it's the bloody truth."

Hightower regarded Malcolm for a moment and then looked away. The dance floor was still packed with twenty or thirty couples. On the perimeter and along the bar, the remainder of the guests were gabbing, laughing, and flirting. Hightower was proud of the evening's turnout, even if Wainright was furious. And now that Malcolm was being coy, he decided he'd done all that he could do to unwind the brief mystery of the evening.

"Well, all right, Malcolm. If that's your story, so be it. I'm off to find someone who'll intrigue me with wild, slanderous tales. You obviously don't wish to entertain my needs. So, piss off," he said, landing a hand on Malcolm's shoulder and winking at him.

"Piss off I shall," Malcolm said. He flagged down a bartender, pointed to his glass, and winked back at Hightower. "To a long life."

# CHAPTER

# FORTY

An irrational assortment of thoughts flashed through Stuart's mind between the moment he felt the hand grasp his arm and the moment his head collided with a cold, dense object. Flashlights. That was his first thought. Why on earth had they not thought to bring flashlights? Next was his mother. She'd be worried and angry that he was risking his life chasing down something her father had been involved with. His mother morphed into Prima. All he saw were her eyes, but he knew it was her, and there was something else he knew but couldn't articulate. Finally, his rent check. The day's date, the first of the month, flashed in front of his eyes. His check would be late. He'd be evicted. Where would he live? All of this shot between his synapses in a fraction of a second. Later, when he briefly had the ability to recall this memory, he would remember that his rent was automatically drawn from his bank account, as it had been from the time he moved into the apartment.

These visions swam together to form a vivid dream. He was standing in his office, gazing out the window, a window that typically looked out upon Park Row. But instead, he was looking over a vast, glaringly white beach. The beach was empty and immaculate. The bluest, clearest sea water he'd ever witnessed rippled against the pristine sand. He felt the urge to jump just as he heard his name.

"Stuart!"

The beach vision vanished into blackness. A blackness he realized he was now seeing because he realized his eyes were open.

"Stuart! Wake up! Are you okay?"

Consciousness rumbled in, followed by pain. His right temple throbbed. He pried a hand from underneath his stomach and jabbed at the side of his face. It was wet. Blood.

"I'm bleeding," he said. Who was he talking to?

"Okay, okay. Look. I need you to stand up. Kaleb is here. I think he tripped you. He's very badly hurt. Can you stand? Can you help me bring him back?"

Stuart attempted to survey the rest of his body. Nothing else ached, but he was worried about his head. What were you supposed to do if you had a concussion? Stay still?

"My head, Aisha. It's cut. Pretty badly, I think." He felt hands grasp his shoulders and lift. He responded by thrusting his hands alongside his torso and pushing upward. He brought his knees in, then his feet, and stood. The moment he was upright he began to stagger. The darkness surrounding him was splattered with pinpoints of light, then a wash of grey. He felt hands attempt to steady his swaying.

"Can you walk?" Aisha asked.

"I think so," he answered. The pain continued to thump in rhythm with his pulse but the dizziness was slipping away. "Where's Kaleb?" He heard a groan to his right.

"Take my hand again," Aisha said. "I'll lead you both back. Watch your footing. We'll take our time." Stuart felt Aisha grasp his hand. A tug pulled him forward through the darkness.

Aisha managed to guide them back into the clearing where Desta waited with the others. Kaleb collapsed on the dirt just outside of the jungle.

Desta rushed to Stuart and began examining his head. The cut must have looked horrific because Desta seemed afraid to touch it.

"It's a head cut, Desta. They bleed a lot," Stuart said. Desta stared into Stuart's eyes for a moment and then nodded, seeming satisfied. "Help Kaleb. He's in bad shape." Stuart lumbered to the edge of the rock and slid into a sitting position. Blood dripped down the front of his shirt. Aisha and Desta knelt over Kaleb and assessed his wounds. Desta retrieved the flask and held it to Kaleb's mouth. Stuart sucked in a breath, watching for Kaleb's reaction, but there was nothing. Aisha looked up at Desta, her brow furrowed.

"What's wrong? He's not reacting," she said.

"I'm not sure," Desta said. "There was very little left."

Stuart pulled his shirttail up to his face and wiped the blood that had run into his eyes. He hoped the cut hadn't been too deep, just bloody. The pain had receded to a muffled thump across his crown. He pushed himself upright and walked to Kaleb's side.

Desta scooped a few stray globs of liquid into Kaleb's trembling lips.

"Do you need to give him more?" Stuart asked.

"It's gone," Desta said, "I'll have to go back. I … I didn't get much on my first trip. There wasn't time. It's … you have to see it, Stuart. I'm not sure if I can get more."

"What do you mean?" Aisha blurted out.

Desta turned to her, his teeth clenched. "I retrieved what I could," he said.

Aisha seemed to sense Desta's frustration and backed off. Desta held the container upside down over Kaleb's mouth, waiting for another drop or two. Eventually, a bead the size of a small pea appeared around the lip of the bottle. Desta lowered the bottle over Kaleb's lips and shook it. The pea held on for a second, then dropped neatly between Kaleb's teeth.

All three waited, hoping for some reaction to the elixir. There was nothing.

Stuart knelt and placed his fingers against Kaleb's neck. He poked a couple of times and then felt something. He pressed down and detected the distant thump of Kaleb's pulse.

"He's still alive, but barely," Stuart said. "Maybe he doesn't have enough. Maybe there's a certain amount that triggers the reaction, kicks off the healing."

"Could be," Desta said, standing. "I'm not aware of any proper dosage. I don't know if anyone's ever tried to measure it."

"Father, can you take Stuart with you? See if you can get more? We can't give up."

Stuart stood up and grasped the extent of Kaleb's injuries. The fading glow of the sunset edged beyond the western ridge, and long shadows from the rocks and surrounding trees blanketed most of the open space. Kaleb's torso was split by the shadows, but Stuart could still see the deep machete wounds that cut across his chest. His legs were in tatters. Gunshot wounds, Stuart assumed.

Desta gauged the setting sun, and shielded his eyes. He paused, then shook his head.

"I'm concerned. It will be very dark soon," Desta said.

"Go! Go now! There's no time to be concerned," Aisha pleaded. "If we don't do anything, he'll die. And the others, who knows how much more they might need?"

Desta shook his head again. "They'll need nothing more. Once the body begins to react, there's no need for additional elixir."

"Come on, Desta. Let's try it. If it's too dark, we'll come back," Stuart said.

Desta sighed. "Okay, you're right. We have to try." He looked at Stuart. "Bring the empty containers and wineskins. We'll take every drop we can."

Stuart clapped and jogged to his pack. He had two small plastic bottles with screw tops and three wineskins of varying sizes. Desta and Aisha carried Kaleb over to the other men.

"Keep an eye on each of them," Desta said to Aisha. "Give them a few bits of food and water if they want it. They'll need their strength for the return." He turned to Stuart and said, "Come with me," motioning him toward the far side of the outcropping.

As they rounded the corner, Stuart realized the massive rock was cloaked in shadow. The matter that infiltrated the surface continued to shimmer as if lit from within. The absence of sunlight seemed to dampen the hypnotic sensation he'd felt earlier. From this side, Stuart could see how large the rock formation was. Thick green moss shrouded large patches of rock at its highest points. Several jagged spires shot at least thirty feet upward. Desta, already several yards ahead of Stuart, paused, turned, and pointed at the stone. As Stuart got closer, he noticed a narrow chasm that cut into the side of the stone at a sixty-degree angle.

"It's through here," Desta said. He stepped into the crevice and disappeared between the rock walls. Stuart found where he thought Desta had entered, but hesitated. It appeared the opening had closed behind Desta. Stuart leaned forward and examined the stone face but saw nothing but rock. He poked his index finger where he thought the gap had been and it continued, unimpeded, into an invisible space. The entrance was naturally camouflaged. He smiled, then placed his foot into the crack, hovered in place, waiting to touch ground, and found something solid. He stepped forward and found the thin hidden steps that had been chiseled into the rock.

Once he was inside the structure, he spotted Desta about twenty feet ahead at the top of the crevice. The moss grew thicker on the walls the higher he climbed, and he realized the growth created more camouflage for the rocks. From above, the colossal outcropping would blend into the surrounding plant life.

He joined Desta at the top and peered over the crest of the ledge. It was nearly impossible to distinguish what lay before them. Pointed rock, shadow, and thick moss combined to create an impenetrable texture.

"Now what?" Stuart asked.

"Just follow me," Desta said. The old man took a step downward and then a sharp left. They continued along the narrow fissure in the rock as the path zigzagged through the stone, diving deeper into the formation. After a pair of hairpin turns, Stuart realized they'd probably dropped back even with or below the ground level outside the formation. The fissure opened wider and Stuart could now see the steps below his feet. He stopped briefly and looked back. The path had disappeared, blended between the shadow, the moss, and the uneven texture of the rock. He turned back and saw Desta several yards below him.

"Come, come," Desta said, waving him forward.

Stuart hopped down the last few steps and joined Desta in a narrow natural hallway. The stone walls shot ten to twelve feet above their heads. Desta turned and advanced along the corridor. Stuart followed closely behind as the pathway bent in a gradual curve to their left. The wall to their right, the outer wall, leaned inward at fifteen to twenty degrees, mirrored by the lean of the inner wall. Stuart realized that again, from above, the top of the outer wall overlapped the inner wall, virtually erasing the existence of their path.

The arc of the channel tightened. They were spiraling toward the center of the structure. While the ground was finely stained with dust and dirt, the walls and surroundings seemed impossibly pristine. The moss didn't grow on the inner walls nor on the ground. No stray branch, misguided root, or discarded leaf tainted the structure. Stuart swiped the wall with his index finger. He drew it back and saw that nothing came away. No dirt, no dust. The stone was as smooth as polished marble.

When he looked up, he saw that Desta had stopped again. He stepped forward and realized the hallway ended, and an arched entryway opened to their left. He peered through the opening into an enclosed, oval shaped chamber, constructed from the same rock. The interior was featureless.

Desta said, "This way," and led them through the archway.

The ceiling was formed by a translucent material that looked like cloudy diamond, carved into layered, inconsistently shaped pentagons that produced a protective roof. The sparse external light scarcely illuminated the ceiling. Stuart tore his eyes from the ceiling and returned to the walls of the room. There was nothing, save him and Desta.

"Where's …" he started. Desta stepped to the wall and indicated a rectangular opening. Like the whole of the formation, it was hidden by the nature of the stone. The opening was approximately two feet wide and three feet high and started about three feet from the floor. At first, Stuart thought the opening was empty, but as he got closer, he could see light reflecting in deep blues and purples off of something hidden just below the surface.

As he continued to examine the space, he could see a much more intricate surface that lined the interior. There was a faint recessed panel about six inches on the back wall of the niche. He leaned toward Desta's side and peered into the opening.

He expected to see more of the crystalline stone structure they'd encountered in the rest of the structure. Instead, the panel appeared to be fashioned from some type of metal.

Aside from heavily treated metal sculptures he'd seen at various street art shows in Manhattan, Stuart could think of nothing that came close to the luster and beauty of the metallic surface. Almost imperceptible, intricately detailed engravings swirled across the surface, highlighted by narrow rainbows from an oil-like veneer. Completely organic shapes emerged out and disappeared into the surface randomly. The absence of any straight line or edge was both startling and comforting.

"What is it?" Stuart said, extending a hand to brush the surface. Desta's hand shot out like a cobra strike and yanked his hand away from the interior.

"The well. The fountain."

"How does it work? Where does the ... the liquid come from?" Stuart asked.

"Watch," Desta said. He reached into the opening and stroked a rounded rectangular piece that rose from the surface of the panel. The interior surface went black. Stuart had a sensation of movement. He heard a low hum and saw another similar shape open in the middle of the panel. The metal surrounding the new opening seemed to melt as the rectangle spread before them. Stuart heard an electronic *click* and the opening froze. A polished, platinum rod extended from the center of the rectangle, protruding out beyond the rock frame, and stopped. Desta looked at Stuart and smiled. He tugged a bottle from his pack and placed it under the end of the rod and tapped the top of the rod. The hum began again, a bit louder this time, and the rod shuddered. Desta watched the rod, holding the bottle steady, but nothing happened.

"Do you see? Nothing ..." Desta muttered. He tapped the rod harder. There was no change. He tapped again and one small drop of the purple fluid emerged from under the rod, hung for a moment, and then dropped into the bottle.

"Is there some kind of limit? Have we exceeded our—I don't know— daily allotment?" Stuart asked.

"I ... I can't say, Stuart. This ... I've never heard of it not producing."

"Tell me, have you been here before? I noticed that you seemed to check the map we brought, but I had the feeling this wasn't your first time."

Desta continued to concentrate on the rod for another beat, then backed up.

"I have," he sighed. "But this is only my third time. I came with

Malcolm the first two times, over twenty years ago. I wasn't sure it was still here. I … I wasn't confident I'd find it after all this time."

"Why didn't you tell us? You made it seem like—"

"I had a pact with Malcolm. I was never to speak of this to anyone. In turn, Malcolm was extremely generous. He compensated me well for acting as a guide."

"Compensated?"

"Both monetarily and … and in other ways." Desta motioned toward the rod weakly.

"The fluid? Is that what you mean?"

"Yes. Malcolm was mindful about who he shared this discovery with. I doubt that you're aware, but he planted—hid—small amounts of the liquid throughout the world, in case he needed it and wasn't in Ethiopia or near his home. In return for helping him return to this place, he provided me with vials of the liquid. I've secured them in case of an emergency. For obvious reasons, this is a difficult landmark to locate. I was very anxious I wouldn't be successful this time."

Stuart paused to process what Desta had just shared with him. His grandfather had discovered this fountain decades ago and had been visiting it regularly, he presumed, to draw from its reserves.

"So, what did he do with his share? You said he stored it, but where? Did he share it with anyone else?"

Desta didn't react at first, and then shrugged. "I heard him once say that he kept some in banks, safe deposit boxes, in major cities. Paris, Rome, Moscow, Tokyo. He didn't elaborate, and I didn't press."

"Do you know how often he visited? I mean, who else knows about this place? Who else has some of this liquid?"

"I think he came frequently after the first time I accompanied him. He claimed to discover this location in 1938. I first came with him in … 1968? Sixty-seven, perhaps? I would see him from time to time after that, in Addis Ababa. He would usually say something like, 'Visiting me mum,' with a wink, you know. I knew what he meant."

"Did he teach you how to use it? How to draw from it?"

"On our second visit, without my asking, he showed me exactly how to get to this part of the … monument, he called it, and how to draw from the fountain."

Stuart regarded the rod and the machine that was housed behind the rock wall. He noticed that the life had seemed to come back to the surrounding metal. The fluidity, the rainbow of reflections had returned. Desta's hand came into view again, tapping the rod lightly. They waited. Nothing happened.

"I realize this sounds crazy, but do you think it's empty? Tapped?" Stuart said.

Desta sighed and crouched down under the rod. "I suppose it's entirely possible. If so, then perhaps we've achieved some degree of success."

"How long has this been here? Was Malcolm the first to find it?" Stuart asked.

"I have no idea, Stuart. I can't believe Malcolm was the first. There have been numerous myths about similar fountains, pools of youth, of healing, for centuries. Herodotus was the local legend. Knowing that this one actually exists has always led me to believe that others knew either of this source, or others like it."

"Others?" Stuart asked.

"Of course. The Ponce de Leon legend? It was fairly prominent in its time. I have to believe that something similar exists, or existed, in Florida."

"Does it, this liquid, I mean, does it … prolong life? Allow you to live longer, as well as heal you?"

Desta nodded. "In a way. We've just seen what it can do to mortal wounds. Not only are those men healing, it's likely they extended their lives by ten, perhaps twenty years. You won't notice. They won't get visibly younger, at least not to a noticeable degree. It seems to work like a … a pause button on a remote control, you know? It suspends aging."

The ceiling darkened after Desta finished speaking.

"The sun. It's set. We should go," Desta said.

"But what about the fountain? We're out of liquid. Kaleb's not healed. He's not reacting to the liquid. We need to try again."

"No," Desta said shaking his head. "It's either empty, or it has decided to stop its flow to us."

"'It's decided? It, like it has a brain? This fountain is alive?"

"No, no. Well, at least I don't believe so. It's a machine. It's just not of this world. It doesn't follow our rules. And now it's decided we are done."

Desta stepped away from the opening. Stuart lingered a moment longer, still mesmerized by the intricate swirls that ran across the metallic surface.

Aisha's horrific scream snapped him back to reality.

# FORTY-ONE

I t took Prima two sentences to pull Christoff away from Parnell's door. Bailey wasn't even sure that it was what she said, but more how she said it, that distracted Christoff. Regardless, Bailey remained outside of Parnell's room until Prima appeared to transfix Christoff with her charm. Bailey watched her mannerisms, her facial expressions, and was mesmerized by how she drew the slimeball into her world. Just by watching the back of his head, Bailey could easily read Christoff's one-track mind—I will have this woman. It took him a moment, but he quickly realized and appreciated Prima's strategy in distracting Rupert's boss. Bailey gave her one last glance and slipped into Parnell's room.

The nurses had gone, and Parnell seemed to be resting calmly in his bed. The vital signs monitor chirped regularly in time with Parnell's pulse, and Bailey could see Parnell's thin chest rising and falling. He pushed the door closed and rushed to Parnell's side, digging in his pocket.

He extracted a thin, oval shaped flask of brushed nickel. Bailey glanced back at the doorway again and unscrewed the top of the flask. Once it was open, he checked his back again, then leaned over his friend. Parnell's lips were barely parted. Bailey slipped an index finger between Parnell's lips and eased his teeth apart. Parnell did nothing to resist. Instead, he stirred and his mouth opened wider. Bailey positioned the flask against his lips for a two count, then withdrew it. He spun the cap onto the container and thrust it into his sport coat pocket. Bailey stepped back and watched. For several seconds nothing happened, then Parnell's pulse jumped. A moment later his body shook beneath the thin white sheet. Parnell's eyes shot open wide as his body stiffened into a rigid arc.

The monitoring equipment in Parnell's room picked up the physical change. Parnell's pulse doubled almost immediately and his breathing halted. A second later, Bailey heard the alarms go off down the hall at the nurses' station.

The nurse who originally spoke to Bailey burst through the door and stopped herself when she saw Bailey.

"What happened?" she asked, wide eyed and out of breath.

"I'm not sure," Bailey said. "I stopped in to say goodbye when … things, this machine, started to beep loudly. He … he had some sort of spasm."

"Spasm?" the nurse asked.

"Yes, his whole body … tensed up, jumped, arced, just as the alarm went off."

The nurse scowled at Bailey, then marched around to the far side of Parnell's bed. From what Bailey could tell, Parnell was still rigid, just not springing from the mattress. His pulse was peaking at 160. The nurse placed her hand on Parnell's forehead. The moment her hand contacted his skin he seemed to relax. A few seconds later his pulse dropped back to 88.

The nurse looked up at Bailey, her forehead scrunched. "Odd. He's very warm, but, I suppose, not entirely abnormal. Did anything else happen while you were with him? Anything aside from the … spasm?"

Bailey shook his head and pushed his lower lip out. The nurse seemed to accept his response and returned her attention to Parnell.

"I'll be back with the clipboard. I want to document any changes in his status."

Bailey nodded and grinned as she exited the room. Once the door closed, he rushed to Parnell's side. A drop of the liquid hung in the corner of Parnell's mouth. Bailey pulled a handkerchief from his pocked and dabbed the purple drop from his friend's lips. He stepped aside and walked to the opposite end of the room and sat in one of the metal chairs. Bailey could still see the digital readout on the equipment. Parnell's pulse had edged back up over 100. He noticed a smaller number off to the bottom right of the pulse read-out. It read 105.7. Oh, God, he thought. It's his temperature.

The nurse nearly rushed back through the doorway, a doctor in tow. The physician, an Asian woman, glanced at Bailey and approached the side of Parnell's bed. The nurse stationed herself across from the doctor.

"Is it necessary for him to be here?" Bailey heard the doctor ask. She had posed the question while focusing on the equipment. The nurse turned her head slowly toward Bailey, stared at him for a moment, her face void of expression, and then said, "Yes. I think it's okay. Mr. Sumner seems to show more signs of recovery when his friend is here." She turned back to face Bailey, and he caught a slight smile in her dark eyes.

"Well, his spell is wearing off. The patient's pulse is rising again and his body temp is dangerously high. Quick, bring several cold packs. We'll see if we can take it down. What have you given him lately?"

The nurse rattled off drug names Bailey didn't recognize. The physician seemed to ponder this information and then said, "Give him 1,500 milligrams of Tylenol."

The nurse nodded and dashed out of the room. The doctor was inspecting Parnell's face and neck. She leaned in close to his face at one point and remained motionless. She stood upright again, did something to one of the monitors, and then turned to face Bailey.

"I'll ask you the same question. What have you given him lately?"

Bailey stood, a bit unsteady, and straightened his sport coat. He cleared his throat, avoiding eye contact, and then looked at her. "Given? Me? Why, nothing. What would I give him? I'm not a doctor. I'm only here to give him my thoughts, my blessings. He's a very dear friend."

The doctor pursed her lips, and then walked up to him. She was a good six inches shorter than Bailey and appeared wiry and fit beneath her immaculate coat. "If you truly want to save your friend's life, you need to be honest with me. He was severely dehydrated. To be honest, I am shocked that someone of his age could have survived that level of dehydration. There were … still are, a number of imbalances that we're attempting to stabilize. And while it's possible his body might have reacted the way it apparently did on its own—an extreme pulse and a fever spike—I'm skeptical. Especially after near-cardiac arrest. Our pharmaceutical approach is critical right now. A misstep, an improper dose, could kill him. So, I'll ask you again, what have you given him lately?"

This time Bailey locked on her eyes. He let himself begin to smile, but kept his lips tightly controlled. He breathed in slightly and said, "Doctor …"

"Yee," the doctor said flatly.

"Doctor Yee, you must understand. I've done nothing to jeopardize this man's health." Bailey then allowed the smile to spread across his face and let his head drop slightly to the side. Dr. Yee pursed her lips, took a deep breath, and then turned away from him. The nurse returned carrying bulky white rectangular packets. She helped Dr. Yee place them around Parnell. The nurse then handed a syringe to the doctor. Dr. Yee checked the measure and then injected the fluid into Parnell's IV.

"I'd like you to remain here in the room," Dr. Yee said to the nurse. "I'll stop by a bit later to check on him." Dr. Yee glared at Bailey and left the room.

The nurse busied herself by rechecking the various monitors and tubes connected to Parnell. Once she had completed her check, she sat in one of the chairs. Bailey watched the largest monitor and saw that Parnell's pulse had settled into the seventies, and his temperature was just above normal. The nurse caught him checking Parnell's vital signs and shook her head at him.

CHAPTER

# FORTY-TWO

Near the top of the steps, Stuart's right ankle slid and buckled beneath him. He felt a pop that sucked the wind from him. He collapsed onto his right elbow, the bone smashing into the unforgiving rock. Stuart began huffing, attempting to blow the searing pain from his body. It felt as if he'd slipped his foot into bubbling magma. The burn intensified as he tried to lift his foot off the ground and balance on his left leg. Another scream ricocheted off the walls.

"Get up!" Desta said. He was already ten yards in front of Stuart. "We've got to help her!"

Stuart didn't think there was any way he could propel himself forward another ten feet, let alone navigate the steps that led back to the jungle floor. The formation was completely draped in shadow now. Twilight was brief in these parts. Stuart pulled in another deep breath and nodded. He hopped, one shaky step at a time, to demonstrate his ability to actually move forward. Desta disappeared.

He heard more commotion from outside, voices, a brief scream.

"Screw it," he groaned, balancing on his left leg. He used his right hand to lean against the wall as he continued onward. While the bouncing intensified the pain, the combination of movement and agony propelled him forward, surging his adrenaline. He found a tolerable rhythm and made his way down the precarious slope.

He didn't trip until he was within sight of the exit. To avoid landing on his ankle, he swiveled to his right. His right heel skidded on the stone and sent him sprawling forward, his head slamming into the wall and reopening the gash on his forehead. Blood streamed back into his eyes. Stuart cursed and forced himself upright, dizzy and shaking from the pain. He started the hobble-skip again and somehow ended up back in the clearing without another fall.

Stuart made his way around the corner of the rock, still using the wall as a crutch, when a body tumbled toward him in a cloud of dust. Stuart's first instinct was to try to catch the person. It resembled Desta in the darkness. He lost his balance and fought to stay upright as the body skidded to a stop next to him. He heard a deep moan. It didn't sound like Desta. A second later another figure, shrieking, flailing, flew around the corner and dove onto the person on the ground. Stuart heard a wet slap as they collided. Sharp grunts followed repeated slaps. Stabs. Stuart realized it was Aisha slamming a knife into her attacker.

"Aisha!" Stuart yelled. "Aisha, you can stop! You can stop!" He tried to bend down and catch her arm but couldn't stop her savage attack. After a few more swings, she stopped, panting, glaring at her attacker. She was crying. Stuart wrestled the bloody knife from her hand and steadied himself.

"Get my dad," she said between sobs. "He's back there."

Stuart abandoned his hopping strategy and galloped awkwardly toward the others. His adrenaline had peaked, eradicating the pain. A fury he couldn't recollect, or even process, tore through his system, driving his legs forward. Finally, the three men came into view, still prone, but he didn't see Desta; a cry rang out and he spotted something writhing near the edge of the jungle. Stuart began to run. There was no pain. All he could think of was reaching Desta.

When he was within a few yards, he realized Desta was wrestling with another attacker. He raced forward and dove toward both men. He landed hard, smashing into someone's hip. The men scrambled, separating. Stuart rolled to his right and came face to face with Desta's assailant. Without a conscious thought, Stuart swung Aisha's knife and drove it into the attacker's neck. The man's body shuddered and collapsed beneath him, gurgling. Stuart thrust himself upward and stabbed into the attacker's body, screaming, plunging, and stabbing in the dark. After what seemed like an endless outburst, Stuart collapsed, heaving and whimpering.

He rolled away from the lifeless body and onto his back. His chest felt as if it was about to erupt. As he continued to suck in air, the pain in his leg came crashing back.

"Father? Stuart? Where are you?" he heard Aisha call.

"Over here," Desta said. He sounded weak.

Aisha slid along the dirt beside them. Stuart rolled onto his side and saw her next to Desta.

"How is he?" Stuart said.

"I'm not sure yet. He's alive, but … but he's hurt."

Aisha stretched out next to her father. They began whispering in their native tongue. Stuart closed his eyes and tried to ignore the throbbing that shot through his leg and ankle. He heard them continue to debate. Finally, there was silence for a few moments, and he felt Aisha move next to him.

"We're going stay here for the night. We can't go anywhere now. Kaleb, Hakim, and Grima are healing, but they'll need to rest tonight before they can make the trip back."

"What about your father?"

"I think he's going to be okay."

Stuart tried to weigh the decision to stay. A large part of him wanted to collapse into the dirt and pass out. Another wanted to get as far away from the Simien Mountains as possible, regardless of the danger or discomfort.

"We'll have to help Dad on the trip back. He was cut deeply in one leg. He may not be able to walk on his own."

Aisha looked over at Kaleb, Hakim, and Grima, and shook her head. Kaleb hadn't moved since they'd laid him down next to Grima. Hakim and Grima were in different positions. Hakim in a tight fetal position and Grima sprawled lengthwise, half on his stomach and half on his side. One of them was snoring.

Desta was sitting up now while Aisha examined him. He grunted from time to time as she moved him or pushed on different areas. She let out a loud sigh, then got up to retrieve her bag. She returned and began bandaging her father's wounds. Desta lay back down once she began treating him again. Stuart watched as she worked, amazingly without emotion, cleaning cuts, efficiently covering and securing gauze and tape. She leaned over and whispered into Desta's ear for several moments, kissed his forehead, and patted his shoulder gently before standing.

"I'm worried about waiting here long. Those two men ambushed me. It seemed like both had been wounded earlier, but they were like rabid dogs," Aisha said. "There may be others, and I'm not excited about waiting around to see if more arrive."

Stuart's ankle had gone numb again, but he could feel the intense swelling. Aisha helped her father move closer to the other men, then came back to Stuart.

"We can't risk a fire tonight," she said. "It's already getting cold, but we don't want to attract any stragglers." She helped Stuart to his feet and supported him as he hopped over to Desta.

Aisha unpacked three energy bars from one of the packs and gave one to Stuart and one to Desta. It tasted dry and remotely stale to Stuart, but he'd abandoned his particular tastes long ago. He devoured his while Aisha and Desta savored each small bite. He recognized the patience that had been developed in a society where all food was precious and respected. Stuart felt ashamed of his voracious appetite.

Aisha seemed to sense Stuart watching her and said, "What is it? What are you staring at?" Stuart blushed but was relieved that his reaction was probably masked by the darkness. "Don't worry about it, Stuart. I spent years in Europe. I've lived outside of the stark conditions of this country. But it's a habit I'll never break. Eating slowly, deliberately, for me it brings peace."

Before turning in, Aisha checked on the recovering men. The progress of their healing was unimaginable. The tiny bit of elixir Kaleb had received worked wonders. He'd originally looked as if he'd fallen into a thrasher, but was now completely healed. No open cuts, no scabs, no scars. Grima, who had suffered significant wounds as well, was unscathed, other than his tattered clothing. Hakim's injuries had seemed to be mostly internal, but he was sleeping soundly. Desta was in the worst shape. From what Stuart could see, the bleeding had stopped, but he was an older man who had taken a vicious beating. Even in the rising moonlight, Stuart could see the bruising on his face and arms. Aisha urged Stuart to sleep first and promised she would wake him in two or three hours. Stuart tried to protest but he knew his fatigue was showing. He gathered his pack beneath his head and was asleep before he could even think about sleep.

# CHAPTER
# FORTY-THREE

The room was bright, filled with the morning sun's light that blurred his vision. Slowly, the hazy objects began to take shape. Silver bars, a piece of furniture, an orange chair, and small flashing lights leaked into focus. Bailey slid up in his chair and rubbed at his eyes. As soon as moved, he felt the smallest muscles in his legs and lower back begin to rebel, to cramp, daring him to continue movement. His mouth tasted like he'd fallen asleep with a tissue in his mouth. He sucked at the insides of his cheeks and sat upright. The world around him fell into focus and, across from him, he saw his friend Parnell sitting upright and smiling.

"Parnell!" Bailey coughed, leaning forward in his chair.

"Good morning, you old hag," Parnell said, grinning widely. Even though it appeared as if he'd dropped twenty pounds from his already bony frame, the sight of Parnell's skeletal grin was overwhelming. Bailey shoved himself from his chair and careened across the tile to the foot of Parnell's bed.

"What in God's name, man?" was all Bailey could manage.

"Don't give me that rubbish, Bailey Honeybourne. You act as if you don't know how I could be in this condition. Tell me, what's that you've stashed in your breast pocket? A bit of whiskey? A nip o' scotch, hmm? Not likely so, I'd imagine."

Bailey moved around to the side of Parnell's bed. He smiled so hard his cheeks ached.

"You know me well enough to know that I don't give up secrets so quickly. Especially in a place as tightly managed as this," Bailey said, motioning to the ceiling. "How ... how are you feeling? Are you truly as well as you seem?"

Parnell looked down, regarding the subtle lumps beneath the stark white sheet, and nodded. "Can't complain, to be honest. I'm rather disappointed in these," he said, raising his bandaged hands. "I'll have to relearn all of that bloody Mozart, I suppose."

Bailey laid a hand on Parnell's shoulder. "I wasn't sure it would work, you know. I distinctly thought, 'This will be the one time it fails. It will have rotted, spoiled, or lost its power.' You've no idea how relieved I am."

Parnell laughed and looked around the room. "You don't suppose they'll allow me to leave, do you? A quick recovery is likely to draw unwanted attention, right?"

There was something irresistibly spry and youthful in Parnell's energy and enthusiasm. Bailey felt himself blush from the relief he felt seeing Parnell's recovery. His old friend was right, though. His sudden improvement would be a problem. Cardiac arrest, or at least being on the verge of it, would normally keep him in the hospital another day or two. Ditto for the wounds on his hands. Although Bailey couldn't see what lay beneath the bandages, he was certain there would be fresh, pink skin growing over the rough nubs, the bloody, scabbing stumps having dissolved overnight. That alone would generate pandemonium.

"I'd like nothing more than to get you out of here as quickly as possible," Bailey said. "I'm not so sure your physicians will have the same enthusiasm."

"Definitely not. We need an escape plan," Parnell said.

Bailey spun around as one of the nurses, a new one, strolled into the room. "Mr. Sumner," she said, shocked. "You … what are you doing sitting up? Your body is fighting to recover. Now lay back down and get some rest."

Parnell and Bailey glanced at each other and burst into laughter. The nurse frowned and planted her hands on her hips. "No shenanigans, you two. We were kind enough to look the other way while your friend slept the night in that frightful chair, Mr. Sumner. It's not kind to make fun of those who are looking out for your best interest."

Bailey backed away and allowed the nurse to continue her checkup on Parnell's condition. A look of disbelief swept over her face as she progressed through her examination. After every area she checked, she gawked at Parnell. Her process slowed until she finally stopped.

"Mr. Sumner, what in God's name happened? Last night, just before I left, you were going into cardiac arrest. I was worried that when I returned this morning you would … that you would not be with us. And now," she said, spreading her arms out before her, "look at you! You are a new man."

Parnell couldn't help himself. He smiled broadly and blushed. The nurse's expression shifted from that of wonder to concern. She put her hands on her hips and bit her bottom lip.

"I don't understand it," she said, more to herself than to Parnell or Bailey. She shook her head and walked out of the room, glancing back at Parnell before she exited.

"This could be a problem," Parnell said as soon as she was gone. "One of those doctors will be down here sooner than we'll want. They'll be asking questions, Bailey. Questions that neither you nor I will want to answer."

Bailey patted his chest pocket, the lump from the flask showing through slightly, and smiled.

"I'm serious, Bailey. I want to get out of here. We *need* to get out of here. I'm assuming Stuart is still in Africa, correct?"

"Yes, he is. He's with Desta."

"In Ethiopia? You left him there with Desta? Alone?"

"Parnell, our circumstances became complicated rather quickly. When Stuart arrived in Addis Ababa and told me you had disappeared, I knew I had to leave. I also knew that I needed to make sure that one of us made it to the fountain. Before them."

Parnell hung his head and slumped. "Are they going to destroy it?"

The fate of the fountain wasn't something Bailey had spoken to Stuart about. Instead, he'd given the instructions to Desta. And he wasn't convinced Desta would take the necessary steps to complete his request. Desta knew there was no value that could be placed on the liquid the fountain produced. The old Ethiopian himself had benefited from the elixir's properties in the past. It was impossible to predict what form of selfishness might overtake any man once they reached the fountain, if they reached it.

"It's what I asked Desta to do. And if that wasn't possible, to drain it," Bailey said, finally.

"Do you think he'll follow through?"

"When I left them at the university, I was fairly confident, but now … it seems like it's been such a long time … I don't know."

"I guess there's little we can do by wondering at this point. We need to focus on our own situation. Getting me out of here."

"Are you feeling well enough to walk?"

Parnell laughed, too loudly, and said, "Walk? Are you joking? I feel as if I could sprint out of here and cap it off with cartwheels. That stuff is potent, Bailey. You remember."

"Let me check the hall. We'll have to get you unhooked quickly." Bailey stepped over to the open door and checked both directions. He returned and said, "It's clear for now. Quickly, let's get these things off of you."

Parnell reached into his gown, about to pull off an EKG pad.

"Wait!" Bailey yelled, waving his arms. "The minute you are disconnected an alarm will sound. The nurses will come running."

Parnell slumped. "We've got no choice, Bailey. We'll have to make a run for it."

Bailey paused, then closed his eyes and nodded. "You're right. You're right. Just be ready to run once we get the wires off. Now, stand up."

Parnell wasted no time unhitching himself from the IV. They both yanked off the ten or twelve EKG pads, tearing mats of brittle grey and black hair from his chest and back. The alarm sounded. Parnell stripped the oxygen mask off and started for the door.

"Wait, you don't have any clothes here," Bailey said. "They probably destroyed what you arrived in, or else kept it for evidence."

"Get that plastic sack over there," Parnell said, pointing to a drawstring bag hanging on the coat hook on the far wall. "It looks as if my wallet and other effects are in it."

Bailey grabbed the bag and followed Parnell into the hallway. They went right and ran toward the green Uscita sign at the end of the hall. The alarm continued to beep from behind them.

"Faster," Bailey whispered, pulling alongside Parnell. "Take the stairs."

Although they'd gained speed, the exit sign seemed to pull further away from them.

As they finally reached the stairwell door, loud voices came from down the hall. Bailey felt Parnell stutter. He pulled his friend forward. Someone said, "Sumner." Bailey sprang toward the door and shoved it open. Parnell, barefoot and flailing in his thin gown, dashed through behind him.

Parnell shot past Bailey and leaped down the stairs, two at a time.

"Wait!" Bailey shouted. "Up. They're coming after us. Come on, go up a flight." Bailey turned and climbed toward the next floor. Parnell skidded to a stop at the landing and came back up the stairs as if he were fifty years younger. As they reached the next floor, Bailey heard the door below them open. Bailey halted Parnell outside the door leading into the upper floor's hallway. He held a finger up to his lips as Parnell collided with him.

Two anxious voices echoed in the stairwell in Italian, then footfalls downward. Bailey nodded to Parnell and eased the door open. They snuck out onto the hospital floor. No one was in eyesight.

"Call Prima," Parnell said. "Have her meet us at the Emergency Room entrance." Bailey found his phone and called Prima's apartment. He was lucky. She was home and waiting to hear from him. He asked her to find something temporary for Parnell to wear and where to meet them. He hung up and gave Parnell the thumbs up.

"The elevators are down the hallway that intersect with this one, to the right," Bailey said. "Hurry. We can take the elevator and make our way to the emergency room."

"I can run faster than you," Parnell said, grinning, and took off down the hall.

"Bastard!" Bailey hissed and trotted after him.

They passed the nurses' station and, as Bailey feared, there were at least three nurses behind the counter. They seemed shocked at Parnell's blurring presence followed by that of a less agile older gentleman.

"Not to worry!" Bailey called out, at a loss for anything more reassuring. Parnell swerved around the corner and disappeared. When he rounded the corner, Parnell had already reached the elevator bank and was punching the call button.

Bailey caught up with Parnell, puffing heavily.

"We'll never make it," Bailey said, looking up at the lit elevator number above them.

"Shut up!" Parnell barked. "We've made it this far. If Prima can get moving, she'll be waiting for us when we get outside."

The elevator finally rang and opened to their right. Parnell darted in, his gown flapping behind him, and careened into a group of people dressed in black. Bailey followed on his heels but barely squeezed into the elevator. An elderly woman, a good foot shorter than Bailey, frowned and slammed her cane into the tiled floor. Behind her stood two much younger, taller men and two teenage girls. They seemed to ignore Parnell and focused their frustration upon Bailey. He paused a moment and then bowed, whispering, "My apologies," over and over as the door closed behind him.

The descent seemed eternal. The elevator stopped four more times before it settled on the ground floor. The family they shared the elevator with didn't budge. When the doors opened at the lobby level, Bailey grabbed Parnell's wrist and yanked him out before the old woman could move. Parnell took two long strides forward then skidded to a stop. Bailey crashed into him.

"Take my arm," he said, thrusting an elbow out toward Bailey. "We've got to make this look like I'm just going for a short walk."

"Through the emergency room? Really?" Bailey said, hesitant to take Parnell's arm.

"Shut your trap and do what I say. We just have to make it out the doors." Parnell began to shuffle again. The family in black was overtaking them, splitting into two groups as they passed. Both girls and one of the younger men glared at them as they passed. Bailey forced a smile and a shrug.

When they reached the receiving area, Parnell paused. There were only a handful of people seated in the plastic chairs. Several administrators were milling around the front desk. Two of them looked up as Bailey and Parnell edged into their frame of vision. Neither looked friendly.

Parnell moaned and slowed his pace even more. Bailey glanced at the nurses and smiled, nodding, and pulled Parnell toward the large automatic doors at the far end of the room. As they turned, Bailey couldn't see if they were watching. He simply pretended he knew what he was doing.

"At worst," Parnell whispered, "they'll try to drag us both back into the hospital. If Prima gets here quickly, I can make a break for it."

"Are you mad? They'll have security after you before you make it three steps into the car park."

"Play the part, Bailey. We're just going for a stroll."

Bailey tried to remember how long it took Prima to get them to the hospital the night before. He knew it hadn't taken long, but the drama of her driving had warped time. There would be no way they could loiter outside the hospital for more than a few minutes before someone came after them. As he thought through all of this, they made it through the first set of automatic doors. As the second set opened they heard the scream of a siren and stopped. A moment later, an ambulance sped into the porte cochère and skidded to a stop. Bailey pulled Parnell through the last set of doors and onto the sidewalk to their left.

Two paramedics jumped from the ambulance cab and sprang the rear doors open. The automatic hospital doors shot open again and two white jacketed men ran out to meet the ambulance. They guided a gurney from the rear of the vehicle, dropped the wheels, and rushed it back through the doors.

The flurry of activity took any attention away from them. He tugged Parnell and both men trotted away from the entrance into the main parking area. Landscaping at the nearest corner provided a makeshift shield. They darted behind the row of towering shrubs and stopped on the shaded sidewalk. They certainly weren't hidden, but the shade and the hedge made Bailey feel less vulnerable.

"Bailey, we can't wait here. It's broad daylight."

There definitely weren't any other patients wandering outside the hospital, especially in a gown. Bailey spotted a row of benches situated across from the emergency room entrance, lining a median strip alongside the parking area. The benches faced away from the hospital. Bailey tore off his sport coat and tossed it to Parnell. He threw it on and followed Bailey to the benches.

"We'll see Prima from here, and I think you'll be a little less conspicuous," Bailey said. A taxi drove behind them and slowed, but the driver continued on.

"How quickly can we get to Addis Ababa?" Parnell asked.

"We?"

"Yes, *we*. You and I have to help Stuart, assuming he's still alive."

"Do you think they would kill him?" Bailey asked.

"They murdered his grandfather and got nothing. They maimed me and left me for dead. What would stop them from slaughtering Stuart, especially once they've followed him to the fountain. I'm confident Helmut's direction to his minions was very clear. No witnesses."

Bailey heard the faint squeal of tires and looked to his left. Just then, there was a disturbance at the emergency room entrance. Both men turned and saw a handful of white-cloaked staff, led by Dr. Yee, marching from the porte cochère toward them.

"Bloody hell," Parnell said, and stood. The tire squeal returned, closer now, and Bailey swung around to see Prima's Mercedes accelerating along the perimeter of the parking lot. She pulled up, slamming on the brakes beside them. Bailey saw that the staff members were now running. Parnell opened the car door and dove into the rear. Bailey nearly tripped off the curb and fell into the backseat next to Parnell. Prima punched the accelerator and rocketed out of the lot.

Bailey fumbled over Parnell's legs and finally brought himself upright in the seat. He looked up at the driver's seat expecting to see Prima but instead found Rupert, who was swinging the steering wheel hard to the right. Prima was wedged into the passenger seat, which she'd brought forward to allow them to enter. Bailey tumbled over against Parnell as they screeched through a turn.

"Thank God you got there when you did, Rupert," Bailey said.

Rupert nodded and said, "Right. We've accelerated our plans. We're going straight to the airport."

"From here?" Parnell said.

"I reserved seats on a flight that leaves in just over an hour. That gives us just enough time to get to the airport. We'll land in Addis Ababa just after 3:00 p.m.," Prima said. "Parnell, you have your passport, correct?"

Parnell looked at Bailey and said, "Yes, well, I believe so." He loosened the string on the bag and pulled out his wallet and passport.

"Excellent. Bailey?" Prima asked.

"As always," Bailey said, patting his breast pocket.

Once the car pulled out onto the highway, Rupert brought his speed down in line with the surrounding traffic.

"So, Parnell," Rupert said. "Good to see you. How are you feeling this morning? I'd say, you look a tad more chipper today than you did last night."

"Yes, well, I'd feel a lot more comfortable if I could escape this blasted gown. I'm just glad my blooming arse isn't hanging out."

"Oh, I almost forgot," Prima said. She leaned down to her feet and pulled out a small duffel bag. She turned in her seat and presented it to Parnell.

"You're not likely to win any fashion awards, but it was the best I could do on short notice. My father and brothers have left a number of things in my flat over the years."

"Outstanding," Parnell said. He unzipped the duffel and pulled out a red and white rugby shirt, a pair of lime green boxer shorts, and what once had been dress khakis that were now covered in paint splatter. At the bottom were a pair of dark wool socks, loafers, and a simple leather belt.

"Please pardon my impropriety," Parnell said, "but I'm going to change immediately. Prima, I must warn you that the nude body of a … mature gentleman can be shocking." Prima giggled, spun dramatically in her seat, and stared out the window.

As Parnell squirmed out of his gown, Bailey said, "Rupert, how long do we have until Christoff learns of our escape? Do you think we'll actually make it through the airport without being spotted?"

Rupert and Prima exchange a glance and a grin.

"I think we'll be unmolested," Rupert said.

"I should hope so," Parnell chimed in from within his rugby shirt. His arms were swimming through the material seeking exit.

"Prima and I convinced Christoff to join us last night for a grappa or two."

"Or six," Prima said.

"Oh, Rupert. You didn't …"

"We did nothing illegal or unethical. We simply needed time to explain our situation to Christoff. Believe me, it was far from simple."

"He didn't begin to smile until the third grappa was gone. Then," Prima said, throwing her hands up, "Voila!"

"He did make it to his hotel, didn't he?" Bailey said.

"Of course! We rode in a taxi with him. I promised him we'd contact him when we decided to leave the city, and he promised to delay his reaction to that information. He told us he couldn't do much about the hospital, which explains why the physician's contingent was stalking you when we picked you up. But he won't put any type of Interpol alert out until we've departed Rome."

Bailey paused and looked out the window. He felt as if he'd forgotten something. This string of events seemed too easy, too perfectly orchestrated. Would Christoff really allow them to leave Rome after the prior night's events? Although he hadn't seen a newspaper nor heard the morning news, he had to assume the press had trumpeted the killings through the city.

"I'm afraid I'm somewhat skeptical, Rupert. Men were murdered last night. How—"

"Not murdered, father; they were killed. Self-defense. We rescued a kidnapping victim."

"I understand that, but there's still protocol to follow. Why didn't we have a guard outside Parnell's room? Or at least on the floor?"

"Dad, dad. We took care of it. Trust me. After we left you, the Interpol team finished their initial screening of the men who were working with Helmut. Each of them had multiple outstanding warrants. They're connected to the Cuntrera family, based here in Rome. Christoff's presence in the city enabled him to be the hero rather than the goat. Because of what we shared with him, he knew the true story, but he was able to brag to the Interpol brass about solving an international kidnapping and landing wanted Mafioso. The bastard will likely get a promotion out of it."

"And you'll keep your job," Parnell added. Bailey looked at his partner and laughed. The clothes hung on Parnell's skeletal body like limp sails. He looked like a deflated clown.

"Exactly," Rupert said. "Exactly."

# CHAPTER

# FORTY-FOUR

Stuart awoke in bright sunlight. He felt oddly refreshed given he was sleeping in clothes he'd worn for three straight days on dirt and rock, and less than twelve hours earlier he'd killed a man. It finally registered with him. As he replayed the scene in his mind—what brief flashes of it he could recall—it unfolded like a surreal, out-of-body experience. It was as if it were something he'd witnessed from afar. The detachment he felt was troubling. There should be some degree of remorse, right? Some terror that accompanies the realization that he was responsible for the death of another human being? Instead, he felt … invigorated.

The second notion that struck him was that he'd slept through the night. Aisha was supposed to have woken him for the second watch. He rolled onto his side and pushed himself up. Aisha, Kaleb, Grima, Hakim, and Desta were sitting in a small circle near the edge of the clearing, eating and chatting. Desta acknowledged Stuart's movement and waved, smiling. Aisha followed with a wave, too. He attempted to stand, but his body rebelled. A shockwave of searing muscle pain ratcheted up his hamstrings, through his rear, and deep into his lower back. He waited, afraid his entire body might seize. Then the burning in his ankle kicked in, alleviating any feeling of guilt he had for sleeping so long and not relieving Aisha.

"Ah, the great warrior arises," Kaleb said.

Stuart felt himself blush and limped to the group. He rubbed a hand through his hair, knocking clouds of dust down over his face.

"Aisha, why didn't you wake me last night? I had second shift."

They all laughed.

"You were unconscious before your head hit your pack," she said. "Besides, about an hour or so after you fell asleep, Kaleb and Grima were jumping with energy."

"Jumping?" Stuart asked.

"It's a … side effect of the liquid, Stuart," Desta said. "Roughly speaking, once the chemicals have completed their healing, there's often a residual effect that appears to convert into adrenaline, or something quite similar."

"It's very difficult to describe," Grima said. "Adrenaline, yes, but something else, too. Happiness, confidence, extreme—"

"That sounds more like cocaine," Stuart said. All of his cohorts looked at him with scowls. "College. A weak moment. Actually, a lonely moment. But memorable."

They looked at one another and exchanged knowing grins.

"We buried Lebna over near the rocks," Aisha said. She pointed to a long mound of dark red dirt alongside the outcropping. "Kaleb and Hakim … took care of the others."

"And then we waited to see what would come next," Desta said. "So far," he said, surveying the camp, "we've been alone."

"That may not last long," Aisha said. "You should eat something, Stuart, and then we'll begin our trek. We don't know who we may run into on our way back. There may be more."

Stuart watched Desta. The man seemed fatigued and slow-moving.

"Desta, are you well enough to travel?" Stuart asked.

Desta continued eating without looking up. "I will not lie. I'm in pain, and I'm tired, but we need to get to safety, and these mountains won't provide that for long. My wounds are beginning to heal."

Shortly thereafter, the group gathered their packs and prepared to leave camp. It was half past seven but the temperature felt as if it had already soared into the nineties. Stuart was coated with sweat from merely getting his pack rearranged and onto his back. His brief breakfast and ration of water did little to ease the soreness reverberating through his body. Aisha elected to lead the group back into the jungle. Desta stepped in behind Stuart and in front of Kaleb.

"Desta," Stuart said, "I can't help feeling that we've … that we've led an incomplete trip."

"Are you asking me in a nice way why we came?"

Stuart paused. As he reflected on the past few days, he realized that *had been* his point. Men had been killed—Aisha's friends and colleagues. Yes, they had verified the location and existence of Malcolm's fountain of youth, but now what? The fountain was either empty or had some unknown governor in place that limited what it bestowed to its visitors. And now, with the dead buried or "taken care of," and the injured either healed or, in Desta's case, slowly healing, they were headed back. A round trip to nowhere.

"The men we've encountered. The men who chased us on the highway, who have been tracking us through the mountains—I feel they were acting upon a strong suspicion of its whereabouts," Desta said.

"So, it was a race of sorts?"

"Yes, assuming they knew the area well, we were racing them to it. They didn't know the exact location, but they knew that either we'd lead them to it or that they would find it on their own."

It was still troubling. What would've happened if Desta hadn't arranged for this trek? Would the group who had murdered Malcolm and kidnapped Helmut and Parnell still have pursued the notion that the fountain was somewhere in the Simien Mountains?

As if reading his mind, Desta said, "I suppose that still doesn't completely justify our effort, does it?"

Stuart continued forward and raised his hands, shrugging.

"Bailey Honeybourne is a good man," Desta said. "Our paths don't cross often, but through our mutual, say, connection with The Kilimanjaro Club, I've heard of both his exploits and his legendary generosity and compassion. When he asked me that day at the university to lead a group to the fountain, I didn't question his request. I knew he would only ask such a favor if he felt it was absolutely necessary."

"But, Desta, you're an intelligent, well-educated man. When a distant acquaintance shows up unexpectedly and asks you to march to your possible death, don't you question his request? Even if you trust and respect him? Aren't you thinking, 'Does this make sense? Is this foolish?'"

Desta laughed. "I suppose something like that ran through my mind. Many years ago, I was in need of a significant favor. A favor I didn't even know could be provided. Bailey was there for me in my time of need, even though I never asked him for help."

"What did he do for you?"

Desta laughed again and clapped a hand on Stuart's shoulder. "Some other time, my friend. Some other time." The old man was silent for a few steps and then added, "I can tell you that I felt obligated to protect the fountain. As you saw, it's not something you or I or anyone can ever remove, but it can certainly be found. At least I believe it can be found by those who have … perhaps earned the right to find it."

"I'm not sure I follow," Stuart said.

"That's understandable. I'm being perhaps a bit coy. As I told you, I've only been to the fountain two other times in my life. On the first trip I was blindfolded until we reached the rock formation. I had no idea how we found it. And I was blindfolded on the way back, too. The second time

Malcolm took me without the blindfold. This was my first opportunity to find it on my own."

"But what does that have to do with earning the right to find the fountain?"

"It's just a theory of mine—highly unproven. But I know these mountains well. I grew up hiking and exploring the very areas we've been traveling through. Never in my life had I happened across the rock formation that holds the fountain. But yesterday, there it was."

"So … the fountain found you, found us, rather than us finding it?"

"That's one way to look at it."

"Do you think it's safe? Or does it matter anymore?"

"You're referring to the dry well we ran into? I don't know. Some of the local legends claim that our fountain has been in existence for centuries. If that's true, and if men like us have been visiting it, or if the fountain itself has found men who seek it, then one must assume that at some point the fountain will be emptied."

"Do you really believe that? Of all the times for the fountain to run dry, you think we end up witnessing the end? I don't know, Desta."

"You're a skeptical man, Mr. Mancini," Desta said, laughing. "Your New York is showing. But I understand your questions. And I have no answers. It could be that we were given what we needed."

Stuart shook his head, amused and a little frustrated with the professor's mystical explanation.

"I believe we have done what we were destined to do. Now we must save ourselves."

Later that morning they emerged from the thick jungle and returned to the barren, rocky landscape that would dominate the remainder of their journey. The heaviness of the air lifted in the open spaces but the intensity of the sun became suffocating. The air was completely still and the red dirt and boulders amplified the sun's heat. The group made a few brief stops throughout the middle of the day, but progress seemed to slow. They had little water left, and Aisha, remaining in the lead, set their pace deliberately to minimize the rate of their dehydration. From Stuart's perspective, nothing seemed to diminish his thirst or the volume of sweat that coated his skin. His memory of their trip into the valley was almost nonexistent, but he felt as if they were moving much slower than they had during the trip into the canyon. If his assumption was accurate, then it could take up to four days to get back to civilization.

Civilization. It was an odd, unfamiliar thought. For the first time in days, he wondered what Heath was doing, what was happening at D'Artagnan. He realized his own disappearance must have appeared suspect given Helmut's vanishing. What were they suspecting? Were they looking for him? Did they even consider him missing? Just as Heath had said, Stuart had certainly earned the time off. It was unlikely the world, or at the very least D'Artagnan, would end during his absence. It was an oddly comforting, and unexpected, thought.

The remainder of the first day passed by in a heat-shrouded blur. Aisha propelled the team forward in a silent march. Even during the brief breaks no one spoke. Once Aisha made the move to continue, they all fell in step. Somehow Desta kept pace. Stuart fully assumed they would be helping, or perhaps carrying, Aisha's father through a portion of their trip. Instead, Desta plunged forward, head down, arms barely moving with his strides, never muttering a complaint.

As they finished building a small fire and scattered out along the rim, Stuart asked Desta, "How far did we make it today? When do you think we'll get back?"

At first, he didn't think Desta was going to answer. Then the old man leaned over toward Stuart and said, "We're over halfway. We'll be back at the car, assuming it's still there, tomorrow evening, maybe afternoon if we maintain this pace. Aisha is the master."

Stuart rocked back against the ground and stared into the star-spattered night sky. Tomorrow. He let himself ponder the possibility and fell asleep smiling.

# CHAPTER

# FORTY-FIVE

The jostling shook him back into consciousness. When Stuart opened his eyes, he was staring directly into the sun. Vertigo kicked in as he rolled his head back and tried to get his bearings. The sun blinded him momentarily, and then it was eclipsed by a dark round orb. Stuart covered his eyes, attempting to erase the white flashes that veiled his vision. Something else broad and white entered his field of vision. Kaleb's smile.

"Hello, Mr. Stuart," he said.

Stuart finally realized what was happening. He felt some form of support beneath his head, shoulder blades, lower back, rear, and legs. He craned his neck and saw the back of Hakim, or perhaps it was Grima, leading the way with the makeshift stretcher. Stuart laid back, closed his eyes, and peeled his tongue from the roof of his mouth.

"Kaleb, what happened?" Stuart said.

"Oh, you fainted. Boom!" Kaleb said, laughing.

"I … I think I'm better. Can you stop? Can I try to walk?"

"Oh, I don't know. Aisha gave us very strict orders."

"How long have you been carrying me?"

Kaleb leaned over Stuart again, blocking out the sun, and smiled. "Don't you worry, Mr. Stuart."

"Really, I mean it. I'm feeling better. I feel fine. Please stop so I can walk."

"Aisha!" Hakim called from in front of him. "Mr. Stuart is awake. He tells us he wants to walk."

A moment later Aisha came into his field of vision. The stretcher didn't provide enough support to allow him to sit up. He turned and squinted at her. She walked backwards alongside him and smiled.

"So, you're back with us, eh?" Aisha asked.

"Yes. It's hot, Aisha. These men have been through enough. Let me walk. Give them a break."

She looked up at Kaleb, still walking backwards, and nodded at him.

"Whoa!" Kaleb called to Hakim. They skidded to a stop and set the stretcher on the ground. Stuart rolled off, trying to look as if he'd recovered, but the truth was that he felt weak and disoriented. Water and even some of that fibrous bread sounded good. He fought his way to his feet and tried to knock the dust from his clothes.

"I feel bad asking, but … could I have a sip of water? And … and maybe some of that bread?"

Kaleb laughed and swung his canteen in front of Stuart. "Please, take a big drink. If you take a big enough drink, I will share my kocho with you."

Stuart took a long draw from the canteen. The water tasted sour and saturated with foreign minerals, but he could feel his body sucking in each drop. He swallowed and handed the canteen back to Kaleb.

"And now your dessert," Kaleb said. He handed Stuart another square of the bread with an exaggerated bow.

He heard footsteps behind him and turned to see Desta's vivid smile.

"You woke up just in time for the home stretch," Desta said.

"I'm sorry. I'm so embarrassed. I—"

413

"No apologies, Stuart," Desta said, raising his hand. "We live here. Although this was a difficult journey, it's something we're accustomed to. You, on the other hand, are just learning."

"We're almost through the pass," Aisha said. "We have a mile, perhaps less, until we're back at the car."

Grima and Hakim joined them, and while Stuart was still ashamed that he'd passed out and had to be carried up the valley during the hottest part of the day, he could see that each of them was genuinely happy he was up and feeling better. The emotion rushed through him, so he approached each of them, thanking and hugging them individually. Desta laughed at Stuart during the entire production.

"Come, we're that much closer to home," Desta said after Stuart finished thanking Aisha. "We'll leave the stretcher here unless you're feeling dizzy again. How is your ankle?"

"Sore as hell," Stuart said, "but I don't care." He retrieved his pack from Kaleb, who had apparently been carrying it all along, and added, "Let's go, please."

The final mile passed quickly. Stuart gnawed on the kocho, scanning the walls of the pass as the sun fell upon his back. Thick brush and rock started to fill in the edges of the broad path, closing off his ability to see more than a few dozen yards ahead. The path snaked through the undulating pass, weaving around Volkswagen-sized boulders, and fell in elevation. Finally, they passed through a long arc of overgrown brush that emptied into a wide lot. It took Stuart a moment to realize where he stood. A hundred yards beyond them was a dust-colored sedan that blended into the landscape. Aisha, who had continued to lead them through the pass, stopped short and held Grima back. Stuart glanced back at the car again and saw what had stopped her. There were two other vehicles parked on the other side of the sedan.

"Did you have more than one vehicle?" Desta asked his daughter. Aisha stared forward and shook her head.

"What now?" Desta asked.

"Shh," she answered. No one moved. Stuart's first thought was that the cars belonged to the men who'd ambushed them. There had been at least five or six attackers, perhaps more. It made sense that they needed two cars.

"Something doesn't feel right," she said. "I smell it."

Stuart watched Grima and Hakim lift their noses into the air and sniff.

"She's correct," Hakim said. "Fumes. I smell it, too. Those cars have just arrived."

Aisha took a step back, nearly hitting Grima. A figure emerged from behind the furthest car.

"Okay, get ready to—"

"Wait!" Stuart yelled, louder than he had meant to. The figure came into focus. He instantly recognized the stout, sport-coat-clad body.

"Bailey!" Stuart yelled. He waved his arm and jumped, triggering a bolt of pain. He saw Bailey pause, then the man began waving wildly. Stuart broke into a hobbled sprint toward him.

# CHAPTER

# FORTY-SIX

There were fewer than two dozen guests scattered through the club. A lone, local pianist filled the gaps of silence with renditions of popular standards from the 1930s and 1940s. Carl, the only bartender on staff for the evening, measured out three Kamikaze shots for the Chicago contingency that had laid claim to the far end of the bar during the past few evenings. Groups of two, three, and four members gathered in the main and adjacent rooms.

In the trophy room, Bailey Honeybourne was slicing through the wine cap of a Methuselah of Château Lafite Rothschild. Parnell, Desta, Stuart, and Prima sat in the worn leather chairs and love seats facing a roaring fire. Bailey was sharing an old story about one of his first expeditions as a member of the club.

Three days had passed since Bailey, Parnell, and Prima rendezvoused with Stuart, Desta, and the others outside of the Simien Mountains. After sleeping for nineteen straight hours, Stuart had joined his new friends on a chartered flight from Addis Ababa to Nairobi. Every muscle in his body had seemed to throb and threatened to cramp with each movement. Bailey had booked him into a suite at the famed Norfolk Hotel. He'd spent the following day resting on the teak lounge chairs adjacent to the pool, dozing off and on, relishing the inactivity and trying to process everything that had happened to him in the past two weeks.

Before boarding the flight to Nairobi from Ethiopia, Stuart placed a call to Heath at D'Artagnan. For the first time in years, he felt the tension in his chest as the phone rang, anxious about how his boss would react to both his disappearance and his resurfacing. His call rolled over to Heath's voicemail. He let out his breath, thankful—and embarrassed at his relief—that he could leave a message rather than speak directly to Heath. Stuart's mind drifted for a second during Heath's greeting, then he heard a click. Heath's voice, not a recording, popped through the receiver. Stuart cleared his throat in an effort to regain his composure and address Heath. He was greeted by loud, sincere laughter. Heath was hooting at the sound of Stuart's voice. Once he calmed down, Heath hit Stuart with a barrage of questions. Was he okay? Where in the hell was he? Was he coming back? How did it feel to be a multi-millionaire?

Heath went on to explain that Rhinegold, Fletcher and Hobbes had devised a way to proceed with the merger during Helmut's absence. When news of Helmut's death reached New York, Fletcher and Hobbes contributed an additional million dollars to each of the principals of D'Artagnan to compensate for their embarrassment.

"You know, you still have a job at the new organization, if you actually decide to come home," Heath said.

"I appreciate that, Heath."

"There's no rush, though. We're all taking a bit of a break over the next few weeks. Then we'll start the transition in earnest. Feel free to hang out in Africa, or wherever the hell you feel like going, until you're ready to come back. You deserve it. I honestly didn't realize the depth of work you put into this deal until we wrapped up the final steps. We wouldn't be here without your diligence."

"It's what I do," Stuart said. "I'm going to spend a few days in Nairobi, then I'll likely be back in New York."

"Again, no rush. Just give me a call when you get back to town. We'll get dinner. A great big dinner!"

Stuart agreed and thanked Heath again for the time off and the good news. He let out a deep sigh after hanging up and allowed himself a broad smile.

During that first day at the Norfolk Hotel, Stuart mentally listed the firsts that he'd racked up since being accosted by Bailey and Parnell. First time in Italy. First time in Africa. First belly dance. First souk. First car chase. First real backpacking trip. First dead body. First miracle. First … murder. And on top of it all, though not a true first, the welcome feeling of caring for someone outside of his family and colleagues. He doubted Prima shared the same invigorating stirrings he felt, but it was reassuring to know he had the capability to let himself be swept up by someone from both a sensual and intellectual standpoint.

On the following day, Bailey and Parnell sought him out to check on his physical and—he'd assumed—mental well-being. They ate lunch at the Lord Delamere Terrace in the hotel, overlooking the haphazard chaos flooding Harry Thuku Road. Bailey commandeered the conversation, recounting for Stuart the pride he took in Rupert's risk to assist them. After hearing the details of Parnell's confinement and torture, Stuart continued to be amazed at how fit and well Parnell appeared.

"Both of you obviously had more than a distant awareness of Malcolm's *secret*," Stuart said. "How long had you known? Have either of you been to the site?"

"We've known about the elixir for ages. We were some of the first, and only, people who Malcolm trusted with the information. He was very generous, your grandfather. He was very deliberate about providing Parnell and me with carefully measured amounts of the elixir over the years. He gave it to us under the strict understanding that we would assist him in storing certain amounts in safe deposit boxes throughout the world. His greatest fear was that someone he cared for would be caught someplace where we couldn't access the liquid quickly when we needed it most," Bailey said.

"When we thought about it, which we deliberately chose not to, it was a meaningless contingency plan. Even if we stashed flasks like Bailey's in twenty, thirty cities throughout the globe, it was unlikely that we'd be conveniently close to the hiding places in a time of need," Parnell added.

"Still," Bailey said, "there is a tremendous feeling of confidence that comes from knowing you have access to something so powerful if needed. We've always sought to carry a small portion with us, whenever possible, of course. But one simply never knows."

Both older men looked away from the table. Bailey watched the blades of the rattan paddled ceiling fan whir above their heads while Parnell seemed to have found something of interest across the busy street.

Parnell broke the short silence first. "Not long after Malcolm shared his healing potion with us—that's what he called it, healing potion, oddly enough—he never seemed to think of it as something that would or could prolong his own life, or the life of someone else. He focused only on its healing properties; he told Bailey and me of the first miracle. One of the men he traveled with had taken a wicked fall and landed on the splintered end of a dead branch near a trail. According to Malcolm it left a gaping puncture wound. The kind that fails to bleed much but looks appalling. Anyway, they were fortunate to be near the fountain and when they reached it, one of the other guides rushed to give the injured man some of the potion. Malcolm said he sat and watched the actual healing, mesmerized by the rapid change in tissue."

"I know he realized that if used correctly, the fountain's bounty could bring positive change. We're still not entirely sure what that means," Bailey said.

"No, not entirely," Parnell repeated. "But we have a strong inkling." He paused and took another drink. "So, as I was saying, that experience is what solidified the fountain's product for Malcolm.

"Well, years later, I was in Cape Town about to embark on a sailing trip to the Antarctic," Parnell continued. My wife, Catherine, had traveled down with me and brought her younger sister. Two days before we were to set sail, Catherine and Janice left Cape Town by rail to rendezvous in Johannesburg. I remember standing in my rented flat, rummaging through the small trunk I planned to take with me, when a young man, no more than twelve or thirteen, knocked meekly at my door. He asked if my name was Parnell Sumner and I, of course, replied, 'Yes.' The boy then took a decisive step backward. I'll never forget that vision. He'd been standing in the rather dim light that came from the bedside lamp. Then he took that step backward, just into the edges of the shadow. He wore a dusty, tattered white shirt and an odd sort of cap. In that half-light he looked like a ghost. He stood completely still for what seemed like an eternity. I realized that I hadn't moved nor spoken either, so I said. 'Is there something I can do for you?' That's when I saw his hand. Just above his waist, this tiny hand held out a piece of paper, or an envelope. I couldn't tell. 'Is that for me?' I asked. He nodded, just barely, and lifted his hand an inch or two higher. I walked over, probably a bit too quickly—I was losing my patience, you see—and snatched the paper from his hand. It was folded in half, and I recognized it was a telegram. I opened the message and read a very brief note. It was about the train that Catherine was on. It had derailed two hundred miles outside of Cape Town. 'Many casualties,' it had said. 'Catherine Sumner among the injured.'

"I somehow conned the handyman at the boarding house into letting me borrow his wreck of a lorry. I remembered my small flask of elixir and took to the road. I'd never driven in South Africa. The roads were horrendous. Pavement for a few miles if one was lucky and then suddenly, without warning, a rock-laden field of dried mud. I drove like a bat out of hell. I made the three hundred twenty kilometers in under four hours, a miracle given the conditions. When I arrived at the scene of the train wreck, it was pandemonium. There were fifteen or twenty railcars, all originally loaded with travelers. It seemed like every car had disintegrated in the accident. Clothing, bodies, food, plates … socks, toothbrushes … sundry items strewn in every direction. It took me ages to find the infirmary, which they'd established in the activity room of a nearby school. The dead and wounded were lined up side by side. The wails, unearthly screams, and shouts were deafening. The racket ricocheted off the tile walls and blended into a shrill. No one knew where any specific passengers were. I noticed a few who hadn't survived or were unconscious had crude nametags tacked to their clothing. I searched frantically, screamed Catherine's name until I was hoarse," Parnell said, his voice cracking.

"Finally, after an eternity of searching, I found her. She was in the very center of the room, wedged between two old men. Her eyes were closed and she looked asleep. Peaceful. Her mouth cocked open just a tad, just like when she slept at home in our bed. She seemed unscathed and my heart leapt. I rushed over to her, shoved the old men aside as best I could, and grabbed her face to wake her. But before I could move again, I froze. Her cheeks were cool. Not cold, just cool, and in a room where the temperature had to have risen into the nineties. I slapped at her cheek lightly and called her name, but she was completely unresponsive, limp.

Then I happened to glance down near her waist. The bottom third of her flowered skirt had turned a ruddy brown, and I knew instantly that it wasn't mud. I scrambled down, and before I even made it to her waist, I realized what had happened. Her right leg was missing, severed just below her hip. She'd probably bled to death in a matter of minutes—before I had even received word of the accident. I was desperate, crazed. I yanked out my flask and doused her lips, trying to channel the spilt liquid into her mouth, kissing her, calling her name. But …" Parnell looked down and took a deep breath.

"I've told Parnell that my theory is that the fountain and its water are cursed, but I'm not convinced he believes me," Bailey said.

Parnell shook his head and looked up. "It was just a horrible coincidence, the saddest irony I could ever imagine. Here I was, in possession of the most incredible substance known—or rather unknown—to man, something that could likely heal any human, and I couldn't save my wife."

There was silence at the table for a few moments, then Stuart said, "I'm so sorry, Parnell. I had no idea. I knew, or I guess assumed, that your wife was no longer … with you, but …"

Parnell smiled, his eyes lagging behind the effort of his cheeks. "We all have tragedy in our lives, Stuart. It just comes in different forms for each us. It creates a part of our unique story. I know that I was extremely lucky to have had Catherine in my life for those few short years, and I wouldn't trade that for anything."

Stuart watched Parnell closely for the next several minutes. Bailey kicked off an inane soliloquy regarding tea quality in African countries, speaking mainly to himself, while Parnell and Stuart soaked in the atmosphere. Stuart understood how the pain from Parnell's distant loss created a harrowing paradox. The very substance that had failed to save Parnell's bride had saved his own life. And then again, perhaps Parnell wasn't thinking of himself at all, but merely recalling the joy of his earlier, balanced, married life.

Parnell suddenly cleared his throat and leaned forward, clasping his glass with both hands, forearms flattened against the worn wooden table.

"Speaking of tragedies," Parnell started, "I don't believe we ever adequately addressed your estrangement from Malcolm. Here you've spent the past several days chasing after Malcolm's most prized possession, or discovery I suppose is more accurate, and … well, what convinced you to do so?"

"I … well, I'm not sure I'll ever be able to supply a satisfying answer."

Bailey looked at him and cocked his head, raising an eyebrow.

"Truth is, it was a minor detail in my life, my childhood. I never pushed my mother on the issue. His name was like … like a swear word. Verboten. I mean, I do remember a time or two—I must have still been very young—when she would catch herself talking about him. Sometimes it was to me, sometimes to … friends, I suppose. Not my father, though. I can't ever remember the two of them ever discussing him. It was just … a given, I suppose. I never asked why."

"You mean to say that you truly don't know *why* your mother cut him off?" Parnell said.

"Not precisely, no. I suppose I put together that he had done something unforgivable. Not to her directly, I don't think, but I believe it was to her mother."

"Alice. She died when your mother was …" Bailey said, glancing up to the ceiling.

"Nineteen or twenty," Stuart said. "I'm not going to come up with anything concrete, but my memory always conjured the thought of my mother being … disgusted rather than hurt. Does that make any sense?"

Parnell nodded, twirling the ice cubes in his glass round its perimeter and frowning. "I know what you mean. Still, as you said, that's no concrete evidence."

"Do either of you know of anything he may have done to cause their fallout?" Stuart asked. He suddenly found himself hungry for the history that, indirectly, brought him to where he was today. Stuart noticed that although neither Bailey nor Parnell answered him, they were exchanging a glance. "Well? Do you?"

"Stuart, were you aware that Malcolm had an older brother? Gavin?" Stuart shook his head and said, "No."

"Gavin Buckley was something of a war hero. He and Malcolm were very close. Malcolm's role in the war was … diminished, at least compared with that of his brother. Malcolm was deaf in one ear, a result of a childhood accident. Anyway, Gavin flew for the RAF, and Malcolm, who slipped through enlistment, was relegated to an intelligence team based in London when his disability was uncovered. Malcolm never saw combat," Parnell said.

"I met Gavin before I ever knew Malcolm," Bailey said. "It was very odd. He and Malcolm could have been identical twins, they looked so much alike. But their personalities were like opposite sides of a coin. As Parnell said, Gavin was the war hero, oozing charisma, chutzpah, testosterone," Bailey added, lifting his arms and pretending to flex his biceps. "While Malcolm was somewhat withdrawn, intellectual, and while not effeminate by any means, certainly not what's referred to these days as a manly man, you know?"

"Anyway," Parnell jumped in, "a year or so after Malcolm married Alice, Gavin disappeared while on a mission, here in Africa. Finding Gavin quickly became Malcolm's obsession. He spent months searching for his brother throughout most of sub-Saharan Africa, fighting for special dispensation from his superiors. I gather his absences were not well accepted by his new bride. Your mother was born in the early days of Gavin's disappearance, and Alice never seemed to recover from the pregnancy. Her health slowly, but steadily, deteriorated. I honestly don't know what happened. They never divorced, but Malcolm wasn't in attendance often. I don't believe I ever met your mother or saw Alice after Gavin's disappearance."

"Although it's more of a curiosity to us, I know that both of us, especially as of late, have wondered why Malcolm wasn't a part of your life," Bailey interjected.

Stuart sat back, trying to assimilate everything he'd just learned. It was a thousand times more than his mother had ever shared or that he'd ever ventured to discover.

Once Bailey managed to draw the massive cork from the wine bottle, Prima jumped up and offered to help him manage the pouring into each wine glass. They both caught a fit of giggles attempting to position themselves around the colossal bottle, and at one point Bailey, seeking leverage, crouched and turned, poking his nose directly into Prima's cleavage. That move alone was nearly enough for both of them to topple to the floor in laughter, leaving the bottle to crash down with them. Somehow Prima caught the bottle, like she was wrangling an angry piglet, and Bailey grasped the neck. Together they shuffled around to each person's glass and slopped in a few ounces of the Bordeaux.

Bailey lifted his glass and cleared his throat. Just as he was about to speak, Parnell stood and interrupted his old friend.

"I realize that we're about to partake in a particularly fine wine that would no doubt continue to come to life through adequate breathing, but I'm afraid if we allow Bailey the opportunity to propose a toast, we'll all be quaffing vinegar by the end."

Bailey laughed and mouthed, "Touché," and Parnell winked at him.

"I feel that I, and perhaps not much more so than the rest of you, have earned the opportunity to first honor each of you. It was your efforts that not only saved my life but, at least temporarily, protected an invaluable secret that, in the wrong hands—of which there are many—could have been disastrous. So, to my old and new friends, I thank you." Parnell raised his glass and was joined by those around him, and drank.

"Stuart," Bailey said, walking toward him, "come with me a moment. I want to show you something."

"Certainly," Stuart said, joining him.

"It's in another part of the club," Bailey said, leading him out of the trophy room doors and into the main room.

"Not unlike the New York club, this original facility has a number of rooms to host our members. Most are public, meaning that members and special guests are allowed to socialize in them, but we always have a few smaller rooms that are reserved for members only. Here in Nairobi, our founders built a lounge reserved for its members. It's at the end of the hall."

Bailey led him down a short, wide hall adjacent to the stage. Diminutive gas-lit sconces cast an orange glow along the walls. The passage ended with two hand-carved wooden doors. Stuart noticed a thin brass plate above the doors that read The Kilimanjaro Room – Members Only, Please.

"I think you might enjoy this," Bailey said as he pushed down on the brass lever-style doorknob. The door popped and creaked as he guided it inward. Bailey fumbled along the near wall for a switch and flipped it. A parade of small light fixtures lining the walls flickered to life. The room reminded Stuart of the sitting room where he'd joined Bailey and Parnell at the New York club. This room, too, was furnished with leather club chairs and sofas. The paneled walls were covered with hundreds of individual picture frames. Most, from what he could tell at first glance, were black and white.

"Let's look over here," Bailey said. He motioned toward the wall to their left, midway down the length of the room. Bailey reached the spot he'd indicated and, with a finger to his lips, began scanning the frames. "Yes, here it is. Come here, Stuart," he said. Stuart joined Bailey, who pointed to one of the larger frames—an eight-by-ten—at eye level. Stuart moved in to get a closer look. It was a group photo of at least a dozen men in traditional hunting clothes—khaki pants, multi-pocketed shirts, billed hats, and a pith helmet or two. Another eight or ten extremely tall, thin African men framed the group. Those men were bare-chested and in loincloths. Most grasped long spears.

"See here? The third bloke from the left. The one with the wild mustache and glasses?"

"Yes," Stuart said, squinting. The picture was slightly out of focus and badly faded.

"That, my young man, is Malcolm Buckley. I believe this was after his very first safari."

Stuart looked again and tried to make out the man's features. He looked, to some degree, familiar, but then perhaps Stuart was trying too hard to see a resemblance or recognize the man's face.

"I honestly can't tell you I recognize him, Bailey. I'm sorry."

"No need for apologies. I simply thought you might like to see him in his heyday. Look," Bailey said, pointing to their right. "Here are a few more snaps of Malcolm."

Bailey pointed at four smaller photos. Each of them had fewer subjects. Stuart picked out Malcolm immediately. The shots were taken at closer range, and it was easier to see the details of Malcolm's features.

"These were taken several years later, I believe. Ah, look! Here's Parnell with Malcolm!" Bailey jabbed his index finger toward another nearby frame.

Stuart slid down and smiled as he recognized Parnell. Between Malcolm and Parnell was a huge lion, obviously dead, its enormous head held up by a local man. Parnell and Malcolm were posed stoically, rifles poised at their sides.

"That lion was only a small part of that expedition. You'll have to ask Parnell to recite that story to you sometime."

Quaint, typewritten captions were pasted below the photographs, identifying the subjects and offering a brief summary: Mssrs. Buckley and Sumner flaunt the result of an errant rifle shot. May 1951.

Bailey toured Stuart around the perimeter of the room. He was amazed at the number of photographs of his grandfather, and of his new friends. They found several color pictures that had been taken in recent decades on the opposite side of the room. Malcolm appeared in fewer safari-like pictures but was prominent in several that had been taken at the club. A common theme he noticed in the more contemporary shots was the glee and camaraderie that was apparent between Malcolm and his colleagues. Arms slapped around shoulders, heads yanked in together, enthusiastic toasts surrounded by broad smiles. It was obvious Malcolm was an admired colleague who enjoyed the life he led with the club.

"I know I told you this before, back when Parnell and I accosted you in the Oak Room, but your grandfather *was* a very special man. His presence at this club, and many others, was exceptional and endearing. He was always one of the first to ask about the travels of fellow members, whether they were men or women he'd just met, or long-time friends. And somehow he managed to demonstrate the perfect level of humility and storytelling skill that allowed him to draw in loyal and entranced audiences wherever he visited."

Stuart wandered back along the walls, admiring the pictures again. An odd mixture of emotions flowed through him. First, he was concerned about his mother. He'd been completely out of contact with her for over two weeks, something that had never happened before. Second, he was sincerely thrilled to learn about the fascinating life, or at least a part of the life, that his maternal grandfather had lived. And finally, he was simultaneously resentful and proud that this man he never knew had accomplished such amazing feats.

"I … I really don't know what to say, Bailey. Other than to thank you for sharing this with me. To me, Malcolm never existed. I pictured him rotting away in some ancient European prison cell, shackled to a wall, hanging by his wrists, or cackling away like Renfield in an equally medieval insane asylum. Never in my life did I imagine him to be this person, this amazing individual that you are showing me this evening."

Bailey listened but didn't comment. Instead, he allowed Stuart to continue perusing the informal gallery. As he paid more attention to the individual photos and their captions, more and more familiar names and faces leapt out at him. Charlie Chaplain, Dwight Eisenhower, Ernest

Hemingway, and Winston Churchill were in multiple shots. Nothing in the captions denoted who was a member and who was simply an honored guest. Stuart decided he could pose that question to Parnell and Bailey later.

"We should join the others," Bailey said after a few more minutes. "Not that they'll miss us, but the food has likely arrived." He laughed at his own joke and waved Stuart out the double doors.

Before they arrived back at the Trophy Room, they heard laughter and Prima's screech from the main hall. When they turned the corner to the room, they saw Desta and Prima attempting to pour more wine. Prima was laughing so hard that tears ran down her cheeks.

"Thank God you've returned," Parnell said. "Desta's about to recreate the Nile in this very room from an extremely expensive wine. Hurry!"

They got the wine bottle back under control, and a trio of servers arrived with oval silver trays of hot and cold hors d'oeuvres. The sight of "normal" food continued to trigger a Pavlovian response in Stuart's appetite. He waited as patiently as possible before neatly loading a cocktail plate with shrimp, a multitude of cheeses, crackers, and cherry tomatoes. He sank back in his chair, a full glass of wine and a serving of amazing food in front of him, and absorbed the warmth and pure joy his new friendships.

# CHAPTER

# FORTY-SEVEN

The following morning, Stuart sat in one of the white rattan lobby chairs, sipping a cup of incredibly strong African coffee and reading a four-day-old *Wall Street Journal*. It was early, just past six, and he realized upon waking that he'd suddenly reached a point of being rested. It was a feeling he'd nearly forgotten—one that had been a simple part of his routine for years. His only regret was that he didn't have appropriate clothes for a run. He thought it would have been fascinating to jog through the early morning streets of Nairobi. Instead, he had dressed and gone for a short walk around the property before settling into his present seat.

From behind him he heard the steady, confident click of heels across the marble tiled floor. He looked up from the paper and saw a familiar form pass by, headed toward the front desk. Prima was dressed in a sleek navy suit, carrying a laptop-sized briefcase. The concierge, a short man with neatly trimmed jet-black hair and comically large glasses, greeted Prima as she approached. Stuart watched as she slid her bag onto the counter and began presenting a set of papers to the man. The concierge's smile never broke, but Prima became more and more animated as she spoke. The concierge nodded to her and backed away, disappearing through a swinging door behind the front desk. Prima turned, placing a hand on her hip, and shook her head. She was staring into the distance when she must have recognized Stuart in her peripheral vision. She shot upright and waved at him, taking quick steps toward his chair. Stuart set his paper on the side table and rose to greet her.

"What are you doing up so early?" she said, kissing him on both cheeks. He tried to return the gesture smoothly but knew he came off rigid and awkward. His clumsiness didn't appear to bother her.

"I woke up this morning and felt the best I have in weeks. Maybe not that long, but it seems like it."

Prima laughed. "I understand," she said.

"What about you? Is there a problem?" he asked, pointing toward the front desk.

"Oh," Prima said, "my flight reservations are incorrect. I had asked the concierge to book me on a flight back to Rome this afternoon, and I just reviewed the paperwork this morning—they have me flying out tomorrow afternoon instead. I doubt the flights will be full. I just want to avoid any unnecessary charges; plus, I have commitments tomorrow."

Her energy was impressive, as was her attitude. Even though it was clear she was anxious about getting her flight changed, and not getting hit with a charge, her face was lit with enthusiasm. If the audio had been turned off on Prima's speech, an observer would have guessed she was talking about a much-anticipated vacation or celebration. Stuart knew that he had probably been cued to respond, but he was distracted by her presence. Her skirt and jacket twirling with her gestures, sending subtle wafts of exotic soaps and lotions into the air.

"Stuart?" she asked, catching him in his trance.

"I'm sorry. Coffee's not kicked in just yet."

She laughed and bit her bottom lip. That gesture was equally distracting.

"I was just wondering when you were flying back to the States?"

"Oh, I'm not sure yet. Soon. I haven't booked a flight. I'd planned to do that today."

"You know, you are welcome to spend some time in Rome, if you'd like. I can get you into a fantastic hotel, give you some time to tour more of the city. It might be good to spend a few days resting on another continent."

Stuart felt his mouth drop open, but no sound came out. He didn't know how to interpret her invitation. Was it personal? Meaning she wanted him to come to Rome *with* her? Or was it sympathetic, as in, "You need to get your rear out of Africa ASAP or you'll crumble." Again, his mind locked. He stared into the woodwork that covered the front desk rather than into Prima's eyes.

"Ms. Valdocci?" the concierge called from the desk.

"Oh, hold on a moment. But think about it," she said, walking backwards toward the concierge. "You didn't see much of our beautiful city your first time through."

Stuart watched her turn and trot over to meet the concierge. Doubt tended to dominate his thoughts during these rarest of moments when a woman demonstrated a social interest in him. True, she'd never mentioned a boyfriend nor fiancé nor, frankly, any other man during their few times together. From what he gathered she worked nearly nonstop and was hugely dedicated to the operation of the club. He was amazed she allowed herself to even make this trip. Perhaps she'd justified the time away by telling herself and others that she would be visiting the original club in Nairobi.

When his thoughts came back to the present, he saw Prima was wrapping up with the concierge. She had her laptop bag open and was filing away the small stack of paper he'd handed her. Prima zipped up her bag and strode back to him. He fought to keep his focus on her face.

"Well? What do you think?"

It was a question he was afraid he couldn't answer. It was heavily loaded.

"I … well, I certainly appreciate the invitation, but I think …" and then it hit him. Not that he was looking for an excuse to say no, but something had been pulling at him, something was stopping him from booking a flight to Rome. "I do need to get back to see my mother. I've been loyal about seeing her every few weeks. Not that she'll remember if I visited recently or not, but …"

Prima raised a hand and closed her eyes, smiling. "No explanation necessary. I'm sorry, I had forgotten about your mother. I'd do the exact same thing."

"It's just that …"

"Stuart, really, you don't have to explain. I feel a bit embarrassed that I … well, that I was thinking of my interests more than yours. I would expect your need to visit the office as well. It sounds like you have a lot of interesting and rewarding work ahead of you."

Stuart exhaled and looked down at the floor. "I'm honestly not thinking of work. Thankfully, the reward part is pretty much a given. I have a decision to make, I suppose, about whether I continue on with this new organization. It's been impossible to fully appreciate through all of this."

"Again, Stuart, I understand perfectly. You've had quite an adventure. Something that I'm a bit accustomed to, at least from spending time with our members who get involved in similar situations. You, on the other hand, have spent most of your adult life in the formal business world. I can't imagine the shock your system has gone through."

Stuart hesitated, unsure of how to respond again to Prima's comments. He knew he needed to get back to New York, even if only for a few weeks. He could spend a week in Boston with his mother, and then focus on what his next steps were with the new organization. That part of his future seemed exceptionally blurry at this point. Prima interrupted his brief daydream by stepping toward him and embracing him. She kissed him on the cheek again, lingering, and pushed herself away, keeping her hands on his shoulders.

"The wonderful thing is that since you're a member you can always visit me at the Rome club whenever you feel like you need another getaway. Right?"

Stuart nodded and kissed her cheek. She slid her hands down his arms and caught his fingers, squeezing before she released him. "Have a safe trip home. And let me know when you are ready to visit Rome in a more casual setting. Promise?"

"I will," Stuart said. Prima took a couple steps back, waved, and spun away, her heels clicking back down the corridor.

There was a sudden emptiness in the pit of his stomach that seemed to drain the energy from him and trigger some form of nostalgia. It was both a familiar and distant feeling, something he couldn't remember experiencing since he was much younger. Flashes of memories flickered through his mind—his father's funeral, the first day of first or second grade, driving away from college after graduation, his mother not recognizing him for the first time. And although most of these memories were somber, there was a warmth, a renewal he felt in letting his thoughts pass through those previous moments.

"May I help you?"

Stuart snapped back into the present and saw that the concierge had come from behind the desk.

"I'm sorry. Lost in my thoughts."

"That's quite all right, sir. You looked concerned."

"No, not concerned. Just … thinking."

"Very well. Please let me know if there's anything I can do for you."

Stuart nodded, looking out the windows adjacent to the front desk.

The floor-to-ceiling glass opened up upon the gardens in the courtyard. He spied Bailey and Parnell stepping from behind a wall of shrubs on one of the paths. They were talking, or at least Bailey was, then they both stopped, looked up toward him, and smiled. A second later Prima was in front of them, greeting them both with cheek kisses.

"As a matter of fact, there is something you can help me with." The concierge had started to step away, but spun on his heel and faced Stuart. "I need to book an airline ticket."

"Excellent," the concierge said, clasping his hands in front of his chest. "Please join me over at the desk and we'll arrange your travel."

Stuart nodded absently, watching his friends interact in the courtyard. Prima was talking, gesturing with a mesmerizing mix of grace and energy, her fingers darting to graze the arms of Bailey and Parnell from time to time.

"Sir?" the concierge called. He'd already positioned himself behind the desk.

"Yes, thank you," Stuart said. He retrieved his coffee mug and newspaper and walked across the lobby to the front desk.

"Now, do you know where you'd like to go?"

"That, my friend, is an excellent question," Stuart answered. He pulled his wallet from his pants pocket, selected a credit card, and slid the card and his passport to the concierge.

# ACKNOWLEDGMENTS

When I was thirteen years old and in the eighth grade, I read Ray Bradbury's *R is for Rocket*. That was when I knew I wanted to be a writer. So, it's taken me decades to make good on that dream, and I certainly didn't make it to this point alone.

I would like to thank Trent Reznor and Nine Inch Nails for providing much of the soundtrack that accompanied my writing. At ten o'clock at night, when the kids were finally in bed, and I somehow survived a full day of "real" work, I needed a sonic infusion to push me through my nightly writing.

I would like to thank Scott Edelstein for offering insightful advice and assistance.

Michael Garrett's editorial expertise in the early stages saved me from the embarrassment of amateur errors reaching the next phases of the editing process. I am forever indebted to the brilliant and patient Erika M. Weinert—The Werd Nerd—who performed her editorial wizardry with the final manuscript. The equally talented and professional Carly Catt delivered a flawless document with her proofreading prowess. Victoria

Wolf created an incredible new cover and interior design, and Kirsten Jensen kept me sane, held me accountable, and gave me invaluable guidance and support through the entire process. Endless thanks to you all!

For a good portion of these last forty-five years, Karen Casey has been a loyal, incomparable champion. Her contagious optimism, perspective, and sincere care propelled me through the completion of this manuscript.

Special thanks to my parents, David and Sandy, who've read just about everything I've written and always offer encouragement and love. Also, a conglomeration of friends and family who have provided, probably unknowingly, inspiration and support—Sherry, John P., Rick, Nick, Dave, Betsy, Brian, Ali, and Sophie.

Finally, and most importantly, this novel would never have begun, let alone been finished, without the unwavering support of my wife, Gretchen.

# ABOUT THE AUTHOR

Ron Lamberson is a novelist and freelance writer, having previously endured a Purgatory-like existence as an HR professional. Ron has published three novels, including *The Poachers of Immortality* and *The System*. He has a bachelor's degree in Creative Writing from Purdue University and an MBA from Indiana University. Ron is a passionate traveler, having visited over twenty countries on five continents, and a Disney freak. He spends some of his free time struggling to learn guitar, attending concerts, and avoiding injury on the tennis court. He is an unabashed fan of the bands Nine Inch Nails and Toto—don't judge. He is *not* a fan of the long-term effects of gravity on his body, most '70s soft rock, or attempting to maintain his lawn. Ron is currently working on his next novel while living his dream life as a husband, father, and dog wrangler. You can learn more about Ron at www.ronlamberson.com.

# BOOK CLUB ADVENTURES

Ron loves connecting with readers, sharing insights, and celebrating the awesomeness of book clubs. As a special gift to book clubs everywhere, Ron will join your discussion in person (for Denver area groups) or via Zoom. Contact Ron at ron@ronlamberson.com to discuss availability and the cool genres your book club loves to explore.

# OTHER BOOKS BY
# RON LAMBERSON

Read *The Poachers of Immortality,*

Book Two of

The Kilimanjaro Club Adventure Series

Made in United States
Orlando, FL
23 November 2022

24939298R00267